THE LOGIC OF SOCIAL SCIENCE

The Logic of Social Science

James Mahoney

PRINCETON UNIVERSITY PRESS
PRINCETON AND OXFORD

Published by Princeton University Press
41 William Street, Princeton, New Jersey 08540
6 Oxford Street, Woodstock, Oxfordshire OX20 1TR

press.princeton.edu

Library of Congress Cataloging-in-Publication Data

Names: Mahoney, James, 1968– author.
Title: The logic of social science / James Mahoney, Princeton University Press.
Description: Princeton, New Jersey : Princeton University Press, [2021] |
    Includes bibliographical references and index.
Identifiers: LCCN 2020049205 (print) | LCCN 2020049206 (ebook) |
    ISBN 9780691217055 (hardback) | ISBN 9780691214955 (paperback) |
    ISBN 9780691214993 (ebook)
Subjects: LCSH: Social sciences—Research. | Social sciences—Methodology.
Classification: LCC H62 .M23578 2021 (print) | LCC H62 (ebook) | DDC 300.1—dc23
LC record available at https://lccn.loc.gov/2020049205
LC ebook record available at https://lccn.loc.gov/2020049206

British Library Cataloging-in-Publication Data is available

Editorial: Bridget Flannery-McCoy and Alena Chekanov
Production Editorial: Natalie Baan
Cover Design: Wanda España
Production: Erin Suydam
Publicity: Kate Hensley

Cover art by Fernand Léger, *Mechanical Elements*, 1924. Oil on canvas, 91.4 x 66
cm (36 x 26 in.) © 2021 Artists Rights Society (ARS), New York / ADAGP, Paris.
Photo: Yale University Art Gallery, Charles B. Benenson, B.A. 1933, Collection

This book has been composed in Adobe Text and Gotham

Printed and bound by CPI Group (UK) Ltd, Croydon, CR0 4YY

Dedicated to my children,
Maya and Alexander

CONTENTS

ILLUSTRATIONS

Tables

Figures

PREFACE

The Logic of Social Science offers new principles for designing and conducting research in the social sciences. The book is both an argument for the use of certain tools and a user's guide for working with these tools. The word *logic* in the title has a double meaning. On the one hand, it refers to the book's concern with the underlying structure, or "logic," of social science research. The book explores the often hidden assumptions that go into the production of social research. On the other hand, the reference to logic alludes to the tools discussed here, which are explicitly rooted in logic and set theory. The book draws on the resources of logic and its set-theoretic extensions to formulate methods appropriate for social science research.

The book is divided into three parts: ontology and epistemology, methodological tools, and explanatory tools. Part I, on ontology and epistemology, begins with the problem of essentialism in the social sciences, exploring the cognitive nature of this problem and the reasons that a solution is so challenging. I develop a general approach—what I call *scientific constructivism*—as an alternative to an essentialist orientation for the social sciences. I show how scientific constructivism and set-theoretic analysis fit together quite naturally as the foundation for a non-essentialist social science.

The second part of the book develops set-theoretic tools for assessing the validity of propositions and theories in the social sciences. Specifically, I develop set-theoretic methods for building and defining categories; for working with a regularity model of causality; for using evidence and generalizations to evaluate the truth of propositions; for carrying out counterfactual analysis to assess propositions; and for leveraging the logic of sequences to understand the relative importance of causes. I conclude Part II by discussing a set-theoretic version of Bayesian analysis for knowledge accumulation in the social sciences.

Part III focuses on tools for formulating propositions, explanations, and theories in the social sciences. I examine the alternative theory frames and normative traditions that shape research in the social sciences. I discuss several of the most important theoretical constructs—event, process, actor, object, rule, institution, resource, and power—that are used to build explanations of social phenomena. I consider the role of sequences and causal chains in social science explanations, including by offering new tools for constructing explanations of critical events and path dependence.

The scope and complexity of this book invite various uses and readings. For readers interested in short summaries of the book's arguments, it is possible to start with the introduction to the book and the introductions to each chapter. This approach will allow readers to decide for themselves which topics they wish to explore in greater depth. Readers who are primarily interested in the argument about scientific constructivism can focus on the introduction and chapters 1 and 2. For Part II, readers should start with chapter 3, but the remaining chapters (4–7) can be read in any order. With Part III, it is not essential to read the chapters in order; each chapter can stand alone, as an independent essay. For all readers, the glossary at the back provides one-sentence definitions of important terms used in this book.

———————

I wish to acknowledge and thank the many people whose comments, insights, and support were essential for the completion of this book. As I do so, however, I want to stress that these individuals may not always agree with the ideas presented in the book. Let me therefore express my gratitude to the following individuals without implying their endorsement of my arguments.

I would first like to acknowledge five talented scholars who coauthored methodological articles with me while they were in graduate school at Northwestern University: Rodrigo Barrenechea, Laura García-Montoya, Erin Kimball Damman, Kendra Koivu, and Rachel Sweet. These individuals worked with me on the following topics: counterfactuals and Bayesian analysis (Rodrigo Barrenechea), critical events (Laura García-Montoya), set-theoretic tests and sequence analysis (Erin Kimball Damman and Kendra Koivu), and set diagrams (Rachel Sweet). I am grateful to these colleagues for allowing me to draw on our collaborations in this book. It is simply heartbreaking to note that Kendra Koivu died as I was nearing completion of the book. The memory of her enthusiasm for methodology inspired me as I worked through the final rounds of revision.

Many graduate students provided valuable feedback on chapters and work related to the manuscript. Let me thank the following former or current students: Laura Acosta, Mariana Borges Martins da Silva, Marissa Brookes, Isabel Castillo, Christopher Day, Daniel Encinas Zevallos, Emilio Lehoucq, Claudia López Hernández, Pilar Manzi, Erin Metz McDonnell, Salih Noor, Silvia Otero Bahamon, Andrew Owen, Diana Rodríguez-Franco, and Matthias vom Hau. Rahardhika Utama helped me with the references, and Rodrigo Barrenechea helped me to construct the figures. I want to express special thanks to Jennifer

Cyr and Matthew Lange for providing me with detailed comments on the entire manuscript.

The material in Part I, concerning ontology and epistemology, addresses philosophical issues that may be unfamiliar to social scientists. For help with clarifying and presenting these ideas, I am grateful to the cohorts of graduate students who read drafts of chapters 1 and 2 for my course on case-study and small-N methods. I also received helpful comments on these ideas at various stages of development from Andrew Abbott, Gabriel Abend, Robert Adcock, Kenneth Bollen, Patrick Jackson, Neil Gross, Ian Hurd, Tianna Paschel, Douglas Porpora, Isaac Reed, Hillel Soifer, David Waldner, and Alexander Wendt.

I started working on the methodological ideas in Part II more than twenty years ago. I would like to thank the following teachers and colleagues who shaped my methodological thinking over these years: Andrew Bennett, David Collier, Colin Elman, Peter Evans, Tulia Falleti, John Gerring, Diana Kapiszewski, Jack Levy, August Nimtz, Charles Ragin, Benoît Rihoux, Carsten Schneider, Jason Seawright, Eric Selbin, Kathryn Sikkink, Lisa Wedeen, and Christopher Winship. I would also like to thank my past and present colleagues at Brown University and Northwestern University who share my love for comparative and historical social science: Bruce Carruthers, Anthony Chen, Patrick Heller, José Itzigsohn, Ann Orloff, and Monica Prasad. For helpful comments on specific chapters in Part II, I am grateful to Tasha Fairfield, Jack Goldstone, Alan Jacobs, Ingo Rohlfing, Kenneth Shadlen, Dan Slater, Richard Snyder, Nina Tannenwald, Eva Thomann, Claudius Wagemann, and Deborah Yashar. I extend a special acknowledgement to my long-time coauthor Gary Goertz, who provided helpful comments on all chapters.

In writing and rewriting the chapters in Part III, on explanatory tools, I was regularly inspired by my years working with Dietrich Rueschemeyer at Brown University and by my conversations with the late Arthur Stinchcombe at Northwestern University. I was fortunate to learn about theory development from these two great masters. My work on the temporal dimensions of social science research has spanned my whole career. I wish to thank the following scholars for helping me with the development of the ideas in Part III: Peter Hall, Paul Pierson, Theda Skocpol, the late Charles Tilly, and Wolfgang Streeck. I need to express a special thank you to Kathleen Thelen for all that she has done for me personally and for the social science community more generally.

This book was copyedited by Nancy Trotic in the midst of the COVID-19 pandemic. Nancy's skill at expressing ideas using the English language made the book much clearer, while her talent at grasping set-theoretic logic led to many important substantive improvements in the book's arguments. It was a pleasure to work with Bridget Flannery-McCoy, my editor at Princeton

University Press. I also want to thank Erik Crahan at the Press for encouraging me on this work over many years.

Finally, I want to express my deepest gratitude to my family, starting with our dog, Cleo, who was a source of unconditional love for us throughout her whole life. My spouse, Sharon Kamra, deserves a medal for supporting my work even as it focused on increasingly abstract topics. While my mind may sometimes have been in a different world, our amazing children, Maya and Alexander, kept my feet firmly planted on the ground during the many years over which I wrote this book.

THE LOGIC OF SOCIAL SCIENCE

Introduction

The Logic of Social Science introduces principles and methods for set-theoretic social research. Most of the book is focused on describing in some detail how these principles and methods can be substantively applied. However, the book's starting point is the argument that set-theoretic analysis offers a correction to the bias of essentialism as manifested in the social sciences. Let me begin with this problem.

Essentialism is an innate bias in which human beings understand the world as consisting of entities that possess inner essences, which endow the entities with an identity and a certain nature. Social science researchers adopt this orientation when they treat their categories as corresponding to things "out there" in the external world that possess properties and dispositions. This understanding of categories is useful for everyday life; it is how we comprehend and often successfully manipulate the world around us. In fact, all human cultures and civilizations depend on essentialism. Nevertheless, I argue that an essentialist orientation to categories is not appropriate for the *scientific* study of social reality.

I build the case against essentialism on the back of an impressive interdisciplinary literature developed over decades of research. Following this literature, I conclude that essentialism distorts perception and reasoning in profound ways. Our understanding of social science categories as entities that exist in the external world with identities and tendencies derives from our built-in essentialist bias. Our social categories do not actually exist with properties and powers. If we recognize the bias of essentialism, I argue, we find that the goals of contemporary social science need to be adjusted. We cannot hope to derive valid findings about an external social world that exists independently of human beings and of ourselves as researchers.

This book is driven almost entirely by a positive agenda: it seeks to develop a set of practical tools for pursuing a social science that does not engage in essentialism. Most of the book concerns specific procedures that scholars can put to use directly to build theories and propositions and to evaluate the validity of those theories and propositions. Many of the tools discussed are inspired by what qualitative social scientists are already doing in their research (Goertz and Mahoney 2012). Qualitative researchers routinely assume that social categories are necessarily and deeply infused with their substantive knowledge. For these researchers, this book offers a new set-theoretic foundation and a new set-theoretic toolkit for the pursuit of non-essentialist research.

This book is committed to science as a mode of discovering truths about the world. This commitment makes the book accessible to all scholars who believe that evidence and logic should be the basis for arriving at inferences and conclusions. For social scientists who work under essentialist assumptions, the book seeks to stimulate a new discussion and debate about essentialism and its consequences for the production of knowledge in the social sciences. It asks researchers to temporarily set aside their skepticism (i.e., adjust their "priors") to the point that the book's arguments can receive a fair hearing.

———————

Scientific constructivism is the approach that I develop to undergird a non-essentialist social science. A scientific constructivist approach assumes that categories do not stand in an approximate one-to-one correspondence with entities in the natural world; social science categories do not carve nature at its joints (or even approximately at its joints).[1] Instead, the meaning and efficacy of social science categories depend on collective understandings among communities of individuals located in particular places and times. The entities in the natural world to which a given social science category refers are heterogeneous and largely uncomprehended (and perhaps incomprehensible). These entities are regarded as instances of a given category because the human mind constructs them in this way. Scientific constructivism is designed to recognize and accommodate the profoundly mind-dependent nature of social science categories.

Scientific constructivism is fully committed to science as understood in a conventional way. *Science* consists of generalizable and public procedures for using evidence to rationally derive beliefs about the truth of propositions concerning the actual world. The methods discussed in this book provide explicit rules for researchers to follow in order to use evidence to logically assess propositions that could be true or false. These methods can be used to evaluate descriptive, causal, and normative statements about constructed categories that exist by virtue of collective understanding.

Both constructivism and science have advocates in philosophy going back centuries and continuing today. Yet the two orientations often stand in opposition to one another in the social sciences (Wendt 1999). Advocates of constructivism tend to be skeptical of science when defined in a conventional way and applied to the social world. They believe that the human-constructed nature of categories obviates the possibility of a science of the social world that uses evidence to arrive at valid conclusions about causal regularities and law-like propositions. Constructivists commonly embrace epistemologies that depart radically from the scientific epistemology of the natural sciences.

For their part, advocates of science often reject constructivism as a depiction of reality and as an approach for the social sciences. They view the concerns of constructivism as reflecting a set of philosophical issues about the nature of reality that are largely irrelevant to the actual practice of social science. They assume that social science categories exhibit an approximate correspondence with actually existing entities of the external world at some level of analysis. They believe that the methods used in the natural sciences are, in principle, appropriate for the social sciences because the subject matter of the natural sciences and that of the social sciences are not fundamentally different.

The scientific constructivist approach of this book joins constructivism and science in a harmonious, truth-seeking alliance. Scientific constructivism is committed to the proposition that the categories of the social sciences do not correspond coherently—i.e., in ways that humans can comprehend and represent—to mind-independent substances, properties, and processes. It endorses the view that human categories function despite an often massive referential disconnect with the natural kinds of the world. It embraces the idea that one task of the social sciences must be to understand how and why particular categories are constructed. It welcomes normative inquiries into the effects of socially constructed categories, including effects on the behavior of the individuals to whom these categories may refer.

Scientific constructivism simultaneously insists that these inquiries follow scientific methodologies that are rooted in logic. The book assumes the validity of transcendental principles, including especially logic, that are requisite in order for researchers to make valid inferences and rationally evaluate the truth of propositions. Scientific constructivist research is focused on contingent propositions whose truth is established on the basis of logical reasoning and constructed evidence from the actual world. Scientific constructivism offers general principles for understanding the social construction of categories, the relationships among these categories, and the consequences of the categories for human beings' experienced reality. At the core of the approach is the encounter between sensory information derived from the natural world, constructed categories in the mind, and methods rooted in logic, whose validity transcends human experience.

Bringing constructivism and science into an alliance is necessary for the flourishing of a social science focused on the rational discovery of truth. However, building the bridge for this alliance is no easy feat. Simply endorsing or justifying scientific constructivism is not sufficient for the task. Any viable scientific constructivist approach must consist of clear guidelines for conducting non-essentialist social research. It must offer well-developed ideas about the procedures that scholars can use to carry out analyses that recognize the mind-dependent nature of social categories. The approach needs principles for formulating categories and propositions, assessing propositions using evidence, and interpreting and reporting results. The approach must not remain on a philosophical plane; it must consist of practical tools that scholars can put to use in designing and conducting social science research. To develop this kind of approach—one consisting of specific and usable procedures for conducting research that is both constructivist and scientific—is the goal of this book.

———

A scientific constructivist approach responds to two challenges facing the social sciences. The first challenge is to recognize and take fully into consideration the implications of scientific research that suggests an essentialist approach is not appropriate for the social sciences. More than thirty years ago, Lakoff (1987) summarized two decades of research across various disciplines showing that categories do not derive meaning from their correspondence to entities in the natural world. Members of a category share no inherent essences or fundamental properties that make them members of the category. Rather, category meanings are located in cognitive models that structure thought and that reflect both human culture and human sensorimotor constitution. In the last twenty-five years, experimental laboratory research in psychology has shown that essentialism is a built-in human bias that emerges early in life as a non-optional mode of categorizing and comprehending reality (Gelman 2003; Newman and Knobe 2019). Essentialist assumptions bias human reasoning concerning categories ranging from race, gender, and caste to money, education, and democracy. Most recently, work in neuroscience offers additional reasons for rejecting the notion that the mind is anything like a mirror of nature. Sensory input from the natural world is transmitted across ensembles of neurons that vary greatly in the density of their connections. Even if our sensory neurons could directly track natural divisions in the world, the categories of which we are consciously aware reflect a heavily processed summary of this sensory input—a summary that is deeply affected by preexisting brain encodings and our current neural activation state, as well as by the inherent limitations of our brain's neural mechanisms.

The implication of this research is that our social categories do not map onto the structure of a mind-independent external reality. Social scientists seemingly have no other choice than to embrace some kind of constructivism, at least in the minimal sense of acknowledging an inescapable role for human minds in creating and sustaining social categories. Yet embracing even this minimal constructivism is difficult, because mainstream social science methods depend on the assumed truth of essentialism. These social science methods are not appropriate for the study of categories that require shared beliefs for their existence. Letting go of essentialism involves letting go of both human intuitions and longstanding approaches to social research. It involves acknowledging that our intuitions about categorization are mistaken and that social science research must correct for the illusion of essentialism.

The second challenge is to embrace constructivism while remaining fully committed to the pursuit of science. The most radical constructivists reject science in conjunction with rejecting realism—i.e., they reject the proposition that an actual world consisting of a structured set of entities exists independently of human beings. Other relativists are agnostic about an external reality and argue that the issue is irrelevant because the truth-value of propositions depends entirely on human thought and language. Still other relativists are realists about the external world but argue that logic is not part of the structure of this world; instead, they believe, logic is an artifact of the kind of bodies and brains that human beings happen to possess. In all of these approaches, truth, reason, and objectivity are optional ideas that depend on human beings for their meaning. What is true from one conceptual viewpoint may be false from another; no viewpoint can be privileged as objective. Under this radical constructivism, scientific propositions about the natural world can be both true and false, depending on how you look at them.

By contrast, this book rejects both skepticism about reality and relativism about truth; it fully embraces realism and objective truth. More extreme relativists fail because they cannot account for the fact that scientific categories predict and shape the sensory input we receive from the external world. Extreme relativism provides no insight into our ability to use categories to successfully manipulate and control the natural world and to predictably and meaningfully interact with one another in the social world. Scientific theories are useful precisely because they capture approximate truths about reality. Other forms of relativism fail to appreciate the indispensability of so-called Western thought for understanding the world. Although scholars may assert that logic is an optional and dispensable tool, their words and reasoning betray them. In order to advance arguments, marshal evidence, and reach conclusions, they, like all of us, must accept transcendental notions of logic, truth, and objectivity. Meanwhile, they leave as a mystery the issue of why logic works so well for understanding and controlling the world if it is unrelated to the world.

I propose that set-theoretic analysis offers a way out of essentialist social science without falling into relativism or anti-realism. Set-theoretic analysis for the social sciences is well suited for constructivist research because it requires the analyst to engage in an ongoing exchange between ideas in the mind and evidence from the world (Ragin 1987, 2000, 2008; Schneider and Wagemann 2012; see also Lamont and Molnár 2002). The categories of set-theoretic analysis are infused with substantive knowledge; they explicitly embody the beliefs of the researcher, who calibrates the boundaries of the categories included in the analysis. Set-theoretic researchers do not measure categories by neutrally describing features of an ontologically objective reality that already exists with an identifiable structure. Instead, they *construct* and *calibrate* categories on the basis of shared understandings concerning the meanings of the categories. If these shared understandings change, the calibrations of the categories also change. In set-theoretic analysis, one's understanding of the meaning of a category establishes the basis for how one reports about the structure of the social world. Categories *literally* help construct the content of the social world.

Although set-theoretic analysis is well suited for constructivist research, a commitment to constructivism is not requisite for the use of set-theoretic analysis. Set-theoretic analysts who embrace essentialism can work under the assumption that a set is simply a group of entities that all share one or more essential properties. These analysts can employ some of the tools developed in this book. However, I show that set-theoretic tools fit most naturally within a constructivist approach in which the mind-dependence of categories is explicitly recognized. I develop the tools of set-theoretic analysis under constructivist assumptions, for social scientists who seek to pursue scientific constructivist research.

To reconfigure set-theoretic analysis for constructivist research, I conceptualize the "sets" of set-theoretic analysis as mental phenomena that are ontologically prior to the entities they categorize. Briefly, I argue that set-theoretic analysts can avoid essentialism by conceiving of sets as actually existing bounded spaces in the mind's representational system that human beings use to understand and classify sensory input from the natural world. Sets are created from and instantiated by an interaction between the mind and the natural world; sets are entities that *exist* as conceptual spaces in the cognitive machinery of the mind. When sets are understood in this way, the toolkit of set-theoretic analysis encompasses a nearly comprehensive methodology for conducting scientific constructivist research.

Under this set-theoretic methodology, social categories refer to particular entanglements of human understandings and aspects of objective reality. They are interactions between conceptual spaces in human minds and entities from the natural world. The social categories of interest to social scientists cannot be reduced to the natural kind constituents of their individual referents. A category such as *capitalist country* refers to complex and heterogeneous entities in the natural world. Knowledge of the various natural kinds that compose each instance of a capitalist country is irrelevant to understanding what it is that all instances of capitalist countries have in common. The ultimate commonality shared by all the instances is their membership in the conceptual space for *capitalist country* within human minds. This conceptual space reflects the meanings of the category for the individuals who use and understand the category. The existence and utility of *capitalist country* depend on shared knowledge and shared understandings of its meaning among communities of individuals. With constructivist research, social categories such as *capitalist country* are not imagined to be ultimately composed of instances with *shared* mind-independent properties. Instead, social categories are treated as conceptual spaces embedded in the cognitive machinery of individuals that are used to comprehend heterogeneous natural entities as meaningful and homogeneous social entities.

This book develops practical and ready-for-use set-theoretic tools under this constructivist understanding of categories, as well as developing a full-blown set-theoretic approach for scientific constructivist research in the social sciences.

————

The pursuit of a set-theoretic social science involves some significant departures from business as usual. Analyzing all categories as sets is a far-reaching transformation for social research. We almost unavoidably view social reality as composed of variables for which individual cases possess particular values. Our language almost forces us to speak as if social categories are natural kind entities existing in external reality, with identities and dispositions. To think about and discuss categories as sets located in the mind that construct heterogeneous natural entities as instances of a given kind requires a deliberate effort, and it takes some practice to do it consistently and do it well. The good news is that many qualitative researchers already think about categories as sets in an informal way (Goertz and Mahoney 2012). These analysts are familiar with the kinds of research questions, theories, and methods that are possible and appropriate within set-theoretic analysis. This book is an invitation for qualitative researchers to embrace the basic premise of scientific constructivism: that social categories do not have a coherent relationship with entities in the natural world or stand in any kind of approximate one-to-one correspondence with natural kinds. It is an invitation for them to conduct constructivist set-theoretic analysis explicitly, rigorously, and imaginatively.

The idea that a set-theoretic social science is a departure from a variable-oriented social science is not controversial. However, methodologists do debate the extent to which set-theoretic methods have value added when compared to other methods, such as regression analysis (see Thomann and Maggetti 2020 for a literature review). Critics of set-theoretic analysis operate under the essentialist assumption that the purpose of a methodology is to report about the objective features of a mind-independent world. From the perspective of this book, however, the question is not whether set-theoretic analysis is a worthy approach in the pursuit of essentialist social science. Instead of arguing about the value added by set-theoretic analysis under essentialist assumptions, this book proposes that the more important and prior questions are (1) whether we need a non-essentialist methodology that accommodates the mind-dependence of social categories and, if so, (2) whether set-theoretic analysis can be that methodology. I argue that the answer is yes to both of these questions.

The focus of this book concerns how to use set-theoretic analysis in the study of categories that depend on shared human beliefs and understandings for their existence. These mind-dependent categories include most of the important categories in the disciplines of sociology (excluding parts of demography), political science, cultural anthropology, and economics. Scholars in these disciplines work almost exclusively with categories that fall into the mind-dependent camp. A few of the categories that are important in these disciplines—such as age, sex, morbidity, and death—exist in large part independently of human minds (some scholars, though not all, would exclude race and intelligence from this camp). In psychology, researchers in subfields such as neuropsychology and behavioral genetics work with largely mind-independent categories. By contrast, psychologists in subfields such as social psychology and educational psychology work with mostly mind-dependent categories. In still other subfields, such as abnormal psychology and developmental psychology, the mind-independent status of categories may vary or be the topic of debate. Insofar as researchers do study mind-independent categories, I view them as engaging in natural science research, for which essentialism is the appropriate point of departure. By contrast, I view scholars who work with mind-dependent categories as engaging in social science, for which constructivism is the appropriate point of departure. This book is directed at the latter group of scholars.

––––––

The scope of this book is restricted in two important ways. First, it focuses mainly on macroscopic research in the social sciences. The examples tend to be studies of large-scale processes and events, such as revolutions, democratization, development, and war. The main categories and units of analysis are aggregate groups, such as social movements, organizations, socioeconomic classes, states, and political systems. This macropolitical and macrosocial orientation reflects my own substantive areas of research and expertise. The focus is consequential because it means that the categories analyzed here are clear-cut examples of human-constructed, mind-dependent categories. If this book were more concentrated on the micro level—such as on individuals and their biological and physiological properties—it would need to say much more about the analysis of natural kinds. As it stands, the book offers principles and methods for research that falls squarely into the social sciences, defined as the study of mind-dependent categories.

Second, the book concerns mainly tools for case-study and small-N research—i.e., research that develops and evaluates propositions about a single case or a small number of cases. I do not focus on questions related to the evaluation of propositions concerning trends or tendencies that apply to large samples or large populations of cases. The focus on case-study and small-N research reflects, again, my own areas of interest and expertise. Fortunately, a scientific constructivist approach can be readily developed by starting with small-N research. The individual case is a convenient point of departure, because set-theoretic analysis for the social sciences is fundamentally rooted in a case-based logic. Trends or averages in populations exist only because of the features of the individual cases. A focus on individual cases also permits direct engagement with important philosophical literatures concerned with the mind, logic, cognitive models, categories, causality, normative beliefs, possible worlds, counterfactual analysis, certitude, and scientific truth. Although I do not address medium- and large-N set-theoretic methods in this book, these tools are well developed in the literature (e.g., Ragin 2008; Rihoux and Ragin 2009; Schneider and Wagemann 2012; Oana, Schneider, and Thomann forthcoming) and could be recast for constructivist rather than essentialist research.

This book is divided into three parts. Part I (chapters 1–2) concerns ontology and epistemology, introducing both scientific constructivism and set-theoretic analysis. This part establishes the conceptual foundations for the rest of the book. Part II (chapters 3–7) introduces and discusses specific methodological tools for evaluating propositions in the social sciences. Individual chapters in this part focus on tools for analyzing categories and causality, developing and using set-theoretic tests, carrying out counterfactual analysis, using sequence analysis for causal assessment, and employing Bayesian inference with evidence from case studies. Part III (chapters 8–11) discusses how set-theoretic analysis can be used in conjunction with a range of theoretical tools—what Stinchcombe (1968) calls tools for "inventing explanations." Individual chapters in this part concern theory frames and normative orientations, theory-building categories, critical event analysis, and path dependence. The book concludes by considering some of the implications of scientific constructivism for what it means to be an individual living in a society.

PART I

Ontology and Epistemology

1

Scientific Constructivism

This chapter begins to develop a scientific constructivist approach for the social sciences. The first section identifies the contrasting subject matter of the natural sciences and the social sciences: I propose that the natural sciences are primarily concerned with the analysis of natural kinds, whereas the social sciences are primarily concerned with the analysis of human kinds. The differences between natural kinds, human kinds, and partial natural kinds are identified and discussed. I focus much attention on how social scientists—unlike natural scientists—must work with mind-dependent categories that exist by virtue of implicit collective understandings.

The second section of the chapter explores how the default essentialism of social science researchers leads them to analyze human kinds as if they exist in the world as mind-independent entities. It shows how essentialism is both a built-in human bias and an entrenched social science orientation. I argue that social scientists need research procedures that assume that categories are produced from, and refer to, an interaction between the mind and the natural world.

The third section starts to build the foundation for the alternative to essentialism: a constructivist orientation. Using insights from a variety of disciplines, I introduce a conceptual space model for understanding human categorization. The model proposes that the human mind encompasses a multidimensional hyperspace in which categories exist as conceptual spaces. These conceptual spaces can be analyzed as *sets*, such that categories are mental sets located in the mind's representational space. I discuss how this approach to categories can help social scientists correct essentialist biases and treat human kinds as mind-dependent entities.

The fourth and final section briefly introduces set-theoretic analysis as a methodology for pursuing scientific research within a constructivist orientation. The section examines how set-theoretic analysis provides both a way of expressing logic and a way of applying the conceptual space model of human categorization in the design and practice of research.

Kinds of Kinds

Natural kinds and human kinds are used in classifying entities in the world (e.g., "these entities are *sodium salts*"; "these entities are *peasant revolts*"). But these classifications have different foundations. With natural kinds, one classifies entities as similar because of their shared essential properties—properties that exist independently of human minds. With human kinds, by contrast, one classifies entities as similar on the basis of characteristics that are not mind-independent properties. As a result, whereas one can study natural kinds by analyzing the essential properties that make them what they are, one must study human kinds by taking into consideration the process of mental classification that helps make them what they are.

The basic distinction developed in this section between natural kinds and human kinds is widely discussed in philosophy, in cognitive science, and, increasingly, in psychology. My summary of this distinction draws broadly from this literature, including especially the scientific realist strands within it. It would be too strong a statement to say that I have summarized the consensus view of the difference between natural kinds and human kinds; such a consensus view does not exist. However, my summary is well within the mainstream of this literature. Each component of the definitions presented here will be quite familiar to any scholar who works on the distinction between natural kinds and human kinds. The most novel aspect of my discussion is that I divide categories that are not human kinds into two groups: *natural kinds* and *partial natural kinds*. I do so because it is not clear to me that scientists have discovered any full-blown natural kinds. The category *partial natural kind* refers to entities that approximate the characteristics of natural kinds. Scientists have most certainly discovered many partial natural kinds, allowing human beings to exercise substantial, and sometimes extraordinary, control over the external world.

Table 1.1 provides an overview of the differences between natural kinds, human kinds, and partial natural kinds. For interested readers, an appendix at the end of this chapter discusses the distinction between natural kinds and human kinds in light of the problem of universals.

NATURAL KINDS

Natural kinds are entities that exist in nature independently of human beings. Humans *may* be able to discover these entities, but that discovery is not necessary for their existence. Natural kinds are *ontologically prior* to human beings

TABLE 1.1. Natural Kinds, Human Kinds, and Partial Natural Kinds

	Natural Kinds	Human Kinds	Partial Natural Kinds
Degree of Mind Independence	Full	Minimal	Considerable
Degree of Spatiotemporal Stability	Full	Minimal	Considerable
Causal Powers	Present	Not present	Partially present
Scientific Examples (substantive kinds)	Electron, helium atom, wave packet	Social movement, country, world system	Gene, igneous rock, synapse
Scientific Examples (property kinds)	Spherical shape, pure quantum state, magnetic	Progressive, democratic, capitalist	Mutant, connected, schizophrenic
Scientific Examples (dynamic kinds)	Photon emission, isomerization, nuclear decay	Revolution, economic growth, state formation	Accretion, eruption, neural communication
Everyday Examples (substantive, property, and dynamic kinds)	NA	Teacher, generous, graduation	Dog, green, death

and their activities and cognitions (Browning 1978; Ellis 2001: 63–67; cf. Hacking 1991). Examples of natural kinds *plausibly* include the elementary particles (e.g., quarks, leptons, bosons), the chemical elements (aluminum, hydrogen, gold), various natural properties (conductivities, wavelengths, spatiotemporal intervals), and various dynamic processes (chemical reactions, ionizations, diffractions). Such entities are our best candidates for the substances and processes that compose the mind-independent environment that is detected by our sensory organs.

Natural kinds are constituted by *essential properties*—i.e., the real essences that they possess and by virtue of which they exist (Ayers 1981; Kripke 1980; Oderberg 2007; Putnam 1975; Robertson 2009; Slater and Borghini 2011; Wilkerson 1988). These essences are immutable properties that have the same form across all times and places. Natural kinds are "eternal kinds" (Millikan 1999: 50). For example, atoms of uranium have the atomic number 92 across all spatiotemporal domains.[1] Regardless of its location in space and time, an entity cannot be an atom of uranium if it lacks the atomic number 92 (Hendry 2006).

The essences of natural kinds include *spectral properties* that permit a range of variation among specific instances of these kinds (Ellis 1996: 23; 2001: 79–81). For example, the essence of a field includes the spectral property "strength." Strength is a quantitative characteristic that can assume a range of possible values, some of which find empirical expression in particular fields. All specific instances of a natural kind must possess values on the spectral properties of that kind. Differences in the incidental possession of particular values on a spectral property by instances of a single kind allow for their comparison. For example, one can compare individual fields on the basis of differences in their strengths, quarks on the basis of differences in their flavors, and electromagnetic radiation emissions on the basis of differences in their frequencies.

The essential properties of natural kinds endow them with *causal powers* (Harré and Madden 1975; Salmon 1998; Ellis 2009; Mumford 2009; Mumford and Anjum 2011). These causal powers make the world dynamic and active, rather than stationary and passive. Sulfuric acid has the power to dissolve copper; electrostatic fields have the power to modify spectral lines; and masses have the power to curve spacetime. Causal powers are inherent dispositions; the kinds that possess them behave as their properties require them to behave. Possession of a particular spectral property (e.g., a strength or a charge) gives a natural kind certain causal powers that are different from those of other natural kinds. Incidental possession of a specific value on a spectral property (e.g., a particular strength or a particular charge) by an instance of a natural kind gives that instance a causal power that is different from that of other instances of the same kind with different values on the spectral property.

The existence of natural kinds suggests that quantification and mathematics are built into the fabric of reality. Under *mathematical realism* (or *platonism*), foundational mathematical entities such as sets, numbers, and functions are objective, eternal, indestructible, and real; they exist as abstract objects in all possible worlds, with or without human beings (Colyvan 2001; Hale 1987; Maddy 1990; Nagel 1997; Putnam 1979; Resnik 1997; Shapiro 1997, 2007).[2] Mathematics is real because reality consists of entities and laws (i.e., natural kinds with causal powers) that can be expressed in a precise and general manner (Sher 2013). The reality of mathematics imposes limits on what can possibly be true in science. Mathematics disqualifies as necessarily false descriptions of reality such as $2 + 2 = 5$. By the same token, mathematical realism qualifies logical reasoning as an objective basis for discovering truths about the world. To embrace mathematics is almost by definition to embrace logic; all or nearly all mathematic propositions are true by virtue of their logical form (Frege 1884/1960; Whitehead and Russell 1910/1956). Logic and mathematics exist in a fruitful relationship in which logic provides formal operators for valid reasoning and inference, while mathematics provides tools for describing the formal structure of reality (Sher 2013). Together, logic and mathematics provide essential resources not only for the scientific analysis of the natural world, but also for understanding and analyzing the human-constructed reality that constitutes the subject matter of the social sciences.

HUMAN KINDS

Human kinds lack intrinsic properties and dispositions that define them as kinds. They are ontologically dependent on human beings for their existence. Specifically, they are dependent on human brain activity; human kinds are mind-dependent kinds.[3] Examples include the social roles, institutions, and events that characterize human cultures and societies (e.g., *shaman, nurse, joke, marriage, supper, veto*). Human kinds encompass aggregate substantive entities designated with nouns (e.g., *movements, municipalities, world systems*), the properties of these entities designated with adjectives (*progressive, suburban, capitalist*), and dynamic processes represented as events (*wars, parades, surgeries, birthday parties, filibusters, state collapses*). Nearly all social science concepts are human kinds. Social science can, in fact, be defined as the scientific study of human kinds.

While human kinds depend ontologically on human brains, the *specific instances* of these kinds are not brain states.[4] Rather, the specific instances of a human kind consist of various mind-independent entities—i.e., various natural kinds—that are classified in and by the mind as an instance of a human kind. A specific instance of a hammer, or a specific instance of a social movement, is composed of natural kinds. But the general categories *hammer* and *social movement* are not reducible to or defined by the heterogeneous and mostly unknown natural substances and properties possessed by their various instances. Any two hammers or any two social movements need not share any natural kind constituents at all in order to be instances of hammers or social movements.

The mental classification of human kinds is marked by spatiotemporal instability. At any given moment, people may disagree about whether a certain event is a revolution, whether a certain practice is an act of discrimination, and whether a certain relationship is a strong political tie. Likewise, the entities that are customarily classified as revolutions, acts of discrimination, and strong political ties can change from one period to the next.[5] While it is possible and even desirable to try to define human kinds by presenting lists of distinguishing attributes, these attributes need not have any more referential connection to natural kinds than the human kinds that they define. One defines and clarifies the meaning of human kinds using other human kinds.

Human kinds lack intrinsic dispositions to which causal powers can be attributed. Human kinds are not part of any laws of nature (Bhaskar 1979/1998; Sayer 2000). To be sure, a *specific instance* of a human kind will follow the laws of nature by virtue of the natural kinds that constitute it. For example, perhaps in part because of its specific mass, an individual hammer has the capacity to deliver a certain amount of energy to a target when subject to a force brought on by our muscles. However, the general category *hammer* cannot be defined on the basis of its intrinsic causal powers or its position in a law of nature. The category *hammer* does not have a correspondence to natural kinds that humans can coherently model or represent.

Intersubjective agreement about the meaning of human kinds is common, at least within spatially and temporally bounded communities. We agree, more or less, on what a hammer is. People in all cultures use declarative speech acts to impose status functions on objects that become collectively recognized and often accepted within their communities (Searle 1995, 2015). This intersubjective understanding allows us to communicate intelligibly and to respond to the world in regularized fashions (Churchland 1998; Laakso and Cottrell 2000). Our linguistic representations infuse meaning into our lives and help guide our behavior (Searle 2008).

Human kinds have *reality-creating effects* for human beings (Merton 1948; Berger and Luckmann 1966; Bourdieu 1984; Foucault 1975/1995; Searle 1995; Hacking 1995a; Goodman 1978; Miller 2000; Thomasson 2003; Smith 2010; I. Reed 2011; Elder-Vass 2012). When people impose a function and a label on entities and then tacitly agree about that imposition, they have created a new human reality. Over time, the fact that the category was originally constructed may be forgotten (if even acknowledged in the first place). The ability of human beings to fluidly create their experienced reality by virtue of categorization distinguishes them from other life forms on earth. This remarkable skill is accompanied by an equally remarkable capacity to effortlessly view the constructed categories as if they directly correspond to an objective external reality. Humans cannot help thinking and talking as if their categories refer to entities that are truly "out there" in the world.

The stable expectations associated with human kinds depend on a larger web of preexisting categories that are themselves treated as if they faithfully map an objective reality (Geertz 1973; Taylor 1985). The meaning of any given human kind is dependent on this larger matrix of categories and meanings. We need not know anything at all about the natural kinds that ultimately underlie this semantic web. The reality *as we experience it* is upheld by mostly unconscious collective understandings that strike us as brute facts about an objectively and independently existing reality.

PARTIAL NATURAL KINDS

Categories can vary in the degree to which they are members of the set *natural kind*. True examples of natural kinds (*boson* might currently be our best candidate) have full membership in *natural kind*. Other categories (e.g., *tiger*) have considerable but not full membership (cf. Churchland 1985; Boyd 1991; Lewis 1984: 227–29; Miller 2000; Wendt 1999: 67–77). Human kind categories (e.g., *sixth-grade teacher*) do not have membership in this set, though they can vary in the extent of their distance from entering the set. The category *bronze things* is closer to being a natural kind than the category *shiny things*; the category *human being* is closer to being a natural kind than the category *professor*; and the category *black hole* is closer to being a natural kind than the category *economy*. Categories such as *planet, thunderstorm,* and *rock*—as well as *neuron, plate tectonics,* and perhaps even *life*—do not carve nature precisely at its joints, but they do carve it in ways that approximate these joints, sometimes very closely.[6]

Partial natural kinds[7] are categories with substantial but incomplete membership in the set *natural kinds*; they correspond reasonably well to the structure of the mind-independent world. Partial natural kinds substantially but imperfectly map the substances, properties, and processes of the natural world. They may pick out some but not all of the essential properties of a natural kind; or they may usefully but incompletely describe these essential properties. Partial natural kinds have relatively predictable effects—sometimes nearly deterministic effects—regardless of human ideas and cognitions. Knowledge of partial natural kinds allows humans to have considerable control over the natural world, at times even unfathomable control.

Many of the concepts used in astronomy, biology, cognitive science, earth science, and psychology are partial natural kinds. Some examples include *planet, stellar collision, gene, cell, lion, natural selection, brain, synaptic connection, neurotransmission, volcano, thunderstorm, human being, aging,* and *memory.* These concepts do not carve nature precisely at its joints, but they come at least reasonably close, allowing scientists to make generalizations about their intrinsic properties and powers. If human beings ceased to recognize *elephants, cancerous cells,* and *galaxies,* the entities corresponding to these categories would still function in ways that approximate our best scientific models of these categories. In fact, insofar as one believes that natural scientists have yet to discover any full-blown natural kinds (cf. Dupré 2002; Hacking 2007), nearly all of the core concepts in even physics and chemistry are partial natural kinds. For our purposes, we need not decide whether concepts such as *electron, uranium,* and *ionization* are true natural kinds or simply partial natural kinds that track nature with remarkable effectiveness. We need only recognize that some existing categories approximate natural kinds.[8]

The boundary between partial natural kinds and human kinds is not always clear. An important component of science is precisely the assessment of whether a category is a partial natural kind or "merely" a human kind. For example, researchers actively explore questions of whether psychological states such as *depression* and *happiness* are partial natural kinds or human kinds (Panksepp 2000; Barrett 2006, 2017; Izard 2007). I see the disciplines of psychology, biology, and physiology as centrally concerned with distinguishing partial natural kinds from human kinds that we may mistakenly understand as existing independently of us.

Questions about whether an entity is a partial natural kind or a human kind often arise with respect to the properties of individuals, such as their biological and psychological features (e.g., race, emotional state, personality type). To evaluate whether these traits are partial natural kinds, scientists explore whether they are reducible to partial natural kinds at lower levels of analysis. If a property of a human being reduces coherently to partial natural kinds at a lower level, the property itself is a partial natural kind. For instance, scientists treat eye color as a partial natural kind because it can be modeled and reduced coherently, if not perfectly, to genes and single-nucleotide polymorphisms. By contrast, they debate whether happiness is a partial natural kind, because it is not clear that it reduces coherently to autonomic nervous system patterns or to the brain's neurotransmitters, circuitry, and chemicals (Barrett 2006, 2017).

In the social sciences, similar questions about whether entities are partial natural kinds typically do not arise. Social scientists do not study entities that reduce coherently to natural kinds at lower levels of analysis. For instance, it is fruitless to try to reduce the entity *United States of America* to a set of natural kind properties. The same can be said of general categories such as *country, inflation, democratic transition,* and *crime.* We do not learn about these categories by probing the underlying natural kinds that constitute their individual instances. This irreducible status also applies to most of the social traits of individuals that interest social scientists, such as income, occupation, and education. When social scientists study traits such as gender, race, and intelligence, they analyze them as constructed categories that depend on human beliefs and practices for their existence. To be sure, one might also study these traits to explore whether they partially reduce to natural kinds. Yet insofar as researchers study individual traits that may be reducible to partial natural kinds—such as biological age, biological sex, biological race, innate intelligence, morbidity, and mortality—they are appropriately regarded as engaging in natural science research (or research at the intersection of the natural sciences and social sciences).

The social sciences productively blur into the natural sciences when social scientists explore the ways in which proposed natural phenomena are in part culturally generated entities. Social scientists have produced formidable research on the social construction of illness (Aronowitz 1991; Briggs and Mantini-Briggs 2003; Brown 1995; Epstein 1996, 2007; Hacking 1995b), gender (Fraser 1989; Morning 2009; Ortner and Whitehead 1981; Scott 1986), race and ethnicity (Bonilla-Silva 2006; Brubaker, Loveman, and Stamatov 2004; Duster 2001; Hirschfeld 1996; Nobles 2000), and sexual orientation (Gagnon and Simon 1973; Plummer 1999; Vance 1989). This research shows that categories which authorities and others understand to be natural or biological kinds (e.g., *HIV positive, female, African American, lesbian*) are actually dependent in part on human ideas and practices, in sometimes ironic ways. Likewise, scholars of science find that scientific kinds are evolving entities whose meaning changes quite a lot over time (Kuhn 1970; Barnes 1974; Latour and Woolgar 1986; Nelson 1994; Giere 2006; Nersessian 2010). The success of this research at illustrating the evolution in scientists' understandings of our best candidates for natural kinds (e.g., *electron, gene, quark*) is one reason why I believe that natural scientists have to date probably discovered only partial natural kinds (Arabatzis 2006; Mukherjee 2016; Pickering 1984). Constructivist research repeatedly shows that scientific entities presented as full-blown natural kinds are not fully independent of human beings and their minds.

THE MEANING-REFERENT CONTINUUM

The fact that natural scientists may not have discovered—and may not be able to discover—any full-blown natural kinds points toward the value of viewing the distinction between natural kinds and human kinds as continuous in nature. A continuous view is helpful for thinking about a partial natural kind, which stands between a human kind and a natural kind, though closer to the latter. A continuous view is also helpful for recognizing that the entities that are members of a given human kind sometimes share incidental natural kind properties, even though those properties are not the main defining components of the human kind.

I propose that we think of natural kinds and human kinds as zones located around opposite ends of a continuum. To conceptualize this continuum, I use Ogden and Richards' (1923) semantic triangle, which is summarized in figure 1.1. For our purposes, the crucial aspect of the triangle is the relationship on the right side, between the meaning of a category and the referents of a category. The *meaning of a category* is cognitive in nature, corresponding to the conscious and unconscious understandings, knowledge, and beliefs of individuals, which are grounded in the machinery of brains. The *referents of a category* correspond to the objects and entities in the world that are instances of the category. For example, if the category is *dog*, the meaning corresponds to our beliefs and understandings of *dog*, whereas the referents correspond to the dog entities in the world.

With full-blown natural kinds, the referents of a category alone determine the meaning of the category. The arrow on the right side of the semantic triangle would then run from *referents* to *meaning* without reciprocal feedback (i.e., referents → meaning). The meaning of a category is a reflection of the mind-independent entities that compose the referents; the mind plays no direct role in the constitution of the category. This view of categories captures

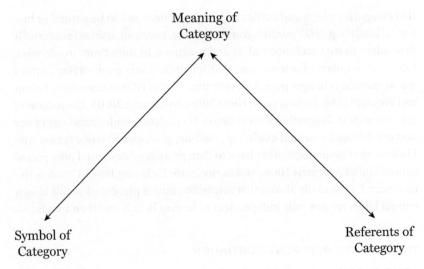

FIGURE 1.1. Ogden and Richards' Semantic Triangle. Adapted from Ogden and Richards (1923).

the logic of an idealized portrait of the natural sciences, one in which natural science categories are simply reports about the structure of objective reality.

With an ideal-typical definition of human kinds, by contrast, the relationship between meaning and referent operates in the opposite direction. Now the arrow on the right side runs non-reciprocally from *meaning* to *referents* (i.e., meaning → referents). Human understandings and beliefs fully constitute the identities and properties of the referents; the mind-independent composition of the referents has nothing to do with the meaning of the category. In the philosophical literature, *radical constructivism* is the view that this relationship applies to all categories. With radical constructivism, all categories depend ontologically only on human cognition and language; they do not map a pre-existing objective reality, even if such a reality exists (Derrida 1982; Goodman 1978; Rorty 1979; Shotter 1993).

I propose that existing categories in the natural and social sciences fall between these two extremes. For all or nearly all existing categories, the relationship between the meaning and the referents is one of mutual constitution and reciprocal causation, just as Ogden and Richards suggested. Individual categories fall along a continuum according to the extent to which the meaning, versus the referents, is the primary constitutive element in the relationship.

Notwithstanding this reciprocal relationship, however, useful categories in the natural sciences and the social sciences fall at opposite ends of the continuum, in what we can think of as the two zones corresponding to, respectively, partial natural kinds and human kinds.[9] With partial natural kinds, the mind-independent composition of the referents primarily determines the meaning of the category, although the beliefs and understandings of researchers have some constitutive role to play. Here, in the mutually constitutive meaning-referent relationship, the referents have the leading role.

By contrast, human kinds are categories whose meaning primarily, or even completely, constructs the identity of the referents. With human kinds, the referents may share certain mind-independent properties (e.g., all professors are constituted in part by oxygen, carbon, and hydrogen), but these properties do not play a significant role in determining the meaning of the category. Rather, the mutually constitutive meaning-referent relationship is such that shared understandings and beliefs come close to fully establishing the similarities required for category membership. Social science categories are rooted ontologically in collective understandings that cannot be reduced to any mind-independent properties that the referents of the categories may share.

The Reification of Human Kinds

Human kinds are reified when they are treated as if they are entities that possess intrinsic properties that endow them with an identity and a disposition. When human kinds are reified, they are understood to be coherent, self-organizing things "out there" in the world. Such reification is an almost unavoidable outcome of the way the mind works and the way language is used. In our everyday lives, we reify the social world on an ongoing basis; we cannot help it. We engage in *psychological essentialism* by viewing the objects and entities around us as if they have inner essences and true natures (Medin 1989; Medin and Ortony 1989; Ahn et al. 2001; Gelman 2003; Newman and Knobe 2019). In social science analysis, this essentialist orientation takes the form of what I call the *property-possession assumption*—i.e., the assumption that social science categories, like natural kinds, possess hidden and causally efficacious properties.[10]

ESSENTIALISM

Essentialism refers to the belief that the members of a category possess hidden properties called *essences* that make them members of the category and that endow them with a certain nature (Medin 1989; Medin and Ortony 1989; Keil 1989; Rothbart and Taylor 1992; Sayer 1997; Haslam 1998; Haslam, Rothschild, and Ernst 2000; Ahn et al. 2001; Gelman 2003; Newman and Knobe 2019; Rose and Nichols 2019).[11] These hidden essences are what all the instances of a given category ultimately have in common. For example, individuals who are members of the category *scientist* are assumed to possess some unobservable though essential characteristics that make them scientists (Knobe, Prasada, and Newman 2013). Our implicit understandings of these essences might differ quite a lot (e.g., the essence of *scientist* might be understood to involve occupational position, the impartial quest for truth, or the application of the scientific method). Nevertheless, the language users in a given community all use the category as if *something* exists that makes it appropriate to call certain individuals scientists.

While we communicate as if specific essences constitute human kinds, "essentialism does not entail that people know (consciously or unconsciously) what the essence is" (Gelman and Diesendruck 1999: 88; see also Medin and Ortony 1989; Gelman 2003; Newman and Knobe 2019; Rose and Nichols 2019). For many categories, the essence is nothing more than a placeholder with unknown content that we simply assume exists. The placeholder structure invites inquiries to discover hidden essences, as well as creative attempts to summarize the underlying similarities shared by all category members (Gelman and Roberts 2017) or perhaps the underlying homeostatic property clusters of categories (Boyd 1991, 2010; Kornblith 1993; Wilson 1999). At the same time, we always have trouble identifying the precise essences of human kinds when asked to do so explicitly—because such essences do not actually exist. The lack of shared essences helps explain why all important concepts in the social sciences defy easy and consensual definition.

An essentialist orientation to the world develops at an early age and does not appear to require any formal training for its acquisition (Gelman 2003). By the time we are adults, it has become a longstanding and basic component of how we experience the world. "Essentialism is a pervasive, persistent reasoning bias that affects human categorization in profound ways. It is deeply ingrained in our conceptual systems, emerging at a very young age across highly varied cultural contexts" (Gelman 2003: 6). The existing evidence supports the proposition that essentialism is "a species-general, universal, inevitable mode of thought," though the specific categories that are essentialized vary greatly across time and space (Gelman 2003: 283; see also Rhodes and Gelman 2009; Bloom 2010; Rhodes, Leslie, and Tworek 2012). Many scholars suggest that ancestral humans evolved a disposition to naturalize human kinds because it was beneficial for their survival and reproduction (e.g., Atran 1998; Kornblith 1993; Pinker 1994, 2002; Sperber 1994). One version of this argument holds that essentialism emerged from cognitive skills that were evolutionarily adaptive (Gelman 2003), including heuristics for making inductive inferences during the first years of life (Cimpian and Salomon 2014; Quillien 2018). By treating entities as if they have essential properties, people can fluently communicate with one another and can predictably and meaningfully act on the world. They can assign functions to objects and create social and institutional facts that exist by virtue of human agreement (cf. Durkheim 1895/1982; Merton 1948; Berger and Luckmann 1966; Searle 1995). A capacity to engage in psychological essentialism may underpin the human ability to discover the inner properties of natural kinds (Bloom 2000).

An essentialist orientation includes the implicit belief that underlying essences can cause other shared traits (besides category identity) among the members of a category. These shared traits often include similarities in the surface-level features, or "perceptual properties," of category members. In the case of *scientist*, one might assume that category members tend to share a certain lifestyle and dress, and perhaps even a typical gender and physical appearance. When asked why category members tend to share certain observable characteristics, people suggest the possession of some common underlying quality (Newman and Knobe 2019). With "identity disruption" experiments, scholars find that children and adults believe that category members can retain their identity despite "unnatural" changes in surface-level appearances. For instance, a scientist is still a scientist even if dressed up to look like a police officer. Only changes that alter *essential properties* can cause category members to lose their identity (Xu and Carey 1996; Rips, Blok, and Newman 2006; De Freitas et al. 2017). For example, one might believe that a scientist whose brain is replaced with a non-scientist's brain is no longer a scientist. Recent experimental work suggests that the essence of a category is closely linked to the imagined purpose, or telos, of the category, much as Aristotle suggested (Rose 2015; Rose and Schaffer 2017; Rose and Nichols 2019).

The imagined shared essences possessed by the members of a category facilitate our ability to make generalizations about the category and its members. Essentialist assumptions provide a logical basis for inductive inference, which is perhaps the primary function of essentialism both evolutionarily and culturally. Human beings assume that essences consist of properties that confer predictable dispositions on category members. They assume that the members of a category have predictable natures, or at least semi-predictable tendencies. When we learn that a case is a member of a category, we generally infer that the case will function or behave like other members of the category. When we hear that an individual is a member of the category *scientist, police officer,* or *artist*, we automatically begin to make inductive inferences based on our understanding of the tendencies of the category. Psychologists have carried out many ingenious experiments that support the proposition that categories promote inductive inferences, by both children and adults (Gelman 2003: chap. 2). The *range* of inferences that one can draw from a category varies, depending on whether the category is a partial natural kind (e.g., *gold*), a living kind (*cat*), a simple artifact (*hammer*), a complex artifact (*computer*), or a social role (*scientist*). Nevertheless, within their range, all of these kinds of categories allow their users to make important inductive inferences (Gelman 2003: 48–52, 137–39). Essentialism underpins human beings' ability to identify and navigate the predictable aspects of both their natural and social environments.

A large literature in psychology and cognitive science has accumulated over the last thirty years in support of the proposition that human beings engage in essentialism for a wide range of categories, including both natural and social categories (for literature reviews, see Gelman 2003 and Newman and Knobe 2019). This impressive research is consistent with important earlier findings in support of the proposition that human beings engage in the objectification of categories (see Lakoff 1987 for a literature review). Within the relevant scientific communities, the proposition that placeholder essentialism is basic to human thought is widely, if not universally, accepted (for a dissenting view, see Strevens 2000; but see also the joint rebuttal of Strevens by eight scientists in Ahn et al. 2001). The best scientific research consistently finds that human beings by default assume that the members of a category possess some perhaps unknowable properties that make them members of the category and give them observable dispositions.

TYPES OF ESSENTIALISM

Human beings engage in essentialism in different ways depending on the kind of essence that is believed to constitute the identity of category members (Rothbart and Taylor 1992; Haslam, Rothschild, and Ernst 2000; Gelman 2003; Prentice and Miller 2007; Newman and Knobe 2019). It is useful to distinguish, on the basis of contrasting understandings of these essences, three types of essentialism: *artifact essentialism*, *innate essentialism*, and *social essentialism* (cf. Bloom 1996; Haslam, Rothschild, and Ernst 2000; Gelman and Hirschfeld 1999).[12] These types imply differences in the extent to which and the way in which essences can change (e.g., Dweck 1998; Dweck and Leggett 1988). They function as different constellations of intuitions, and they may be rooted in distinct information-processing systems of the brain (Quillien 2018). Despite their differences, each type is a full member of the category *essentialism* (on the definition of essentialism, see Newman and Knobe 2019; Rose and Nichols 2019). One implication of this typology is that even constructivist scholars, who recognize that human kinds are historically and socially constructed entities, engage in the reification of human kinds. A commitment to constructivism is not sufficient to avoid it.[13]

With *artifact essentialism*, objects are understood to have essences reflecting the intentions of perhaps hypothetical designers who endow the objects with certain functions (Keil 1989; Dennett 1990; Bloom 1996, 1998, 2010; Keleman and Carey 2007; Rose 2015). We identify hammers, blankets, computers, and airplanes on the basis of assumptions about what the entities were designed to be, rather than only their surface-level similarities. A cup and bowl differ because they were designed for different purposes. A large towel may be more functional for warmth than a decorative blanket, but the former cannot be a member of the category *blanket* because of its presumed design history (cf. Rips 1989). The essences of artifacts can be changed through redesign (e.g., a cup can be remade into a plate), and artifacts may retain some of their identity even when their surface-level features are radically transformed (a shattered glass is still kind of a glass). The utility of artifacts is often linked to their imagined essences (Bloom 1996, 1998; Gelman 2013). The essence of a cup is understood as a history in which a designer created an object for drinking liquids. In turn, a cup is a great object to use for drinking liquids. Beyond their intended functions, most artifacts do not allow for interesting additional generalizations or inductive inferences. Artifacts are not part of the laws of nature. We do not believe that the everyday category *cup* possesses interesting properties that endow its members with intrinsic causal powers worth studying in the natural or social sciences.

With *innate essentialism*, the members of a category are believed to share an inherent and relatively permanent internal structure that gives rise to common surface-level features and predictable natures. Our folk biology regarding species illustrates innate essentialism: we assume the members of a species are born with some hidden inner essence that makes them a certain kind of plant or animal (Atran and Medin 2008; Mayr 1982, 1988). Even children as young as four years old believe that animals sustain their identity despite major changes to their appearance—e.g., a cat remains a cat even if it is changed to look like a skunk (Taylor 1996; Gelman 2003). Cultural variation exists in the extent to which human characteristics are viewed as innate. Categories associated with mental disorders (e.g., *bipolar*), ethnicity (*Jewish*), gender (*male*), race (*Latinx*), and sexual orientation (*homosexual*) are often, though certainly not always, seen as deeply ingrained properties that are beyond the control of individuals (Haslam, Rothschild, and Ernst 2000; Haslam, Holland, and Karasawa 2013; Taylor, Rhodes, and Gelman 2009). Constructivist social scientists view innate essentialism as deeply problematic, because it promotes prejudicial stereotypes about individuals. These constructivists target innate essentialism for exposure, critique, and elimination.[14]

Finally, with *social essentialism*, entities are believed to share underlying essences that are historically and socially acquired, perhaps even voluntarily chosen. But once established, these essences assume an autonomous existence, functioning as an underlying core that makes a category a meaningful, unified, self-organized, and distinct entity in the world (Haslam, Rothschild, and Ernst 2000, 2004; Rhodes and Gelman 2009; Rhodes and Mandalaywala 2017; Waxman 2012). People understand a wide range of ordinary descriptive categories through the lens of social essentialism. These categories include the social characteristics of individuals, such as their occupations (e.g., *lawyer, chef, telemarketer*), their politics (*Republican, libertarian, centrist*), and their personalities (*friendly, talkative, rude*). The categories viewed through social essentialism also include social entities (e.g., *neighborhood, protest movement, county, country, world economy*) and their social characteristics (*diverse, strong, homogeneous, developed, capitalist*). People often believe that cases acquire membership in these categories through a historical process in which the case moves from non-membership to membership. Understanding these social processes is of great interest to historically inclined researchers like myself. At the same time, once a case has acquired membership in a category, we normally feel comfortable treating the case as an entity that exists empirically in the world with the new category identity.

Experimental research finds that categories with socially acquired essences are believed to possess the features of *entitativity*, including coherence, unification, and meaningfulness (Diesendruck et al. 2013; Haslam, Rothschild, and Ernst 2000, 2004; Haslam, Holland, and Karasawa 2013). With entitativity, a category is treated as a self-organized thing or property in the world; the category is believed to be a meaningful, informative, and deeply seated entity (Tsukamoto et al. 2017; cf. Campbell 1958). Entitativity is the main basis of essentialism for social categories. We engage in entitativity even as we readily acknowledge the social construction of a category. We simply cannot help implicitly understanding a category as an informative, cohesive thing, even though we also know that it is mutable and socially constructed.

The extent to which social categories are viewed as coherent, meaningful, and unified entities can vary across categories and contexts (Haslam, Rothschild, and Ernst 2000, 2004; Haslam, Holland, and Karasawa 2013; Prentice and Miller 2007; Karasawa, Asai, and Hioki 2019). At one extreme, some categories are incoherent across all contexts (e.g., *birds that smell like squares*) or arbitrary across all contexts (*birds hatched on Tuesdays between 10 a.m. and 11 a.m. central time*). Some categories are arbitrary across nearly all contexts (*left-handed professors, gas stations with exactly five pumps, countries with flags that contain red, white, or blue*). At the other extreme, many of our ordinary language categories are coherent, meaningful, and unified entities across a wide range of contexts. For example, according to one important set of experimental results, the properties of individuals with high entitativity include (but are not limited to) their specific political orientation (e.g., *liberal*), personality type (*shy*), social class (*upper class*), psychiatric state (*depressed*), and occupational position (*doctor*) (Haslam, Rothschild, and Ernst 2000). Another class of categories with high entitativity are those that are carefully and explicitly defined to function as coherent, meaningful, and unified entities for specific audiences. Important social science categories fall into this group. Social scientists define and measure social categories that are intended to have exceptionally high levels of entitativity for their audiences. While social scientists use categories that may depend on considerable contextual knowledge, the categories are always understood to be very sound, clear, and well-specified ideas for those who possess the requisite knowledge.

Social essentialism is the foundation of our inductive inferences and generalizations about non-artifact human kinds. For example, if we know that a country is populous, industrialized, and ethnically homogeneous, we have a basis for making educated guesses about the wealth and health of its people. In fact, we cannot help starting to make inferences when we hear about a case that possesses these traits. If we learn that an individual is female, educated, and unemployed, our minds automatically begin to generalize about her possible experiences and traits. We may also feel emotions and begin to pass normative judgments in response to that information (Bloom 2010).

Social researchers believe that category essences are at least somewhat malleable, often arbitrary, and human-constructed. A strong version of these beliefs corresponds to what is usually meant by *constructivism* (cf. Bourdieu 1989; Hacking 1999; Smith 2010). Constructivists are scholars who emphasize the socially constructed nature of social categories. However, our built-in essentialist orientation does not disappear when we recognize that category essences are historical achievements and human inventions. We still think and speak about categories in ways that depend on placeholder essences to hold the categories together as entities. We still proceed using a language in which individuals *possess* a sexual orientation, a geographic location, and a level of income. We cannot help communicating as if an individual *is* a Latina, a community *has* a good human rights record, and a city *was* or *will become* progressive. We engage in reification simply by virtue of working and communicating through the orientation with which our species has been built to perceive and understand the world.

Essentialism is so basic to how we think and communicate that it is not apparent how we can truly transcend this viewpoint. Overcoming essentialist thinking and communication is not only a matter of accepting that our linguistic categories function quite well despite their referential disconnection with natural kinds. Nor is it only a matter of accepting the human-constructed and mind-dependent nature of our categories. Rather, to escape essentialism, we need an approach that allows us to comprehend, analyze, and discuss the social world as composed of something other than entities in possession of properties. We need an approach that views human reality in a way that does not correspond to how we ordinarily experience it.

THE PROPERTY-POSSESSION ASSUMPTION

In the social sciences, the implicit belief that human kinds possess essential properties that endow them with an identity and dispositional tendencies can be called the *property-possession assumption*. This assumption is a natural outgrowth of psychological essentialism when extended to social scientific research. The property-possession assumption is used whenever we define and measure our units of analysis (e.g., social movements, neighborhoods, countries) on the basis of properties and attributes that are understood to match empirical features of the world. It is used when we compare our units of analysis using variables (e.g., size of membership, level of resources, degree of economic integration) that are understood to capture variation in a property possessed by the units. It is used when we test hypotheses to see if changes in one property (e.g., level of income) generate a causal process that leads to changes in another property (e.g., political party affiliation).

Methodological work on concepts and conceptualization sometimes explicitly embraces an essentialist approach to social science concepts (e.g., Goertz 2006b, 2020). Whether explicitly essentialist or not, however, nearly all social scientists assume that their concepts reference objects and properties in the external world.[15] A standard view is that the referents of concepts are the phenomena of interest, and "the phenomena of interest are, of course, the entities out there in the world that correspond to the concept" (Gerring 2012: 116). Scholars assume that macro concepts such as *state, democracy,* and *capitalism* aggregate attributes from lower levels of analysis. They assume that the attributes at the very lowest level—the "leaves" on concept trees—are sufficiently differentiated to track properties of the external world. For the purposes of research, they assume that concepts ultimately reduce to measures that correspond to the structure of the mind-independent world. They do so even though these final measures are often variables that are clearly dependent on human constructions, such as household income reports, years of schooling, and GDP per capita.

The property-possession assumption also underpins the measurement of human kinds once they are defined. Standard measurement techniques entail observing and recording the mind-independent properties possessed by the units of analysis. Measurement is understood to be the quantification of physical properties (Campbell 1920). As Stevens (1946: 677) famously put it, "measurement, in the broadest sense, is defined as the assignment of numerals to objects or events according to rules." For Stevens and others, the empirical status of these "objects or events" was never in doubt; the focus was on the appropriate rules for their objective measurement. Social scientists usually assume without comment that the units under study (e.g., individuals, clubs, trade alliances) are marked by characteristics that we can directly or indirectly observe and measure. As Bollen (2002: 611) writes, "The starting point is the objects of study . . . These objects have properties. Properties are characteristics . . . such as self-esteem, intelligence, cohesion, anxiety, etc." (see also Blalock 1982: 24). When the properties are latent (i.e., not directly observable), we must find correlated indicators to measure them. But we still assume that we are measuring a variable (e.g., self-esteem, cohesion, anxiety) that corresponds to a feature varyingly possessed by the cases under study.

The property-possession assumption is built into causal propositions concerning social categories. For instance, consider the proposition that the growth of the state within countries causes a reduction in violence in those countries (Pinker 2011). The proposition assumes that the state is an entity that exists in the world with certain properties and certain dispositions that can endow it with causal powers. Scholars might debate the exact nature of these properties and powers (e.g., the state's coercive powers versus its persuasive powers). They might emphasize different features of the state when explaining this relationship (e.g., enforcement agencies versus educational agencies). But for the proposition to make sense, scholars must assume that states are entities that can be scientifically studied in basically the same way that individuals, earthquakes, and DNA strands can be scientifically studied. The property-possession assumption is vital to the meaning and intelligibility of causal propositions concerning social categories and their causal relationships.

No mental heavy lifting is required to understand the proposition that the growth of the state causes a reduction in societal violence. Our built-in essentialist orientation leads us to view as strange the argument that states are not entities that exist in the world with causal potentials. Essentialism tells us that of course they are. Our essentialist thinking calls forth arguments maintaining that we know that the state exists because we know it has real effects (Wendt 1999, 2004). The essentialist in us says, "Of course the state exists. If it didn't, we wouldn't pay our taxes!" Yet our logical mind is capable of accepting a different conclusion: human kinds, such as the state, do not correspond in any *coherent* way with any natural entities in the world. Rather, the category *state* runs through, and is entangled with, our minds. To understand any relationship between states and violence, we must acknowledge and somehow model the mind-dependent nature of the category *state*.[16]

The commonness of a psychological orientation does not determine its truth (Churchland 1989; Dennett 1987).[17] Understanding reality often depends on departing from our commonsense orientations, helpful as they otherwise may be. A very useful orientation built into our cognitive machinery is *intuitive physics*—i.e., our capacity to anticipate how the medium-sized physical objects around us will behave (Dennett 1987; Pinker 2007; Elga 2007). Yet our intuitive physics is deeply misleading about the true nature of objects and motion; its assumptions are rejected in Newtonian, relativity, and quantum physics (McCloskey 1983). *Scientific physics* is counterintuitive to us, and some of its implications (e.g., nonlocality) are difficult to accept or even comprehend, because they so completely violate our experience. Similar remarks can be made about intuitive biology (Shtulman 2006; Coley and Tanner 2012), intuitive chemistry (Maeyer and Talanquer 2010), and intuitive psychology (Medin and Ortony 1989; Pinker 1997).

This book asserts that *intuitive social analysis* is misleading about the nature of social, cultural, economic, and political categories and their relationships. Intuitive social analysis assumes that social units, such as physicians, social movements, economies, and countries, possess essential properties that constitute them as meaningful entities. It assumes that differences in essential properties explain why different kinds of social units have the potential to behave in distinctive ways: for instance, social movements are by their very nature the kind of entities that can engage in protests, whereas economies are by their nature the kind of entities that can experience recessions. Intuitive social analysis assumes that particular instances of a given human kind can vary in the degree to which or the way in which they possess essential properties. These differences explain variations in how specific instances of a particular kind express their general dispositions: for instance, variations in the resources possessed by social movements may explain their relative tendencies to achieve unified protest, whereas variations in the distribution of wealth within economies may explain their relative tendencies toward recession. Researchers follow their intuitions when they formulate and evaluate hypotheses about the causal relationships that exist among human kinds.

Scientific social analysis requires letting go of these intuitions in order to analyze social categories in a non-essentialist way. A scientific approach to social analysis recognizes that the members of a social category consist of heterogeneous, mostly unspecified, and certainly uncomprehended natural kinds. These naturally diverse entities are instances of a category because they are constructed as an entity—and a particular kind of entity—in the mind. Scientific social analysis assumes that the existence of a social category as a meaningful and coherent entity depends on the ongoing operations of human minds. When working with categories such as *state*, *democracy*, and *capitalism*, scientific social analysis recognizes that the mind plays a central role in their original construction and ongoing constitution. Any causal effects of these categories are entangled with the human minds that allow the categories to exist. Scientific social analysis is constructivist, in the sense that it builds a fundamental role for human minds into the ontology of social science categories.

Scientific social analysis requires researchers to be conflicted: science insists on an understanding of social reality that violates our basic intuitions. The gap between science and intuition can never be completely closed, because essentialism is rooted in neurological machinery shaped by millions of years of evolution (cf. Graziano 2019: 93–94). But it is possible to develop and follow research procedures that reject essentialism. This book develops a set-theoretic approach that not only embraces a constructivist understanding of human kinds in principle, but also provides tools for its adoption in the actual practice of research. This set-theoretic methodology follows the mandate of science to use the rational parts of our brain machinery to overcome the limitations and deeply seated biases of our evolved minds.

Conceptual Spaces and the Constitution of Human Kinds

The constructivist set-theoretic approach developed in this book proposes that a particular instance of a human kind exists when individuals classify unspecified natural kinds as an entity with membership in a set. A *set* is an abstract object produced by and in the human mind; it is a mental phenomenon (see chapter 2 for analysis of the category *set*). By assigning a leading role to mental sets in the constitution of human kinds, we can build an approach that avoids the reification of human kinds, and formulate a usable methodology for substantive scientific constructivist research.

A CONCEPTUAL SPACE MODEL

To explore the ontology of human kinds, we need some working model of the cognitive processes involved in human categorization. Such a model must be consistent with the best insights and findings from scientific work about how the mind creates and uses categories. Of course, scientists face daunting problems in modeling and explaining these representational processes. The vast complexity of our mental machinery (the brain is a dynamic, nonlinear system with billions of neurons and trillions of synapses) and its profound inaccessibility to us (we have no conscious access to the brain mechanisms that interpret and process perceptions) render impossible, with current knowledge, a fully adequate model of all the components of representational processes. Nevertheless, scientists have generated stable conclusions about some of the partial natural kinds that constitute the entities, properties, and processes involved in categorization. These conclusions can help ground a framework for conceptualizing the mind-dependent nature of social categories.

Proceeding with caution, we can say that the classification of an entity as an instance of a human kind (e.g., "this is a neoliberal policy") depends on our sensory neurons, the current activation state of our brain's larger neural population, and the configuration of our vast network of synaptic weights, which have been calibrated from previous experience (Barsalou 1999, 2004, 2016; Churchland 2012; Crick and Koch 2003; Clark 2013, 2016; Edelman and Tononi 2000; Glymour 2001; Gopnik et al. 2004; Jackendoff 1987). In receiving signals from the world, the brain, perhaps actively, makes a cascade of predictions, learning from errors and conveying expectations, possibly functioning as a Bayesian-like prediction machine. Perceptual signals activate relevant detectors in modality-specific areas of the brain; different populations of neurons fire in ways that represent the different perceived features of entities. Crucially, activation patterns are stored by conjunctive neurons for later use, allowing for categorical knowledge. Even thinking about a category can stimulate patterns of neural activation in specific regions in a way that resembles the brain processing that occurred when the category was originally learned. The neural reenactment of modality-specific states is arguably the basis of human categorization. Different members of the same category activate similar neural patterns in similar brain regions. Perceptions are transformed into categories by a distributed brain system that reenacts aspects of its own content to represent the relevant category. This system can be thought of as a simulator for representing the properties, relations, processes, and holistic entities that we perceive as constituting reality.

To go forward, social scientists need a basic model of categorization that is both consistent with the brain processes underlying representation and capable of informing actual social science research on myriad topics. For these purposes, I propose the use of a *conceptual space model* of the mental processes involved in the classification of human kinds (Gärdenfors 2000, 2014; Warglien and Gärdenfors 2013; see also Fauconnier 1994). This model is consistent with the findings of various strands of research on categorization developed over the last fifty years. As formulated here, the conceptual space model is a prototype-based understanding of how the brain represents heterogeneous, unidentified natural kinds as instances of a given human kind. It is part of a family of geometric-spatial models of mental content, such as Churchland's (1989, 1998, 2012) state-space semantics. It draws heavily on work about human categorization from cognitive science, especially Rosch's prototype theory (Rosch 1973, 1978, 1999; cf. Smith and Medin 1981; Lakoff 1987; Prinz 2002, 2015). In addition, the conceptual space model is strongly informed by studies of categorization and representation from philosophy (e.g., Putnam 1970; Fodor 1975, 1998; Margolis and Laurence 1999, 2007b), psychology (e.g., Pinker 1994, 2007; Jackendoff 2002; Carey 2009), and political science and sociology (e.g., Sartori 1970; Goertz 2006b, 2020; Collier and Gerring 2009). The model does not depend on a physicalist and/or reductionist understanding of the human mind;[18] its ideas are compatible with both reductionist and non-reductionist understandings.[19]

The conceptual space model proposes that the mind encompasses a representational hyperspace in which human kinds correspond to bounded locations in that space (cf. Churchland 2012; Gärdenfors 2000; Rosch 1999). Human kinds exist in the mind's multidimensional hyperspace as conceptual spaces— also called *sets* in this book—in which entities can have membership. A *prototype* is a single point located at the center of a conceptual space. The spaces themselves can be most easily visualized as closed shapes surrounding prototype points, though the mind's hyperspace in fact has multiple dimensions

(Gärdenfors 2000; Churchland 2012). In Gärdenfors's (2000, 2014) seminal formulation, categories are intersections of convex regions within larger conceptual spaces, spaces that consist of a number of domains representing various properties.[20] Prototypes are center points within these convex regions. For simplicity, I treat individual regions in the mind's topology as conceptual spaces themselves, retaining the idea that central points correspond with the prototypes of categories.

In this basic conceptual space model, sensory inputs from the natural world are situated as entities in relation to a prototype and its surrounding conceptual space. A human kind is deemed to exist (consciously or unconsciously)[21] when sensory input is processed as an entity with membership in a conceptual space, triggering conceptual space activation grounded in neural reenactment. If the input falls partly inside and partly outside of the space, the category is only partially activated, such that the human kind is deemed to be partially present. When the input is not situated within that space at all, it is regarded as not representing a member of the target category.

Conceptual spaces are forged from an individual's exposure to and engagement with natural kinds, events that calibrate and recalibrate *synaptic weights* (i.e., connections) among brain cells. The neural networks thereby created allow sensory perceptions of natural kinds to register as coherent human kinds seemingly endowed with inherent properties, coherence, and meanings. From the beginning of life, experience wires the brain to perceive the stuff of the world as possessing various similarities and differences. This categorization allows regularities to be stored as information and used unconsciously when we anticipate worldly content and activity. Although experience and learning are vital to the development of conceptual spaces, our brains are built in ways that predispose us to develop spaces for human kinds when exposed to the natural world (Pinker 2002; Jackendoff 2002). It is not an accident that the "blooming, buzzing confusion" experienced by a newborn (James 1890: 488; see also Barsalou 2016) is soon rendered into comprehensible human kinds. Evolution selected brain modules that, when confronted with the natural world, make the neural connections and store the activation patterns necessary to carry out this rendering.

The trajectory from external partial natural kinds to sensory organs to conceptual spaces can be illustrated with findings from research on colors (Kay and McDaniel 1978; Hurvich 1981; S. Palmer 1999; Giere 2006). Here, the partial natural kinds are electromagnetic wavelengths, and colors are categories stored by neural patterns as information and linked to conceptual spaces that can vary across individuals. Accidental features include specific lighting conditions, which affect reflected wavelengths, and the brain's current activation state as it anticipates sensory information. In most cultural settings, scientists can make strong generalizations about the typical range of electromagnetic wavelengths that trigger specific conceptual spaces. For example, hues with wavelengths between approximately 650 and 780 nanometers have high degrees of membership in the category *red*, whereas hues with wavelengths between approximately 500 and 550 nanometers have high degrees of membership in the category *green* (Kay and McDaniel 1978: 625). If one knows the wavelength of a hue, one can make successful predictions about its membership in color categories. Analysts can thus use knowledge of partial natural kinds to predict, with good success, conceptual space activation within cultural communities. Unfortunately, once we move beyond categories that are closely linked to our sensory organs (e.g., the color cones in our retinas), it is far more difficult to generalize about the partial natural kinds that activate specific conceptual spaces, even within spatially and temporally bounded communities.

In the case of human kinds, categories do not reduce solely to the natural kind composition of their referents. Human kinds instead refer to an interaction between entities in the world, on the one hand, and the minds of individuals on the other. The natural kind constituents of a human kind necessarily include the cognitive machinery of the individual who carries out the categorization, as well as the natural kinds that compose the entities to which a category refers. For instance, consider the category *primary school teacher*, which is well understood by, and meaningful to, the readers of this book. We cannot specify the referents of this category by identifying a set of natural kind constituents shared by all primary school teachers. Primary school teachers do not share special natural kind compositions that make them primary school teachers. Instead, they are primary school teachers because we share an understanding of the category *primary school teacher*. We understand this category because of the natural kinds that constitute our brains, which in turn can be understood using a conceptual space model. Categories such as *primary school teacher* are mind-dependent kinds, and part of what they reduce to is the minds of the individuals who share understandings of the categories.

Crucially, the activation of conceptual spaces can stimulate the motor neurons that control our muscles, triggering speech and other complex behavior. As Churchland (1998: 31) notes, "perhaps the primary *function* of activational trajectories is to generate a corresponding sequence of motor behaviors. The administration of motor behavior is almost certainly the original function of activational trajectories, evolutionarily speaking." The brain represents sensory information as categories precisely because such representation is useful for human action; the brain represents the world in order for the body to successfully navigate it (Prinz 2015; Barsalou 2016).

When conceptual space activation occurs, not only does the mind represent sensory input as an entity with membership in a category, but this activation is accompanied by reification, in which the entity corresponding to the sensory input is mentally transformed into an objectively existing substance, property, or process. This external entity is understood to have a mind-independent existence. For example, if the spectral reflection of a given entity activates the conceptual space for a given color (e.g., red), that entity is ordinarily treated as if it literally possesses that color (i.e., as if it possesses redness). The entity may also be reified in other ways; it may be treated as possessing, for example, a certain size, shape, texture, weight, or function.[22] Subsequent behavior toward the entity then proceeds on the basis of the essences that it is perceived to possess. Our understanding of an entity's essences may also shape our feelings toward it, including our emotional judgments (Bloom 2010). What we regard as good, bad, right, or wrong is closely tied to our essentialist casting of human kinds.

The conceptual space model has implications for how social scientists analyze the behavior of individuals. The model suggests the following input-to-action sequence: natural kind input → conceptual space activation → psychological essentializing → behavior. Since the composition of the natural kinds that trigger conceptual activation can rarely, if ever, be known, the starting point and foundation of the analysis is with the conceptual space activation in the actor under study. This activation occurs when input is apprehended as an entity—itself a complex process that involves several different brain regions and is only partially understood (see Leslie et al. 1998; Barsalou 1983, 1999)—and is situated as a member (or non-member) within a conceptual space. At this point in the model, individuals essentialize categories, and on the basis of that essentialist understanding, they perhaps form judgments and feelings, consciously weigh alternative courses of behavior, and carry out actions that they and others understand to be intentional.

For our purposes, however, the main utility of the conceptual space model is to help social scientists consider the place of essentialism *in their own thinking and work*. Although researchers can certainly apply the model to the actors they study, the primary concern from the perspective of scientific constructivism is that they themselves avoid essentialist assumptions in the production of social science. In this regard, it bears repeating that all social scientists need an orientation that avoids hardwired essentialist biases. Even those constructivist scholars who study contested meaning creation currently do so from the default essentialist standpoint of human language and thinking. To overcome essentialism, I argue, scholars must describe the constructivist processes they study in a way that does not itself assume essentialism.

Set-theoretic analysis provides a way of analyzing categories that does not partake in the mind's default essentialism. With this approach, the categories under analysis are assumed to correspond to conceptual spaces in the mind, rather than tracking natural boundaries in the external world. A given category has a one-to-one correspondence with a particular conceptual space, rather than with a particular natural kind at some level of generality. At the same time, categories are created from interactions with the external world, and they make reference to heterogeneous entities that exist objectively in the external world. These objective entities are composed of various natural kinds whose properties are not comprehended and do not coherently map onto particular human kind categories. When distinct and heterogeneous clusters of natural kinds are regarded as similar to one another, it is because they are members of the same conceptual space in the mind's representational system. The one thing that all instances of a given human kind have in common is their activation of a particular conceptual space of the mind.

Constructivist set-theoretic analysis focuses on the *final output phase* of a larger process of meaning-making that takes place in the brain. The set-theoretic approach is not concerned with the neural and chemical processes involved in transforming sensory input into specific categories. Various sophisticated models exist to make sense of these processes, including connectionist models that consider how sub-symbolic systems composed of hidden layers and parallel systems transform sensory input units into category output units (see, e.g., Smolensky 1988; Flusberg and McClelland 2017). These connectionist models assume that the brain engages in a form of associational or analogical reasoning that is possibly not consistent with rule-based and algorithmic understandings of categorization (for a literature review, see Pater 2019; see also Berent and Marcus 2019). With respect to these models and debates, constructivist set-theoretic analysis remains neutral, focusing on only the output units of a longer chain of cognitive work that may or may not be entirely rule-based. Conceptual space activation is a way of describing what takes place during the output phase, when the mind actually classifies entities as instances of a category. Sets are final-stage representational vehicles in complex mental computation processes that involve many other components.

OTHER COGNITIVE PROCESSES

Additional cognitive constructs inform the arguments of this book (especially in Part III). These constructs include the ideas of gestalts and basic-level categorization, which help make sense of the use of whole categories at particular levels of generality in the social sciences. They also include the ideas of image schemas and metaphors, which are centrally involved in both human categorization and theory building in the social sciences.

Human beings perceive the world by forming rich mental images of objects, properties, and processes. Our thoughts consist in part of these images. We do not perceive the world at the lowest possible level of aggregation. Rather, we experience *gestalts*—i.e., whole structures that are psychologically simpler than their parts (Lakoff 1987). For instance, one usually first notices a hammer and not its handle. Nor do we usually see the world as consisting of the first-order constituents that help organize all of human language, such as Thing, Event, Place, Property, or Amount (Jackendoff 1992: 34–35; see also Chisholm 1996; Lowe 2006). If we see a hammer, our first reaction is usually not to classify it as a thing, a hand-held device, or even a tool (though all of these classifications are correct); rather, in our culture, we call it a hammer.

Human beings tend to perceive the entities around them at a *basic level* that reflects their culture and learning, as well as our sensorimotor constitution as human beings (Brown 1958, 1965; Lakoff 1987). Essentialism occurs primarily for basic-level categories within a given community (Gelman 2003). Social scientists build theories using categories that correspond to the basic level of their intended audience, which may consist of highly specialized academics. Part of what it means to be a skilled researcher and effective presenter of ideas is to know how to use categories at the basic level of one's audience. Scientific constructivism offers tools for creating and using non-essentialist categories at the basic level of the particular audiences with whom researchers seek to communicate.

Humans use simple structures called *image schemas* when processing natural kind input to form categories. Image schemas are easily understood, recurring patterns that consist of a small number of parts and their relations; they are permanent and unconscious representations of meaning derived from interactions with the natural world during infancy (Johnson 1987; Lakoff 1987; Mandler 2004; Grady 2005; Mandler and Pagán Cánovas 2014). Examples of image schemas include schematic spatial representations with simple structures, such as containers, paths, and forces, and simple relationships that can exist among entities, such as up-down, center-periphery, and part-whole. As these examples suggest, image schemas are closely related to bodily and perceptual experiences. Image schemas are spatial structures rather than temporal ones; our most basic temporal concepts are spatially imbued, rather than the other way around. Some cognitive scientists believe that image schemas are the fundamental units of categorization. On this view, basic spatial-relational patterns have a special status in thought: they are the organizing devices used to build human categories.[23]

Metaphors are also basic to human thought and language (Lakoff and Johnson 1980; Jackendoff 1990, 2002; Pinker 2007). They help us to move conceptually from image schemas and primitive spatial and force ideas to more abstract concepts, including categories at the basic level. A metaphor can be defined broadly to include most extensions of terms from one domain (a source domain) to another (a target domain).[24] Some metaphors are directly linked to specific image schemas. For instance, the readily processed metaphor SADNESS IS DOWN is linked to the up-down image schema (as with, for example, "the bad news brought her even lower"). Other metaphors, such as LIFE IS A THEATER ("he panics under the spotlight"), are less directly linked to particular image schemas. Some scholars link metaphors to conceptual integration (or conceptual blending), in which cognitive models are combined to inform creative thinking and help make sense of the world (Fauconnier and Turner 2002; Mandler and Pagán Cánovas 2014). Metaphors call attention to the cognitive domains in which semantic leaps are pursued and stylized elements are blended to create new ideas (Fauconnier 1994) that make sense within particular cultures (Quinn 1991). Whereas longstanding metaphors often function in a manner similar to how ordinary categories function, novel metaphors play an important role in creating new meanings. For instance, the metaphor "he's a pain in the neck" involves sense retrieval, whereas the metaphor "metaphors are analogies" involves sense-making (Gentner et al. 2001). We can use metaphors creatively and imaginatively to bring new ideas into the social world.

To take stock, set-theoretic analysis avoids essentialism by making conceptual spaces of the mind (i.e., sets) not only the loci of categorization, but also essential components in the constitution of human kinds. The spaces themselves are partial natural kinds, created from interactions between the mind and the natural world. The individual entities that have membership in these spaces reference substances, properties, and processes in the natural world (i.e., natural kinds). However, those natural kinds are not homogeneous across all entities with membership in a given conceptual space. Hence, instead of focusing on categories that are assumed to stand in correspondence with entities of the external world, constructivist set-theoretic analysis focuses on the conceptual spaces of the mind that are used to represent input from the natural world. These conceptual spaces are the sets of set-theoretic analysis when this methodology is formulated as a constructivist approach to social science research.

Toward a Set-Theoretic Approach

Set-theoretic analysis can serve as a tool for conceptualizing and expressing systems of logic, including the main logics used in this book: propositional logic, Boolean logic, modal logic, and fuzzy logic (Cantor 1915; Hacking 1979; Lewis 1986b; Ragin 1987, 2000; Stoll 1961; Zadeh 1965). Logic is an essential tool of human reasoning and scientific analysis, including quantification and mathematical analysis (Frege 1884/1960). Logic itself is an abstract object woven into the fabric of reality (cf. Sher 2013); the innate ability of human beings to think logically allows them to learn from and control the natural world (Hanna 2006). Logic is not only a part of reality and inherently connected to truth; it is also a necessary tool for describing the world with language (with, e.g., propositions, inferences, and theoretical models). The indispensability of logic can be seen by the fact that scholars who deny its indispensability end up needing it to develop their anti-logic arguments (see the critiques in Hanna 2006: chap. 3; Holt 2018; Nagel 1997: chap. 4; Pinker 2007: 247–48; Warner 1989).[25]

The core ideas of set-theoretic analysis are based on image schemas that correspond to the most primitive structures that human beings use to comprehend reality. Set-theoretic analysis is grounded in the anchoring concepts of human thought. The basic idea of a set, which undergirds set-theoretic analysis and mathematics more generally, is rooted in the containment image schema (Lakoff 1987; Lakoff and Núñez 2000). This image schema is arguably the most primitive concept of all human thought. Set-theoretic analysis uses it in conjunction with other basic image schemas to build a methodology. Some of the more important image schemas that inform set-theoretic analysis are as follows: the center-periphery schema is used for prototype analysis; path, force, and blockage schemas are used with causal analysis; the part-whole schema is used when slicing out observations from cases; and the containment and superimposition schemas are used when analyzing set intersections and partial set membership.

Metaphors are also essential devices in set-theoretic analysis. They are essential because all set-theoretic analysts—like all people—must reason in part by using metaphors (Lakoff and Johnson 1980; Pinker 2007). Set-theoretic analysts use metaphors to build theories about how categories operate and are connected to other categories. They use spatial and force metaphors to reason about causal relationships, path and branching metaphors to conceptualize historical sequences, and container and boundary metaphors to understand category membership. The general metaphors CATEGORIES ARE SETS, NUMBERS ARE SETS, and CONCEPTUAL SPACES ARE SETS open the door to using the tools of logic and mathematics in the analysis of human kinds and their relations. The use of the category *set* as the target domain of metaphors is strikingly common in both everyday and scientific communication. This metaphorical capaciousness allows the category *set* to integrate diverse aspects of human experience and fields of science (cf. Grosholz 1985).

Set-theoretic analysis is congruent with scientific constructivism precisely because the category *set* anchors both conceptual spaces (the locus of categories) and logic (an indispensable component of rational thought and science). When categories are treated as sets, the researcher can view categories simultaneously as (1) conceptual spaces in the mind, which grounds a constructivist ontology, and (2) the basic entities analyzed in logic, which grounds scientific research. This remarkable utility of *set*—as the link between categories, conceptual spaces, and logic—underscores the paramount importance of the containment image schema in human experience, cognition, and reasoning.[26] It is possible that something equivalent to the containment image schema is necessary for apprehending and reasoning about reality regardless of the form of sentient being.[27]

As an everyday example of how one might treat categories as sets, consider the ordinary language category *lie*. How can we know if an entity is a member of this category? Drawing on Sweetser's (1987) analysis, we can elucidate the meaning of *lie* by situating the category within a semantic field of related categories. One way of presenting this semantic field is with a sequence of subset relations that culminate in *lie*: *entity → event → action → speech act → statement → false statement → lie*. The point is not that the brain's machinery actually processes sensory inputs using anything like this sequence; rather, the sequence helps illuminate the meaning of *lie* by calling attention to the kinds of entities that can be lies. If we want to grasp the meaning of *lie*, it is helpful to know that, given our system of categories and meanings, lies are a subset of false statements, which are a subset of statements, which are a subset of speech acts, and so on. In fact, as we know, many people define a lie as simply a false statement.

The subset sequence shows, however, that not all statements with membership in *false statement* also have membership in *lie*. For a statement to have membership in *lie*, we must implicitly understand it to have occurred in a particular kind of speech setting, one in which the speaker is informed and the truth-value of statements matters (Sweetser 1987). This setting is an idealized cultural model of communication with two key assumptions. First, speakers have beliefs, and these beliefs meet socially accepted standards of justification for being true; speakers are well informed and capable of telling the truth. Second, the speech act occurs in a rule-governed setting in which people are expected to be helpful, including by sharing information with one another; a norm regulates the speech environment such that the speaker is supposed to tell the truth and the hearer is supposed to believe the speaker.

A good definition of *lie* is a false statement by an informed speaker in a social setting where the truth counts. This definition underscores that when classifying statements as lies, we need to know about the truth of the words spoken, the speaker's knowledge, and the setting in which the statement occurred. It is not enough to know that the statement was false; an idealized cultural model must also be applicable to the situation. As figure 1.2 shows, we can use set-theoretic analysis to represent the category *lie* as falling at the intersection of *false statement*, *speaker informed*, and *truth-value relevant*. We regard sensory input of an unknown composition as a full-blown lie when we can represent it as an entity with full membership in all three of these sets. We do not know *how*, in real time, our brains process sensory data to determine that the incoming data are an instance of a lie.[28] However, we do know that the category *lie* can be usefully represented using the set-theoretic structure of figure 1.2. These sets function as representational tools that help us grasp what *lie* means in our linguistic and cultural community.

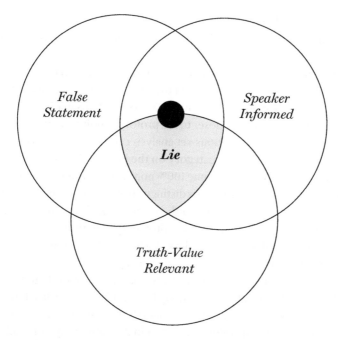

FIGURE 1.2. Conceptual Spaces and the Category of a Lie

Fuzzy-set analysis, or what I prefer to call *continuous-set analysis*,[29] offers rules for measuring and analyzing partial membership, in which one category is partially contained within another (Zadeh 1965; Ragin 2000, 2008). Continuous-set analysis is particularly useful for the study of graded categories that exhibit prototype effects (Rosch 2011: 112). It provides logical steps for carrying out conceptual aggregation and analyzing category relationships when cases are partial members of categories. As an example, imagine that we regard a given statement as a "half lie"—neither a full-blown lie nor a clear non-lie, but right in the middle. We may determine that the statement is a half lie because it has only half membership in one or more of the categories *false statement, speaker informed,* and *truth-value relevant.* For instance, a speech act may have half membership in *truth-value relevant* but full membership in the other two constituent categories. Here, the false statement by the informed speaker is classified as a half lie because it occurs in a setting in which the requirement that the truth-value be relevant is deemed only half present. This setting might be an informal conversation that permits *some* exaggeration and humor (e.g., a relaxed context in which a little joking around is occurring). If confronted with the falsehood, the speaker may insist that he was only kidding, but neutral observers might be only partially convinced, believing that his statement was a borderline lie. In figure 1.2, this half lie is represented by the small solid circle with full membership in *false statement* and *speaker informed* but only half membership in *truth-value relevant*. The figure illustrates how this combination of membership values yields half membership in the target category *lie*.

Continuous-set analysis also allows analysts to differentiate between two or more full members of a category on the basis of their proximity to the prototype point of the category. For example, two statements may each be 100% a lie, but one of the lies may be closer to the prototype point and therefore a better exemplar of a lie.[30] Continuous-set analysis can also be used to distinguish among full non-members of a category on the basis of their proximity to the prototype point. For example, some 100% non-lie speech acts are closer to lies than others. Continuous-set analysis distinguishes these non-lies by comparing their proximity to the boundaries of the category *lie*. Diagrams can often be useful for illustrating differences in the proximity of entities to the prototype point of a conceptual space, regardless of whether the entities are members, partial members, or non-members of the conceptual space.[31]

Finally, continuous-set analysis is appropriate for studying logical relationships of necessity and sufficiency among human kind categories. If membership in category X is necessary for membership in category Y, cases cannot have higher membership values in Y than in X. Conversely, if membership in category X is sufficient for membership in category Y, cases cannot have higher membership values in X than in Y (Zadeh 1965; Ragin 2000, 2008). For instance, if membership in the category *false statement* is a necessary condition for membership in the category *lie*, any given statement cannot have greater set membership in *lie* than in *false statement*. If a statement has 100% membership in *lie*, it will always have 100% membership in *false statement* if indeed falsehood is a necessary condition for a lie. However, under the same rules, if a statement has 100% membership in *false statement*, it may or may not have 100% membership in *lie*—it depends on the context in which the false statement is uttered.

In due course, we shall explore in a more extensive and precise way how set-theoretic analysis is useful for conceptualization, description, causal analysis, and normative assessment in a non-essentialist social science. At this point, we have only scratched the surface of a rich methodology for scientific constructivist research.

————

This chapter has begun to develop an approach for the social sciences that rejects essentialism and replaces it with a scientific constructivist alternative. As summarized in table 1.2, a scientific constructivist orientation differs from essentialist social science with respect to assumptions about the entities under analysis, the nature of categories, the dimensions of comparison, the

TABLE 1.2. Competing Orientations for the Social Sciences

	Scientific Essentialist Orientation	Scientific Constructivist Orientation
Principal Units of Analysis	Entities of the external world	Human-constructed categories
Ontology of Categories	Representations of facets of external world	Representations of interaction of mind and external world
Dimensions of Comparison	Properties possessed by units of analysis	Membership of units in categories
Relationships of Interest	Associations among properties of units	Subset-superset relations among categories
Focus of Causal Analysis	Changes in property possession	Changes in category membership

associations under study, and the focus of causal analysis. By way of conclusion and anticipation, let us briefly consider these differences.

First, the standard essentialist approach seeks to study entities that map the structure and boundaries of an independently existing reality. Valid social science findings are intended to describe features of the actual world as it exists independently of the researcher. Social science is effective insofar as its categories and models approximately describe the objective structure of social reality.

By contrast, a scientific constructivist approach seeks to study entities whose existence depends on collective understandings. Valid social science findings describe features of reality as it is experienced by spatially and temporally grounded communities, including social scientific communities at certain times and places. Social science is effective because scholars can objectively study this experiential reality using logical procedures that separate truth from non-truth.

Second, the prevailing essentialist approach assumes that categories are representations of aspects of the external world. The meaning of a category approximately maps the content of a facet of reality. Scholars can scientifically analyze categories because the structure of reality neutrally adjudicates the appropriate meaning of categories.

By contrast, a scientific constructivist approach assumes that categories are mental representations derived from an interaction between the mind and facets of the external world. The meaning of a category summarizes the way in which the mind groups together as similar heterogeneous facets of reality. Scholars can scientifically analyze categories because they can communicate and share with their audience their understandings of the meanings of categories.

Third, an essentialist approach compares units on the basis of the properties possessed by those units. Comparison across units is the act of recording similarities and differences in the possession of these properties. Scientific comparison is possible because social researchers can directly or indirectly observe these similarities and differences.

By contrast, a scientific constructivist approach compares units on the basis of their membership in categories. Comparison is the act of recording similarities and differences in the extent to which the units of analysis are members of certain categories. Scientific comparison is possible because all human beings share important cognitive structures and because precise communication about category membership is possible using these cognitive structures.

Fourth, an essentialist approach analyzes relationships among the properties possessed by the units under study. Procedures such as those employed in statistics allow scholars to make inferences about relationships that are not readily apparent from the data. These procedures allow scholars to summarize property relationships and degrees of certainty in mathematically precise ways.

By contrast, a scientific constructivist approach analyzes set-membership relationships among the categories under study. Scholars explore the extent to which membership in one category is necessary and/or sufficient for membership in another category. They use the tools of set-theoretic logic to summarize the nature of these relationships in mathematically precise ways.

Finally, an essentialist approach analyzes causality by exploring how changes in one property effect changes in another property among units of analysis. Causality is a feature of the world in the sense that changes in one property objectively produce changes in another property. Scholars study causal effects by manipulating or observing changes in one property and examining how these changes are associated with changes in another property, net of everything else.

By contrast, a scientific constructivist approach analyzes causality by exploring set-membership relations among constructed categories that are understood to be located at different points in time. *Causality* is itself a category that social scientists use to help describe certain kinds of temporal set-membership relations. Scientific constructivist scholars study causality by examining the set-membership relations that characterize categories in a temporal sequence.

In this chapter, I have argued that the best scientific evidence shows that essentialism is not appropriate for the social sciences. Social scientists need a scientific constructivist approach, not because the goals it pursues and the types of results it generates are inherently superior, but because these goals and types of results are appropriate for the social sciences, given its subject matter. The essentialist approach may offer an attractive picture of the social sciences, but if its assumptions are not justified, an essentialist social science cannot actually deliver the things that it promises.

Appendix: A Note on Natural Kinds, Human Kinds, and Universals

It is instructive to view the distinction between natural kinds and human kinds in light of the problem of universals, which concerns the ontological status of *kinds* in relation to *particulars* (Armstrong 1989, 1997; Galluzzo and Loux 2015). Scientific constructivism holds that kinds, or universals, are real entities and that they are indispensable components of science; it rejects the nominalist arguments that only either particulars (Goodman 1951) or concrete physical objects (Quine 1943) exist (see also Goodman and Quine 1947). At the same time, scientific constructivism assigns human kinds an ontological status completely different from that of natural kinds.

According to scientific constructivism, natural kinds are *immanent universals*, in the sense that they do not exist in nature without particulars (or tokens) that possess their essential properties. For instance, if an individual element with the atomic number 130 cannot exist in nature, then the general category for this kind of element cannot exist in nature either. Similarly, because entities exist in nature with an atomic number of 79, the general category for entities with the atomic number 79 (i.e., *gold*) also exists in nature. Scientific constructivism is *aristotelian* with respect to natural kinds, believing that these kinds exist insofar as particular instances of them exist in nature.

In sharp contrast, scientific constructivism holds that human kinds exist as *transcendent universals* in the mind; they are abstract objects that do not require particular instances in the actual world for their existence. For example, *U.S. one-dollar bill* and *U.S. three-dollar bill* are both real categories with the same ontological status. The creation of a three-dollar bill by the Treasury Department would not change the ontological status of this human kind category. Scientific constructivism is *platonist* with respect to the universals that animate human reality. Human kind categories can exist with or without the instantiation (or exemplification) of particulars in the actual world; the existence of human kinds does not depend on the existence of corresponding spatiotemporal entities in the actual world.

Scientific constructivism allows for a diversity of positions regarding other issues surrounding universals. Notably, scientific constructivism does not weigh in on the debate about whether scientists who study natural kinds should always seek the lowest-level kinds in their research. The reductionist position on this issue is that higher-order natural kinds are dispensable (e.g., Galluzzo 2015: 101–8; cf. Armstrong 1997). The alternative view is that higher-level natural kinds play a vital role in scientific explanation (e.g., Ellis 2001).

2

Foundations of Set-Theoretic Analysis

This chapter discusses the conceptual foundations of a scientific constructivist social science. It does so by focusing on several categories that are at the heart of set-theoretic analysis when formulated as a constructivist approach. I begin by analyzing the category *set*, arguing that a new understanding of this category is needed for constructivist research. Scholars normally understand sets to be collections of entities that share one or more properties. I propose that social scientists should instead understand sets as bounded spaces (conceptual spaces) in the representational machinery of human minds. When this understanding is applied, a social category refers to a group of entities that need not share any properties beyond their common membership within a conceptual space. I explore how this understanding of *set* represents a departure from how we typically understand and analyze variables in the social sciences.

I build on this definition of *set* to introduce other categories that are essential to the ontology of a constructivist set-theoretic social science. These categories include *possible worlds*, which consist of the *actual world* and various *non-actual worlds*. Whereas possible worlds can be regarded as real worlds, *impossible worlds* are imaginary and not real. I discuss how these categories are used in the assessment of the validity of propositions and theories. I argue that social science as a theory-evaluating endeavor is guided most basically by the quest to use evidence and logical reasoning to understand whether or not the actual world is a member of a set in which a proposition is true.

I present a set-theoretic framework for defining and using different units of analysis, including *worlds*, *cases*, and *observations*. I explore the meaning of these categories by situating them within both set-theoretic and part-whole hierarchies. I consider how *cases* in the social sciences are human kinds corresponding to the main spatiotemporal units under study. I formulate the category *set-membership observation* to characterize the justified societal facts that social scientists use to assess the truth of propositions.

In terms of epistemology, I examine the meaning of the ideas "certainty" and "truth" within a scientific constructivist approach. In contrast to radical constructivists, I regard these categories as crucial for understanding knowledge generation in the social sciences. I first discuss the meaning of *certain proposition*, defining it as a belief about the truth of a proposition that has intrinsic credibility or the highest degree of credibility. I consider how the data collection and data analysis methods that social scientists use help establish credibility but also necessarily introduce uncertainty into findings. Next, I discuss the meaning of the category *true proposition* for the social sciences, arguing that a true proposition is one that accurately describes one or more facets of experiential reality. Because experiential reality depends in part on shared understandings among communities of people, truth in the social sciences also depends in part on these understandings. Nevertheless, when semantic context is taken into consideration, a proposition about the social world must be either true or false. Truth is relative to particular semantic contexts, but within those contexts, truth is fixed and unequivocal.

Sets

The core concept of set-theoretic analysis is the category *set*. In scientific constructivism, a set is a bounded location in mental space, rather than a collection of elements that share essential properties. This definition differentiates *set* from *variable* as ordinarily used in the social sciences. It also has important downstream consequences for the methodological and theoretical tools that are appropriate for social science research.

PROPERTY SETS VERSUS SPATIAL SETS

In mathematics, sets are abstract objects—themselves not defined—that are used to define all other concepts. They are introduced axiomatically, and their characteristics are specified by the formal axioms themselves (Jech 2011: 3; see also Shapiro 1991; Bagaria 2019). Since Cantor, nevertheless, mathematicians have roughly understood sets as collections of distinct elements. The philosophical problem has always been that collections are metaphysically problematic entities (Armstrong 1989; Galluzzo 2015; Lewis 1983; Merrill 1980). "We know quite a lot now about sets," the set-theoretic mathematician Potter quips, "but one thing we cannot yet prove is that there are any" (2004: 55).

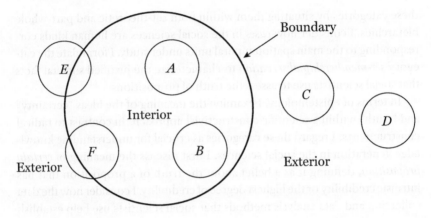

FIGURE 2.1. Illustration of Spatial Set

In the social sciences, the concept of *set* is used interchangeably with *class*, *type*, and *kind*. Normally, all of these concepts are understood in terms of the property-possession assumption: a set, class, type, or kind is a collection of distinct entities that share one or more properties (Tversky 1977). The idea of a set is a way of highlighting the properties that the entities already possess; the shared properties make the entities members of the set. We can label collections that fall under this definition *property sets*. Natural kinds are examples of property sets.

An alternative definition of *set* derives from the containment, or boundary, image schema underpinning the category: a set is a bounded location in space in which entities can have membership (cf. Lakoff and Núñez 2000: 30–31, 43–45). As figure 2.1 suggests, these *spatial sets* have three parts: an interior, a boundary, and an exterior. The interior of a set includes all entities of a given kind that have membership in the set; the exterior includes all entities of a given kind that do not have membership; and the boundary is the partition between membership and non-membership. A core purpose of set-theoretic analysis is to establish the boundary that marks the relative size of a spatial set X vis-à-vis its logical complement, $\sim X$, and to establish X's membership relations with other spatial sets and their logical complements.

With spatial sets, the set is ontologically prior to its members (cf. Bourdieu 1989; Lamont and Molnár 2002). The boundaries of the set determine whether entities are members; the properties of the entities do not determine the set boundaries. Membership boundaries can shift without any changes at all in the properties of the entities. Entities are similar or different because of their set membership. With spatial sets, the set itself constructs similarities and differences among potential membership units.

This containment, or bounded space, understanding of *set* allows entities— which are themselves spatial sets—to have membership, partial membership, or no membership within a set of interest. Entities with membership in a set are permitted to vary in the degree to which they are safely within that set (compare entity A with entity B in figure 2.1), and entities that fall outside of the set may do so to differing degrees (compare C and D). Entities can have varying degrees of partial membership in the set: they may reside partly in the interior and partly in the exterior (E and F). In short, the conception of a set as a bounded space allows entities to be entirely within the set (including with different levels of security), entirely outside of it (including closer to or further from entering it), or partially within and partially outside of it (including to differing degrees).

With spatial sets, the key issue is drawing the appropriate boundary to partition membership from non-membership. For any given set, this boundary is constituted by other sets; analysts draw the boundary line for a set on the basis of these *constitutive sets*. For instance, in figure 2.2, the boundary of set D could be defined by the *intersection* of the more general sets B and C. In that case, B and C would be constitutive sets of D. The boundaries of B and C could themselves be defined by appealing to the still more general sets of which they are members. In turn, these boundaries could be defined by appealing to yet more sets. With set-theoretic analysis, the boundary-establishment process does not bottom out with property sets, material/physical elements, or non-set entities (i.e., urelements).[1] With set-theoretic analysis, it is spatial sets all the way down.[2]

One can envision constitutive sets as a series of sequenced filters, as in figure 2.2. In this imagery, the final set of interest is D. An entity can achieve membership in set D only if it can "pass through" logically prior constitutive filters (we assume that the entity moves horizontally across space from left to right). One can determine if an entity has membership in D by examining if it has membership in the more general sets A, B, and C. If it lacks full membership in any of these constitutive sets, it lacks full membership in D. For example, case 1 has full membership in the constitutive sets A and C, but it lacks membership in set B, so it also lacks membership in set D.

The diagram in figure 2.2 can be used to discuss issues related to the prototypes of categories (Rosch 1973, 1978, 1999).[3] In the diagram, the prototypes are points located at the center of the sets, which is where the letters A, B, C, and D are situated. We can see that the prototypical member of set D (case 2) is a full member of sets A, B, and C, but it does not correspond with the prototypes of these constitutive sets. The prototypical member of set B—which corresponds to case 3—is not quite a member of D, though it is very close to being a partial member. Hence, even though membership in B is necessary for membership in D, the best, or prototypical, example of B is not even a member of D.[4]

In constructivist set-theoretic analysis, human kinds are represented and analyzed as sets in this sense of bounded locations in space. Under this

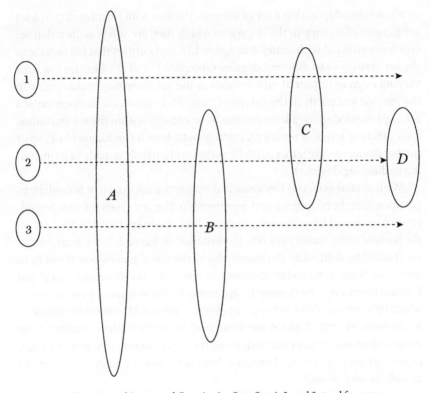

FIGURE 2.2. Illustration of Sequenced Constitutive Sets. Sets 1, 2, and 3 stand for cases.

spatial-set assumption, we arrive at an approach that avoids the property-possession assumption. We move from a material arena of physical objects with properties into an abstract arena of spatial sets contained within spatial sets. Members of a set no longer need to have any intrinsic properties in common (cf. Lewis 1983). Instead, their resemblance to one another is based on their location vis-à-vis bounded spaces. These bounded spaces, or conceptual spaces, are abstract objects that have a virtual but ontologically objective existence within the mind's representational system. The conceptual spaces to which spatial sets correspond are partial natural kinds within this representational system. In turn, conceptual spaces reduce to other natural kinds that comprise mind-independent substances and processes in the brain. However, for the purposes of social science, spatial sets are reduced to other spatial sets, not to underlying brain chemicals and neural material. Specific spatial sets are defined using other spatial sets, which in turn are defined by still more spatial sets, and so on. At no point does this process of definitional elaboration lead to, or reduce to, natural kind properties. Instead, the process continues in an endless progression, and perhaps culminates with definitional circularity.

When social reality is conceived under the spatial-set assumption, we no longer need to make reference to the intrinsic properties of the entities we study. We speak instead of sets and their members and non-members. We ask if entities, whose intrinsic properties are not comprehended, are members of a given set. We ask if a set is a member of another set. We ask about *the extent to which* sets are members of other sets. We inquire about the *proximity* of the members of a set to the prototype point of the set. We recognize that the members of a set are similar because of their shared membership in the set. Set membership replaces property possession as the basis for the definition, measurement, comparison, normative valuation, and overall analysis of categories in the social sciences.

VARIABLES VERSUS SETS

The distinction between the property-possession assumption and the spatial-set assumption maps onto the distinction between variables as conventionally used in the social sciences and sets as used in set-theoretic analysis (cf. Ragin 2000). Just as the property-possession assumption applies to partial natural kinds but not to human kinds, variable-oriented analysis makes sense for the study of partial natural kinds but not human kinds. The problems associated with using variables for social science analysis point toward the value of a set-theoretic approach.

Variables are tools for systematically conceptualizing similarities and differences in the attributes of units of analysis (Gerring 2012: 75–78; Hoover 1984: 22–26; Seawright and Collier 2010: 358). The similarities and differences of units vis-à-vis a given variable can be measured at different levels (e.g., nominal, ordinal, interval, or ratio levels), depending on the phenomenon under study and the data available. Each particular unit has a specific value on a variable of interest, which reflects the way in which or the degree to which the unit possesses the property designated by the variable. The variable itself is the full spectrum of values that units can possess (which can range from two values to an infinite number of values), only some of which may find empirical expression.

Social scientists often study variables because they want to explore whether the differing possession of properties is causally consequential for units. For example, individual households (units of analysis) possess income (a variable) to differing degrees. They also possess certain racial compositions, locations, and sizes (other variables). Researchers might hypothesize that one or more of these variables endows households with certain causal powers, such as the capacity to generate children with certain life chances (a dependent variable). This hypothesis assumes that changes on the independent variable cause changes on the dependent variable. As Abbott (2001: 39) notes, variable-oriented analysis "assumes that the social world consists of fixed entities (the units of analysis) that have attributes (the variables). These attributes interact, in causal or actual time, to create outcomes, themselves measurable as attributes of fixed entities."

By contrast, spatial sets are bounded spaces that exist as real but abstract objects in the hyperspace of the mind's representational system; they have the same "location" as our conscious thoughts and mental images.[5] Spatial sets do not refer to or coherently track specific properties that are literally possessed by external entities. Rather, they are mental instruments involved in the categorization and quantification of sensory input. Humans carve out, organize, and count their experienced reality with conceptual sets that lack a concrete expression in physical space (cf. Balkenius and Gärdenfors 2016). The experienced world is constructed set-theoretically by the representational apparatus of the human mind as it interacts with itself and the natural world. The spatial sets that humans use to classify entities refer to particular ways in which the mind is entangled with (or interacts with) natural kinds.

If categories are analyzed ontologically as sets, their labels (i.e., the words we use for them) must allow—grammatically and logically speaking—for units of analysis to have membership in them (Ragin 2008). The labels must imply a boundary separating membership from non-membership. While this boundary is a clear and unambiguous dividing line, particular units—which are also sets—may have partial membership in both zones. As membership in one zone increases, membership in the other zone decreases (i.e., the unit's percent membership in X + its percent membership in $\sim X = 100\%$). When used to designate particular concepts, set labels often conjoin a noun that corresponds to the substantive kind being studied (e.g., *country*) with an adjective that identifies a more specific type (e.g., *democratic*) to produce the category of interest (*democratic country*). This labeling approach moves away from the practice of distinguishing units of analysis (e.g., countries) and variables (e.g., level of democracy). The typical labels used for variables in the social sciences— such as level of democracy—are generally not useful in set-theoretic analysis, because they cannot be treated as sets in which entities can have membership. A country cannot be a member of level of democracy. Nor can a person be a member of gender, age, income, or level of education—though a person can be a member of *female person*, *person age 50*, *high-income person*, and *highly educated person*. Variables as conventionally used in the social sciences are built from the property-possession assumption: they are treated as categorical or quantitative dimensions that reflect whether, or the extent to which, units possess particular properties. In a social science that avoids this assumption, variables and their labels are replaced with sets and their labels.[6]

With set-theoretic analysis, researchers examine relationships among sets, not relationships among variables. They explore subset-superset relations by inquiring about the degree to which the members of one category form a subset or superset of another category. They note when two categories approximate a subset-superset relationship—i.e., when the members of one category are mostly or completely contained within another category. They note when units that are members of any one condition in a series are also likely to be members of all the conditions in the series. These relationships can be summarized using the ideas of necessity and sufficiency. Unlike the variable-oriented analyst, the constructivist set-theoretic researcher does not treat the relationships as associations among the properties of units. The researcher does not analyze the relationships using the statistical idea of a correlation; the variable-oriented idea of a correlation is replaced with the set-theoretic ideas of set coincidence and subset-superset relations (Ragin and Fiss 2017).

The move from variables to sets has downstream consequences for nearly all aspects of research design. Notably, it shapes the kinds of questions that are asked and answered in the social sciences. Set-theoretic analysts do not summarize the features of cases in terms of their possession of quantified properties.[7] They do not ask questions about the associations among the properties of cases. They do not explore the average causal effect of one property on another. Instead, set-theoretic analysts are drawn to questions such as these: To what extent does a case or group of cases have membership (or partial membership, or no membership) in a category of interest? To what extent is membership in one category or combination of categories necessary for membership in another category? To what extent is membership in one category or combination of categories sufficient for membership in another category? To what extent is a case's membership in one category a non-trivial cause of its membership in another category? To what extent is the membership of one or more cases in a category morally good or bad?

These kinds of questions require the use of methodological tools quite distinct from those used in variable-oriented social science (Ragin 1987, 2000, 2008; Rihoux and Ragin 2009; Rohlfing 2012; Schneider and Wagemann 2012; Thiem, Baumgartner, and Bol 2016; Thomann and Maggetti 2020). They require the use of set-theoretic methods.

Possible Worlds

This section discusses the use of possible world semantics in the social sciences. In philosophy, possible world semantics is a mainstream tool that analysts explicitly use for myriad purposes, including the elucidation of modal logic. In the social sciences, however, analysts only implicitly invoke possible worlds in their research. The following discussion serves as an introduction for social scientists into the ways in which possible world semantics can and often implicitly does undergird social scientific investigation.

KINDS OF WORLDS

Social scientists are interested in studying the *actual world*—i.e., the spatio-temporal arena that we can, in principle, know or affect.[8] Social scientists are not primarily interested in studying *non-actual worlds*—i.e., domains that lack any spatial, temporal, or causal connections to our own. These non-actual worlds may be as real as our own actual world, but they are forever outside the spatiotemporal domain in which we live our lives (Bradley and Swartz 1979; Lewis 1986a).

With a set-theoretic approach, social scientists evaluate the truth of a proposition by exploring whether a set representing the actual world has membership in a set in which the proposition is true. For example, they might explore whether the actual world has membership in the set *Osama bin Laden died in 2011* or the set *Venezuela was wealthier than Colombia in the late nineteenth century*.[9] A basic purpose of social science is to learn whether the actual world is located within sets of interest.

To achieve this end, social scientists must consider non-actual worlds in their research. The need to consider the non-actual is an inevitable consequence of the fact that researchers do not know the set location of the actual world. To rationally update one's beliefs in light of new evidence, one must consider the consequences of the evidence for a world in which a proposition is true and for relevant worlds in which it is false. For example, to learn whether the actual world is a member of the set *Venezuela was wealthier than Colombia in the late nineteenth century*, researchers need to consider possible worlds with membership in this set and possible worlds with membership in its negation set (i.e., its logical complement). Although only one of the two sets can contain the actual world, both sets and their members need to be considered to find out which one contains it.

Social scientists need not consider the full population of non-actual worlds. Notably, they need not study any impossible worlds. *Impossible worlds* are domains in which one or more necessarily true statements are false or in which one or more necessarily false statements are true. I regard as impossible worlds those imaginary domains that violate transcendental truths—including the principles of first-order logic, mathematical theorems and structures, and the fundamental laws of physics.[10] Examples of impossible worlds are make-believe universes in which $2 + 2 = 5$, $X = \sim X$, and lines are four-dimensional objects. I do not consider these impossible worlds to be part of reality. Although I can formulate a sentence about a make-believe world in which a triangle has four sides, or a world in which helium is heavier than air, I do not regard these worlds as real domains.

The worlds that social scientists do study are *possible worlds*. A possible world is a spatiotemporal domain that does not violate a transcendental truth

(Lewis 1986a; cf. Bradley and Swartz 1979; Divers 2002; Girle 2003; Hale 2013; Menzel 2015; Stalnaker 2003, 2012). A possible world is a *maximal* domain, in that it includes all parts that have any spatiotemporal relationship to one another; it is a *closed* domain, in that its parts do not bear any spatiotemporal connection to any other world.[11] There is a possible world in which Hillary Clinton was elected president of the United States in 2016. There is a possible world in which Bigfoot walks in the Pacific Northwest. There is a possible world in which dragons and unicorns exist. In fact, there is a possible world in which we are all just brains in a vat (Putnam 1975, 1981).

As a modal realist, I happen to regard all possible worlds as real in the same sense that human kinds are real: possible worlds are mind-dependent representations of a reality composed of natural kinds (cf. Lewis 1986a).[12] Thus, I assign possible worlds the same ontological status as experienced reality; possible worlds are as real as the actual world as we experience it. However, the set-theoretic tools discussed in this book do not require one to embrace modal realism. One can employ all of the techniques in this book without adopting a realist view of possible worlds. One can use possible worlds under the assumption that they are hypothetical domains that exist in a person's imagination, without corresponding to any natural kinds in any real domain (cf. Stalnaker 2003, 2012).[13]

Not all possible worlds are candidates for being the actual world. We do not live in a world in which Hillary Clinton was elected president of the United States in 2016. Nor do we live in a world in which dragons and unicorns exist. These domains are possible worlds, but they are non-actual worlds—i.e., possible worlds that are not the actual world. Most, but not all, analysts believe that we have sufficient evidence to regard a world with Bigfoot as a non-actual world. Meanwhile, scholars continue to explore whether the actual world might be a world in which we are brains in a vat (Putnam 1975), simulations (Bostrom 2003), or Boltzmann brains (Carroll 2017).

Social scientists work to locate the actual world vis-à-vis categories of interest through the study of possible worlds. The actual world is one possible world; all other possible worlds are non-actual worlds (see figure 2.3). Set-theoretic analysis is designed to evaluate propositions by using knowledge about constructed facets of the actual world to determine whether some possible worlds are non-actual worlds. For example, consider the proposition that Osama bin Laden died in 2011. Set-theoretic analysis focuses on the distribution of possible worlds across a set in which the proposition is true (set X) and a set in which the proposition is false (set $\sim X$). Let us assume that most of the possible worlds with membership in set X assume and require that Osama bin Laden lived in Pakistan in 2011 (set k). Let us also assume that we discover evidence ($\sim k$) that conclusively shows that, in fact, bin Laden was not living in Pakistan in 2011. We must then eliminate as non-actual many of the members

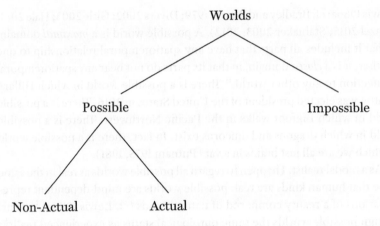

FIGURE 2.3. A Set-Theoretic Typology of Worlds I

of set X, because the actual world is not a member of set k, as they assume and require. The result will be a change in the distribution of possible worlds across sets X and $\sim X$, such that we have greater confidence than before that the actual world resides in set $\sim X$.

Figure 2.4 presents a set diagram of the distinction between impossible worlds, possible worlds, non-actual worlds, and the actual world (cf. Bradley and Swartz 1979: 6). The entities that have membership within this full typological space are *worlds*—i.e., closed and maximal spatiotemporal domains that cannot, even in principle, affect one another. A basic goal of social science research is to learn whether the actual world is a member of a set in which a proposition is true or whether it is a member of a set in which the proposition is false. With respect to figure 2.4, one can imagine introducing a subset into the space that contains all possible worlds. This new subset would contain some, but not all, possible worlds. Let us stipulate that this subset contains all possible worlds in which a proposition of interest is true. Set-theoretic analysis is designed to determine whether this subset contains as one of its members the actual world. If it does, the proposition of interest is true.

With this perspective, we first conceive the totality of everything[14] as the set of all worlds (i.e., all closed, maximal spatiotemporal domains). We then divide these worlds into possible worlds (reality) and impossible worlds (not reality). We then carve up the possible worlds into non-actual worlds and the actual world. Using the actual world, as we shall see, researchers continue to slice up reality into sets. They situate the actual world as a member of categories that designate cases. They then situate these cases as members of categories that designate observations. The observations are the evidence that researchers use to estimate the set location of the actual world vis-à-vis propositions of interest.

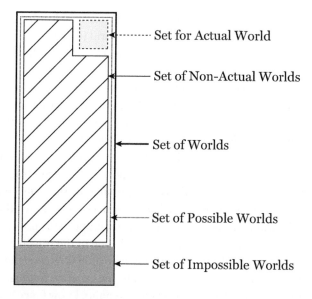

FIGURE 2.4. A Set-Theoretic Typology of Worlds II

USES OF POSSIBLE WORLD SEMANTICS

In this section, I call attention to three ways in which possible world semantics informs scientific constructivism and set-theoretic analysis. The discussion of these different uses suggests that social scientists already implicitly assume or directly employ possible worlds quite extensively in their research.

First, possible world semantics helps to define the rules of modal logic (Bradley and Swartz 1979; Divers 2002; Girle 2003). Modal logic concerns propositions that have qualifiers such as necessarily true, possibly true, possibly false, and necessarily false. Although possible worlds are not the only way in which one can understand modal propositions, they do provide perhaps the easiest way to grasp such notions (Girle 2003: 3).[15] For example, consider the following definitions:

True proposition: A proposition that is true in the actual world (e.g., Donald Trump was elected president of the United States in 2016).

False proposition: A proposition that is false in the actual world (e.g., Hillary Clinton was elected president of the United States in 2016).

Necessarily true proposition: A proposition that is true in all possible worlds (e.g., squares have four sides).

Necessarily false proposition: A proposition that is false in all possible worlds (e.g., $X = {\sim}X$).

Contingent proposition: A proposition that is true in at least one possible world and false in at least one possible world (e.g., Donald Trump would have lost the 2016 presidential election without Russian help).

In the social sciences, contingent propositions about the actual world are the focus of research. In this book, I shall refer to them simply as *propositions*. Part II of this book concerns primarily the evaluation of propositions; Part III concerns primarily the formulation of propositions.

Modal logic helps to define science more generally: *science* is the study (using evidence and logic) of contingent propositions that are true in at least one possible world and false in at least one possible world. Science does not study propositions that are necessarily true or necessarily false. The goal of science is to determine whether the actual world is one of the possible worlds in which a proposition is true or whether it is one of the possible worlds in which the proposition is false. Unfortunately, no matter how good the evidence and how sound the reasoning, science can never generate findings that lack all uncertainty (Popper 1934/1968). Scientists cannot know for certain the set location of the actual world; they cannot generate findings that turn contingent propositions into necessarily true or necessarily false propositions.

Second, possible world semantics provides a means of deriving and using Bayesian analysis within a scientific constructivist framework (see chapter 7 on Bayesian analysis). This book embraces the argument that the use of Bayes' theorem (or its equivalent) defines what it means to rationally update one's beliefs about the truth of propositions in light of evidence. To adopt an epistemologically scientific approach to evidence requires one to follow Bayes' theorem in the assessment of the truth of propositions. Bayesian reasoning is a basic component of scientific epistemology, regardless of whether one is studying partial natural kinds or human kinds.

Possible world semantics provides essential tools for understanding Bayesian reasoning in a set-theoretic framework. To begin to see why, consider again the idea that our beliefs about the likelihood that a proposition is true reflect our understanding of the relative proportion of possible worlds in a set in which the proposition is true (X) versus a set in which the proposition is false ($\sim X$). New evidence from the actual world can lead us to become more or less confident in the truth of the proposition by asymmetrically eliminating possible worlds from sets X and $\sim X$. The discovery of evidence k requires us to eliminate all possible worlds that assume and require $\sim k$. If evidence k thereby removes more possible worlds from set X than from set $\sim X$, its discovery will have changed the distribution of possible worlds across sets X and $\sim X$. Specifically, a greater proportion of possible worlds will now be located in set $\sim X$, reducing the likelihood that the actual world is located in set X. We will have less confidence that the proposition is true as a result of evidence k.

Third, possible world semantics allows one to conduct counterfactual analysis in case-study research (see chapter 5 on counterfactual analysis). With counterfactual analysis, researchers directly analyze non-actual worlds in order to learn about the actual world (Fearon 1991; Tetlock and Belkin 1996b; Levy 2008). For instance, imagine that we wish to assess the following proposition: If Hillary Clinton had been elected president in 2016, fewer people would have died from COVID-19 in the United States in 2020. To evaluate whether the actual world is a member of the set in which this proposition is true, researchers can investigate what would have happened under a Clinton presidency. Although a world in which Clinton is president is non-actual, analyzing it is useful for evaluating the effect of the election of Donald Trump on health policy during the pandemic. The events that unfold in a non-actual world in which Clinton is president (but in which nearly all other features are the same as in the actual world) can offer insight into the difference-making aspects of Trump's election for outcomes such as mortality rates.

Counterfactual analysis is an essential methodology for explaining outcomes in particular cases. Researchers *must* consider counterfactual cases in order to explain why specific outcomes take place within individual cases. In fact, they must consider two different kinds of counterfactual cases: first, counterfactual cases that are similar to cases in the actual world except that one or more potential causal factors are changed; and second, counterfactual cases that are similar to cases in the actual world except that potential causal factors operate in contexts that are changed in specific ways. Both kinds of counterfactual cases take place in possible worlds that are very similar to the actual world but that differ in specific ways that provide inferential leverage to researchers evaluating propositions about the actual world.

Units of Analysis

This section introduces a constructivist and set-theoretic approach for defining and using different units of analysis. I consider the relationship between part-whole hierarchies and set-theoretic hierarchies in conjunction with defining the categories *world*, *case*, and *observation* as employed in constructivist set-theoretic analysis.

HIERARCHIES OF UNITS

The category *unit of analysis* references a class of constructed spatiotemporal entities at a particular level of generality. In scientific constructivist research, the main units of analysis are (1) worlds, (2) cases, and (3) observations. As figure 2.5 illustrates, these units can be situated in a part-whole hierarchy: observations are parts of cases, and cases are parts of worlds.[16] More specifically,

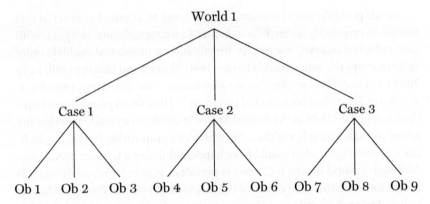

FIGURE 2.5. A Part-Whole Hierarchy: Worlds, Cases, and Observations. Ob = observation.

observations are constructed spatiotemporal parts of cases, and cases are constructed spatiotemporal parts of worlds; worlds are maximal, closed spatiotemporal domains. The analyst normally studies one or more cases from the actual world (e.g., Mexico and Argentina). From these cases, the analyst discovers and uses various observations—facts and evidence about the cases—to assess the propositions under study.

At the same time, these three units—worlds, cases, and observations—can be situated within a set-theoretic hierarchy (see figure 2.6). With a set-theoretic hierarchy, a specific world (e.g., the actual world or a non-actual possible world) is a subset of a category referring to worlds with a specific case (e.g., *worlds with eighteenth-century France*), which is in turn a subset of a category referring to cases with a specific observation (e.g., *cases with peasant revolution*). Perhaps counterintuitively, the overarching superset corresponds to the observation category, whereas the smallest subset corresponds to the world category. Thus, the most disaggregated part in figure 2.5 is the largest set in figure 2.6, whereas the fully aggregated whole in figure 2.5 is the smallest set in figure 2.6. One way to make intuitive sense of the set-theoretic hierarchy is to recognize that the set for a given observation contains actual and possible cases (i.e., a given observation has multiple case members), and the set for a given case contains various possible worlds (i.e., a given case has multiple worlds as its members). Hence, the order of the set sizes is: observations > cases > worlds. It does not make sense to imagine that more worlds exist than cases or that more cases exist than observations.

As an illustration, consider the following statement: "A peasant revolution occurred in eighteenth-century France." In this statement, the three units of analysis are as follows: (1) the implicit *world* is the actual world, (2) the *case* is eighteenth-century France, and (3) the *observation* is a peasant revolution. The category for the observation—*peasant revolution*—includes as its

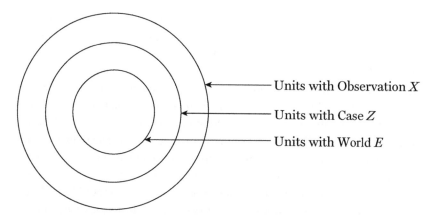

FIGURE 2.6. A Set-Theoretic Hierarchy: Worlds, Cases, and Observations

members several actual cases and many other possible cases. The category for the case—*eighteenth-century France*—includes as its members the actual world and other possible worlds. Thus, the actual world and other possible worlds have membership in both *eighteenth-century France* and *peasant revolution*. The former category (*eighteenth-century France*) is a member of the latter category (*peasant revolution*).

A set-theoretic hierarchy also applies to the relationship between worlds and propositions: worlds are members of sets for propositions. Specifically, possible worlds are members of a set in which a given proposition is true and a set in which that proposition is false. By definition, a contingent proposition contains at least one possible world member in both a set in which the proposition is true and a set in which the proposition is false. The question of interest is whether the actual world is one of the possible worlds that have membership in the set in which the proposition is true. Set-theoretic methods are designed to help researchers answer this question.

CASES

In set-theoretic social science, an individual *case* is one member of a category corresponding to a constructed substantive unit of analysis; the category itself designates a *type* of case.[17] Common examples of the categories that designate types of cases are *voter, household, movement, organization, municipality, country,* and *international system*. For instance, the individual case of Mexico is a member of the substantive category *country*. Specific cases are members of many substantive categories. Some of these categories may be regarded as necessary for the case's membership in the category designating the case itself. For example, Mexico's membership in *sovereign polity* might be regarded as necessary for its membership in *country*. Other categories of which an individual case is a member are regarded as incidental to its membership in the category designating the type of case. For example, Mexico is a member of *ethnically heterogeneous society*, but its membership in that set is incidental to its membership in *country*. Set-theoretic analysts describe the distinctive features of a particular case by discussing the incidental sets of which it is a member. Similarities and differences in membership in incidental categories allow for the comparison of different cases of the same type. For instance, the cases of Mexico and Guatemala share membership in some incidental sets (e.g., *ethnically heterogeneous society*) but not others (e.g., *federal system of governance*).

In macro social science, the cases under study are human kinds.[18] For example, the entity called Mexico refers to a complex clustering of incomprehensible natural kinds that are classified in the mind as a coherent entity with coherent parts. When one asks whether Mexico and Puerto Rico are members of *country*, one is inquiring about the membership of complex entities in a category. One might conclude that the entity Mexico is a full member of this set, whereas the entity Puerto Rico is a partial member. Obviously, the correct answer depends on what we mean by the category *country* and in what other sets (e.g., *sovereign polity*) we believe Mexico and Puerto Rico to have membership. However, the correct answer does not depend on our understanding of the natural kinds that compose Mexico and Puerto Rico. For all intents and purposes, these natural kinds are irrelevant to what we believe is the right answer. We can state this point more generally: knowledge of the natural kind composition of entities is irrelevant when determining their membership in macro social science categories.

In set-theoretic analysis, two kinds of cases must be distinguished: actual cases and non-actual cases. An *actual case* is a unit of analysis that contains the actual world as a member.[19] For example, the actual case *Mexico* contains the actual world as a member. The size of the N of any study corresponds to the number of actual cases under analysis. A case study examines one actual case. A small-N study examines a small number of actual cases, such as 2–20 cases. A large-N study examines a large number of actual cases, typically more (often many more) than 100 cases (cf. Lijphart 1971).

A *non-actual case* is one that does not contain the actual world as a member; non-actual cases contain only non-actual worlds as members.[20] Counterfactual cases are non-actual cases. One can compare non-actual cases: for example, one can compare a Hillary Clinton presidency to an Al Gore presidency. However, in the social sciences, analysts who consider non-actual cases usually compare them to actual ones. For example, they compare an Al Gore presidency to the George W. Bush presidency. An implication is that the number of cases systematically compared and analyzed in a given study need not correspond to the number of actual cases under analysis. A case study of an individual presidency could systematically analyze several non-actual presidencies. Nevertheless, I follow the convention of defining the N of a study as the number of actual cases under systematic analysis.

SET-MEMBERSHIP OBSERVATIONS

A *set-membership observation* is a belief held with very high certitude that an actual case has membership in a specific category (e.g., France 1975 is a member of *industrialized country*; Donald Trump in 2019 is a member of *U.S. President*).[21] Within a given community, set-membership observations are *facts* about cases.[22] For example, we treat it as a fact that the case *Mexico* has membership in the categories *country with Mexico City as its capital* and *country in which Vicente Fox was president*. Indeed, we naturalize these facts and proceed as if they reflect essential and indisputable properties of Mexico: "Mexico City *is* the capital of the country Mexico" and "Vicente Fox *was* a president of the country Mexico." While the finality and certitude of set-membership observations can never be absolute, social scientists treat them as definitive pieces of information and valid descriptions of experiential reality for the purposes of proposition evaluation (cf. Hempel 1980; Hudson 1994; Hunt 1994; Sayer 1992: 65–72).

Set-membership observations concern the membership of actual cases, rather than non-actual cases, in categories of interest. We have sensory access only to the actual world, not to any other possible worlds. We cannot detect, even indirectly, any possible world besides the actual world. The set corresponding to a particular set-membership observation contains either one or multiple actual cases. For example, Mexico is the only actual case that has membership in the set *country with Oaxaca as a coffee-producing region*. By contrast, the set *significant coffee-producing country* has multiple actual cases as members (e.g., Brazil, Vietnam, Colombia, Indonesia, and Ethiopia). The set designating any given set-membership observation is itself a member of sets at higher levels of generality and contains within it sets at lower levels of generality. Thus, we can say with a very high degree of certitude that the case of Colombia has membership in the set *major coffee-producing country*, as well as in *coffee-producing country* (a superset) and *major coffee-producing country with many small and medium-sized farms* (a subset). Depending on research goals, one may seek and use set-membership observations at more general or more specific levels of analysis.

Researchers use set-membership observations to assess whether or not the actual world is a member of a set in which a proposition is true. For instance, consider whether or not the actual world is a member of the set *Russian interference was an important cause of Donald Trump's election in 2016*. As of 2020, analysts seem undecided on this question, because of insufficient evidence; some believe that the universe of possible worlds is distributed fairly evenly across the set in which the proposition is true and the set in which it is false. To move forward, researchers can use set-membership observations that asymmetrically reduce the range of possible worlds in the two sets. For instance, some of the worlds in which the Russian-interference proposition is false require that Vladimir Putin did not personally authorize a major operation to interfere in the U.S. election. If a researcher discovers evidence that we agree definitively shows that the actual world is a member of a set in which Putin did authorize large-scale interference, we eliminate as non-actual those worlds that assume the opposite. The consequence is a shift in the distribution of possible worlds, such that the set containing possible worlds in which Russian interference was an important cause of Trump's victory is now more likely to contain the actual world.

It bears emphasizing that social science evidence does not consist of "brute facts" about reality; even the most credible set-membership observations depend on collective understandings among a community of people for their truth (cf. Churchland 1988; Elder-Vass 2012; Fodor 1988; Searle 1995; Smith 2010). Scholarly debate about the validity of propositions in case-study and small-N research may turn precisely on the truth of particular set-membership observations. For example, in scholarship on late colonial Chile, historians do not agree about the extent to which this case is a member of the set *strong export economy in colonial Spanish America* (Barbier 1980: 158–59; Cavieres 1996: 53). The issue is important to theories of postcolonial development that propose that Chile's membership in *isolated and marginal colonial territory* was necessary for its subsequent membership in *wealthy postcolonial country in Spanish America* (Mahoney 2010). If late colonial Chile lacks membership in *strong export economy*, then the proposition that its marginal colonial status enabled its development escapes falsification.

In summary, set-membership observations are the evidence and facts that social scientists use to evaluate propositions and theories. They are beliefs characterized by high certitude about the membership of a case in a category; they are understood to be accurate descriptions of experiential reality for the purposes of analysis. From the perspective of an essentialist social science, these observations are simply facts about cases. In scientific constructivist analysis, they are treated as justified societal facts. Either way, set-membership observations correspond to the evidence that scholars use to evaluate propositions and theories.

Certitude and Truth

This section fleshes out the conceptual distinction between *certain proposition* and *true proposition* in scientific constructivism. Both of these categories are treated as sets in which particular propositions can have membership. In addition, particular propositions can be closer to or further from the proto-types of these two categories. In the social sciences, however, propositions cannot correspond to the prototypical member of *certain proposition* or the prototypical member of *true proposition*.

THE CATEGORY *CERTAIN PROPOSITION*

Regarding the meaning of *certain proposition*, Bertrand Russell provides a use-ful starting point: "A proposition is certain when it has the highest degree of credibility, either intrinsically or as a result of argument" (1948: 396; see also Popper 1934/1968; Firth 1967; B. Reed 2011). Propositions have intrinsic credibility when they are logical or mathematical truths. Propositions also have intrinsic credibility to the extent that they strike us as involuntary, self-evident, and fixed realities immune from cognitive and theoretical influence (Fodor 1983, 1984; Hudson 1994). The members of a community quickly and easily agree about whether these propositions are true (cf. Feyerabend 1958: 145). Intrinsically certain propositions may include statements whose truth is required for countless other propositions that are known to be true. For instance, consider the proposition that George Washington was the first president of the United States. For this proposition to be false, a vast sea of other propositions that we know to be true would also need to be false. The proposition is highly credible in part because so many existing truths assume and require this belief. Intrinsic justification can also apply when the truth-making process that establishes a given proposition as true is regarded as infallible and identical to the process that establishes countless other propo-sitions as true (e.g., repeated, direct visual observation by many individuals). Calling into question the truth-making process for the individual proposition would raise doubts about multitudes of other propositions about which we feel certain.[23]

If a proposition cannot be said to have intrinsic credibility, analysts must demonstrate that they nevertheless have *sufficient reason* for being certain about its truth (Russell 1948; Melamed and Lin 2020). This demonstration usually consists in part of showing how one's work follows existing procedural norms within the social sciences (cf. Bourdieu 1991; Hempel 1980). The field of social science methodology is specifically concerned with elaborating the systematic procedures that provide researchers with sufficient reason to hold their beliefs with high certainty. These procedures are much broader than the application of statistical significance tests, which are now often criticized (see, e.g., McShane et al. 2019); they are basic methods that scholars use to gather data and make inferences from those data. These methods are ultimately rooted in logic, and their procedures provide reason for scholars to believe that they generate valid findings. Nevertheless, uncertainty in social science research arises because its methods cannot be applied in an ideal way, and because the methods themselves are inadequate for eliminating all uncertainty.

It is helpful to break down social science methodologies into two groups. A *data collection methodology* concerns procedures for finding, collecting, and reporting information. In the social sciences, data collection methodologies include techniques for carrying out interviews, leading focus groups, conducting ethnography, implementing experiments, coding newspapers, analyzing archival materials, using secondary source materials, and more. Social scientists often distinguish types of data according to the method through which the data were gathered (e.g., archival data, ethnographic data, survey data, and so on). By contrast, a *data analysis methodology* consists of explicit and replicable procedures for making inferences from data. Data analysis methodologies can be thought of as the epistemological tools that social scientists use to derive new knowledge from existing knowledge. These tools include both quantitative techniques, such as experiments and regression analysis, and qualitative techniques, such as Mill's methods and qualitative comparative analysis (QCA).

Uncertainty inevitably arises with the application of data collection and data analysis methodologies in the social sciences.[24] With data collection, uncertainty is produced because even raw data are generated through social processes that shape the existence, nature, and meaning of the data. In the social sciences, the bottom-level data are not in fact "raw" in the sense of unconstructed and uncontaminated by the workings of human minds. The human-dependent nature of data introduces uncertainty into research in various characteristic ways, depending on the specific data collection technique. With secondary source material, uncertainty exists because the author of the secondary source may select a biased sample of primary sources and impose his or her interpretation onto the material in ways that are not transparent (Goldthorpe 1991; Lustick 1996). Likewise, one cannot take primary sources at face value, as authentic representations of the world as it was in the past. Primary sources are human-created artifacts that reflect the beliefs of their creators and the context in which they were produced (Presnell 2013). Similar remarks can be made about data collected through interviews, focus groups, and ethnography (Kapiszewski, MacLean, and Read 2015; Cyr 2019; Geertz 1988). Uncertainty exists because the subjects under study and the researcher are human beings reporting about a social reality that they help to construct. Researchers bring to the data collection process their own worldviews and biases, and the actors whom they observe or engage bring their own belief systems and understandings. Uncertainty exists on both sides of this "double hermeneutic": uncertainty about the subject's ability to accurately represent social reality; and uncertainty about the researcher's ability to accurately represent the subject's representations of social reality (Giddens 1984). One cannot be certain that a different researcher would arrive at exactly the same results; subjects may not respond in the same way, and a different researcher might "see" a different reality.

With respect to data analysis, the gold standard is a *truth-preserving methodology*, in which the analysis yields conclusions that must be valid provided that the input data are valid. A truth-preserving methodology might have the slogan "valid data in, valid conclusions out." Unfortunately, with the exception of purely deductive tests, in which conclusions are logical entailments of premises (Sundholm 2000), social science modes of data analysis are not fully truth preserving. Instead, they use partial generalizations to reach uncertain conclusions. The logically inductive nature of social science methods ensures the introduction of uncertainty into findings, even if the input data are valid. Social scientists cannot use the laws of the social world to infer why one event follows another or to explain why a given trend exists within a population. Instead, as constructivist scholars emphasize, they must use generalizations that consist of social categories that are related to one another in ways that are not stable across all times and places. From a constructivist view, uncertainty is introduced because the very categories that are used in social science generalizations are contingently bound in time and space; they are subject to scope conditions whose range can never be known for certain.

Beyond the uncertainties raised by the use of logical induction with constructed categories, social science findings are uncertain in the same way that all scientific findings are uncertain. Objective reality in the natural sciences and experiential reality in the social sciences provide a basis for adjudicating among competing theories, models, and categories. However, the truth of a finding depends on the theories, models, and categories that are used to understand the workings of objective reality or experiential reality. The discovery or formulation of new theories, models, and categories can always overturn even firm conclusions about the validity of propositions (Hudson 1994; Hunt 1994; Sayer 2000). In science, propositions are always false in at least one possible world. Scientists can never be 100% certain that the actual world is one of the possible worlds in which the proposition is true (Tichý 1978; Oddie 1981, 1986). The existence of uncertainty is inevitable with scientific research.

Given this inherent uncertainty, it is appropriate to speak of *highly certain propositions*, rather than *absolutely certain propositions* (Popper 1934/1968; Sayer 2000; Gadenne 2015). The kind of truth sought in the sciences—whether the natural sciences or the social sciences—must be highly certain truth, rather than absolutely certain truth. Scholars in the discipline of mathematics may be able to prove theorems and arrive at absolute truths (cf. Hacking 2014), but the same cannot be said for scholars in the natural and social sciences.

THE CATEGORY *TRUE PROPOSITION*

Scientific research uses evidence and logic to try to determine with a high degree of certitude whether a given proposition is a member of the category *true proposition*. I understand the category *true proposition* to be more or less equivalent to *accurate proposition*; a true proposition is a correct depiction of objective or experiential reality (cf. Weston 1987, 1992).[25] In the natural sciences, true propositions identify natural kinds and accurately describe their properties, powers, and relations. In the social sciences, true propositions identify and accurately describe human kinds and their set-membership relations. Because human kinds depend on human minds for their existence, social scientists cannot use external reality as the sole basis for identifying true propositions. Rather, the identification of a true proposition depends in part on shared beliefs about the meanings of categories—meanings rooted in the conceptual spaces of human minds.

I use the label *truth-dependent semantic context* to refer to the shared meanings and assumptions on which truths in the social sciences depend. A truth-dependent semantic context consists of shared understandings about (1) the meanings of the main categories under analysis, and (2) the background cognitive models on which the meanings of these categories depend. Unlike the natural sciences, which sometimes seek truths that apply across nearly all contexts, the social sciences seek to capture truths within localized semantic contexts. In the social sciences, the scope of a true proposition is set by the semantic context in which that proposition bears a particular meaning. To be a member of *true proposition*, a given proposition must be consistent with larger matrices of meaning that can only ever be partially specified.

The dependence of truth on semantics in the social sciences does not commit one to epistemological relativism (Boyd 1990; Sayer 2000; David 2016; cf. Goodman 1978; Lakoff and Johnson 1980; Lakoff 1987; Putnam 1981). This dependence does not mean that a proposition is true in one semantic context and false in another. Rather, the implication is that a proposition *requires* a particular semantic context in order to embody a certain meaning and exist as a certain kind of proposition. Outside of this context, the proposition carries a different meaning, and is not the same proposition. Here we need to recall that categories *are* meanings, as embedded in cognitive spaces that are entangled with entities in the natural world. If the meaning of a category changes, the *identity* of the category changes. Likewise, if the semantic context of a proposition shifts, the proposition turns into a different proposition. The semantic context of a proposition is partly constitutive of the proposition. Hence, when one says that a proposition is relative to a particular semantic context, one is asserting that the proposition *consists* in part of, and presupposes, the meanings and cognitive models that compose that context.

Within a semantic context, an individual proposition is a member of either *true proposition* or *false proposition*. An appropriately formulated proposition in the social sciences cannot be a member of both or neither of these categories in the actual world. The *meaning* of a proposition depends on a semantic context, but truth is not relative within that context. Truth is epistemologically objective; a single right answer exists about the truth of a proposition. A true proposition is the description of experiential or objective reality that emerges once all relevant evidence and all relevant theories have been fully considered (cf. Boyd 1990; Hempel 1965; Popper 1934/1968). For the reasons that we have explored, social scientists can never be *certain* about the truth of a proposition. But that uncertainty is not an artifact of an inherent relativism regarding truth. Statements about human kinds are either right or wrong depending on evidence derived from the social world. Experiential reality provides a sufficient basis for adjudicating truth, with varying certitude, among competing theories and propositions.

In addition to *accurate proposition*, two other categories—*comprehensive proposition* and *precise proposition*—are useful for understanding how close a given proposition is to the prototypical true proposition. A *comprehensive proposition* is one that omits no necessary information and contains no unnecessary information ("the whole truth and nothing but the truth"). A *precise proposition* is one that is formulated without vagueness or ambiguity. The *ideal-typical true proposition* (the prototypical true proposition) is one that has 100% membership not only in *accurate proposition*, but also in *comprehensive proposition* and *precise proposition*.

Individual propositions with full membership in the set *true proposition* (or with full non-membership) can be closer to or further from the ideal type of this category. The degree of a proposition's membership in the category *comprehensive proposition* and the degree of its membership in *precise proposition* reveal its proximity to the prototype point of *true proposition*. For example, the true proposition that the United States contains between 48 and 52 states is closer to the ideal type than the true proposition that the United States contains between 1 and 100 states. The former has greater membership in the category *precise proposition*. Propositions that are false also vary in the extent to which they approximate the ideal type of *true proposition*. For example, the 100% false proposition that the United States contains exactly 47 states is closer to having membership in the set *true proposition* than the 100% false proposition that the United States contains exactly 23 states. The former proposition is closer to being a member of the set *accurate proposition* than the latter. Or consider the following two true propositions: (1) the current population of the United States is at least one person, and (2) the current population of the United States is at least 325 million people. Both propositions are accurate and thus 100% members of *true proposition*, but the latter has greater membership in *comprehensive proposition,* bringing it closer to the prototype point of *true proposition.*

The inability of scientists to discover 100% certain propositions that match the ideal-typical truth is *not* an artifact of the lack of epistemologically objective truth. To the contrary, the existence of 100% true propositions whose certainty can be rationally assessed depends on an objective reality structured by natural kinds (Aronson 1990). If objective truths are not found in the world, it is hard to know what one might mean by *truth* and *certitude* (cf. Tarski 1944; Hodges 2018; Gómez-Torrente 2019). The existence of an objective reality that is logically structured allows science to reach rational conclusions about the truth of propositions, including propositions about human kinds.

———

This chapter has introduced foundational concepts for set-theoretic analysis when conducted from a scientific constructivist orientation. These foundational concepts are *sets, worlds, cases, observations, propositions, certainty,* and *truth.*

The concept of *set*—defined as a bounded location in space—is the most basic category in constructivist set-theoretic analysis. A set can have other sets as its members (or partial members), and a set can be a member (or partial member) of other sets. Sets are essential tools for understanding social categories in the social world and for building the categories that social scientists use to study that world.

The categories *world, case,* and *observation* are conceptualized as sets at different positions within a set-theoretic hierarchy of units of analysis: worlds are subsets of cases, which in turn are subsets of observations. *Worlds* divide into possible worlds and impossible (imaginary) worlds, with possible worlds being the focus of social science. The actual world is one particular possible world—the one in which we reside and the only one to which we have sensory access. The main units of analysis in social science research are *cases,* which can be most readily conceived as spatiotemporal parts of worlds. Social scientists examine not only actual cases, but also non-actual, or counterfactual, cases. Analysts do not look at whole cases, but focus instead on particular aspects of cases, which correspond to *observations*—sets in which cases and worlds can be members. A *set-membership observation* is an observation for which the researcher is nearly certain that the actual world is a member. Set-membership observations are the societal facts and evidence on which social scientific analysis depends.

Propositions are statements about observations, cases, and worlds that are either true or false. Propositions in the social sciences are constituted by social categories and their relationships, as well as the semantic context in which those categories and relationships bear specific meanings. In the social sciences, the category *true proposition* is defined as an accurate statement about a facet of experiential reality. The prototypical true proposition is a member of the set *accurate, comprehensive, and precise proposition.*

Although propositions are either true or false in the actual world, researchers can never know with 100% certainty whether a proposition is true or false. The sources of uncertainty include limitations inherent in all scientific methodologies and limitations specific to particular social science methodologies. Nevertheless, this book will show that when social scientists use set-theoretic methodologies with set-membership observations, they can arrive at highly certain conclusions about the truth of propositions.

PART II

Methodological Tools

3

Set-Theoretic Methodology

With set-theoretic analysis, researchers study *relationships among sets*, not relationships among variables. When studying set relations, analysts do not ask questions about the extent to which one property is associated with another property. Rather, they ask questions about the extent to which one set is a member of another set. *Set-membership relations* are at the heart of set-theoretic methodology.

This chapter considers five set-membership relations: necessary, sufficient, necessary and sufficient, INUS, and SUIN relationships.[1] To describe these different types, I use the language of condition-to-outcome relationships. A *condition* is the set that helps constitute or cause another set, called the *outcome*. With a necessity relationship, to take one example, the condition (set X) is a superset of the outcome (set Y), such that an entity must be a member of X to be a member of Y. Each of the five set-membership relations can be defined and illustrated according to its particular condition-to-outcome membership pattern. The language of condition-to-outcome relationships accommodates both constitutive relationships (e.g., X constitutes Y) and causal relationships (e.g., X causes Y). One important difference between a constitutive relationship and a causal relationship concerns time order: X and Y are coterminous with a constitutive relationship, whereas X precedes Y with a causal relationship.

The framework in this chapter offers tools for making logical conclusions about the relative importance of individual conditions in the explanation of a given outcome.[2] The guiding rule is simple: a condition (X) becomes more important in the explanation of an outcome (Y) to the extent that membership in X is necessary and sufficient for membership in Y. For instance, if we discover that two conditions are each necessary for a given outcome,[3] we can evaluate their relative importance by exploring which one comes closer to also being sufficient. The importance of any individual condition can be measured according to how closely it approximates a necessary *and* sufficient condition.

Set-membership relations are used for both working with categories and studying causality. On the categorization side, a set-theoretic framework offers tools for defining terms. Good definitions, in turn, are one way to promote collective understanding about the meaning of categories, especially among individuals who already share many similar frames and background assumptions. Two modes of category definition are discussed in this chapter: a classic mode and a family resemblance mode. With the *classic mode* of category definition, membership in each condition is necessary for membership in the outcome, and membership in all conditions is sufficient for membership in the outcome. With the *family resemblance mode*, membership in an individual condition—or an individual combination of conditions—is sufficient but not necessary for membership in the outcome; at least two distinct conditions or combinations of conditions are each sufficient for membership in the outcome.

On the causal analysis side, the focus of this chapter is *token causality*, which concerns the causes of particular outcomes in specific cases. Three models of token causality are discussed: causal power models, counterfactual models, and regularity models. I argue that each of these models offers a useful set of tools for scientific analysis, though the primary domains of application for each one vary. Specifically, causal power models are most appropriate for the analysis of natural kinds; counterfactual models are most appropriate for the analysis of partial natural kinds; and regularity models are most appropriate for the analysis of human kinds. Since this book is concerned with the study of human kinds, regularity models are the focus of attention. This chapter discusses the kinds of causes that are associated with regularity models of token causality; and it proposes an inclusive understanding of cause, placing much of the burden of causal analysis on differentiating more important causes from less important ones.

Types of Set-Membership Relations

Set-theoretic methodology focuses on the membership relations that exist between one or more conditions and an outcome. This section considers five such relations, each of which can be helpful for the purposes of category definition and causal analysis.

NECESSARY CONDITION

A condition is necessary for an outcome when an entity must have membership in the condition in order to be a member of the outcome. A relationship of necessity can be purely definitional and tautological. For example, an entity must be a member of the condition *shape* in order to be a member of the

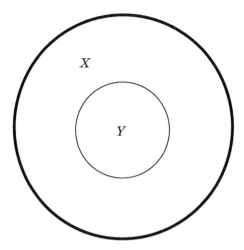

FIGURE 3.1. Set-Theoretic Conceptualization of a
Necessary Condition

outcome *square*. Alternatively, membership in a necessary condition can be
temporally prior to and causally required for membership in the outcome. For
example, with respect to the case of the United States, membership in the set
Donald Trump is elected president was causally required for membership in the
subsequent set *protests occur against the Trump presidency*.

Various techniques exist for defining necessary conditions in the social sciences. Necessary conditions can be defined using aristotelian two-valued logic,
probability theory, and calculus (Goertz 2003a). They can also be defined using
statistical frameworks, such as the potential outcomes framework (Seawright
2015). Consistent with the approach of this book, I employ a set-theoretic
definition of a necessary but not sufficient condition:

> X is a necessary (but not sufficient) condition of outcome Y if X is a
> proper superset of Y.

As figure 3.1 illustrates, any case that is a member of set Y must also be a member of set X. However, a case's membership in X does not ensure that it is also
a member of Y. Thus, X is necessary but not sufficient for Y.

SUFFICIENT CONDITION

Membership in a condition may be sufficient—but not necessary—for membership in an outcome. When this is true, a case that has membership in condition X must also have membership in outcome Y, though not all cases with
membership in Y have membership in X. From a set-theoretic perspective, a
sufficient but not necessary condition can be defined as follows:

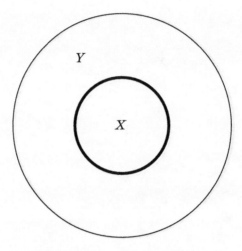

FIGURE 3.2. Set-Theoretic Conceptualization of a
Sufficient Condition

> X is a sufficient (but not necessary) condition of outcome Y if X is a
> proper subset of Y.

Figure 3.2 illustrates a sufficiency relationship. Any case that is a member of set X must also be a member of set Y. However, a case can achieve membership in Y without being a member of X.

NECESSARY AND SUFFICIENT CONDITION

An individual condition is necessary *and* sufficient for an outcome if a case must have membership in the condition to have membership in the outcome *and* if the case's membership in the condition ensures its membership in the outcome. In set-theoretic terms, a necessary and sufficient condition is defined as follows:

> X is a necessary and sufficient condition of outcome Y if X is an equal set
> of Y.

As figure 3.3 shows, the set-theoretic relationship is one of perfect overlap (X and Y are supersets and subsets of each other, though not *proper* supersets and subsets). Any case that is a member of one set must and will be a member of the other set. The membership or non-membership of a case in one set perfectly predicts its membership or non-membership in the other.

INUS CONDITION

Simultaneous membership in *multiple* conditions may be sufficient for membership in an outcome. The individual conditions are neither necessary nor

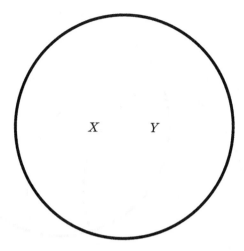

FIGURE 3.3. Set-Theoretic Conceptualization of a
Necessary and Sufficient Condition

sufficient; rather, they are part of an overall *combination* of conditions that is
sufficient for the outcome. The individual factors in the *sufficiency combination*
are INUS conditions, an acronym created by the philosopher J. L. Mackie:
"An *insufficient* but *necessary* part of a condition which is itself *unnecessary*
but *sufficient* for the result" (Mackie 1965: 246; see also Mackie 1980; Ragin
1987; Wright 1985, 2011). In set-theoretic terms, an INUS condition can be
defined as follows:

> *X* is an INUS condition of outcome *Y* if the set created by the
> intersection of *X* and one or more conditions is a proper subset
> of *Y*.

Figure 3.4 presents a set diagram to illustrate this idea. In the diagram,
neither *X* nor *Z* is necessary or sufficient for *Y*. The absence of necessity is
illustrated by the fact that a case can achieve membership in *Y* without being
a member of either *X* or *Z*. Likewise, the absence of sufficiency is clear from
the fact that some cases are members of *X* or *Z* but not of *Y*. However, the
space where sets *X* and *Z* *intersect* is a proper subset of *Y*. This intersection
set meets the set-theoretic criteria for sufficiency. Any case that is a member
of *both* X *and* Z must also be a member of *Y*. Thus, *X* and *Z* are INUS conditions for *Y*.

SUIN CONDITION

A final kind of condition is used when an analyst regards the constitutive attributes of a necessary condition as individual conditions themselves. This type is
called a SUIN condition: a *sufficient* but *unnecessary* part of a condition that is

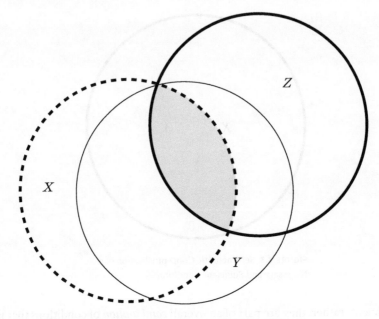

FIGURE 3.4. Set-Theoretic Conceptualization of INUS Conditions

insufficient but *necessary* for an outcome (Mahoney, Kimball, and Koivu 2009). With a SUIN condition, constitutive features that are sufficient (but not necessary) for the existence of a necessary condition are analyzed as individual conditions themselves. In set-theoretic terms, a SUIN condition is defined as follows:

> X is a SUIN condition of outcome Y if Y is a proper subset of the union of X and one or more conditions.

Figure 3.5 presents a set diagram of a SUIN condition. In this figure, neither X nor Z is necessary or sufficient for Y. However, the set created by the union of these conditions is a superset of Y. Since membership in this overarching condition is necessary for membership in Y, X and Z are SUIN conditions of Y. As we shall see, SUIN conditions play an important role in counterfactual analysis.

In sum, five kinds of set-membership relations—necessary, sufficient, necessary and sufficient, INUS, and SUIN—are used in set-theoretic analysis.[4] These relations inform both modes of defining categories and approaches to distinguishing causes.

Modes of Defining Categories

A central challenge of social science is to provide definitions that help a community of individuals to achieve collective understanding about the meaning of social categories. Because these categories are mind-dependent entities,

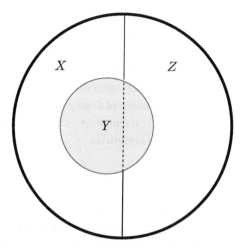

FIGURE 3.5. Set-Theoretic Conceptualization of SUIN Conditions

analysts cannot adequately define them by appealing to their natural essences, objective properties, or inherent causal powers. They cannot identify necessary and sufficient conditions that physically constitute these categories. Instead, social scientists must adopt a semantic approach to categories that focuses on their stipulated meaning. With this approach, category analysis involves meaning clarification, in which the goal is to enhance understanding and communication among a community of individuals.

Meaning clarification with a set-theoretic approach can be pursued in part—but only in part—by offering a formal definition of the category in question. Other techniques of clarification include providing examples of the category, using the category in one or more sentences, discussing the field of related terms in which the category is situated, and identifying the cognitive models and background assumptions required for the category to make sense. With respect to human kinds, all of these tools can help promote intersubjective understanding about the meaning of a category.

Set-theoretic analysts define a category by identifying the coterminous conditions of which it is a subset and/or for which it is a superset. These defining conditions are the constitutive sets that establish the boundaries for membership in the category of interest. The constitutive sets are themselves defined by other constitutive sets, which in turn are defined by still more sets, and so on. At no point does the process of definitional elaboration lead to mind-independent properties. Instead, as with dictionary definitions, the process continues in a seemingly endless progression, perhaps culminating in circularity.

Here I discuss two modes of category definition: (1) a classic mode, based on individually necessary and jointly sufficient conditions; and (2) a family resemblance mode, based on INUS conditions (Goertz 2006b, 2020; cf. Wittgenstein 1953/2001). Both modes specify precise criteria for obtaining category membership, though neither mode is intended to capture the actual cognitive processes involved in human categorization. Likewise, while the modes are intended to help clarify the meaning of categories, they do not offer a comprehensive presentation of the full meaning of a category. The use of other tools—including examples, analogies, and test sentences—can supplement these modes and further clarify the meaning of categories.

CLASSIC MODE

The classic mode builds categories with defining conditions that are individually necessary and jointly sufficient for membership in the category (Sartori 1970). For example, one possible definition of *democratic national regime* has three defining conditions: *free elections, universal suffrage*, and *broad civil rights* (countries are the cases that can have membership in these sets). With the classic mode, these conditions are necessary, because if a case is not a member of even one of them, that case cannot be a member of the category *democratic national regime*. The defining conditions are jointly sufficient, because if a case is a member of all of them, that case is definitely a member of *democratic national regime*. As figure 3.6 illustrates, *democratic national regime* is located at the intersection of the three defining conditions. The classic mode uses only the logical AND (not the logical OR) when aggregating defining conditions.

Researchers using the classic mode strive to identify defining features that are *important* necessary conditions. Unlike trivial necessary conditions, for which cases always or almost always have membership, important necessary conditions help the analyst distinguish members of the category from nonmembers. In figure 3.6, the set *broad civil rights* is the most important necessary condition. One can see this by noting that this condition is the smallest superset in the figure and thus comes closest to also being individually sufficient for the category. Of the three necessary conditions, *broad civil rights* does the best job of identifying cases that lack membership in *democratic national regime*. By contrast, the least important defining condition is *universal suffrage*, because this condition does the least work distinguishing members from nonmembers of *democratic national regime*.

Venn diagrams offer a useful way of illustrating case membership in combinations of necessary conditions. With Venn diagrams, the size of the circles is not related to the number of cases in a set. Instead, Venn diagrams include the individual sets and all possible combinations of sets, and they may list the number of cases in each. Figure 3.7 illustrates the use of a Venn diagram for the conditions of democracy in five Central American countries from 1981 to 2000 (N = 100 country-year cases). In this example, 48 of the 100 cases

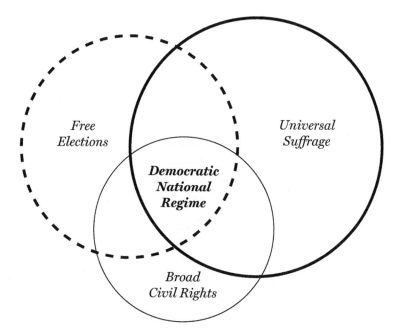

FIGURE 3.6. Illustration of the Classic Mode of Category Definition

have membership in all three defining conditions; these are Central America's 48 country-years with membership in *democratic national regime* during that period (Bowman, Lehoucq, and Mahoney 2005). The figure shows that the three defining conditions have varying degrees of importance as defining elements. In particular, *free elections* is the most difficult condition in which to achieve membership and thus is the most important necessary ingredient. Only 59 of 100 country-years have membership in *free elections*, whereas 84 and 81 country-years have membership in *universal suffrage* and *broad civil rights*, respectively. When a case has membership in *free elections*, it also has membership in *democratic national regime* 81% of the time. By contrast, membership in *democratic national regime* is accompanied by membership in *universal suffrage* and *broad civil rights* 57% and 59% of the time, respectively.

Venn diagrams are also helpful for illustrating the idea of *diminished subtypes* of democracy (Collier and Levitsky 1997). Scholars form diminished subtypes of democracy to characterize cases that are missing membership in one specific defining condition of *democracy* and are thus less than full members of the category. To label these cases, scholars commonly place an adjective in front of *democracy* that highlights the condition in which the case lacks membership. In figure 3.7, for example, 11 country-years would be members of *democratic national regime* except that they lack membership in *broad civil rights*. These 11 country-years might be called cases of *restricted democracies*.

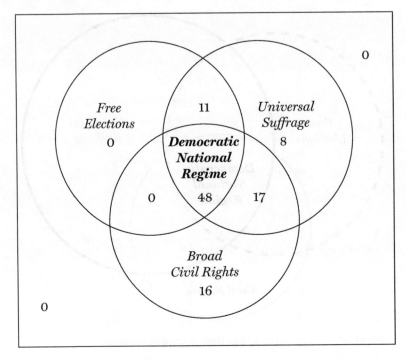

FIGURE 3.7. Venn Diagram of Defining Conditions of Democracy: Central America, 1981–2000

Diminished subtypes require cases to have membership in one or more *negated* defining conditions. For example, restricted democracies are cases that have membership in three necessary and jointly sufficient conditions: *free elections, universal suffrage,* and *not–broad civil rights.* Depending on the membership distribution of cases in the category *broad civil rights* versus its negation, *not–broad civil rights,* it is possible that restricted democracies are more common than democracies (though this is not true with the Central America data). A diminished subtype has the same number of defining conditions as the original category, and it may have fewer, more, or the same number of members compared to the original category (Collier and Levitsky 1997).

FAMILY RESEMBLANCE MODE

In its pure form, the family resemblance mode assumes that membership in no single defining condition is necessary for membership in a category (Barrenechea and Castillo 2019; cf. Collier and Mahon 1993; Goertz 2006b). Instead, membership in different individual conditions, or different individual *combinations* of conditions, is sufficient for membership in the category. Each individual defining condition is either a sufficient condition itself or an INUS

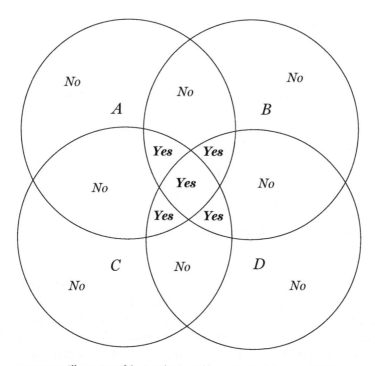

FIGURE 3.8. Illustration of the Family Resemblance Mode of Category Definition. Yes = *early welfare state*; A = *public health insurance*; B = *workman's compensation*; C = *unemployment compensation*; D = *old-age pensions*. Derived from Hicks (1999).

condition that is part of a combination of conditions that is sufficient for membership in the category. INUS conditions are neither individually necessary nor individually sufficient for membership; they combine into a *sufficiency combination*—i.e., a package of conditions that is sufficient, but not necessary, for membership in the category of interest. With the family resemblance mode, the logical OR is used to capture the distinct sufficient conditions and/or sufficiency combinations that lead to membership in the category.

For example, imagine that a scholar defines a category as requiring membership in any three of four defining conditions. If these conditions are labeled *A, B, C,* and *D,* there are five distinct ways to achieve membership in the category: *ABC~D, AB~CD, A~BCD, ~ABCD,* and *ABCD.* Figure 3.8 makes the point visually, with a set diagram for Hicks's (1999) definition of the category *early welfare state.* Hicks argues that to qualify for membership in this category, countries must be members of at least three of four INUS conditions representing major social provision programs (*public health insurance, workman's compensation, unemployment compensation,* and *old-age pensions*). No single set of programs is required; rather, five different membership combinations are each sufficient for membership in the category.

With a hybrid version of the family resemblance mode, the analyst includes one or more necessary conditions along with two or more INUS conditions (Barrenechea and Castillo 2019). In this hybrid mode, all cases with membership in the category of interest share membership in one or more defining conditions but not all defining conditions. For example, one might define the category *nineteenth-century democracy* as requiring membership in the condition *free elections* and in either *broad suffrage* or *broad civil rights*. The following equation summarizes this definition:

$$X \,\&\, (A \vee B) \rightarrow Y, \tag{3.1}$$

where $X = free\ elections$, $A = broad\ suffrage$, $B = broad\ civil\ rights$, and $Y = nineteenth\text{-}century\ democracy$. The equation reads, "The combination of X and either A or B (or both) is sufficient for Y." Here, X is a necessary condition and A and B are INUS conditions for Y. The equation combines aspects of the classic mode and aspects of the family resemblance mode.

Clear definitions of categories are desirable—some might argue even necessary—for the purposes of social science analysis. Clear definitions are formal, reproducible, and, ideally, public statements about the meaning of categories, all of which serve the goals of science well. However, even when scholars carefully define categories and achieve collective agreement about their meanings, they should have no illusion that their definitions literally identify the mind-independent substances that objectively constitute the category under analysis. In the social sciences, human kind categories and their definitions are always constructed by virtue of the mind's interaction with a natural reality that is not well comprehended.

A Note on the Category *Causality*

The category *causality* (or *causation*) lacks a singularly correct definition that can be derived from nature. Causality is not a single, monolithic concept; different definitions can be useful for different purposes (Cartwright 2004; see also Anscombe 1971; Godfrey-Smith 2009). By the same token, it seems unlikely that any single definition will ever be entirely adequate for all human purposes (Glymour et al. 2010; see also Skyrms 1984). All existing definitions and models of causality are subject to counterexamples and limitations. Hence, a pragmatic approach to defining causality and employing models of causality seems warranted.

This pragmatic orientation is consistent with what we know about the category *causality* from work in developmental psychology and cognitive science (Danks 2009; Lakoff and Johnson 1980; Leslie and Keeble 1987; Pinker 2007; Sloman 2005; Talmy 1988; Wolff 2007; Wolff and Zettergren 2002). This research finds that causal beliefs are deeply embedded in human cognition, figuring prominently in decision-making, explanation, and prediction, as well as conceptual, counterfactual, and moral reasoning. Causal ideas develop in the first year of life as part of perception, rather than as inferences from perceptions. Cognitively speaking, the notion of causality develops as a subset of primitive force dynamics, which concerns how entities interact with respect to force. Infants, children, and adults experience causal perceptions when an agent exerts a force that changes the movement of a recipient. Depending on whether the agent and recipient have a tendency toward rest or motion, the agent might (1) trigger or reinforce movement, (2) stop or slow movement, or (3) allow or block movement. In the prototypical version of causality, the agent is an intentional human being who uses his or her body to physically change or move an object or person. This prototypical understanding of causality is so basic to thought and language that people tend to reserve the word *cause* for situations that do not match the prototypical case. For instance, when lifting a box or cutting a piece of paper, we do not usually depict the event in explicitly causal terms (e.g., "she caused the box to rise" or "he caused the paper to separate").

By the time we are adults, we embrace several different meanings of the word *cause* and use the category in linguistically ambiguous ways (Kelley 1973; Wolff 2007). We associate causality with correlations, but we also want information about linking mechanisms before attributing causality to a relationship (Ahn et al. 1995). Causal inference and causal perception are likely different cognitive processes, using different parts of the brain. We tend to overestimate our capacity to infer causality, including our understandings of causal mechanisms (Rozenblit and Keil 2002; Tetlock 2005). Formal definitions of causality from philosophy, statistics, and the social sciences capture some aspects of our folk understandings of causality, but not others. No formal definition fully encompasses all the ways in which the human mind perceives causality and makes inferences about it. At the same time, the idea of causality can hardly be abandoned (cf. Russell 1913: 1). Causality is so deeply embedded in our language and thinking that it cannot be dislodged, short of reinventing human perception and inference.

The set-theoretic approach developed in this book is concerned with token (or actual) causality. With *token* causality, one explores whether a specific state of affairs is a cause of a specific outcome in a particular case in the actual world. For example, one asks questions such as, "What were the main causes of the French Revolution?" and "Was the Enlightenment an important cause of the French Revolution?" By contrast, with *type* causality, one explores the causes of general outcomes, asking questions such as, "What are the main causes of social revolutions?" and "Are transformative beliefs a cause of social revolutions?"[5] The particular set-theoretic approach presented here is one of several ongoing scholarly efforts to develop a theory of token causality.[6]

The set-theoretic approach maintains that token causes are ontologically prior to type causes; that is, type causes depend on token causes, but the reverse is not true (cf. Anscombe 1971; Carroll 1991; Cartwright 1989; Lewis 1986b; Tooley 1987). The set-theoretic definition of causality comes close to offering a reductionist definition—i.e., one that does not depend on causal language (see Carroll 2009). However, because the definition includes the requirement that causes precede effects in time, some would argue that it falls back on causal terminology (Tooley 2003: 398). Nevertheless, the set-theoretic definition is a parsimonious one that addresses most standard problems associated with causality (e.g., issues of spuriousness and preemption) and compares favorably with other approaches for the purposes of analyzing human kinds.

Three Models of Causality

In philosophy, three general models of causality compete with one another: causal power models, counterfactual models, and regularity models (Beebee, Hitchcock, and Menzies 2009: pts. 2, 3). My position is that all three of these models are useful, though their primary domains of application are different: causal power models offer useful tools for characterizing the operation of natural kinds, counterfactual models offer tools for studying the effects of partial natural kinds, and regularity models offer tools for understanding relationships among human kinds. Hence, different models of causality are needed for different domains of science. Table 3.1 offers a guide to the following discussion of these models of causality.

CAUSAL POWER MODELS

Causal power models see causality as a power that is an enduring, ongoing state of the world, instead of as a relationship involving spatiotemporally discrete events (cf. Russell 1913, 1948). With *conservation accounts*, causality involves the transfer of properties from one natural entity to another. One particular version suggests that causality is the transfer of energy or momentum, as discovered by physicists (Fair 1979); other versions focus more generally on the preservation of any quantity governed by conservation laws across world-lines (Salmon 1998; Dowe 2000, 2009). *Causal dispositional versions* call attention to the role of unobservable generative entities that necessarily produce relations among observable events (Bhaskar 1975; Ellis 2001; Harré and Madden 1975; McMullin 1984; Mumford 2009; Mumford and Anjum 2011). With disposition models, observable patterns and regularities exist because natural kinds have real causal powers and operate as their nature requires. To take one example, Brownian motion can be explained in light of micro-entities called molecules, whose disposition is to collide with one another when suspended

TABLE 3.1. Three Models of Causality

	Approximate Definition of Token Causality	Ontological Assumptions	Domains of Application	Ten Important Contributions
Causal Power Models	Entity X is a cause of entity Y if: (1) X and Y behave as their natures require them to behave; (2) X intersects with Y in spacetime; and (3) X transfers a nonzero amount of a conserved quantity to Y.	(1) Entities refer to kinds that possess conserved quantities and inherent powers, dispositions, and tendencies. (2) The operation and interaction of entities produce observable effects, including regularities.	(1) Domains in which natural kinds can be isolated. (2) Domains in which natural kinds leave observable traces.	Locke (1690/1980) Hume (1777/1975) Russell (1913) Bhaskar (1975) Harré and Madden (1975) Tooley (1987) Cartwright (1989) Salmon (1998) Mumford (1998) Dowe (2000)
Counterfactual Models	Variable X is a cause of variable Y if: (1) $X=x_1$ and $Y=y_1$ are the actual values of these variables; (2) x_2 and y_2 are other possible values of these variables; (3) an ideal intervention changes the value of X from x_1 to x_2; and (4) the value of Y changes from y_1 to y_2.	(1) Variables refer to properties in the world, and a variable value refers to whether or the extent to which a case possesses a property. (2) An ideal intervention is a manipulation that causes X to change its value without changing the values of any variable that is causally relevant to X.	(1) Domains in which the variables under analysis partially map natural properties and partially mark objective similarities and differences. (2) Domains that allow for experiments and naturally occurring interventions that approximate an ideal intervention.	Hume (1777/1975) Campbell and Stanley (1963) Suppes (1970) Lewis (1973) Rubin (1974) Holland (1986) Sprites, Glymour, and Scheines (1993) Pearl (2000) Woodward (2003) Morgan and Winship (2007)
Regularity Models	Category X is a cause of category Y if: (1) X precedes Y in time; (2) X makes direct or indirect spatiotemporal contact with Y; and (3) X is part of a minimized solution set that is constantly conjoined with Y.	(1) Categories are mind-dependent human kinds. (2) A minimized solution set contains no redundancies.	(1) Domains in which categories are mind-dependent entities. (2) Domains in which collective agreement exists concerning the meaning of categories.	Hume (1777/1975) Mill (1861/1998) Hempel (1942) Hart and Honoré (1959) Mackie (1965) Armstrong (1983) Wright (1985) Ragin (1987) Psillos (2002) Baumgartner (2013)

in a fluid, causing observable movement among pollen grains floating on water. To take another example, the gravitational attraction between two masses can be explained in terms of the curvature of spacetime, a field-like entity whose disposition is to warp in patterns that accord with the Einstein field equations.

Causal power models describe the essential properties of mind-independent entities found in nature (Ellis 2001; though see Mumford 2009: 268–69). These properties endow natural kinds with inherent causal powers and are responsible for dynamism in the world. The challenge facing scientific researchers who study objective reality is to *discover* these causal powers by identifying natural kinds and their dispositions.

By contrast, human kinds do not possess any inherent causal powers. Efforts in the social sciences to identify any inherent tendencies, dispositions, or mind-independent manifestations of human kinds cannot be successful (cf. Bhaskar 1979/1998; Collier 1994; Elder-Vass 2012; Sayer 2000; Smith 2010). Thus, despite a proliferation of definitions of *mechanism* and the development of sophisticated methods for tracing processes over time, even the most talented social scientists cannot discover human kinds with essential causal powers. They may study intervening events and overarching processes when making sense of the connections among human kind categories (Elster 1998; Falleti and Lynch 2009; Glennan 2009; Hedström and Swedberg 1998; Little 2009; Mayntz 2004; McAdam, Tarrow, and Tilly 2001). They may use general theories that posit unobservable entities in order to deduce propositions that can be tested empirically (Jasso 1988; Dessler 1991; Mahoney 2004). And they may employ process-tracing methods to identify and test propositions about the connections among human kinds (Beach and Pedersen 2013; Bennett 2008; Collier 2011; George and Bennett 2005; Hall 2006; Waldner 2012). However, social scientists do not study processes that are literally marked by the conservation of a physical quantity, by the operation of an invariant mechanism, or by the interaction of mind-independent entities with causal powers and dispositions.

COUNTERFACTUAL MODELS

Counterfactual models of causality analyze probabilistic relationships among variables representing specific properties of units of analysis. In this approach, a well-designed experiment is the gold standard methodology for evaluating causality. Statistical work in this tradition often focuses on how to approximate the experimental gold standard in a non-experimental setting in which various threats to validity exist, including confounding variables.

In modern versions of the counterfactual framework, analysts think about causal inference in terms of estimating the average treatment effect (ATE) of an independent variable on a dependent variable (e.g., Rubin 1974; Holland

1986; Morgan and Winship 2015; cf. Pearl 2009). In its basic form, the framework estimates ATE by comparing the difference on a dependent variable (Y) among a large number of units randomly assigned to a treatment ($X=1$) and a control ($X=0$). The core model is:

$$\text{ATE} = \bar{Y}_{(X=1)} - \bar{Y}_{(X=0)}. \tag{3.2}$$

The equation reads, "The average treatment effect is equal to the average value of Y when X equals 1 minus the average value of Y when X equals 0." No control variables are included in this model, because a large number of units are randomly assigned to values on the independent variable, as in an experiment. With observational data, many complexities must be introduced into equation (3.2) to deal with the fact that units are not randomly assigned to their values on X; but the basic understanding of causality remains the same.

With token causality, the model in equation (3.2) is adapted to focus on the individual unit. With an individual unit, the model holds that variable X causes variable Y if, were an ideal intervention to change the value of X, the value of Y would change. Here, an *ideal intervention* is defined as a change on variable X that occurs in such a way that none of the variables that are causally relevant to X are affected by the intervention. With an ideal intervention, the only way in which Y can change is through the change in X (Menzies 2009: 356–60). At the core of the approach is the idea that token causes are *difference-makers*: the counterfactual removal or alteration of the X variable *changes* the value on the Y variable under idealized ceteris paribus conditions.

With this counterfactual framework, variables correspond to properties of the units of analysis. The framework assumes that causality exists among variables irrespective of the investigator's ideas about those variables; causality among variables is present in the social world regardless of whether it is actually discovered by an investigator. Accordingly, the results of an analysis should, in principle, be reproducible and subject to empirical verification in subsequent work by different researchers. The application of the counterfactual model yields results that are *epistemologically objective*, because the entities and causality under study are *ontologically objective*.

Investigators in the social sciences who use the counterfactual framework may acknowledge that the variables and units of analysis are socially constructed entities. However, they do not view the social construction of variables and units as an insurmountable obstacle to valid causal inference. Collective understanding about the meaning, definition, and measurement of variables and units is sufficient to overcome problems that might derive from their constructed nature. Thus, while it is true that concepts such as *democracy* and *development* can mean different things and be measured in different ways, researchers can still objectively assess their causal effects provided that they agree, for the purposes of the research, to define and measure these concepts in one particular way that is transparent and reproducible. With well-designed research, according to this view, analysts using the counterfactual framework can arrive at valid findings about causal effects even with socially constructed concepts.

The position of this book, however, is that researchers who employ a counterfactual theory of causality cannot arrive at sound findings about causal effects if the variables and/or units of analysis are human kinds. The problem is not that the researchers lack intersubjective agreement about the definition and measurement of their variables. Nor is the problem any failings or shortcomings on the part of the researchers. Rather, the problem is that the counterfactual model of causality assumes and requires that variables and units of analysis stand in an approximate one-to-one correspondence with entities of the natural world. Yet this assumption is never met when the variables and units are human kinds (see chapter 1 on natural kinds versus human kinds).

Social scientists who study human kinds cannot effectively model or represent the heterogeneous natural substances and properties to which those human kinds refer. Researchers do not know what actual world changes are introduced with an ideal intervention. What they regard as two repetitions of the same treatment are not the same treatment from the perspective of the natural world. Each treatment corresponds to its own distinctive changes in natural kind properties. For instance, if the treatment is a public policy that is randomly introduced in some districts but not others, researchers lack a basis for assuming that the effects of the public policy are homogeneous across the cases. They do not know what natural properties are being manipulated through the introduction of the policy. Likewise, if a group of countries have the same annual growth rate (e.g., 2%) in GDP per capita, social scientists do not know what this means in terms of transformations of natural kinds within the countries. Yet they can be highly certain that these natural kind transformations are not the same for any two countries.

Statisticians do not discuss these problems of causal heterogeneity in terms of the referential mismatch between social science categories and natural kind entities. However, they do provide an excellent vocabulary from which to explore these issues. For instance, one can discuss the problem in terms of a failure to meet the stable unit treatment value assumption (SUTVA; Rubin 1974). This assumption requires that a treatment ($X=1$) have the same form across all units. Yet if the treatment is a human kind, such as *2% increase in GDP per capita*, this assumption is radically violated. At the level of natural kinds, *2% increase in GDP per capita* entails a mostly unknown and unknowable change that is not constant across any two units. Although contemporary discussions of causal inference often focus on threats to validity related to assignment mechanisms and conditional independence, the problem discussed here is one of conceptual heterogeneity that undermines SUTVA. This problem of conceptual heterogeneity applies not only to treatments, but to all variables, and to the concepts designating the cases themselves (e.g., *district, movement, country*).

From a constructivist perspective, the lack of correspondence between human kinds and entities of the natural world explains ongoing problems with social science research that uses the counterfactual model of causality. The problems manifest themselves in the form of inconsistent results, despite repeated efforts by talented scholars to use this model to generate stable results. Social research using a counterfactual model of causation has not accumulated solid results or a truly progressive body of knowledge about causal effects (cf. Elman, Gerring, and Mahoney 2020). Consider the example of research on the effect of democracy on economic growth. This voluminous research suggests that democracy may promote, prevent, be irrelevant to, or have a nonlinear relationship with economic growth (see Seawright 2010). To account for these huge divergences in findings, scholars point to shortcomings such as missing data, incorrectly specified causal models, and reciprocal causation.[7] This book proposes that a more general and serious problem is at work: the variables and cases do not refer to entities that can be treated as existing in the external world, independently of our ideas about them. Democracy cannot cause economic growth across different countries in the ways proposed by counterfactual models because these categories do not map the structure of an objective reality.

Sober assessments by statisticians also lead to the conclusion that research using a counterfactual model of causality has yielded few stable findings about the causal effects of human kinds. According to Freedman (1999, 2008), studies using statistical models of causality have yielded dozens, but not hundreds, of sound findings about causal effects. These dozens of successful inferences, however, are from studies that focus on partial natural kinds, such as work in the field of epidemiology. It is hard or impossible to identify similarly successful research findings that focus on human kinds (Freedman 2008 offers no examples). This fact may also underlie the skepticism that some natural scientists hold toward the social sciences. The implication of this lack of stable findings is not that valid causal inference is impossible in the social sciences, as radical constructivists suggest. Rather, the implication is that social scientists need an alternative understanding of causality that is more appropriate for the analysis of human kinds.

Non-causal statistical models can be useful for forecasting and predicting future trends and events. Qualified success stories of this kind seem common in the social sciences. For instance, political analysts have made great progress using polling numbers and other quantitative data to predict electoral outcomes, including even, to some degree, the stunning election of Donald Trump in 2016 (Silver 2012, 2016). Sociologists are often successful at predicting major life outcomes (e.g., income and occupation) on the basis of race, class, and gender characteristics (Grusky 2001). Economists use models to forecast trends in the economy, such as inflation, in reasonably successful ways (Eickmeier and Ziegler 2008). To be sure, social science predictions about the social world are far from perfect. Statistical models are better at explaining trends across many cases than at making pinpoint predictions about single cases. Nevertheless, scholars using statistical prediction models increasingly have success stories to tell, to a much greater extent than social scientists working on causal inference with counterfactual models.

Once we move beyond the social sciences into the natural sciences, where the variables and cases under study are partial natural kinds, we find more successful applications of the counterfactual model of causality. Partial natural kinds substantially (though imperfectly) map the substances, properties, and processes of the natural world. They partially pick out entities whose essential properties endow them with causal properties. Partial natural kinds therefore often have discernable causal effects, though probabilistic rather than deterministic. With a large population of cases, interventions that change partial natural kind properties exhibit causal effects in well-designed research.

Examples of successful research focused on partial natural kinds using a counterfactual model of causality can be found in both the physical sciences and the life sciences (see Freedman 2010; Pearl 2018). For instance, Hooke's law, concerning the relationship between the length of a spring and a hang weight, can be summarized precisely with regression equations that accommodate different scope conditions. Statistical studies of the effect of greenhouse gas emissions on climate change have reached convincing findings—including even for individual weather events—although scholars have had difficulty finding full public acceptance of their findings. Research in the field of epidemiology suggests both the promise and the difficulties of using a counterfactual model to study causal relationships among partial natural kinds. For instance, research on the causal relationship between smoking and lung cancer is highly convincing, whereas research on the causal relationship between salt intake and blood pressure remains less convincing. In the field of psychology, research is often directed at the question of whether a given construct—such as bipolar disorder, intelligence, or extroversion—is a mind-independent property found in nature. Recent experimental research in this field has focused explicitly on the issue of whether emotions are natural kinds (see Barrett 2017). The long-standing debate continues over whether mental disorders and certain health problems have a mind-independent existence (Aronowitz 1991; Brown 1995; Epstein 1996, 2007; Hacking 1995b).

The main implication of this discussion is that social scientists are misapplying the counterfactual model of causality when they use it to study human kinds. This model is appropriate for the study of partial natural kinds, not human kinds. The counterfactual model can be helpful to distinguish whether phenomena such as human emotions, diseases, and mental disorders are partial natural kinds or human kinds. However, if one already knows that a phenomenon is a human kind—which is the case for most of the important social science concepts—the counterfactual model is not the right tool for evaluating causal propositions.

REGULARITY MODELS

Regularity models of causality focus on causal relationships among *discrete events*. In these models, causality is a way of describing a particular kind of relationship among events. A regularity theory defines causation between event X and event Y as a relationship that features (1) temporal succession (X precedes Y in time), (2) spatiotemporal contiguity (X makes direct or indirect contact with Y in space and time), and (3) logical regularity (X is part of a minimized solution set that is constantly conjoined with Y) (cf. Hume 1777/1975; Mill 1861/1998; Mackie 1980; Psillos 2002, 2009).[8]

The first criterion requires that event X *begin* before event Y. It does not require that event X *end* before event Y, though it does assume that X as a cause of Y terminates with the occurrence of Y. With token causes, it can be easy to establish temporal succession. In fact, causes may be separated from their outcomes by years, decades, or even centuries.

The second criterion requires that X directly or indirectly make contact with Y in space and time. X has *direct* spatiotemporal contact with Y if it intersects in time and space with Y. For instance, in Hume's (1777/1975) famous example of two billiard balls colliding, the first ball makes direct contact with the second in both space and time.[9] By contrast, X has *indirect* spatiotemporal contact with Y if it sets into motion a series of causally connected events that culminate in Y (Psillos 2002: 25). In the social sciences, macro-oriented analysts usually do not study causes that involve direct spatiotemporal contact with their outcomes. Rather, they study indirect contact, in which a cause and its outcome are connected by virtue of intermediary events.

The requirement for spatiotemporal contact unites a regularity model with qualitative methodologies and approaches that focus on the events that link an initial cause to a final outcome (Beach and Pedersen 2013; George and Bennett 2005; Little 2009; Mahoney and Rueschemeyer 2003). These approaches include historical analyses in which the emphasis is on the overall causal chain, rather than only the relationship between the main cause and the main outcome (Roberts 1996; Mahoney 1999; cf. Abbott 2016). Methodologies consistent with a regularity approach open up the "black box" of causality by identifying and following the linking processes through which a causal factor reaches and affects its outcome. In many traditions of research, these intermediary or connecting events are called *mechanisms* (Bunge 1997; Glennan

1996, 2009; Hedström and Swedberg 1998; Mayntz 2004). The identification of mechanisms is a major component of sequential and path dependence explanations, in which a historical cause establishes a trajectory of change that leads to a final outcome of interest (Capoccia 2015; Clemens and Cook 1999; Grzymala-Busse 2011; Pierson 2004; Soifer 2012; Thelen 1999). Of the different approaches to causation, only regularity models view connecting mechanisms as a part of causation itself. Causal power models see mechanisms as unobservable generative forces, rather than as intermediary and connecting events. Counterfactual models are concerned only with the dependence of Y on X; the identification of a mechanism is not a requirement for causality (Green, Ha, and Bullock 2010).

Logical regularity, the third component of the definition of causation in regularity models, links these models to set-theoretic analysis. For a logical regularity to exist between event X and event Y, X must be directly or indirectly necessary and/or sufficient for Y in the minimized solution set that explains Y. Event X has a *direct logical relationship* with event Y if it is a necessary, sufficient, or necessary and sufficient condition for Y in this solution set. Event X has an *indirect logical relationship* with Y if it is a necessary condition for a sufficient condition for Y (i.e., an INUS condition) or if it is a sufficient condition for a necessary condition for Y (i.e., a SUIN condition) in this solution set. Hence, the five types of set-theoretic relationships discussed in this chapter are at the core of the understanding of causality in regularity models.

The idea of a *minimized solution set* is connected to the concern that regularity models need a means to distinguish spurious relationships from causal ones (Lewis 1973; Cartwright 1989; Hitchcock 2018; Pearl 2000). Modern regularity models of causality (e.g., Graßhoff and May 2001; Baumgartner 2008, 2013; Psillos 2002, 2009; Mahoney and Acosta forthcoming; see also Ragin 2008; Schneider 2018; Schneider and Wagemann 2012; Thiem 2017; Wright 2011) require that regularities be not only stable but also *non-redundant*, which is achieved through Boolean minimization procedures that remove redundancies from both necessary conditions and sufficient conditions to arrive at final solution sets.[10] These minimized solution sets identify conditions and/or combinations of conditions that are *sufficient* for the outcome (i.e., the outcome always follows the condition or combination of conditions).[11] The individual conditions in the minimized solution set can be necessary, sufficient, necessary and sufficient, INUS, or SUIN conditions for the outcome. The requirement that regularities contain no redundancies eliminates findings that include irrelevant conditions or that misspecify the causal role of particular conditions. With respect to the problem of spuriousness, the insistence in regularity models on using only the minimized solution set is analogous to the stipulation of an ideal intervention in counterfactual models: both stipulations are designed to ensure that non-causal factors are not mistaken for causal factors.

Modern regularity models assess token causality through the explicit analysis of both actual cases and possible cases. The examination of possible cases solves the most obvious problems of spuriousness that are held up as counterexamples to regularity models. For example, critics point out that a barometer reading may consistently precede weather patterns and thus be deemed, under a regularity model, to be a sufficient cause of these weather patterns. Yet one can easily construct cases in which barometer readings have no association at all with weather outcomes. Barometer readings do not bear a direct or indirect logical relationship with weather patterns across all possible cases. The barometer reading does not make an appearance in the minimized solution set that explains weather patterns.

A regularity model's definition of token causality follows from its general definition of causality but assumes possible cases. Event X is a token cause of event Y if (1) X begins before Y; (2) X makes direct or indirect spatiotemporal contact with Y; and (3) X is a necessary, sufficient, necessary and sufficient, INUS, or SUIN condition for Y across the universe of relevant cases. The universe of relevant cases includes non-actual cases that are proximate to the actual world but that differ in theoretically important ways. The counterfactual analysis of specific possible cases is essential for evaluating token causality with case studies in the social sciences. The analysis of counterfactual cases allows researchers to estimate the extent to which a given event is necessary and sufficient for an outcome even when the outcome is a one-off occurrence that takes place in a single case.

The requirement that causes and outcomes be logically related to one another distinguishes regularity models from both counterfactual and causal power models. Unlike a counterfactual model, a regularity model allows factors that are not difference-makers for token outcomes to be causes. The regularity approach permits INUS conditions and sufficient but not necessary conditions to be causes of particular outcomes in specific cases. The fact that regularity models accommodate INUS causes is one reason that many scholars favor this approach for the social sciences (in addition to its concern with causal chains). Unlike a causal power model, furthermore, a regularity model understands causal propositions to be statements about discrete events that are temporally and logically related to other discrete events. Regularity analysts can accept the truth of causal power models for natural kinds while rejecting the idea that human kinds have natural dispositions, intrinsic powers, or tendencies.

With scientific constructivism, the events analyzed in regularity models are constructed categories, rather than mind-independent entities. The cause, the outcome, and all of the intermediary events in these models are social categories that depend on a particular semantic context for their meaning. The logical regularity between the cause and the outcome assumes and requires particular constructions of meanings; if the meanings of the categories change, the regularity may change or disappear. With a regularity model, causality is a way in which people describe the temporally sequenced relationships that exist among the mind-dependent events by which they comprehend the social world.

In summary, regularity models direct social scientists to understand the way in which an antecedent event is logically related and spatiotemporally connected to an outcome event. In practice, the causal assessment of an individual event of interest involves two basic steps. First, the researcher must establish the type of logical association that exists between the individual event and the outcome in the minimized solution set. This step establishes whether the event is logically necessary, sufficient, necessary and sufficient, INUS, or SUIN for the outcome. The second part of causal assessment is identifying the intermediary events that connect the individual event to the outcome event. The specification of this causal chain requires the analyst to engage in sequence analysis, in which individual links between events are constructed and analyzed. Both parts are essential to causal analysis in the social sciences.

Tools for the pursuit of this two-part approach to causal analysis using a regularity model are developed throughout this book.

Types of Set-Theoretic Causes

With the set-theoretic approach, the analysis of a causal relationship between two token events requires the analyst to identify the *type* of logical association that characterizes the relationship. This type corresponds to the nature of the association between the main causal event and the main outcome event. The main causal event can be a necessary condition, a sufficient condition, a necessary and sufficient condition, an INUS condition, or a SUIN condition for the main outcome event across all relevant possible worlds. Causal analysis involves making an *inference*, on the basis of evidence and logical reasoning, about which type of association (if any) applies to a relationship between an antecedent event and an outcome event.

A separate aspect of causal analysis involves assessing the *importance* of the cause. Although causes may be regarded as important for many normative or theory-related reasons, set-theoretic analysis focuses on the *logical importance* of a cause. With set-theoretic analysis, causal importance is defined as the extent to which an individual cause is both necessary and sufficient for an outcome. In substantive research, the key issue is often not whether a given event is a cause of an outcome, but whether it is an *important* cause.

A NECESSARY AND SUFFICIENT CAUSE: THE GOLD STANDARD

The idea that a cause is a necessary and sufficient condition for an outcome is not new. Galileo's definition from four centuries ago proposes just that notion: "That and no other is to be called cause, at the presence of which the effect always follows, and at whose removal the effect disappears" (quoted in Bunge [1959: 33]). In set-theoretic analysis, a necessary and sufficient cause is a *maximally important cause*, the gold standard against which the importance of all causes is assessed. Adopting this maximalist definition as the exclusive meaning of *cause*, as Galileo does, has many virtues. The definition avoids the problems of overdetermination (i.e., when multiple sufficient causes are simultaneously present) and triviality (i.e., when unimportant conditions are classified as causes).[12] Defining a cause as a necessary and sufficient condition permits one to evaluate other logical relationships (e.g., a necessary but not sufficient relationship) as partial members of the category *cause*. One can examine how close other relationships come to causality on the basis of their proximity to being a necessary and sufficient cause.

In this book, however, I advocate an inclusive definition of *cause*, allowing five logical relationships to be full members of the set *cause* or *causality* (requiring always that a cause also meet the criteria of temporal succession and spatiotemporal contiguity). My reasoning is that an inclusive approach better captures how the term *cause* is used in the social sciences and in everyday life. Our intuitions about causality do not require full necessity and full sufficiency for an event to be a cause. Not all conditions with 100% membership in the category *cause* are necessary and sufficient causes. Nevertheless, for assessing the *importance* of a given cause, I embrace Galileo's idea of a necessary and sufficient cause. I define a *maximally important cause* as a necessary and sufficient cause.

SUFFICIENT CAUSE

A famous quotation from Hume illuminates the idea that not all causes are both necessary and sufficient for an outcome: "We may define a cause to be an object followed by another, and where all the objects, similar to the first, are followed by objects similar to the second. Or, in other words, where, if the first object had not been, the second never would have existed" (Hume 1777/1975: sec. 7). As many philosophers have pointed out (e.g., Lewis 1973: 181), Hume's "in other words" is no mere restatement of the first definition. Hume's passage proposes two separate definitions: a first corresponding to a sufficient cause, and a second corresponding to a necessary cause.

The idea that sufficient conditions can be causes accords with our sense that a cause is something that, when present, is followed by an effect (cf. Davidson

1967). This understanding of causality plays a central role in social science methodologies, including Mill's (1843/1911) indirect method of difference, the covering-law model of causation (Hempel 1965), and qualitative comparative analysis (QCA; Ragin 1987, 2008). For instance, Mill's indirect method of difference, as conventionally applied in the social sciences, involves the evaluation of causal factors that are potentially sufficient conditions for an outcome. Likewise, the covering-law model proposes that if a set of conditions ($C_1, C_2, \ldots C_N$) obtains, then an event E will follow (Hempel and Oppenheim 1948). With QCA, the analyst uses Boolean minimization procedures to identify conditions and combinations of conditions that are sufficient for an outcome.

A fully sufficient cause exists when the cause is always followed by the outcome across all cases in a population. With a set-theoretic framework, this population of cases includes *possible cases* as well as actual cases. For instance, as noted above, we know that a barometer reading is not a sufficient cause for a weather pattern because a barometer reading is not related to weather patterns across all relevant possible cases. To evaluate a sufficiency proposition, the set-theoretic investigator asks whether *any* relevant case exists in which event X is not followed by event Y. If such a case exists, as it clearly does in the barometer example, the cause is not fully sufficient for the outcome.

In the social sciences, scholars often explore whether a cause is sufficient for an outcome "in the circumstances," where the circumstances are understood to be standard and expected aspects of background context (cf. Hart and Honoré 1985: xxxvii–xlii; Falleti and Lynch 2009).[13] In this formulation, a sufficient cause is followed by an outcome across all cases, under the assumption that certain normal contextual and circumstantial factors are in place. Membership in X is not sufficient for membership in Y across all conceivable cases, but rather only in those possible cases that meet the specified conditions. These conditions include not only a particular semantic context, but also other essential parts of the context that are normally taken for granted. For instance, skipping the final exam is 100% sufficient for a failing grade in my undergraduate course. In making this statement, however, I assume the operation of certain circumstantial and background features, such as that the exam-skippers are enrolled students who do not have a special health status that overrides standard course policy.

NECESSARY CAUSE

Necessary causes embody the counterfactual claim that an outcome would not have occurred if the cause had been absent, though the cause's presence did not guarantee the outcome. A famous example is Barrington Moore's (1966) argument that a strong bourgeoisie was necessary for a revolutionary breakthrough to democracy ("no bourgeoisie, no democracy"). Statistical models of causality assume necessary causes at the case level, because these models define causes as exclusively counterfactual difference-makers (Rubin 1974; Holland 1986; Morgan and Winship 2007). Lewis's original counterfactual model of token causality was also built around necessary causes: "Event *e* depends causally on the distinct event *c* iff[;] if *c* had not occurred, *e* would not have occurred" (1986a: 161–62). Lewis further explains, "My analysis is meant to apply to causation in particular cases. It is not an analysis of causal generalizations" (1986b: 242). To illustrate the ubiquity of necessary condition hypotheses, Goertz (2003b) lists 150 examples from various domains of social science research.

A sophisticated and growing methodological literature—both qualitative and quantitative—is now concerned with the analysis of necessary causes in both individual cases and populations of many cases (Braumoeller and Goertz 2000, 2002; Clark, Gilligan, and Golder 2006; Dion 1998; Dul 2016; Eliason and Stryker 2009; Goertz and Starr 2003; Ragin 1987, 2000, 2008). Some of the key resources from this literature that are used in this book include tools for evaluating *the extent to which* a given factor corresponds to a necessary condition; tools for formally distinguishing trivial necessary conditions from important necessary conditions; and tools for the analysis of chains of necessary causes.

INUS CAUSE

The philosopher Mackie (1965), building on Mill (1843/1911), proposes INUS conditions as another kind of cause. He gives the example of experts' declaring that an electrical short circuit is the cause of a fire. But the short circuit, he points out, is neither necessary nor sufficient for the fire. Rather, "the short-circuit which is said to have caused the fire is . . . an indispensable part of a complex sufficient (but not necessary) condition of the fire. In this case, then, the so-called cause is, and is known to be, an *insufficient* but *necessary* part of a condition which is itself *unnecessary* but *sufficient* for the result" (p. 245). As Mackie suggests, the idea that an INUS condition can be a cause is consistent with our intuitions. INUS conditions are regarded as causes in legal contexts and in everyday explanations of events (Hart and Honoré 1985). In the social sciences, the QCA methodology is centrally focused on identifying individual factors that are INUS conditions (Ragin 1987, 2000, 2008; Schneider and Wagemann 2012; Thomann and Maggetti 2020). Even scholars associated with the counterfactual model of causality may view probabilistic causes as INUS causes. For example, Shadish, Cook, and Campbell (2002: 5) write that "most causes are more accurately called inus conditions."

Analyses using INUS conditions address a central problem associated with sufficient causes. The problem is that no single factor ever seems sufficient for an outcome; minimally, the condition's efficacy requires many routine background conditions to be in place. For example, Goldhagen (1996) argues that virulent anti-semitism was sufficient to produce the motivational basis for the

Holocaust in Germany. However, his argument assumes the presence of count-less trivial background conditions that were also necessary for this outcome, ranging from air, gravity, and human life to the existence of modern states, societies, and national belief systems. Given that these conditions were also necessary, it is not, strictly speaking, correct to say that anti-semitism was enough by itself to generate the motivational basis of the Holocaust. Instead, what Goldhagen surely means is that anti-semitism was an INUS cause that approximated sufficiency, requiring only the presence of ordinary background conditions to produce the outcome.

In fact, INUS causes are what most scholars actually examine when they study sufficient conditions and necessary conditions. First, when scholars make sufficiency assertions, they normally do so by implicitly or explicitly assuming a particular scope within which the assertion applies ("in the cir-cumstances"). This assumption means that the condition is actually an INUS cause that needs to combine with other conditions to form a sufficiency com-bination. Second, when scholars make necessary condition assertions, some possible exceptions normally exist in which the outcome occurs without the necessary condition. For example, when Moore claims that a strong bourgeoi-sie was necessary for an early route to democracy, his assertion does not have the force of a deterministic physical law; one can construct possible cases that violate the assertion. Most necessary conditions are actually INUS conditions that are almost always present when the outcome occurs.

Scholars who work within a regularity model of causality sometimes refer to approximate sufficient causes and approximate necessary causes. Strictly speaking, these conditions are actually INUS causes that are almost always followed by an outcome (with an approximate sufficient cause) or that almost always precede an outcome (with an approximate necessary cause), or both (with an approximate necessary and sufficient cause).

SUIN CAUSE

The fifth and final type of set-theoretic cause—a SUIN cause—is used primar-ily with counterfactual analysis. Condition Z is a SUIN cause of outcome Y if (1) Z is a non-trivial sufficient condition for X, which is a non-trivial neces-sary cause of outcome Y; and (2) Z and X are coterminous and prior to Y. For example, consider the proposition that *not-democracy* is a necessary cause of interstate war (i.e., a war occurs only if at least one of the countries involved is not a democracy). This proposition suggests that membership in the set *military government* is a SUIN cause of membership in the set *war*. *Military government* is sufficient (but not necessary) for membership in *not-democracy*, which is causally necessary (but not sufficient) for membership in *war*.

We shall return to the idea of a SUIN cause in chapter 5, when we explore the counterfactuals used to assess propositions about necessary causes. We will see that many counterfactual assertions suggest that an event that occurred in the actual world is a SUIN cause of an outcome. One example we will explore is the counterfactual statement that if Al Gore had won the 2000 presidential election, the United States would not have invaded Iraq—an assertion implying that the election of George W. Bush was a SUIN cause of the Iraq War.

———

The discussion of types of causes in this section has focused on the logical associations that can exist between a causal event and an outcome. While the identification of a particular kind of logical association is a crucial part of causal analysis, it is not the only component. Scholars must also analyze the causal sequence, or chain of intermediary events, through which the initial causal event makes spatiotemporal contact with the outcome of interest. The analysis of this sequence is required for the demonstration of causality. If an analyst cannot connect a causal event to its outcome, the event has not been established to be a cause within the requirements of a regularity model.

In addition, qualifying as a cause of an outcome is not enough for an event to merit special attention in research. A good explanation of an outcome need not consider every single causal factor. Rather, a good explanation will call attention to events that are *important causes* and thus warrant discussion and sustained consideration. Important causes are those that come reasonably close to the gold standard of causation: a necessary and sufficient cause. Many of the methods and tools in this book are intended to assist analysts with the assessment of causal importance, including by leveraging the sequence of intermediary events that connects a cause to its outcome.

Continuous-Set Analysis

The discussion in this chapter has treated categories as sets in which cases either do or do not have membership—e.g., a case is a member of either X or $\sim X$. Yet dichotomous measurement is not required or assumed in set-theoretic analysis. Rather, this approach is built around the idea that cases have *varying degrees of membership* in a category. Dichotomous measurement applies only when the categories under analysis are constructed such that cases must be fully in or fully out of the category boundaries. Most categories in natural language are not constructed as dichotomous sets (Lakoff 1987).

With continuous-set analysis, cases are measured and compared according to the degree to which (or percent to which) they are members of sets (Zadeh

1965; see also Ragin 2000, 2008; Schneider and Wagemann 2012). Some cases may be full members of a set, others may be full non-members, and still others may have varying degrees of partial membership. Set boundaries still exist, and they are sharp and bright, not blurry and hazy. However, the boundaries are penetrable, or permeable, allowing for partial membership.

To code case membership, researchers conventionally use a continuous scale ranging from 1.0 (full membership) to 0.0 (full non-membership), with an infinite range of partial membership values in between. For example, a membership value of 0.75 means that a case has three-quarters (75%) membership in a set and one-quarter (25%) membership in its logical complement. If set-membership values range continuously from 0.0 to 1.0, the formula for calculating membership in the logical complement (or negation) of a category is simply $\sim X = 1.0 - X$.

Continuous-set analysis does not use a conventional level of measurement (e.g., nominal, ordinal, interval, or ratio). The measurement of continuous sets assumes a meaningful minimum (no membership), a meaningful maximum (full membership), and an infinite range of values in between. The anchors of no membership and full membership are similar to the categorization scale of nominal measurement; the continuous range of membership values between these anchors is similar to the degree-of-difference scale of interval measurement. However, no conventional level of measurement corresponds exactly with continuous-set measurement.

When continuous-set analysis is used for defining categories, cases are assessed not for the extent to which they possess a property, but for their degree of membership in the category of interest. For example, in figure 3.9, the primary boundary defines the category *democratic national regime*; hypothetical country cases are represented by small circles. These countries have varying degrees of membership within the category.

With an *ideal-typical category*—which Max Weber (1978) defined as an idea construct that does not appear perfectly in the actual world—two practical approaches exist for coding case membership. One approach is to create a coding rule that prohibits any actual case from obtaining full membership in the ideal-typical category. For instance, following Dahl (1971), one might argue that the category *democratic national regime* is an ideal type in which no actual country is or can be a full member. Actual countries may be full members of the category *polyarchy*, but they inherently fall short of full membership in *democratic national regime*, in the same way that bowling balls and other round objects fall short of full membership in the category *perfect spherical shape*.

A second approach is to consider the ideal type as the prototype point of the category and prohibit cases from having membership in, or overlapping with, that prototype point. Cases with full membership in the category must be distinguished according to their proximity to the prototype point. For instance,

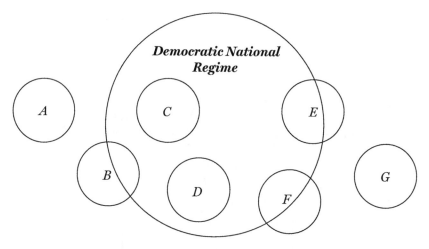

FIGURE 3.9. Illustration of Continuous-Set Membership. Set-membership values: country A, 0.0; country B, 0.3; country C, 1.0; country D, 1.0; country E, 0.7; country F, 0.5; country G, 0.0.

in figure 3.9, one of the two cases with full membership in *democratic national regime* (country C) is closer to the prototype point than the other case (country D). In effect, the prototype point of an ideal-typical category functions like a *white hole*—a region in conceptual space that cannot be entered from the actual world.[14] For measurement purposes, researchers may choose to apply a "second-level" measure (cf. Zadeh 1972; Arfi 2010) that captures the extent to which cases that are full (100%) members of a category approximate the unobtainable ideal type.

A case's membership value in a category is a function of its membership values in the conditions that define that category. These defining conditions are sets themselves, and thus cases are allowed to have partial membership in each of them. Continuous-set analysis uses logical aggregation rules to arrive at the membership values of cases in the category of interest. These rules of aggregation vary depending on whether the category is defined using the classic mode (i.e., with the logical AND only), the family resemblance mode (i.e., with at least one logical OR; see Zadeh 1965; Ragin 2000; Goertz 2006b), or some hybrid combination (see Barrenechea and Castillo 2019).

If the defining conditions are individually necessary and jointly sufficient for membership in the category, the intersection of these conditions is the zone of interest, and the logical AND is the relevant operator. With the logical AND, the analyst uses the *minimum membership value* of a case's membership among the defining conditions as the case's membership value in the overarching category. To return to the example of *democratic national regime*, this category might be defined by three conditions that are individually necessary and jointly sufficient: *free elections, universal suffrage,* and *broad civil*

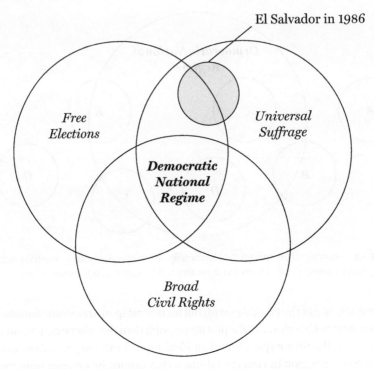

FIGURE 3.10. Illustration of Continuous-Set Aggregation: El Salvador in 1986

rights. With continuous-set measurement, one identifies the degree to which a case has membership in each of these three defining categories. The case's *lowest*, or *minimum*, membership value among the three necessary defining conditions corresponds to its overall membership in *democratic national regime*.

In the set diagram in figure 3.10, for instance, the case of El Salvador in 1986 is coded as having the following membership values: 0.5 for *free elections*, 1.0 for *universal suffrage*, and 0.0 for *broad civil rights* (Bowman, Lehoucq, and Mahoney 2005). Accordingly, El Salvador in 1986 receives a value of 0.0 for the category *democratic national regime*, because 0.0 is its minimum value among the three defining necessary conditions. Thus, even though El Salvador in 1986 has partial membership in *free elections* and full membership in *universal suffrage*, it has no membership in the overarching outcome of *democratic national regime*, because it completely lacks membership in *broad civil rights*. The diagram illustrates a general rule of aggregation with the classic approach to category definition: a case cannot have *greater* membership in the overarching category of interest than in any of its defining conditions.

With the family resemblance mode of definition, by contrast, membership in any particular defining condition is not necessary for membership in the outcome category. Instead, the defining conditions are either sufficient or INUS conditions for the outcome category. For instance, one might define the category *eighteenth-century democratic national regime* as requiring membership in any one of three conditions: $A \vee B \vee C \rightarrow Y$, where $A = $*free elections*, $B = $*broad suffrage*, $C = $*broad civil rights*, and $Y = $*eighteenth-century democratic national regime*. Here A, B, and C are each sufficient conditions for Y; thus, the union is the zone of interest, and the logical OR ($\vee$) is the appropriate operator. When aggregating with the logical OR, a case's *highest*, or *maximum*, membership value among the defining conditions corresponds to its membership in the overarching category. For instance, *England in 1790* might have membership values for conditions A, B, and C of 0.75, 0.25, and 0.50, respectively. Accordingly, England's membership value for *eighteenth-century democratic national regime* would be 0.75. With individually sufficient conditions, a case's membership in the union of these conditions will always be equal to its highest membership value among the individual conditions. With INUS conditions, the same idea applies: a case's membership in the category of interest will be equal to its highest membership value among the different *sufficiency combinations* that each ensure membership in the overarching category.[15]

Causal analysis with continuous sets uses these same aggregation rules for specifying logical relationships. With a necessary cause, a case's membership in the antecedent causal category must be *greater than or equal to* its membership in the outcome category. Figure 3.11 presents an illustrative set diagram, in which membership in temporally prior X is necessary for membership in temporally subsequent Y. The figure includes three cases whose (X, Y) membership values are, from top to bottom, $(0.5, 0.5)$, $(1.0, 1.0)$, and $(1.0, 0.0)$. For any case, a membership value in X cannot be less than a membership value in Y. This pattern exists because X is a superset of Y, such that it is impossible for a case to have *less* membership in X than in Y. Cases must have membership values in the X set that are greater than or equal to their membership values in the Y set. In short, for any necessary cause X, membership values in X must be greater than or equal to membership values in Y for all cases.

As figure 3.12 shows, the opposite pattern applies to a sufficient cause: membership values in X are *less than or equal to* membership values in Y. In this example, the (X, Y) values for the three cases are, from top to bottom, $(0.5, 0.5)$, $(1.0, 1.0)$, and $(0.5, 1.0)$. Because this example is a sufficient cause (i.e., X is a subset of Y), one cannot conceive of a case that has greater membership in X than in Y. For any sufficient cause X, membership values in X must be less than or equal to membership values in Y for all cases.

With continuous-set scatterplots, such as in figure 3.13, cases are situated in a two-dimensional space in which the X axis and Y axis correspond to the percentage of membership (from 0% to 100%) in the sets X and Y. With a necessary cause, cases must fall on or below the bisecting diagonal line. This

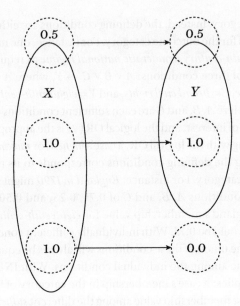

FIGURE 3.11. Membership Values with a Necessary
Cause

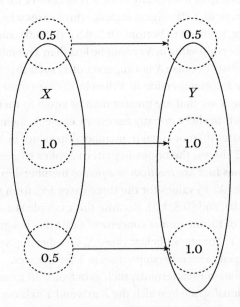

FIGURE 3.12. Membership Values with a Sufficient
Cause

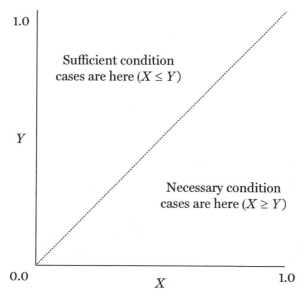

FIGURE 3.13. Location of Cases for Necessary Condition and Sufficient Condition with Continuous-Set Scatterplot

rule is another way of stating the principle introduced above for a necessary cause: membership values in X must be greater than or equal to membership values in Y. With a sufficient cause, cases must fall on or above the bisecting diagonal line. This rule restates the principle for a sufficient cause: membership values in X must be less than or equal to membership values in Y. Cases that fall exactly on the bisecting line (i.e., X value $= Y$ value) are consistent with both necessity and sufficiency. With a necessary and sufficient cause, all cases would fall on this line, because their membership value in X would equal their membership value in Y.

Set diagrams and continuous-set scatterplots complement each other. As figure 3.14 illustrates, when cases are situated on a continuous-set scatterplot, necessary causes become increasingly important for the outcome as cases approach the bisecting diagonal line. Analogously, sufficient causes become increasingly important as cases approach the line. One can think about the bisecting diagonal line in terms of set diagrams: it is the point of perfect overlap, where X and Y are equal sets (i.e., $X \leftrightarrow Y$).

As a concrete illustration, consider figure 3.15, which plots the continuous-set membership values for 15 Latin American countries in the categories *nineteenth-century strong liberal elites* (X) and *twentieth-century economically developed country* (Y).[16] The results are consistent with the hypothesis that prior membership in *strong liberal elites* is necessary for subsequent membership in *economically developed country*. No case has a membership value for X

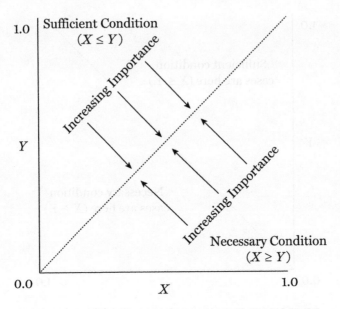

FIGURE 3.14. Illustration of Increasing Importance with Continuous-Set Scatterplot

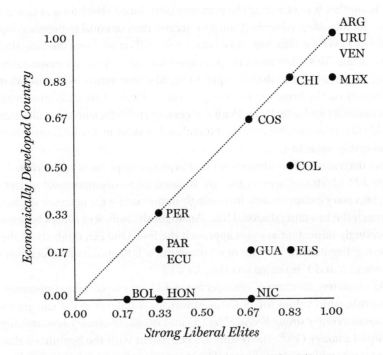

FIGURE 3.15. Continuous-Set Scatterplot of a Necessary Condition for 15 Latin American Cases

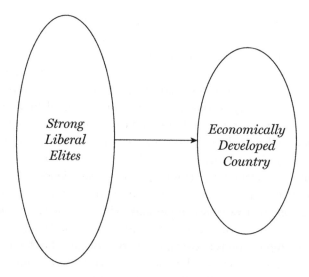

FIGURE 3.16. Set Diagram Derived from Continuous-Set
Scatterplot

that is less than its membership value for Y. However, the figure also suggests
that X is not a maximally important necessary cause. One can see this by noting that several cases are well off the bisecting diagonal line. Indeed, whereas
the data are 100% consistent with necessity, the "coverage" statistic for these
data—which is a continuous-set measure of the importance of a necessary
or a sufficient condition[17]—is 0.68 (Ragin 2008; Schneider and Wagemann
2012). The implication is that this condition may be a necessary cause, and
even a critical cause (see chapter 6 on critical events), but it is not a maximally
important cause.

The finding in the scatterplot in figure 3.15 can be summarized visually with
a simple set diagram, as in figure 3.16. To reflect the causal necessity relationship, the diagram is constructed such that cause X is a superset of outcome Y.
The coverage statistic (0.68 in this example) is used to calculate how large the
superset X is in relation to Y. Although the set diagram does not contain all of
the information in the scatterplot, it does highlight the set-membership relationship between the two categories. The arrow in the figure also emphasizes
the connection between the categories, a connection that would need to be
unpacked in terms of intermediary linking events before one could reach any
firm conclusions about causality.

———

It is easy to both underestimate and overestimate the extent of change to existing research practices that accompanies the use of set-theoretic methods in

the social sciences. On the one hand, analysts must recognize that the application of these methods is a big departure from the use of mainstream variable-oriented methods built around the property-possession assumption. The employment of set-theoretic methods entails the study of logical relationships among categories rather than statistical associations among properties. Set-theoretic methodology encompasses modes of category definition (e.g., the family resemblance mode) and kinds of measurement (e.g., continuous-set measurement) that are largely foreign to contemporary social science. Likewise, set-theoretic methods for the study of causality consist of techniques that are not used explicitly in contemporary social science. Whereas social scientists currently pursue causal analysis by working to isolate the net effects of variables on other variables, or perhaps to identify the efficacious powers of social science categories, set-theoretic methods are designed to summarize set-membership relations between categories located at different points in time. Under a set-theoretic methodology, causal inference involves the use of a regularity model of causality that focuses on logical connections between mind-dependent categories.

On the other hand, analysts must recognize that the application of set-theoretic methods does not necessitate other important kinds of changes. Crucially, the use of set-theoretic methods need not shift attention away from the main topics and issues that animate research in the contemporary social sciences. Researchers can continue to study phenomena such as economic inequality, political violence, and racial injustice. They can continue to ask questions about the causes and consequences of globalization, democratic breakdowns, and market-oriented reforms. Researchers who prefer to use quantitative methods with a large number of cases in order to study general categories may continue to do so; likewise, those who prefer to use qualitative methods, analyze a small number of cases, and study particular categories can retain these emphases. Nor do researchers need to shift the kinds of methods that they use to gather their data—such as archival, interview, and ethnographic methods—when using set-theoretic methods. Indeed, the qualities that we associate with excellence in research, such as creativity, knowledge, and diligence, remain the same. Set-theoretic methods are intended to provide a stronger foundation for scientific research; they are not intended to displace existing areas of substantive interest, styles of conducting analysis, or the very hallmarks of scholarly excellence in the social sciences.

4

Set-Theoretic Tests

This chapter explores how analysts use set-membership observations to evaluate propositions of interest, including descriptive propositions (e.g., case Z is a member of category X), causal propositions (e.g., case Z's membership in X is an important cause of its membership in Y), and normative propositions (e.g., case Z's membership in X is morally wrong). The search for set-membership observations is a core activity in research precisely because these observations enable analysts to evaluate propositions that could be true or false. By themselves, however, set-membership observations are only isolated societal facts—i.e., individual beliefs held with high certitude about the set-theoretic membership of the actual world vis-à-vis particular categories. To be used in the assessment of a proposition, set-membership observations must be combined with set-theoretic generalizations.

Set-theoretic generalizations are findings or assumptions about the set-membership relations that exist between two or more categories. Set-membership relations can assume any of the five condition-to-outcome relationships discussed in chapter 3 (necessary, sufficient, necessary and sufficient, INUS, and SUIN relations). For instance, the assertion that X is a necessary condition for Y is a set-theoretic generalization. Proposition assessment in case-study and small-N research combines set-membership observations with set-theoretic generalizations to *logically derive* conclusions about the truth of contingent propositions.

This chapter specifically examines the use of *set-theoretic tests* in the assessment of contingent propositions about specific cases.[1] These tests combine set-theoretic generalizations (e.g., all members of X are members of Y) with set-membership observations (e.g., case Z is a member of X) to reach conclusions (e.g., case Z is a member of Y). The discussion focuses on two kinds of tests:

TABLE 4.1. Implications of Set-Theoretic Tests for Propositions

	Necessity Test	Sufficiency Test
Proposition Passes Test	Preservation	Confirmation
Proposition Fails Test	Disconfirmation	Diminution

necessity tests and sufficiency tests. A *necessity test* proposes that the existence of a specific set-membership observation is a necessary condition for a proposition to be true. More precisely, a necessity test proposes that the membership of the actual world in a set-membership observation is a necessary condition for its membership in the set *proposition is true*. A *sufficiency test* proposes that the existence of a specific set-membership observation is a sufficient condition for a proposition to be true. More precisely, a sufficiency test proposes that the membership of the actual world in a specific set-membership observation is a sufficient condition for its membership in the set *proposition is true.*

With respect to a proposition under study, one of four results follows from its passing or failing a specific set-theoretic test (see table 4.1). If the proposition passes a necessity test, the result is *preservation* of the proposition; if it fails, the result is *disconfirmation*. If the proposition passes a sufficiency test, the result is *confirmation* of the proposition; if it fails, the result is *diminution*.

With a necessity test, as figure 4.1 shows, the membership of the actual world in X (i.e., *observation is present*) is necessary for its membership in Y (i.e., *proposition is true*). If the actual world has membership in X, thus passing the necessity test, the proposition is not fully confirmed, but it is preserved. Passing a necessity test also lends some support in favor of the truth of the proposition. By contrast, if the actual world does not have membership in X, thus failing the test, the proposition is disconfirmed.

With a sufficiency test, a specific set-membership observation is sufficient to establish the truth of the proposition of interest (see figure 4.2). The actual world's membership in X (i.e., *observation is present*) ensures its membership in Y (i.e., *proposition is true*). Failing a sufficiency test does not fully disconfirm the proposition. However, a failed sufficiency test does mean that the proposition is less likely to be true. A failed sufficiency test diminishes confidence in the validity of the proposition.

The discussion so far assumes that set-theoretic tests are deterministic: a failed necessity test fully establishes the falsity of a proposition, whereas a successful sufficiency test fully establishes its truth. In practice, however, set-theoretic tests never remove all uncertainty; the certitude of the inferences derived from these tests cannot be absolute (see chapter 2). The extent to which a test removes uncertainty depends on the strength of the set-theoretic generalization that is used with the test. In turn, the strength of the generalization

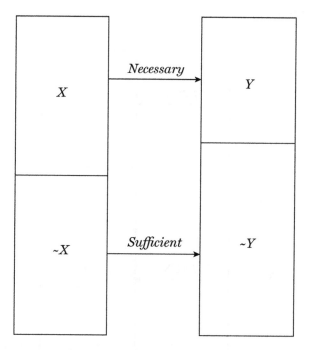

FIGURE 4.1. The Logic of a Necessity Test. X = observation is present; Y = proposition is true.

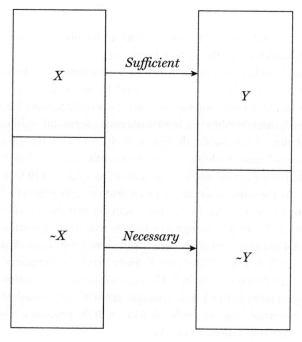

FIGURE 4.2. The Logic of a Sufficiency Test. X = observation is present; Y = proposition is true.

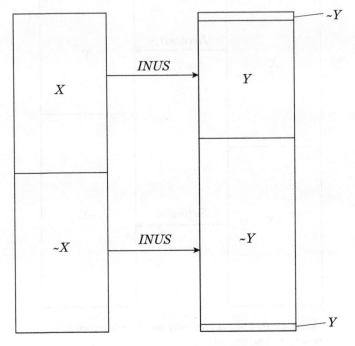

FIGURE 4.3. A Non-Deterministic Necessity Test (90% Necessary).
X = observation is present; Y = proposition is true.

can be assessed on the basis of the extent to which it embodies a fully necessary and/or fully sufficient set-theoretic relationship.[2]

The logical mechanics of approximate, or non-deterministic, versions of the set-theoretic tests can be illustrated with set diagrams. In figure 4.3, membership in X is an INUS condition that is nearly necessary for membership in Y. More precisely, membership in X is 90% necessary for membership in Y. With this formulation, it is possible, though unlikely, for a proposition to be true in the absence of membership in X. Said differently, membership in Y almost always requires the actual world to be a member of X, but 10% of cases are exceptions. By the same token, the actual world's membership in ~X is nearly sufficient for its membership in ~Y. The discovery that the actual world lacks membership in X is nearly enough to conclude that the proposition is false.

Figure 4.4 illustrates an approximate sufficiency test. Here, X is an INUS condition that is nearly sufficient for Y. More precisely, membership in X is 90% sufficient for membership in Y. Hence, membership in X is almost always followed by membership in Y. Likewise, the actual world's membership in set ~X is almost required for its membership in ~Y. If the proposition is false, the actual world is likely a member of ~X.

The degree to which a *successful* necessity test offers *positive* support for a proposition depends on the difficulty of the test. Passing a *difficult* necessity

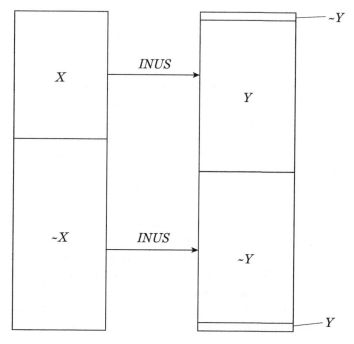

FIGURE 4.4. A Non-Deterministic Sufficiency Test (90% Sufficient).
X = observation is present; Y = proposition is true.

test lends significant positive support in favor of the truth of the proposition; passing an *easy* necessity test does not. The relative difficulty of a necessity test is determined by the extent to which a proposition's membership in X is necessary *and* sufficient for its membership in Y. For example, consider a deterministic necessity test in which all possible worlds with membership in set Y are also members of set X (as in figure 4.1). Here, the relative difficulty of the test is determined by the extent to which membership in X is sufficient as well as necessary for membership in Y. As X approaches the threshold of also being sufficient for Y, fewer possible worlds have membership in X, and therefore the necessity test becomes harder to pass. Said differently, a necessity test becomes more difficult to the extent that it is more difficult for the actual world to be a member of X. If it is difficult but required for the actual world to be a member of X, and if the researcher establishes that the actual world is a member of X, many possible worlds that previously had membership in $\sim Y$ are eliminated. As a consequence of this elimination, the actual world more likely resides in set Y.

The extent to which a *failed* sufficiency test *counts against* a proposition also depends on the difficulty of the test. Here, however, the failure of an *easy* sufficiency test counts heavily against a proposition, whereas the failure of a *difficult* sufficiency test does not count significantly against it. With a sufficiency test, the relative difficulty of the test is determined by the extent to which membership in set X is necessary as well as sufficient for membership in set Y. For example, consider the deterministic test in figure 4.2. As X approaches the threshold of also being necessary for Y, a greater proportion of possible worlds have membership in X, such that the sufficiency test is easier. If the actual world turns out to be a member of $\sim X$, thus failing the easy sufficiency test, many possible worlds that previously had membership in Y are eliminated. As a consequence, it is more likely than before that the actual world resides in $\sim Y$.

We may summarize these various distinctions about set-theoretic tests as follows. First, the tests use set-membership observations and set-theoretic generalizations to pass judgment on the truth of propositions. Depending on whether the test is a necessity test or a sufficiency test, and depending on whether a proposition passes or fails the test, one of four outcomes will result: preservation, disconfirmation, confirmation, or diminution.

Second, the extent to which a test is deterministic varies depending on the extent to which the set-theoretic generalization used in the test is a fully necessary or fully sufficient relationship. In practice, set-theoretic generalizations only approximate the deterministic standards. Thus, a failed necessity test will not fully eliminate a proposition, nor will a successful sufficiency test fully confirm a proposition.

Third, the extent to which passing a necessity test (preservation) supports a proposition, and the extent to which failing a sufficiency test (diminution) counts against a proposition, also varies depending on the difficulty of the test. Passing a difficult necessity test supports a proposition to a greater degree than passing an easy necessity test. Failing an easy sufficiency test counts against a proposition to a greater degree than failing a difficult sufficiency test. The difficulty of a test corresponds with the extent to which a set-membership observation is both necessary and sufficient for the truth of a proposition.

A last comment about the use of the term *test* is in order. This term may suggest that the researcher has carefully thought out and specified the set-theoretic operations prior to the discovery of the relevant set-membership observation. With this sequence, the researcher first identifies the targeted set-membership observation X and the set-membership generalization, before the analysis of any data. The test then involves the analysis of data to discover whether the actual world is a member of X or $\sim X$. While this sequence may sometimes characterize case-study and small-N research, often it does not. Frequently, the researcher's discovery of a specific set-membership observation suggests a set-theoretic test that had not been previously identified. The discovery of the set-membership observation occurs before, not after, the formulation of the set-theoretic test. Later in this chapter, we will return to issues regarding the timing of the discovery of a piece of evidence relative to the timing of the specification of a set-theoretic test.

Descriptive Propositions

This section considers descriptive propositions that have the generic form "case *Z* is a member of category *X*." When social scientists discuss the facts of a case, they are assuming the truth of various descriptive propositions. In most cases, descriptive propositions function as set-membership observations that are treated as societal facts. However, in some cases, the validity of a descriptive proposition is either unknown or a matter of debate. These latter propositions are the focus of set-theoretic tests for descriptive purposes. For instance, consider the following two propositions: (1) Donald Trump was elected president of the United States in 2016; and (2) Vladimir Putin authorized an operation to interfere in the 2016 U.S. presidential election to help Donald Trump win. Both of these propositions are descriptive statements that could be true or false. The first statement is true with the highest degree of credibility in our society—i.e., it is a societal fact. By contrast, the truth of the second statement depends on the discovery of one or more set-membership observations and the use of one or more set-theoretic generalizations.

The discussion here will explore how necessity tests and sufficiency tests can be used to establish the truth or non-truth of descriptive statements. To provide substantive examples, the presentation draws on selected aspects of the arguments in Skocpol (1979) and Drèze and Sen (1989). These scholars do not explicitly use set-theoretic tests. However, they do implicitly use these tests to establish the truth of contested facts about the cases under analysis.

NECESSITY TESTS

In *States and Social Revolutions*, Theda Skocpol (1979: 118–20, 144–47) makes the following descriptive assertions: Eighteenth-century France was characterized by rural community solidarity; nineteenth-century Prussia (east of the Elbe) lacked rural community solidarity. These assertions can be formulated as set-theoretic propositions: Eighteenth-century France is a member of the category *rural community solidarity*, whereas nineteenth-century Prussia is not. Are these propositions true? How can we know?

To use a necessity test to evaluate a descriptive proposition about an individual case, the analyst explores two basic questions. First, the analyst asks whether the case is a member of all categories that are known to be *necessary* for membership in the category of interest. Membership in these categories is requisite for the proposition to be valid. Skocpol (1979: 115–17) asserts that, almost by definition, peasants' possessing some land and having some autonomy from landlords and state agents (conditions *A*, *B*, and *C*) are necessary ingredients for a case to be a member of the category *rural community solidarity*. Prussia is not a member of conditions *A*, *B*, and *C*; set-membership observations reveal that peasants controlled at most only tiny plots and were under the close supervision of Junker landlords. Hence, the case of Prussia fails a necessity test—i.e., it lacks membership in conditions that are necessary to be a member of *rural community solidarity*. By contrast, France passes the same test on the basis of set-membership observations: French peasants controlled substantial land as smallholdings and lived in villages free from supervision by royal officials and landed elites.

Second, to evaluate a descriptive proposition using a necessity test, one can ask about auxiliary traces that would have been left behind if a case had membership in the category of interest. This kind of necessity test builds on the idea that membership in a category is often *sufficient* for membership in subsequent trace categories that are not themselves the target of analytic interest. If one can show that the case does *not* have membership in one or more of these trace categories, then one can infer that the case does not have membership in the target category. In other words, a *necessary* condition for a case to be a member of the target category is that the case have membership in any auxiliary categories for which membership in the target category is *sufficient*.

As an illustration, consider Jean Drèze and Amartya Sen's (1989) descriptive proposition that the state of Kerala in India is a member of the category *high female status*, whereas most states in the federal system of India are not. The authors reason that if a case has membership in *high female status*, it must have membership in certain other categories, such as *high female literacy* and *high female longevity*. They then point to set-membership observations that show that India in general is not a member of these categories. Thus, India as a whole fails the necessity test, and the authors conclude that India is not a member of *high female status*. By contrast, the individual state of Kerala has membership in the categories, passing the necessity test. Kerala may have membership in *high female status*.

Failing a necessity test leads to the approximate disconfirmation of a proposition; it is a way in which a proposition about a case is falsified. By contrast, passing a necessity test lends supporting evidence in favor of the proposition to the extent that the test is difficult to pass. The necessity test above is an example of a relatively difficult test. It is unusual for a state in India to have membership in *high female literacy* and *high female longevity*; most states do not have membership in these sets. Hence, the necessity test requires Kerala to be a member of sets in which it is not easy or typical to achieve membership. The ability of Kerala to pass the test therefore substantially increases confidence that the category *high female status* contains the actual case of Kerala as one of its members.

SUFFICIENCY TESTS

A sufficiency test can explore whether a case is a member of a particular category by inquiring about the case's membership in auxiliary traces for which the particular category is a *necessary condition*. This test builds on the idea that membership in a given category may be an essential ingredient for membership in subsequent trace categories. If one can show that a case has membership in one or more of these trace categories, then one can infer that the case is also a member of the target category. If membership in a target category is necessary for membership in a subsequent trace category, a case's membership in that trace category is *sufficient* to confirm a proposition stating that the case has membership in the target category.[3]

This kind of sufficiency test is the implicit method used to infer the existence of most "basic historical facts," including most set-membership observations.[4] Analysts know that certain events occurred in the past because these events leave behind traces that otherwise could not possibly exist. We have smoking-gun proof that Abraham Lincoln existed: how else can we explain the millions of primary and secondary records depicting his life and actions? Likewise, we have incontrovertible proof that what we understand to be massive peasant revolts took place in eighteenth-century France. These revolts were necessary for countless traces of evidence that have persisted until today, including a large number of sources describing features of the revolts that have been scrutinized by historical experts.

The authenticity of historical facts is questioned when traces that should be present are absent. For example, some authors contend that Kerala is marked by high morbidity rates for both males and females, deriving this conclusion from self-reported data about illnesses in the state. Yet Drèze and Sen (1989: 221–22) argue that these reports are not strong evidence that Kerala is a member of the category *high morbidity*. They note that indicators of self-reported morbidity are often misleading insofar as a researcher is interested in physical illness as opposed to issues related to health communication. They note that if Kerala were a member of *high morbidity*, we would observe other visible traces in recorded health outcomes. The absence of these traces leads Drèze and Sen to question the authenticity of the "fact" that Kerala is a member of *high morbidity*.

The consequence of a proposition's passing a sufficiency test depends on the strength of the set-theoretic generalization that is used in the test. The degree to which the generalization approximates a necessity and/or sufficiency relationship dictates the degree to which a successful test ensures the truth of a proposition. When we assert indisputable facts, such as that Abraham Lincoln was an actual person, we implicitly assume deterministic set-membership generalizations. While the generalizations that underpin our belief that Lincoln existed as a real person are not 100% infallible, we treat them as if they were, for the purposes of analysis.

Finally, the extent to which failing a sufficiency test counts against a proposition depends on the difficulty of the test: failing an easy sufficiency test counts more heavily against a proposition. For example, consider Drèze and Sen's (1989: 221) assessment of the proposition that Kerala is a member of the category *low-calorie-intake region*. Although good data on calorie intake are not available for Indian states or regions, the authors assert that a high incidence of significant undernutrition in Kerala would offer a strong confirmation of this proposition. Yet the data indicate that Kerala is not a member of *significant undernutrition*. Thus, the proposition that Kerala is a member of *low-calorie-intake region* fails a sufficiency test. Moreover, membership in *significant undernutrition* is common throughout India and the developing world, such that this sufficiency test was relatively easy to pass. The failure of the easy test counts as non-trivial disconfirming evidence for the proposition that Kerala is a member of *low-calorie-intake region*.

Causal Propositions

If we agree that a particular case is a member of antecedent event X and subsequent event Y, how can we know if its membership in X causes its membership in Y? For example, given that eighteenth-century France was a member of the set *rural community solidarity* before it was a member of the set *peasant revolution*, how can we decide if its membership in the former set was a *cause* of its membership in the latter set?

This section considers how necessity and sufficiency tests can help analysts evaluate causal propositions. The discussion builds on the regularity model of causality introduced in chapter 3. With a regularity model of causality, the researcher not only establishes that a causal event stands in a logical regularity relationship with an outcome event across all possible cases, but also demonstrates that the causal event is linked to the outcome event through a series of intermediary events that compose a causal chain. The links in the chain between the main causal event and the outcome are the mechanisms through which the cause achieves spatiotemporal contact with the outcome. Following this approach, I use the term *intervening mechanism* for an event that stands as a link in a causal chain. The intervening mechanism is both an outcome of an initial cause and a cause of a final outcome. The identification and analysis of intervening mechanisms are indispensable components of the set-theoretic analysis of causal propositions.

NECESSITY TESTS

A necessity test identifies a category in which a case's membership is *necessary* for the proposition to be true. With a causal proposition, the essential category in which the case must have membership is an intervening mechanism linking sets X and Y. More specifically, a necessity test of the proposition that X causes Y in case Z requires that case Z have membership in an intervening mechanism (M) in the causal chain $X \rightarrow M \rightarrow Y$. The specific procedures for using this kind of necessity test vary depending on whether the proposition under consideration states that membership in X is a necessary cause of membership in Y (including when X is a combination of SUIN causes) or that membership in X is a sufficient cause of membership in Y (including when X is a sufficiency combination of INUS causes).

Let us first assume that one is evaluating a proposition stating that X is a necessary cause of Y. For example, Skocpol (1979: 121–26) proposes that France's antecedent membership in *rural community solidarity* (X) is a necessary cause of its subsequent membership in *peasant revolution* (Y). To carry out a necessity test, Skocpol could draw on existing general knowledge and identify a mechanism (M) that is known to be *sufficient* for the outcome (Y). To pass the necessity test, membership in *rural community solidarity* (X) must be necessary for membership in the intervening category M.[5] In other words, if we know that temporally intermediate M is sufficient for Y, we can logically deduce that X must be necessary for M if it is a necessary cause of Y.

This kind of test depends on (1) preexisting knowledge that membership in M is sufficient for membership in Y, and (2) set-membership observations that establish that membership in X is (or is not) necessary for membership in M. The leverage gained from the test derives from the fact that X is temporally closer to M than to Y, and hence it is easier to evaluate a link between X and M than a link between X and Y. To continue with the Skocpol example, the historical literature establishes that certain specific rural rebellions that occurred in parts of France in 1789—composed centrally of struggles against seigniorial practices, especially in the north and northeast—were events sufficient (i.e., enough by themselves) to generate France's membership in *peasant revolution* (Y). Accordingly, Skocpol explores whether the causal factor—*rural community solidarity* (X)—was necessary for these specific anti-seigniorial revolts (M). She notes that the literature shows that the revolts were made possible by the assemblies and organizations that existed in the relevant peasant villages. Peasant communities with "considerable property, community autonomy, and antiseigneurial solidarity . . . [featured] a preexisting potential for antiseigneurial revolts" (p. 125). In her judgment, the proposition passes the necessity test: membership in *rural community solidarity* (X) is necessary for membership in *widespread anti-seigniorial revolts* (M), which in turn was sufficient for membership in *peasant revolution* (Y).

The consequences for a causal proposition of passing a necessity test will vary depending on the difficulty of the test. If the intervening mechanism in the test is an important sufficient cause of the outcome (i.e., the mechanism comes reasonably close to also being necessary for the outcome), the test will be more difficult to pass. In the Skocpol example, the mechanism is a series of anti-seigniorial revolts taking place in strategic parts of France. Although these revolts may not have been essential for a peasant revolution (i.e., peasant revolts that took place in other parts of France may have brought about the same result), they were the events that most readily and obviously generated France's membership in *peasant revolution*. In that sense, the necessity test seems fairly difficult: the mechanism is an important sufficient condition for peasant revolution in France. Hence, Skocpol's hypothesis passes a fairly difficult necessity test and, by doing so, receives non-trivial confirmatory support.

For a proposition that X is a *sufficient cause* of Y (including when X is a sufficiency combination of INUS conditions), a necessity test can be carried out in conjunction with any mechanism (M) that is *necessary* for Y. For the proposition to pass the necessity test, membership in X must be sufficient for membership in M. If X is not sufficient for M, the proposition fails the test, and one concludes that the causal proposition is likely disconfirmed. The assumption is that if X really is causally sufficient for Y, as the proposition states, X must be sufficient for any intervening mechanism that is necessary for Y.

For example, Drèze and Sen (1989: 223–25) consider and reject as false the proposition that membership in *progressive public policy* (X) was a sufficient cause of membership in *high female status* (Y) in Kerala. They arrive at this conclusion by emphasizing Kerala's membership in the category *female-male ratio greater than unity* (M). They follow scholars who believe that membership in this category is a necessary condition for membership in the *high female status* outcome. Kerala's membership in *progressive public policy*, however, is not sufficient for its membership in *female-male ratio greater than unity*. Rather, Kerala's female-male birth ratio has cultural roots going far back in time, including a partially matrilineal system of inheritance. Thus, the proposition fails the necessity test: membership in *progressive public policy* (X) was not a sufficient cause of membership in *high female status* (Y). We discover this because X is not sufficient for membership in *female-male ratio greater than unity* (M), which is believed to be approximately necessary for membership in Y.

SUFFICIENCY TESTS

Sufficiency tests to assess causal propositions also require the analyst to ask about the presence of an intervening mechanism linking X and Y. Again, the specific tasks that need to be carried out vary depending on whether the proposition under consideration is that X is a necessary cause of Y or that X is a sufficient cause of Y.

If membership in the potential cause (X) is hypothesized to be *necessary* for membership in the outcome (Y), the analyst can run a sufficiency test by identifying an intervening mechanism (M) in which membership is known to be necessary for Y. The analyst then determines whether membership in X is necessary for membership in M. If membership in X is necessary for membership in a mechanism that is known to be necessary for Y, then X itself *must* be necessary for Y.

The assumption behind the test is that although we may not know whether membership in X is necessary for membership in Y, we do know that membership in M is necessary for membership in Y. We then use set-membership observations to decide whether membership in X is necessary for membership in M. The advantage is that it is easier to decide whether X is necessary for M than whether X is necessary for Y. This is true because X and M are closer to one another in time than are X and Y. As several analysts suggest, causal links between proximate events can be intuitively obvious, especially with necessary causes (Abbott 1992; Goldstone 1998a; Griffin 1993; Roberts 1996). Chains of linked necessary causes provide a good opportunity for the analyst to carry out a sufficiency test: the analyst can show how case membership in an initial cause was essential to put the overall sequence in motion, culminating with case membership in the outcome.

As an example, let us return once more to the proposition that Kerala's membership in *progressive public policy* (X) was a sufficient cause of its membership in *high female status* (Y). One way to try to confirm this proposition is to look for an intervening mechanism (M) in which membership is necessary for subsequent membership in *high female status* (Y). Drèze and Sen's discussion suggests that *gender-equitable education* is such a mechanism: "It would be surprising if a greater level of female education—and less gender inequality in the sharing of education—had not contributed to better prospects of a plausible life for women, both through raising the status of women and through increasing female economic power" (1989: 224). The question becomes whether Kerala's membership in *progressive public policy* was necessary for its membership in the intervening mechanism *gender-equitable education*. The authors suggest that the answer is affirmative: "Public policy [in Kerala] put much greater emphasis on general education and literacy than was the case in the rest of India, and the emphasis on female education was particularly exceptional" (p. 223). Hence, they find that (1) membership in *gender-equitable education* (M) was a necessary cause of membership in *high female status* (Y); and (2) membership in the antecedent *progressive public policy* (X) was necessary for membership in *gender-equitable education* (M). Given these findings, it follows that the core causal proposition is true: *progressive public policy* was a necessary cause of *high female status*.

Finally, let us consider a proposition in which membership in the cause (or combination of causes) is believed to be *sufficient* for membership in the outcome. To carry out a sufficiency test, one locates an intervening mechanism that is established as a sufficient cause of the outcome. One then shows that membership in the cause is sufficient for membership in this mechanism. The assumption is that if membership in the cause (X) is sufficient for membership in an intervening mechanism (M) that is known to be sufficient for membership in the outcome (Y), then the cause itself *must* be sufficient for the outcome.

This kind of set-theoretic test is routinely carried out by detectives and medical examiners. For example, a medical examiner during an autopsy may establish a proximate mechanism sufficient for death and a more remote cause sufficient for this mechanism. A proximate sufficient cause of death might be the transection of the left internal jugular vein. A sharp-force injury inflicted with a knife might be sufficient for this transection. The conclusion that follows logically is that the knife injury is sufficient for the death.

In the social sciences, this kind of test is often carried out in conjunction with arguments about a mechanism composed of multiple factors that is sufficient for the outcome of interest. For example, Skocpol (1979) holds that France's membership in the combination of *peasant revolution* (X_1) and *state breakdown* (X_2) was sufficient for its membership in *social revolution* (Y). That is, she holds that the following relationship is true: X_1 & $X_2 \rightarrow Y$. In turn, she works to show how three INUS causes—*international pressure* (A), *dominant class political leverage* (B), and *rural community solidarity* (C)—were jointly sufficient for membership in *peasant revolution* and *state breakdown* (Goertz and Mahoney 2005). To the extent that she can plausibly show that membership in the combination of A, B, and C was enough to generate membership in both *peasant revolution* and *state breakdown*, she can then assert that this combination of INUS causes was also sufficient for membership in the outcome of social revolution itself. Her overall argument is thus A & B & $C \rightarrow X_1$ & $X_2 \rightarrow Y$. Stated in words, Skocpol finds that the combination of *international pressure*, *dominant class political leverage*, and *rural community solidarity* was approximately sufficient for the combination of *peasant revolution* and *state breakdown*, which in turn was approximately sufficient for *social revolution* in France.

Empirical examples of set-theoretic tests help illuminate the logic of causal assessment in small-N and case-study research. The appendix to this chapter provides three more examples of these tests from famous works on historical democratization in England.

Normative Propositions

In case-study and small-N research, normative propositions have the generic form "category X is a member of category Y for case C," where X is a specific event or institution and Y is a normative category that contains an evaluative descriptor such as *right, wrong, good,* or *bad*. For instance, one might assert that the category *French Revolution* is a member of the category *positive event in human history* for the case of the world. Or one might assert that the category *neoliberal policy program* is a member of *detrimental economic policy program* for one or more Latin American cases. One purpose of social science analysis is to evaluate the truth of explicitly normative propositions using evidence and logic.

In this section, I draw on Norman Furniss and Timothy Tilton's book *The Case for the Welfare State* (1977) to illustrate the use of set-theoretic tests with normative propositions. Furniss and Tilton evaluate whether the category *social welfare state* is a member of the category *justified political-economic system* for the advanced industrial countries. Their definition of *social welfare state* reflects a commitment to the general normative tradition of egalitarianism (see chapter 8 on normative traditions). Furniss and Tilton understand *social welfare state* as the pursuit of equality of living conditions via social policy and the broadening of the locus of political power via social empowerment. The authors contrast *social welfare state*, which has Sweden as its exemplary actual world member, with two other political-economic systems: the *positive state*, which has the United States as an exemplary member, and the *social security state*, which has Britain as one of its members.

Their discussion of the category *justified political-economic system* makes clear that their findings assume and require an endorsement of egalitarian values. The findings do not extend beyond the scope of this normative tradition. Specifically, they assert that, in order to assess their argument, one must first embrace the values of equality—"the conviction that all persons have the same right to live a full and satisfying life"—as "an essential attribute of a just society" (1977: 29).

NECESSITY TESTS

A basic kind of necessity test asks about the auxiliary conditions (trace categories) that follow from the normative category under study, exploring whether the outcome of interest is a member of these auxiliary conditions. The analyst begins with the knowledge that the normative category Y is sufficient for a subsequent condition Z. The test then requires that the event or institution X be a member of this condition Z in order for the proposition to avoid disconfirmation.

For instance, scholars might start with the following set-theoretic generalization: the normative category *justified political-economic system* (Y) is nearly sufficient for *strong citizen approval of political-economic system* (Z). The assumption is that *justified political-economic system* leaves behind as a trace *strong citizen approval.*[6] While this trace may or may not precede *justified political-economic system*, it almost always follows it. The logical implication is that countries that are members of *social welfare state* (X) for a certain amount of time should be members of *strong citizen approval* if the proposition (that a social welfare state is a justified political-economic system) is true. The membership of *social welfare state* in the *strong citizen approval* trace category is nearly necessary for the validity of the proposition.

Passing this kind of test preserves a proposition and lends at least some positive support in its favor. With the case of Sweden, Furniss and Tilton suggest that the proposition receives non-trivial support because the necessity test is fairly difficult. Most countries are not members of *strong citizen approval*, and thus membership in this required category cannot be taken for granted; in fact, for Sweden in the 1970s, scholars have pointed out that citizens exhibit strong approval for the social welfare system even though many of them had also lived under a different system (Brooks and Manza 2007). They still strongly prefer the social welfare state, despite knowledge of and experience with the positive state alternative. In sum, membership of *social welfare state* in the category *strong citizen approval* is required, but is not easily obtained. Thus, the successful necessity test provides non-trivial support in favor of the proposition.

A different kind of necessity test inquires about conditions that temporally or logically precede the normative category under study. The test specifically targets prior conditions that are necessary for membership in the normative category. For a proposition to pass the test, the event or institution must itself be a member of the conditions that are necessary for the normative category. For example, if membership in the category *politically free society* is necessary for membership in *justified political-economic system*, as Furniss and Tilton suggest, then the category *social welfare state* must be a member of *politically free society* if it is to have membership in *justified political-economic system*.

This kind of necessity test helps identify the range of cases that are appropriate for evaluating a normative proposition. For instance, one might argue that countries must first be members of the categories *democratic country* and *developed country* in order to be members of *justified political-economic system*. The reasoning is that countries that lack membership in these prior categories also lack essential requisites for membership in *justified political-economic system*. In a sense, the set-theoretic test establishes the scope of the analysis: countries that do not meet certain conditions are excluded from the possibility of being members of the normative category.

SUFFICIENCY TESTS

A basic kind of sufficiency test focuses on an auxiliary condition (Z) in which a case can have membership only if it already has membership in the normative category (Y) under study (i.e., membership in condition Y is necessary for membership in condition Z). The analyst explores whether the event or institution under study (X) has membership in this auxiliary condition (Z), knowing that this membership is approximately sufficient for membership in the normative category (Y). For example, the analyst might begin with the generalization that *justified political-economic system* (Y) is an approximate necessary condition for *political empowerment of disadvantaged societal groups* (Z), as Furniss and Tilton suggest. The idea is that nearly all unjust political-economic systems yield unjust results, including the ongoing disempowerment of less powerful groups. For their empowerment, a justified system is required. The set-theoretic test takes the following form: if *social welfare state* (*X*) is a member of the category *political empowerment of disadvantaged societal groups* (*Z*), it is also very likely a member of *justified political-economic system* (*Y*). This conclusion follows because membership in *political empowerment of disadvantaged societal groups* nearly requires prior membership in *justified political-economic system.*

We can see the logic of this test at work in Furniss and Tilton's argument that for Sweden, *social welfare state* is a member of *justified political-economic system.* The authors support this argument by pointing to various indications that *social welfare state* is a member of the category *political empowerment of disadvantaged societal groups.* They remark that "the most striking testimonial to the success of the Swedish welfare state is the extent to which traditional class barriers have been razed. Everyday phenomena reveal the presence of substantial social equality" (1977: 140). The membership of *social welfare state* in *political empowerment* provides strong confirming evidence for Furniss and Tilton's argument, insofar as we accept that *justified political-economic system* is necessary for *political empowerment.*

Failing a sufficiency test does not disconfirm a proposition; it will only count against a proposition to the extent that the test is easy to pass. For example, this same test would have resulted in failure if the proposition had been that *positive state*, which has the United States as an exemplary member, is a member of *justified political-economic system.* Furniss and Tilton call attention to much evidence illustrating that *positive state* is quite far from being a member of *political empowerment of disadvantaged societal groups.* Yet its non-membership in this category has only slightly damaging consequences for the proposition, because this sufficiency test is hard to pass: it is very hard for a society to obtain membership in *political empowerment of disadvantaged societal groups.* Hence, the fact that *positive state* lacks membership in this category does not strongly support the argument that *positive state* is also not a member of *justified political-economic system.*

Finally, a sufficiency test can be built around the generalization that one or more prior conditions are sufficient for membership in the normative category under study. For instance, one might start with the generalization that the category *truly democratic process of politics* is sufficient for *justified political-economic system.* This generalization holds that any political-economic system that is formed from a truly democratic process is inherently justified. If one can show that a given system was so formed, one can conclude that it has membership in *justified political-economic system.*

This example raises issues concerning partial membership in the categories used in a set-theoretic test. For instance, an analyst might conclude that the case of Sweden has considerable but incomplete membership (e.g., a 0.75

membership value) in *truly democratic process of politics*. If so, following the rules of continuous-set analysis, the analyst concludes that Sweden has at least as much membership (e.g., ≥ 0.75) in the category *justified political-economic system*. This finding follows necessarily from the generalization that *truly democratic process of politics* is sufficient for *justified political-economic system*. With a sufficient condition, the extent of a case's membership in the sufficient condition is equal to or greater than the extent of its membership in the target category (see chapter 3 on set-theoretic analysis with partial set membership).

In conclusion, normative propositions do not have a special status with respect to set-theoretic tests. One uses the same procedures to evaluate a proposition stating "*X* is morally good" as to evaluate a proposition stating "*X* is an instance of *Y*." With scientific constructivism, all social categories are understood to be mind-dependent entities that require shared beliefs for their existence. Thus, the fact that the truth of normative propositions depends on our beliefs does not differentiate normative propositions from other kinds of propositions. What makes normative propositions distinctive is that their evaluation often depends on set-theoretic generalizations associated with an overall tradition of normative beliefs. For example, Furniss and Tilton, in their 1977 study, explicitly draw on generalizations associated with moral egalitarianism. A scholar who rejects moral egalitarianism may also reject its generalizations. For this reason, scholars working from different normative traditions (see chapter 8) may have difficulty reaching similar conclusions regarding the truth of specific normative propositions.

Deduction and Induction

Do set-theoretic tests involve an inductive or a deductive mode of explanation and reasoning? The answer to this question helps to clarify the ways in which set-theoretic tests are used in case-study and small-N research. However, the answer varies depending on what one means by inductive versus deductive analysis. The definition of these terms in the field of logic is different from their definition in the field of empirical social science. Both definitions are useful for elucidating the mechanics of set-theoretic tests, but they need to be distinguished clearly.

DEFINITIONS FROM LOGIC

In the field of logic, the concept of *deduction* refers to a mode of reasoning in which the truth of the premises of an argument guarantees the truth of the con-clusion of the argument (Copi and Cohen 1994; Hacking 2001). Analysts who use set-theoretic tests prefer to employ deductive analysis in this specific sense. They try to derive conclusions that follow logically and necessarily from a set of premises. Their premises include set-membership observations that are treated as societal facts and one or more set-theoretic generalizations that are treated as true. The approach resembles in some ways the deductive-nomological (D-N) model of explanation (Hempel 1942; Nagel 1961; Popper 1934/1968). Along the same lines as the D-N model, set-theoretic tests evaluate propositions about particular cases using societal facts and regularity statements. However, set-theoretic tests place the D-N model on a constructivist footing, rather than a positivist or empiricist foundation. The categories used in set-theoretic tests are mind-dependent entities, and the relationships between these categories are also mind-dependent entities that do not have an existence independent of human beliefs. Hence, the regularities that inform set-theoretic tests are bounded in space and time, within particular truth-dependent semantic contexts.

An *inductive* mode of reasoning is used when the truth of the premises does not guarantee the truth of the conclusion: the premises, even when they are all true, yield a probabilistic prediction about a conclusion (Hempel 1942; Hacking 2001). Whereas propositional logic is a mode of deductive analysis, statistics is a mode of inductive analysis. To be used effectively in the analysis of individual cases, inductive reasoning requires that the analyst draw on strong generalizations. One needs to begin with a strong regularity statement to be able to infer that an event is likely to occur (or not occur) in an individual case. Highly probabilistic generalizations prohibit such inferences and are of limited use in the assessment of propositions about individual cases (Hempel 1942; Scriven 1959; Costner and Leik 1964; Railton 1978).

Although case-study researchers seek to use fully deductive tests, they must engage in logical induction, because their generalizations only approximate necessity and/or sufficiency. Set-theoretic tests yield uncertain conclusions about the validity of propositions (see chapter 2 on uncertainty). The degree of certainty generated by any given test—i.e., the strength of the test—depends on exactly how close its generalizations are to being necessary and/or sufficient relationships.

When researchers cannot use deductive analysis, they can compensate for this inability by carrying out multiple inductive tests and thus achieving higher confidence in their findings. A proposition that passes a single inductive test is not well supported unless it is a very strong test. But a proposition that passes several inductive tests may receive considerable support even if each test uses generalizations that only approximate the deterministic ideals (Goertz and Mahoney 2012).

DEFINITIONS FROM EMPIRICAL SOCIAL SCIENCE

In the social sciences, deductive analysis is defined by the formulation of concepts, propositions, and theories prior to the analysis of the evidence used to evaluate those concepts, propositions, and theories. Under this definition, concepts, propositions, and theories *precede* data collection and analysis. By contrast, inductive analysis involves the use of evidence and data analysis to generate concepts, propositions, and theories that had not been previously formulated. Under this definition, case-study and small-N researchers engage in inductive reasoning when they develop concepts, propositions, and theories using hitherto unexamined cases and evidence.[7] Likewise, statistical researchers engage in inductive analysis when they pursue specification searches and run exploratory tests of the data.

When applied to set-theoretic tests, the social science concepts of deduction and induction concern whether the test is designed prior to the analysis of set-membership observations. With a deductive set-theoretic test, the analyst first designs the test and then examines the specific evidence needed to carry it out. For instance, when writing a proposal for research, a case-oriented analyst may identify a set-theoretic test to be carried out. In the actual research, the analyst works to establish (or not) the case's membership in one or more categories, as specified in the test. Implementing a deductive set-theoretic test is analogous to the work of a detective who searches for pre-targeted evidence that will help solve the mystery. From some (non-Bayesian) epistemological standpoints, deductive analysis is regarded as a superior mode of inference, because the test is conceived prior to the analysis of the data. For instance, empiricist epistemologies advocate a sharp separation between the "context of justification" and the "context of discovery" (Popper 1934/1968). The investigator first specifies the kind of evidence that can justify a belief about the truth of a proposition. The investigator then works empirically to discover whether that evidence is present.

Yet in practice, social researchers often implicitly carry out empirically inductive set-theoretic tests under Bayesian assumptions. While learning about a case, they may discover that it has membership in a category that can be used to evaluate the proposition of interest. For example, they may come across an unexpected yet essential piece of data concerning a mechanism, much as a detective might stumble upon an unanticipated but decisive clue in the course of an investigation. Although not looking for specific data, the analyst may be generally hunting for useful pieces of evidence that can inform set-theoretic tests not yet conceived. With inductive research, the discovery of a specific set-membership observation *precedes* and *causes* the formulation of a set-theoretic test. This process may be easier to accomplish if the researcher is ready to run a set-theoretic test if and when appropriate evidence is found. Skilled researchers may not be able to anticipate the specific set-membership observations that will prove highly useful, but they know where to look to find these kinds of observations, and they are ready to use the observations if they are discovered.

Set-theoretic tests are powerful tools when inductively formulated as a response to the discovery of useful evidence that was not fully anticipated. Like detectives, researchers begin their investigations with propositions to be evaluated and different theories and hunches. In the course of gathering evidence, they discover unforeseen but welcome set-membership observations that bear on their conclusions. They almost simultaneously formulate and carry out set-theoretic tests in light of these discoveries.[8]

To sum up, set-theoretic researchers strive to develop tests that are logically deductive, but in practice they must use logical induction. They compensate for the lack of deductive tests by employing strong inductive set-theoretic tests and multiple inductive tests. They may occasionally formulate these set-theoretic tests prior to analyzing the main evidence. More commonly, however, they formulate and evaluate set-theoretic tests in conjunction with the discovery of relevant but not fully anticipated evidence.

––––––

Set-theoretic tests involve both searching for set-membership observations and using and developing set-theoretic generalizations. To excel at the data collection end of set-theoretic testing, the analyst must have a strong understanding of the subject matter. The possession of expert knowledge provides access to useful pieces of evidence—i.e., set-membership observations—that simply may not be available to those less familiar with the subject matter (cf. Tansey 2007).

To excel at designing good set-theoretic tests, one must possess knowledge of relevant existing generalizations, perhaps established from studies of other cases. These generalizations need not be "universal laws," but ideally they will approximate necessary and/or sufficient conditions. Set-theoretic researchers typically employ multiple tests using diverse evidence when assessing a given proposition. Hence, when evaluating the overall strength of an inference with set-theoretic analysis, one must consider the various pieces of evidence and the multiple tests that inform the inference.

Appendix: Examples of Set-Theoretic Tests: Explaining Democracy in England

This appendix discusses causal propositions from three famous studies of democratization in historical England. Each of the examples involves the use of a set-theoretic test with an intervening mechanism. Although all of the examples focus on early democratization in England, they concern propositions that do not necessarily compete with or contradict one another.

MOORE ON THE ENCLOSURE MOVEMENT

In *Social Origins of Dictatorship and Democracy: Lord and Peasant in the Making of the Modern World* (1966), Barrington Moore famously proposes that the enclosure movement in England (between 1760 and 1832) was a necessary cause of the parliamentary democracy that developed in this country after the mid-nineteenth century (pp. 20–39). The core support for the argument involves a *sufficiency test* concerning an intervening mechanism that links the enclosure movement and the construction of parliamentary democracy. This key intervening mechanism is the destruction of traditional peasant society.

Moore uses cross-case comparisons to reach the generalization that democratization could not have gone forward during this world-historical period within a society marked by a powerful traditional peasantry. Wherever the peasantry was large and entrenched, Moore finds, the result was reactionary fascism (e.g., in Germany and Japan), communism (Russia and China), or premodern backwardness (India). When stated set-theoretically, this argument holds that membership in *not–strong traditional peasantry* was a necessary cause of membership in *parliamentary democracy* for societies as they followed their pathways to the modern world.

Moore uses the historical literature—especially the work of Tawney (1912, 1941) and Campbell (1942)—to establish that in England, the enclosure movement was essential to the process through which the traditional peasantry was removed. Without the enclosures, he argues, the smallholding rural villages and traditional peasant society would have persisted. In set-theoretic terms, England's membership in *the enclosure movement* was necessary for its membership in *not–strong traditional peasantry*.

Thus, in terms of set membership, the argument is that *the enclosure movement* was a necessary cause of *not–strong traditional peasantry*, which was a necessary cause of *parliamentary democracy*. For Moore, these facts add up to strong support for the proposition that the enclosure movement was necessary for England's parliamentary democracy. In addition, since the enclosure movement was an unusual event in the early modern world (Moore treats it as perhaps the main factor that sets England apart from the rest of the world), one can regard it as an important necessary cause—even a critical event—for England's democratic outcome (see chapter 10 on critical events).

LUEBBERT ON LIB-LABISM

In *Liberalism, Fascism, or Social Democracy: Social Classes and the Political Origins of Regimes in Interwar Europe* (1991), Gregory Luebbert argues that an alliance between liberal parties and the labor movement (*Lib-Lab alliance*) before World War I was nearly sufficient (in the historical context of Europe) for England's open political-economic regime (*liberal democracy*) during the interwar period. A key component of this argument involves a *necessity test* with an intervening mechanism: *moderate labor movement*. Luebbert's comparative analysis suggests that this mechanism is a necessary cause of membership in *liberal democracy* for interwar Europe. If the proposition is correct, membership in *Lib-Lab alliance* must, in turn, be sufficient for membership in this mechanism. A sufficient cause of an outcome must be sufficient for all intervening mechanisms that are necessary for the outcome.

In this test, Luebbert employs the set-theoretic generalization that *moderate labor movement* was necessary for *liberal democracy* during the interwar period in Europe. This generalization derives from an analysis of England and other European cases where strong labor movements were present. In these cases, "labor peace and discipline, and by correlate the stability of the political order . . . would require a fundamental break with the liberal model" (p. 10). Only if labor was docile and without class consciousness could liberal democracy prevail.

Given this generalization, the necessity test involves showing that membership in *Lib-Lab alliance* was sufficient for membership in *moderate labor movement*. Luebbert summarizes the evidence for this conclusion as follows: "The message to be drawn from the historical material is unambiguous: very few British workers had much use for class politics precisely because Lib-Labism gave them a measure of confidence, however small, that was sufficient to undermine a more comprehensive vision" (p. 25).

It is important to recognize that the form of this argument is a necessity test, not a sufficiency test. The ability of the case to pass the test does not provide decisive evidence that the proposition is true (though failing the test would have practically falsified it). The test is convincing in that it draws on a set-theoretic generalization that Luebbert carefully develops through systematic cross-case comparisons elsewhere in the book. Moreover, the necessity test is not easy to pass. Moderate labor movements were the exception rather than the rule, and finding any condition sufficient for these movements is difficult. Passing this necessity test therefore lends positive support to the proposition that *Lib-Lab alliance* was sufficient (in the context of England during the interwar period) for *liberal democracy*.

DOWNING ON MEDIEVAL CONSTITUTIONALISM

In *The Military Revolution and Political Change: Origins of Democracy and Autocracy in Early Modern Europe* (1992), Brian Downing argues that three conditions during the medieval period in England (and in Europe more generally) were necessary for the emergence and consolidation of democracy: *balance of power between crown and nobility (A), decentralized military systems*

(B), and *peasant property rights* (C) (pp. 19–26). He argues that if England had lacked membership in any one of these conditions, it could not have embarked on its path toward membership in *liberal democracy*.

Downing develops this argument by showing how the conjunction of the three conditions was necessary for membership in a more proximate mechanism: *Western constitutionalism*. Downing defines *Western constitutionalism* by membership in (1) *strong local government*, (2) *parliamentary bodies*, and (3) *rule of law*. Although *Western constitutionalism* is not sufficient for *democracy*, it is an essential ingredient for that outcome. Downing establishes this generalization by contrasting Western Europe to other regions of the world that did not achieve membership in *democracy* during the nineteenth and early twentieth centuries.

The structure of Downing's argument is thus as follows:

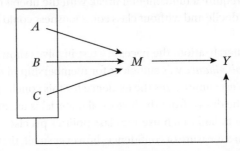

Here A is *balance of power between crown and nobility*; B is *decentralized military systems*; C is *peasant property rights*; M is *Western constitutionalism*; Y is *liberal democracy*; and → stands for a necessity relationship.

The set-theoretic test leverages Downing's cross-case finding that M is necessary for Y. Downing works to convince readers that A, B, and C are each necessary for M. He is aided in this effort by the fact that A, B, and C are temporally proximate to M and suitable for counterfactual analysis. Once he has persuaded us that A, B, and C are necessary for M, he reasons logically that these three factors must also be necessary for Y, given that M has been established to be necessary for Y.

Overall, then, the set-theoretic test parallels the Moore example above. Downing has carried out a sufficiency test of the proposition that three conditions from the medieval period were causally necessary for liberal democracy in England.

5

Counterfactual Analysis

(coauthored with Rodrigo Barrenechea)

A counterfactual is a "subjunctive conditional in which the antecedent is known or supposed for purposes of argument to be false" (Tetlock and Belkin 1996a: 4; see also Goodman 1947; Weber 1949). A well-known example is, "If Al Gore had been elected president in 2000, the United States would not have invaded Iraq" (see Harvey 2012). In case-study research, counterfactual analysis is intended to help analysts evaluate the effect of an actual world event by considering what would have happened if the event had not occurred, or had occurred differently. These evaluations involve the formulation of structured "what if" arguments that systematically consider aspects of a possible case in which an analytically important counterfactual antecedent is in place (Lewis 1973). The analyst considers what happens in this possible case with respect to the occurrence of an outcome, or outcomes, of interest.

   The counterfactual analysis of possible cases is a major tool of causal inference in small-N and case-study analysis (Fearon 1991, 1996; George and Bennett 2005; Goertz and Levy 2007a; Harvey 2012, 2015; Lebow 2010; Levy 2008, 2015; Tetlock and Belkin 1996b; Tetlock and Parker 2006). Researchers use counterfactual analysis to explore causal regularities, even though only one or a small number of actual cases are analyzed. Through the construction of appropriate counterfactual cases, they gain the leverage needed to estimate the extent to which a condition is necessary and sufficient for an outcome.

   In this chapter, we seek to provide concepts and tools for the assessment of causal propositions in case-study research, working explicitly within the set-theoretic approach and its regularity model of causality. The chapter treats all events—whether actual or non-actual—as constructed categories whose meaning depends on particular semantic contexts. With counterfactual analysis, the focus is on non-actual events that take place in possible worlds other than the actual world. Counterfactual statements are, specifically, causal propositions about non-actual events. We propose that in order to analyze non-actual events as causes, scholars must use many of the same tools as are used in the study of actual events. They must employ set-theoretic tests to help establish whether one non-actual event is a cause of another non-actual event. They must also study the chain of intermediary events that link a counterfactual antecedent with the outcome of interest.

The first part of the chapter distinguishes different types of (1) counterfactual cases and (2) counterfactual statements. Counterfactual cases are differentiated according to the kind of change that is introduced to the actual world to create the counterfactual case. The discussion focuses on cause-varying counterfactual cases, which introduce a change to the causal factor of interest; and context-varying counterfactual cases, which introduce a change to a specific aspect of the context in which a causal factor operates. Counterfactual statements are differentiated according to the *type of cause* that is used in the statement. For instance, a case study might examine a proposition holding that X was nearly a *necessary cause* of Y in case Z. Alternatively, a case study might examine a proposition holding that X was nearly a *sufficient cause* of Y in the context of case Z. We consider the different kinds of analysis that must accompany propositions about different kinds of causes.

The next two sections of the chapter focus on the trade-offs involved in selecting particular possible cases for counterfactual analysis. Some of these trade-offs concern whether a possible case is more proximate or less proximate to the actual world. The *minimal-rewrite rule* holds that useful possible cases are quite close to the actual world. Yet analysts may seek to understand what would have happened if a major change had been introduced into the actual world. As we shall see, they can address this problem in part through the analysis of context-varying counterfactual cases that keep the causal factor in place but that counterfactually change aspects of the context in which it operates.

This chapter also explores the advantages and disadvantages of formulating (1) more specific versus more general counterfactual statements, and (2) more plausible versus more important counterfactual statements. The discussion shows why these two issues are intimately connected. In general, researchers prefer more specific counterfactual statements, because they are clearer, more precise, and thus more important. However, more specific and more important counterfactual statements are less likely to be plausible. The chapter examines why more important counterfactual statements are necessarily less plausible, and it offers tools for researchers to formulate counterfactual statements as precisely as possible while still keeping them plausible.

The chapter concludes by situating the role of counterfactual analysis within the broader range of methodological and analytic tools discussed in this book. Counterfactual analysis is crucial to the study of all aspects of causality, including the causal chain that connects X and Y. At the same time, counterfactual analysis depends on other methodological tools, including the set-theoretic tests discussed in the previous chapter.

Types of Counterfactuals

This section develops two typologies of counterfactuals that are essential for the effective employment of counterfactual analysis in the social sciences. The first typology concerns the *types of counterfactual cases* that provide the most leverage for the assessment of causal necessity versus causal sufficiency. The second typology concerns the *types of counterfactual propositions* that are used in the analysis of different kinds of causes in case-study research.

CAUSE-VARYING AND CONTEXT-VARYING COUNTERFACTUAL CASES

Two kinds of counterfactual cases are used in causal analysis. *Cause-varying counterfactual cases* introduce a change to a potential causal factor in order to assess the extent to which that factor is necessary for an outcome. *Context-varying counterfactual cases* introduce a change to a particular aspect of context in order to assess the extent to which a potential causal factor is sufficient for an outcome.

These two types of counterfactual cases are studied in order to address problems associated with learning about causal necessity and sufficiency in case-study research. The standard set-theoretic tools for determining the extent to which X is necessary and sufficient for Y require a medium to large number of actual cases (Ragin 2008: chap. 3; Schneider and Wagemann 2012: chap. 5). In case-study research, however, analysts cannot directly use these tools, because they are analyzing a single actual case. The X and Y scores for the one actual case under study are normally $X = 1$ and $Y = 1$, which is consistent with both necessity and sufficiency. However, the researcher does not know what would have happened with respect to membership in Y if the case (1) did not have membership in X, or (2) did not have membership in a particular contextual condition.

To estimate the extent to which X is necessary and sufficient for Y, the analyst carries out the counterfactual analysis of one or more carefully selected *non-actual cases*. The specific type of counterfactual case that is needed depends on whether the analyst is studying causal necessity or causal sufficiency.

To assess causal necessity, the analyst constructs one or more non-actual cases in which membership in the causal factor of interest X is replaced with membership in a specific version of ~X. The analyst holds constant all else regarding membership in contextual and circumstantial categories, except for the changes needed to arrive at the specific version of ~X. Some versions of ~X require fewer revisions to history than others; these counterfactual cases are *more proximate* to the actual world. In the assessment of causal importance, X is *more necessary* for Y to the degree that proximate possible cases are consistent with necessity. A possible case is *consistent* with necessity when a particular version of ~X is not followed by the outcome of interest (i.e., cases in which $X = 0$ and $Y = 0$ are consistent with necessity). A possible case is *inconsistent* with necessity when a particular version of ~X is followed by the outcome of interest (i.e., cases in which $X = 0$ and $Y = 1$ are inconsistent with necessity). These inconsistent counterfactual cases, in which $X = 0$ and $Y = 1$, violate the proposition that X is required for Y. When assessing *the degree to which X is necessary* for Y, one uses the tools of critical event analysis to estimate the size of the change to the actual world that is needed to create these $X = 0$ and $Y = 1$ cases (see chapter 10 on the development of these tools).

To estimate causal sufficiency, the analyst constructs possible cases by holding membership in X constant (identical to the actual world) but introducing changes to membership in individual aspects of context and circumstance. The aspects of context for which case membership is changed correspond to theoretically relevant conditions that are potentially necessary for the outcome (on the identification of theoretically relevant conditions, see chapter 10). Under this approach, X is more sufficient for Y to the degree that proximate possible cases with changed membership in an aspect of context are consistent with sufficiency. A possible case is *consistent* with sufficiency when a case with X in a changed context is followed by the outcome of interest (i.e., cases in which $X = 1$ and $Y = 1$ are consistent with sufficiency). A possible case is *inconsistent* with sufficiency when a case with X in a changed context is not followed by the outcome of interest (i.e., cases in which $X = 1$ and $Y = 0$ are inconsistent with sufficiency). These inconsistent counterfactual cases, in which $X = 1$ and $Y = 0$, violate the proposition that membership in X assures membership in Y. When assessing *the degree to which X is sufficient* for Y, one uses, again, the tools of critical event analysis to estimate the size of the change to context that is needed to create these $X = 1$ and $Y = 0$ cases.

Cause-varying counterfactual cases are the main focus of the best literature on counterfactual analysis in political science, sociology, and psychology (Fearon 1991, 1996; Harvey 2012, 2015; Lebow 2010; Levy 2008, 2015; Tetlock and Belkin 1996b; Tetlock and Parker 2006). These counterfactual cases are closely connected to the study of necessary conditions (Goertz and Levy 2007b). When one asserts that Y would not have occurred but for X, one is making a counterfactual statement about the necessity of X for Y. This kind of case is the starting point for modern counterfactual theories of causality (Rubin 1974; Holland 1986; Morgan and Winship 2015), including Lewis's (1986b) original counterfactual definition of causality. Because cause-varying counterfactual cases must be close to the actual world to be useful, they typically involve contingent events as causes; a case's membership in a contingent event can be changed without radically rewriting history. Below, we shall explore this connection between cause-varying counterfactual cases, causal necessity, and causal contingency.

The use of context-varying counterfactual cases for the study of sufficiency helps address some of the problems that arise when a large event is proposed to be a cause. For example, structural theories of international wars propose macro causal factors related to the balance of power in the international system. One might argue that the actual world's membership in *breakdown in the balance of international power* was an important cause of its membership in *World War II*. Counterfactual analysis is not directly useful for assessing the necessity effects of this causal factor, because its counterfactual removal requires a massive historical rewrite. However, researchers can engage in the counterfactual analysis of the sufficiency effects of *breakdown in the balance of international power* by altering individual aspects of context and exploring whether the world still ends up with membership in *World War II*. For instance, one might create a more proximate case that retains membership in *breakdown in the balance of international power* but that has Hitler dying during World War I (cf. Rosenfeld 2005). The question would then be whether the world still ends up with membership in *World War II*. If so, one could use this context-varying counterfactual case as evidence for the sufficiency effects of *breakdown in the balance of international power* for *World War II*.

In short, the two types of counterfactual cases used for causal assessment in case-study research are (1) cause-varying counterfactual cases, which change membership in X but hold constant membership in contextual conditions; and (2) context-varying counterfactual cases, which hold constant membership in X but change membership in a specific contextual condition. The former type of counterfactual case is used for the assessment of causal necessity, whereas the latter type is used for the assessment of causal sufficiency. The literature on counterfactual analysis mainly considers counterfactuals that are relevant to the study of necessity. However, counterfactuals for the study of sufficiency are equally important.

CAUSAL TYPES AND COUNTERFACTUAL PROPOSITIONS

Counterfactuals can be linked to any of the five logical conditions discussed in this book. However, propositions involving necessary conditions and SUIN conditions provide the most traction for counterfactual analysis. These propositions are useful because they hold that the alteration of membership in the antecedent condition can or must change membership in the outcome. By contrast, sufficient conditions and INUS conditions are associated with less useful counterfactuals, because the alteration of membership in these conditions does not yield a change in membership in the outcome.

One type of counterfactual proposes that if a case had not had membership in a particular antecedent category, then it would not have had membership in a particular outcome category (Levy 2008: 629; see also Weber 1949; Lewis 1973). For example, consider the following statement: Without membership in the category *strong bourgeoisie*, England would not have had membership in the category *democratic route to modernity* (cf. Moore 1966: 418; see the discussion in the appendix to chapter 4). Following Goertz and Levy (2007a: 9–10), we use the label *necessary condition counterfactual* to designate counterfactuals that are derived from propositions that assume that membership in an actual world antecedent set is essential for membership in an outcome set. The corresponding counterfactuals require that membership in the negated antecedent is sufficient for membership in the negated outcome.

Figure 5.1 depicts a necessary condition counterfactual, showing how a case must first acquire membership in set X (*strong bourgeoisie*) to obtain subsequent membership in set Y (*democracy*). A case that is a member of set $\sim X$ (*not–strong bourgeoisie*) is ensured subsequent membership in set $\sim Y$ (*not–democracy*). This logic underlies Moore's famous maxim "no bourgeoisie, no democracy" (1966: 418). The figure illustrates this relationship in two ways. Figure 5.1a presents separate set diagrams for the outcomes Y and $\sim Y$. By contrast, figure 5.1b includes both outcomes in a single diagram and adds a temporal component, offering a vivid presentation of the logic of Moore's maxim.

With a valid necessary condition counterfactual, the set for the actual world antecedent (set X) will always be larger than the set for the actual world outcome (set Y). A core implication is that a necessary condition counterfactual proposes that a higher proportion of possible cases lack membership in the outcome category than in the cause category. In the context of Moore's research, the implication is that a possible case in which democracy does not occur in England is closer to the actual world than a possible case in which England lacks a strong bourgeoisie. No possible Englands exist that have membership in *democracy* without also having membership in *strong bourgeoisie*, although some possible Englands do have membership in both *not-democracy* and *strong bourgeoisie*. Under the same logic, consider the counterfactual "If George W. Bush had not been elected president in 2000, the United States would not have invaded Iraq." If this counterfactual is valid, the non-actual event in which the Iraq invasion does not occur is closer to the actual world than the non-actual event in which Bush does not win the election. No possible cases exist in which Bush is not elected and the invasion occurs; however, possible cases do exist in which Bush is elected and the invasion does not occur.

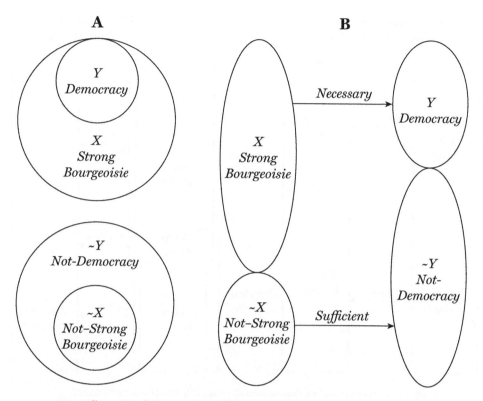

FIGURE 5.1. Illustration of a Necessary Condition Counterfactual

The set *George W. Bush is not elected president* is not equal to the set *Al Gore is elected president*. Rather, the latter is a subset of the former. Thus, the following two counterfactual statements are not identical:

C1. If George W. Bush had not been elected president, the United States would not have invaded Iraq.

C2. If Al Gore had been elected president, the United States would not have invaded Iraq.

The first statement (C1) is a necessary condition counterfactual. When formulated and analyzed as a set-theoretic proposition, this statement implies that membership in the category *George W. Bush is elected president* is a necessary condition for membership in the category *United States invades Iraq*; equivalently, the absence of membership in *George W. Bush is elected president* is a sufficient condition for the absence of membership in *United States invades Iraq*. By contrast, the second statement (C2) is not, strictly speaking, a necessary condition counterfactual; it does not state or imply that the actual world

**Necessary Condition
Counterfactual (C1)**

**SUIN Condition
Counterfactual (C2)**

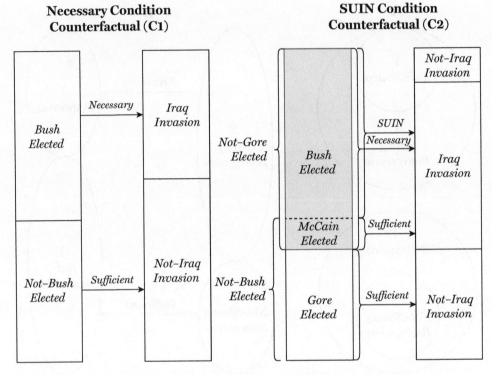

FIGURE 5.2. Necessary Condition Counterfactual versus SUIN Condition Counterfactual

antecedent is necessary for the outcome. If analyzed set-theoretically, this statement suggests that membership in *Al Gore is elected president* is *sufficient* for membership in *United States does not invade Iraq*. However, C2 does not suggest or imply that membership in *Bush is elected* is necessary for membership in *United States invades Iraq*. It allows for membership in *United States invades Iraq* without prior membership in either *Bush is elected* or *Gore is elected*.

One must therefore distinguish between necessary condition counterfactuals and SUIN condition counterfactuals (see figure 5.2). A SUIN condition is a *sufficient* but *unnecessary* part of a factor that is *insufficient* but *necessary* for an outcome (see chapter 3 for an explanation of SUIN conditions). With a SUIN condition, one analyzes an individually sufficient constitutive attribute of a necessary condition. For example, the appropriate set-theoretic reading of C2 is that *Bush is elected* is a SUIN condition for *United States invades Iraq*. We know this because in the statement, membership in *Gore is not elected* is a necessary condition for membership in *United States invades Iraq*. Membership in *Bush is elected* is sufficient (but not necessary) for membership in *Gore is not elected*.

A necessary condition counterfactual and a SUIN condition counterfactual are related, but they differ in important ways. A necessary condition counterfactual embodies two logically equivalent propositions: (1) membership in the specific actual world antecedent is necessary for membership in the actual world outcome, and (2) membership in the negation of the actual world antecedent is sufficient for membership in the negation of the actual world outcome. By contrast, a SUIN condition counterfactual *does not entail any necessity claim*; it only embodies a sufficiency claim about a specific negated antecedent. The sufficiency claim concerns *one subset* of the negated antecedent. For instance, if event X had not occurred in one specific way, then event Y would not have occurred; but if event X had not occurred in another way, event Y would still have occurred.

Figure 5.2 illustrates the difference between the two counterfactuals. The first diagram shows a standard necessary condition counterfactual. In the second one, the actual world antecedent is a SUIN condition. The SUIN condition counterfactual allows for the following statements: (1) membership in the category *Al Gore is elected president* is sufficient for membership in the category *United States does not invade Iraq*; and (2) membership in the category *John McCain is elected president* is sufficient for membership in the category *United States invades Iraq*. This example contains two different subsets of *George W. Bush is not elected president*, one of which is sufficient for the non-invasion set and the other of which is sufficient for the invasion set. SUIN condition counterfactual statements propose that membership in at least one subset of the negated antecedent condition is sufficient for membership in the negated outcome, whereas membership in other subsets of the negated antecedent condition is sufficient for membership in the actual world outcome.

Both necessary condition and SUIN condition counterfactuals are useful, because they must (necessary condition) or can (SUIN condition) reference counterfactual antecedents that change the actual world outcome. Whether scholars formulate one type rather than the other depends on whether they are interested in evaluating all versions of the negated antecedent or one specific version. For various reasons, including data availability, existing theory, and normative considerations, an analyst may wish to explore one specific way in which the antecedent could be negated, yielding a SUIN condition counterfactual. In other instances, a necessary condition counterfactual may seem more appropriate—e.g., if the antecedent set is dichotomous, if one subset of the antecedent set is nearly necessary and sufficient for the antecedent set, or if one believes that membership in the actual antecedent was indeed necessary for the actual outcome.

Assertions about conditions that are sufficient for outcomes create problems for counterfactual analysis (Goertz and Levy 2007a: 19–23).[1] The core difficulty is that a sufficient condition yields a counterfactual in which the outcome remains the same. When membership in an antecedent category is sufficient but not necessary for membership in an outcome, then membership in at least one other category or combination is also sufficient for the same outcome. Membership in the actual world outcome is *overdetermined* (cf. Przeworski and Teune 1970); the outcome remains inevitable, even in the absence of membership in a particular category that is sufficient for the outcome (Koivu 2016).

Ceteris paribus, the removal of an individual sufficient condition will not generate a change in outcome, because at least one other condition (or combination of conditions) is still sufficient for the outcome. Thus, with a sufficient condition, one can formulate a sufficient condition counterfactual that proposes, "Even if Bush had not been elected, the Iraq invasion would still have occurred." However, the ceteris paribus clause, requiring that all other conditions remain the same, may not apply or may not even be possible. Specifically, the introduction of the counterfactual antecedent ($\sim X$) may require additional changes to the case that have the effect of removing other sufficient conditions, such that the outcome is possible. Hence, an alternative way of expressing a sufficient condition counterfactual is to emphasize the enabling effect of $\sim X$ on $\sim Y$ (Koivu 2016)—for example, "If Bush had not been elected, the Iraq invasion may have been avoidable."

Finally, one may believe that membership in the category *Bush is elected* contributed as much as anything else to the invasion, even though membership in this category was, by itself, neither necessary nor sufficient for membership in *United States invades Iraq*. Here the assumption is that Bush's election was an important INUS cause: it combined with one or more other events to produce at least one combination of factors that was sufficient for the overdetermined invasion.

If a case lacks membership in one category that is an INUS condition, the case may still, ceteris paribus, have membership in the outcome category.[2] To produce non-membership in the outcome category, the case must lack membership in at least one condition from each sufficiency combination. The relative difficulty of applying cause-varying counterfactual analysis with INUS conditions depends on the number of sufficiency combinations (i.e., the extent of equifinality) and the degree to which individual INUS conditions approximate being necessary conditions (i.e., the degree to which individual INUS conditions appear in multiple sufficiency combinations). For example, if only two pathways exist to *United States invades Iraq*, the analyst can develop a relatively parsimonious counterfactual statement by negating membership in one INUS condition in each of the two combinations. The resulting counterfactual would change the outcome. But if there are many pathways to the outcome and most of them are constituted by non-recurring INUS conditions, then one must

TABLE 5.1. Types of Counterfactual Statements in Case-Study Research

	Status of Actual Antecedent (X) for Actual Outcome (Y)	Status of Counterfactual Antecedent ($\sim X$ or A) for Negated Outcome ($\sim Y$)	Example
Necessary Condition Counterfactual	Necessary $X \& Z \rightarrow Y$	Sufficient $\sim X \vee \sim Z \rightarrow \sim Y$	If George W. Bush had not been elected president ($\sim X$), the United States would not have invaded Iraq ($\sim Y$).
SUIN Condition Counterfactual	SUIN $\sim A \& B \rightarrow Y;$ $X \vee \sim Z \rightarrow \sim A$	Sufficient $A \vee \sim B \rightarrow \sim Y$	If Al Gore had been elected president (A), the United States would not have invaded Iraq ($\sim Y$).
Sufficient Condition Counterfactual	Sufficient $X \vee Z \rightarrow Y$	Necessary $\sim X \& \sim Z \rightarrow \sim Y$	Even if George W. Bush had not been elected president ($\sim X$), the United States still would have invaded Iraq (Y) provided other conditions (Z) were still in place.
INUS Condition Counterfactual	INUS $(X \& B) \vee Z \rightarrow Y$	INUS $\sim Z \& (\sim X \vee \sim B) \rightarrow \sim Y$	Even if George W. Bush had not been elected president ($\sim X$), the United States still would have invaded Iraq (Y) provided other conditions (Z) were still in place.

Note: The symbol & is the logical AND, $\vee$ is the logical OR, and $\rightarrow$ is sufficiency. Y is *United States invades Iraq*, X is *Bush is elected president*, A is *Gore is elected president*, and Z and B are unspecified events or conditions.

negate membership in many categories in order to negate membership in the outcome.

Table 5.1 provides a summary of the preceding discussion. The table shows that the different kinds of counterfactuals derive their names from the logical status of the actual world antecedent condition. The examples underscore why propositions about necessary conditions and SUIN conditions lend themselves to cause-varying counterfactuals: these propositions allow for counterfactual statements in which the negation of the cause produces a change in the outcome. The examples also suggest why sufficient condition and INUS condition counterfactuals are less useful in the social sciences: they require the analyst to negate the actual world's membership in multiple categories in order to generate a counterfactual proposition in which the outcome must change.

The Minimal-Rewrite Rule

The minimal-rewrite rule holds that the most useful counterfactuals are those that require the fewest changes to the actual world (Tetlock and Belkin 1996a: 23–25; see also Weber 1949: 180–84). Intuitively, "miracle" counterfactuals, whose antecedents require massive changes to history, seem problematic or even absurd. An example of a miracle counterfactual is, "If Napoleon had had nuclear weapons, the French Empire would have expanded across the globe." While the counterfactual may be true, the implausibility of its antecedent renders it unhelpful for the purposes of scientific inference. A set-theoretic approach helps to show why this is so, by making explicit the logic underpinning the minimal-rewrite rule.

In the following discussion, we focus mostly on the application of the minimal-rewrite rule to cause-varying necessary condition counterfactuals. However, as we briefly discuss, this rule also applies to context-varying sufficient condition counterfactuals.

PLAUSIBILITY, ENABLING COUNTERFACTUALS, AND CONTINGENT EVENTS

Minimal-rewrite, or *plausible*, counterfactuals are preferred to *maximal-rewrite*, or *miracle*, counterfactuals in part because changing membership in an antecedent condition requires changing membership in other conditions in the world, including categories prior to the antecedent condition itself. If the changes in category membership required to bring about membership in a counterfactual antecedent are massive or implausible, the researcher may be unable to use counterfactual analysis to effectively assess a proposition. One cannot sustain the primary counterfactual of interest without specifying the "enabling counterfactuals" (Lebow 2010: 51–57; see also Goodman 1947: 117–21) that are requisite for membership in the counterfactual antecedent. For example, in order to achieve membership in the counterfactual antecedent *Al Gore is elected*, one must specify enabling counterfactuals, such as *several hundred voters in Florida decide to vote for Gore rather than Bush*. In addition, this counterfactual requires other enabling counterfactuals that connect a Gore victory to membership in the outcome *United States does not invade Iraq*. To sustain the tenability of the primary counterfactual of interest, these enabling counterfactuals before and after the counterfactual antecedent must themselves be plausible. Hence, the minimal-rewrite rule applies not only to the primary counterfactual antecedent, but also to its associated enabling counterfactuals.

The minimal-rewrite rule explains why small events, accidents, and discretionary choices yield plausible counterfactuals. With these contingent occurrences, one can construct a possible case that lacks membership in event *X* but that is otherwise quite similar to the actual world. As an illustration of more maximal and more minimal rewrites, consider the two different necessary conditions that Soifer (2015) identifies to explain Chile's membership in *strong state apparatus*: (1) *highly centralized urban population,* and (2) *deployment of competent officials from the center to the peripheries to execute state-building projects.* Of the two categories, the latter is associated with a more minimal-rewrite counterfactual: it is easier to reconstruct Chilean history so that the case lacks membership in *deployment of competent officials.* By contrast, the counterfactual attached to the former condition requires a more maximal rewrite: many historical and geographical features would have to change to create a Chile that lacks membership in *highly centralized urban population.*

Membership in the counterfactual category *Gore is elected president* is plausible because the actual vote was so close; it is relatively easy to envision a different vote total in Florida. Contingent events such as an assassination, an individual policy choice, the outcome of a specific military battle, or a natural disaster are often used to create plausible counterfactuals. Empirical illustrations of path dependence, such as the adoption of the QWERTY keyboard format or the choice of post-independence stabilization strategy in African countries (see chapter 11 for a discussion of these examples), invoke early contingent historical events that could have easily turned out differently. Critical event analyses often focus on choices and agency for which one can readily imagine a case's having membership in a different category at a key historical moment. The correspondence between small or contingent events and plausible counterfactuals directs historical explanations toward singular events and idiographic causes, as opposed to factors and variables associated with more general theories (Levy 2015). Likewise, the quest to find plausible counterfactuals may lead one to emphasize contingent choice and agency, rather than structure.

It does not follow from this discussion that counterfactual analysis always leads scholars to emphasize the importance of contingent events as causes. First, the results of a counterfactual analysis need not lead to the conclusion that small events are the decisive causal movers in history. It is quite possible that a counterfactual that posits a small event as an antecedent will be deemed false upon investigation. For example, Harvey's (2012) rigorous analysis of the Gore counterfactual (discussed later in this chapter) leads him to the conclusion that the invasion of Iraq was more plausible than not under a Gore presidency. His analysis points to the causal power of historical and situational forces that favored membership in this outcome, regardless of whether the actual world had membership in *Gore is elected* or *Bush is elected.* When initially plausible counterfactuals are deemed dubious or incorrect, one may conclude that large events, structure, history, and impersonal situational forces carry the explanatory day.

Second, the counterfactual antecedent under consideration may be a contingent aspect of context in which a structural cause of interest operates. For example, in an explanation of the U.S. invasion of Iraq, the main causal factor under study may be *liberal expansionism in a unipolar world*. To test the proposition that this causal factor is sufficient for *United States invades Iraq*, the researcher would explore whether liberal expansionism still generates the war in a context in which Gore is elected. If the war still occurs under a Gore presidency, the proposition has passed a relatively difficult test. The upshot is that the minimal-rewrite rule may require that the analyst alter a contingent aspect of a case for the purposes of analysis. However, it does not follow that the analyst must treat that contingent condition as the main causal factor. Instead, the counterfactual antecedent may be one aspect of the context in which a non-contingent causal factor occurs and unfolds.

SET THEORY AND MINIMAL REWRITES

The tools of set theory provide a basis, grounded in logic, for understanding why contingent events can offer plausible antecedents in counterfactual explanations. Figure 5.3 illustrates two necessary condition relationships. In both cases, X is a superset of Y (and thus a necessary condition for Y). With a non-contingent antecedent, however (in the diagram on the left), X is a large superset in relation to Y; there are many possible cases with membership in X but not in Y. Membership in X is necessary for membership in Y, but it does not come close to also being sufficient. With a contingent antecedent, by contrast (in the diagram on the right), X not only is a superset of Y, but comes close to perfectly overlapping with Y. Nearly all possible cases with membership in X are also cases with membership in Y. Said differently, relatively few possible cases exist with membership in X but not in Y.

The *utility* of a necessary condition counterfactual varies depending on whether X is a large or a small superset in relation to Y. A *trivial counterfactual* employs a necessary condition antecedent X that is a very large superset of Y, such that the vast majority of possible cases have membership in X but not in Y. For example, as illustrated in figure 5.4, the following counterfactual is trivial: "If George W. Bush had not been elected president, the United States would not have invaded Iraq at sunrise on March 20, 2003." The trivialness in this example is related to the specificity of the outcome: the outcome is so specific that nearly all *not–Bush elected* cases lack membership in the outcome set. When the outcome is a very small set, a necessary

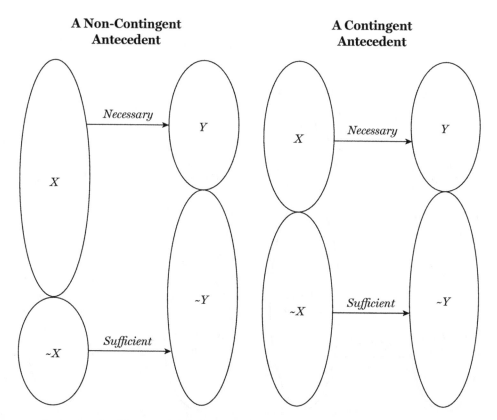

A Non-Contingent Antecedent

A Contingent Antecedent

FIGURE 5.3. Small Events and Plausible Counterfactuals

condition counterfactual can avoid trivialness only by referencing an actual world antecedent that is also a very small set (see the Rule of Causal Contingency in chapter 10).

A necessary condition counterfactual becomes more important to the degree that the actual world antecedent approximates a sufficient condition as well as a necessary condition (cf. Goertz 2006a; Hart and Honoré 1985; Ragin 2008; Schneider and Wagemann 2012). With an *important* necessary condition counterfactual, it is difficult to construct a possible case with membership in the outcome but not in the actual antecedent. For instance, the counterfactual holding that membership in the *not–Bush elected* set would have led to membership in the *not–Iraq invasion* set is logically more important to the extent that membership in the *Bush elected* set nearly ensured (i.e., was sufficient for) membership in the *Iraq invasion* set. The upshot is that when two necessary conditions for a given outcome are proposed, one can often say something about their relative importance by using counterfactual

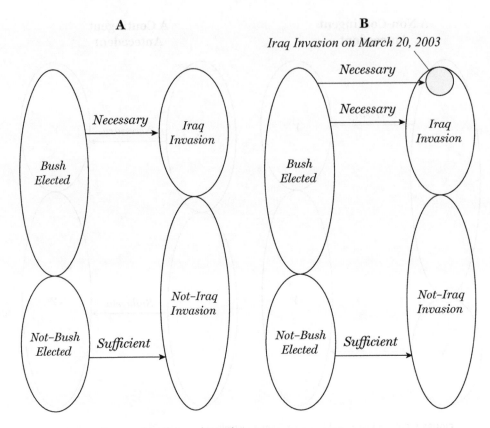

A

B
Iraq Invasion on March 20, 2003

FIGURE 5.4. Outcome Specificity and Trivialness

analysis. In particular, if one necessary condition entails a minimal rewrite and the other entails a more considerable rewrite, then the former is a more important cause.

THE END OF THE COLD WAR

As an illustration of how counterfactual analysis can be used to assess causal importance, consider the debate between Robert English (2007) and Stephen Brooks and William Wohlforth (2007a, 2007b) about the causes of the end of the Cold War. English asserts that materialist factors, in particular the long-term economic decline in the Soviet Union, "were a necessary but clearly insufficient condition for the Cold War's peaceful end" (p. 239). He argues that ideational factors—especially Gorbachev and "new thinking"—were also necessary for Soviet retrenchment. As he points out, "Whatever one believes about the old thinkers' acquiescence in Gorbachev's initiatives, it remains inconceivable that they would have launched similar initiatives without him"

(p. 245). English suggests that ideational factors were more important than materialist factors because the former "developed and operated independent of material pressures" (p. 249).

Brooks and Wohlforth initially do not deny that ideational factors may have been a necessary ingredient (2007b: 196). However, they argue that ideational factors were not decisive causes—that they mainly shaped the specific form of retrenchment, rather than determining whether or not it occurred. Brooks and Wohlforth contend that materialist factors, especially the long-term economic decline in the Soviet Union, were more important causes of the retrenchment. "We found that the Soviet Union's declining material fortunes was the key factor that made the new thinkers' ideas saleable to those skeptical of retrenchment" (2007a: 263). They argue that "the Soviets reoriented their foreign policy in large part in response to changing material incentives" and point out that "many of the basic causal mechanisms that are featured in ideational models of this case are to a significant degree endogenous to material changes" (2007b: 200, 235).

Figure 5.5 offers a stylized reconstruction of Brooks and Wohlforth's argument from a set-theoretic perspective. The diagram is intended to represent the logic underpinning these authors' view that ideational factors are endogenous to material factors, and thus that the connection between *new thinking* and *end of the Cold War* is less important than the connection between *Soviet economic decline* and *end of the Cold War*. In the figure, both *Soviet economic decline* and *new thinking* are necessary for *end of the Cold War*. However, *Soviet economic decline* is the more important necessary cause for this outcome, because it is closer to also being a sufficient cause.

Although English allows that *Soviet economic decline* may have been necessary for *new thinking*, he argues that it was not close to being sufficient. He regards other causal factors—such as Gorbachev's personality, the fast pace of events, public opinion, and weaknesses among hardliners—as more important in allowing for *new thinking* (2007: 253). He suggests, moreover, that when compared to material factors, *new thinking* is the more important cause of *end of the Cold War*. Figure 5.6 illustrates the set-theoretic logic of this argument. Here, both causes are again necessary for *end of the Cold War*, but *new thinking* comes closer to also being sufficient. *New thinking* is now the more important of the two necessary causes.

The question arises: How can we know which necessary cause (*Soviet economic decline* or *new thinking*) is more important? How can we know which depiction—figure 5.5 or figure 5.6—is closer to approximating the truth?

These questions can be addressed using comparative counterfactual analysis (Harvey 2015). Specifically, one can compare the plausibility of the counterfactual claims assumed by the two arguments in light of the extent of changes they require to the actual world. In support of English's argument, one can

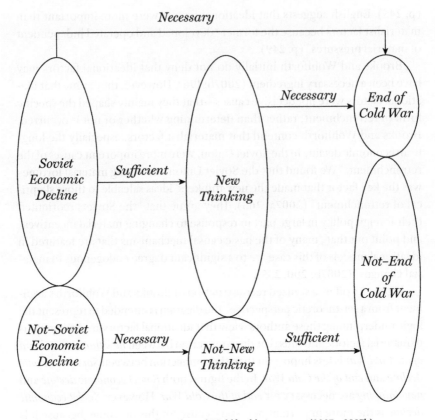

FIGURE 5.5. Stylized Summary of Brooks and Wohlforth's Argument (2007a, 2007b)

argue that a possible world without Gorbachev and new thinking is closer to the actual world than a possible world without Soviet economic decline. While one can formulate minimal-rewrite scenarios in which Gorbachev does not come to power, it is difficult to do the same for scenarios in which the Soviet Union does not decline economically. Thus, a comparative counterfactual argument using the minimal-rewrite rule suggests that the true relationship more likely follows the set diagram in figure 5.6 than the one in figure 5.5. In figure 5.6, *new thinking* is a contingent event, as indicated by the fact that its set is smaller than the *not–new thinking* set. By contrast, *Soviet economic decline* is an expected event, as indicated by the larger size of its set in comparison with its negation. On this basis, English has the upper hand in the debate, because *new thinking* appears to be the more important of these two necessary causes for membership in *end of the Cold War*.

In response, however, Brooks and Wohlforth might argue that *new thinking* was actually *not* a necessary cause of *end of the Cold War*. In a rebuttal to English, they stress that their argument is best understood probabilistically,

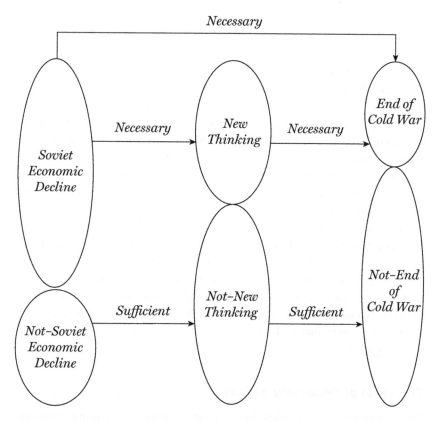

FIGURE 5.6. Stylized Summary of English's Argument (2007)

rather than deterministically (2007a: 266–68). Their rebuttal suggests that they believe that the causes of *end of the Cold War* were INUS causes, each one contributing nonessentially to the outcome. One can assess the relative importance of the two or more INUS causes—such as *Soviet economic decline* and *new thinking* in this example—on the basis of the degree to which they approximate being necessary and sufficient for the outcome. To estimate the sufficiency effects of an INUS condition, one can ask about the other causes that must combine with the INUS condition to produce the outcome. If these causes are common, then the INUS condition exerts substantial sufficiency effects. But if the INUS condition must combine with rare or unusual conditions to generate the outcome, then its sufficiency effects are modest. In this example, it seems reasonable to assume that *Soviet economic decline* needs to combine with relatively small additional causes to produce membership in the outcome, whereas *new thinking* needs to combine with many important structural causes to do so. On this basis, one may conclude that materialist factors are the more important INUS cause: these factors nearly produce outcome membership by themselves (i.e., they are nearly sufficient), whereas ideational factors require the presence of additional and more uncommon causal factors.

The implication of this analysis is that the debate over the end of the Cold War depends heavily on the specific causal claims of the authors involved. If both *Soviet economic decline* and *new thinking* exert mainly necessity effects, then comparative counterfactual analysis suggests that English has the upper hand in the debate: Gorbachev and new thinking are associated with a more plausible counterfactual argument. By contrast, if *Soviet economic decline* and *new thinking* exert primarily sufficiency effects, then Brooks and Wohlforth have the stronger argument: materialist factors come closer to sufficiency than ideational factors.

A more general point about comparative counterfactual analysis follows. A comparative analysis of two necessary condition counterfactuals will tend to favor small events and contingent happenings. By contrast, a comparative analysis of two INUS condition counterfactuals will tend to favor more generalizable, less contingent causal factors. Opposite findings about relative causal importance can emerge depending on whether one believes the actual world antecedents run primarily through necessity or primarily through sufficiency for the outcome of interest.

The Level of Generality of Events

The *level of generality* at which the events in a counterfactual proposition are formulated is linked to (1) the precision of the counterfactual proposition, and (2) the causal importance of the antecedent condition of the counterfactual proposition.

First, the *precision* of a counterfactual proposition increases as the events it proposes are cast in more specific forms. The most precise counterfactuals are those that reference highly detailed particular events. However, as a given counterfactual statement becomes more precise, it also becomes less plausible (cf. Elster 1978; Levy 2015). This trade-off between precision and plausibility can be neatly explicated and illustrated using set-theoretic tools.

Second, the *causal importance* of the antecedent condition in a counterfactual proposition increases to the extent that the antecedent and outcome have a similar level of generality (see the Rule of Causal Contingency in chapter 10). The most important SUIN condition counterfactuals have antecedents that are nearly an equal set with the outcome; the most important necessary condition counterfactuals have antecedents that are only slightly less general than their outcomes; and the most important INUS condition counterfactuals have antecedents that are part of a sufficiency combination that is only slightly less specific than the outcome.

PRECISION

Counterfactuals can be formulated in ways that are more precise or less precise. Consider, for example, the following two counterfactuals (cf. Lebow 2007):

C3. If Franz Ferdinand had not been assassinated, World War I would not have occurred.

C4. If no assassination attempt had been made against Franz Ferdinand, World War I would not have occurred.

C4 is more precise than C3 because it refers to a more specific (less general) counterfactual antecedent. C4 is a specific way in which Franz Ferdinand might have been not assassinated; it is one possible instantiation of C3. In set-theoretic terms, the antecedent of C4 is a subset of the antecedent of C3. This relationship is illustrated in figure 5.7.

Counterfactual statements can always be made more precise by reconceptualizing their events in more specific terms. If a historical event is conceptualized at a more specific level of generality, a smaller proportion of all possible cases are contained within that event. Consider the following counterfactuals:

C5. If Franz Ferdinand had not been assassinated, World War I would not have occurred.

C6. If Franz Ferdinand had not been assassinated, fewer than 10,000 combatants would have died in interstate combat among the great powers between 1914 and 1918.

Both counterfactuals reference non-actual outcomes, but C6 is more precise. Its counterfactual outcome refers to a more specific historical event containing fewer possible cases. C6 is one possible instantiation of C5; it is a subset of C5.

Researchers can make counterfactuals more precise by clarifying the characteristics of events and providing more detail. Consider the following two counterfactuals:

C7. If Franz Ferdinand had not been assassinated, fewer than 10,000 combatants would have died in interstate combat among the great powers between 1914 and 1918.

C8. If Franz Ferdinand had not been assassinated, fewer than 10,000 combatants would have died in interstate combat among the great powers (i.e., Austria-Hungary, Great Britain, France, Germany, the Ottoman Empire, Russia, and the United States) between 1914 and 1918.

C8 is more precise because it defines *great powers between 1914 and 1918*. The clarification delimits the states that constitute the great powers and eliminates

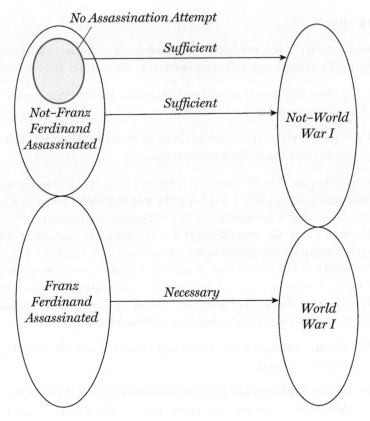

FIGURE 5.7. Cause Specificity and Trivialness

alternative possible definitions. For example, in the opinion of some scholars, Italy and Japan might be considered great powers; alternatively, some scholars would not regard the Ottoman Empire as a great power. C7 is ambiguous about the inclusion or exclusion of these states and therefore allows all reasonable definitions of *great powers*. Defining terms in a more specific and exacting way rules out some possibilities and makes a statement more precise.

One can also make a counterfactual more precise by replacing an unspecified non-event with a specific instantiation of the non-event. A non-event is characterized by the absence or negation of a positive event, such as *not–World War I* or *not–United States invades Iraq*. By transforming a vague non-event into a specific event, one develops a more precise counterfactual. For example, *conflict limited to a local war in Europe in which Russia, Germany, and Britain remain at peace* is a subset of *not–World War I*. Likewise, *military action limited to covert operations to assassinate Saddam Hussein* is a subset of *not–United States invades Iraq*. The more detail that is added to a specific event, the more precise the counterfactual becomes.

As the precision of a counterfactual is increased, however, the counterfactual becomes less plausible; precision and plausibility are inversely related (Elster 1978: 184; Levy 2015: 389). It is easier to imagine a world in which Franz Ferdinand is not assassinated than to imagine a world in which no assassination attempt occurs. The former counterfactual permits all instantiations of the latter plus additional possibilities: it permits an assassination attempt that fails, whereas the latter counterfactual does not. Likewise, it is more plausible to imagine a world in which World War I does not occur than a world in which fewer than 10,000 combatants die in hostilities between 1914 and 1918. The former scenario allows for possibilities (e.g., a local war in Europe that does not become a world war) that the latter does not.

Exactly where a researcher should draw the line between precision and plausibility will vary depending on the domain and the goals of the research. As a practical strategy, one may first assess a less precise, less detailed, and more plausible counterfactual. If the counterfactual is sustainable, it can be stated more precisely and reassessed in this less plausible form. By continuing this process, the researcher can work to determine how precisely the counterfactual can be formulated and still remain consistent with the evidence. More precise counterfactuals are preferred to less precise ones, but all counterfactuals will reach a point where additional precision renders them implausible and unsustainable.

CAUSAL IMPORTANCE

The level of generality of the events in a counterfactual is systematically related to the causal importance of the counterfactual antecedent under investigation. Causal importance increases to the degree that the counterfactual antecedent and the counterfactual outcome have the same level of generality (i.e., to the degree that they are equal sets). For instance, if the counterfactual outcome is a highly specific event, then its antecedent must also be highly specific in order to achieve maximum causal importance. As an illustration, consider the following two necessary condition counterfactual statements, as represented in figure 5.8:

C9. If pre-revolutionary Cuba and Nicaragua had not had authoritarian regimes, they would not have experienced political violence in the 1950s and 1970s, respectively.

C10. If pre-revolutionary Cuba and Nicaragua had not had authoritarian regimes, they would not have experienced social revolutions in the 1950s and 1970s, respectively.

Both counterfactuals treat membership in *authoritarian regime* as a necessary condition for membership in the outcomes (*political violence* in C9

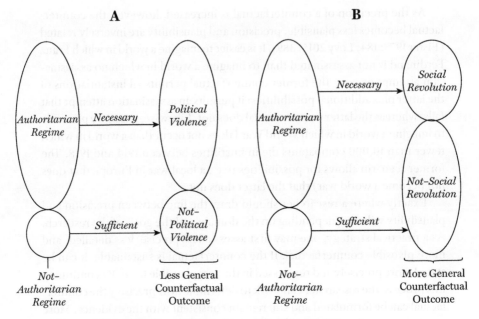

FIGURE 5.8. Relationship of Level of Generality and Causal Importance

and *social revolution* in C10). In both counterfactuals, membership in *not–authoritarian regime* is sufficient for the absence of membership in these outcomes. However, the counterfactual outcome in C9 (*not–political violence*) is a more specific category than the counterfactual outcome in C10 (*not–social revolution*): *not–political violence* is a subset of *not–social revolution*. Consequently, as figure 5.8 shows, the counterfactual antecedent in C9 comes closer to being both necessary and sufficient for its outcome.

As a general rule, with a necessary condition counterfactual, one can increase the causal importance of a counterfactual antecedent by (1) conceptualizing the counterfactual outcome in a more specific way, and/or (2) conceptualizing the counterfactual antecedent in a more general way. The risk one runs with such reconceptualizations, however, is that the effort to increase causal importance may render the counterfactual implausible or false. For instance, with the example above, membership in *not–authoritarian regime* would more plausibly have prevented membership in *social revolution* than in the more general category *political violence*.

While researchers seek both causal importance and plausibility, these goals stand in tension with one another, as illustrated in figure 5.9. It is easier to formulate a plausible counterfactual statement if the antecedent is a relatively trivial condition; it is more difficult if the antecedent is an important cause that approximates a necessary and sufficient condition.

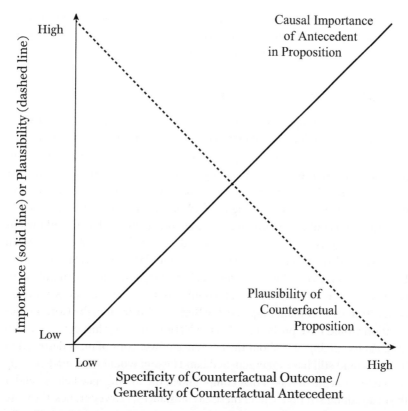

FIGURE 5.9. Relationship of the Specificity of Events to the Importance and Plausibility of Counterfactual Propositions

This section has considered the reasons for this trade-off and identified the ways in which scholars can shift the generality of events to manage the trade-off. Again, the rule for a necessary condition counterfactual is that as one increases the specificity of the antecedent and/or decreases the specificity of the outcome, the counterfactual proposition becomes less plausible but more important.

Counterfactual Causal Chains

Counterfactual assessment involves constructing both forward-looking and backtracking causal chains. With forward-looking causal chains, the analyst builds a counterfactual sequence that connects the non-actual antecedent to the outcome category. This sequence consists of causally connected and temporally ordered non-actual events. With backtracking causal chains, by contrast, the analyst treats the counterfactual antecedent as an outcome itself and looks back in history to identify its causes. The exercise of identifying a causal chain leading to the counterfactual antecedent helps the analyst determine the extent to which the minimal-rewrite rule can be applied to the antecedent.

FORWARD-LOOKING CAUSAL CHAINS

With forward-looking causal chains, the researcher develops the intermediary steps through which membership in a non-actual antecedent is connected in space and time to membership in an outcome. As an example, figure 5.10 presents a stylized summary of Harvey's (2012) analysis of the Gore–no war counterfactual. Harvey argues that if Gore had been elected president, Iraq would have been a central foreign policy preoccupation of his administration. He points out that Gore himself was a foreign policy hawk, and various evidence suggests he would have appointed a hawkish national security team (e.g., Richard Holbrooke was the leading candidate for secretary of state). Under this non-actual Gore presidency, Harvey argues, assertive multilateralism with a coercive military threat would have been carried out as a foreign policy strategy to contain Iraq. Like the Bush administration, the Gore administration would have pushed the United Nations to bring inspectors back to Iraq. Faulty intelligence about the existence of weapons of mass destruction in Iraq would still have emerged. Saddam Hussein would have made largely the same strategic mistakes that compounded the intelligence failures under the Bush administration. Under these circumstances, Harvey argues, the Gore administration would have sought support from Britain and other allies for military action against Iraq, with much of the U.S. public rallying around the flag in support. Harvey concludes that it is more plausible than not to believe that the United States would have attacked Iraq under a Gore presidency.

As figure 5.10 shows, the logic of this SUIN condition counterfactual argument can be cast as a sequence of increasingly important sufficient causes culminating in the Iraq War under a Gore presidency. For either a SUIN condition or a necessary condition counterfactual, the non-actual linking events in the counterfactual chain are sufficient conditions.[3] Each condition in the chain is sufficient for the next condition in the context of the case. "In the context of the case" is the stipulation that the counterfactual case is identical to the actual world except for any changes needed to bring about the starting counterfactual antecedent and any subsequent differences caused by that antecedent. Once an event in the counterfactual chain occurs, it becomes part of the background context for all subsequent events. By focusing on conditions that are sufficient in the context of the case, analysts can explore whether the counterfactual antecedent generates membership in the same outcome as in the actual world. If the non-actual antecedent leads to the same outcome, the researcher has

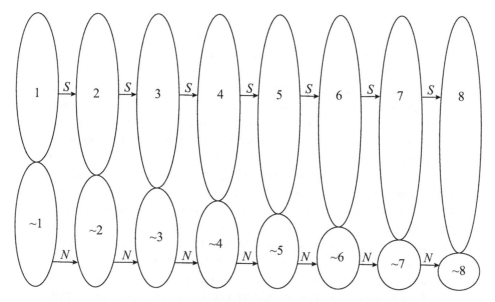

FIGURE 5.10. Stylized Summary of Harvey's Counterfactual Argument (2012). *S* stands for *sufficient*; *N* stands for *necessary*. 1 = Gore is elected president; 2 = Gore appoints hawkish national security team; 3 = Iraq is central foreign policy concern; 4 = UN inspectors are brought back to Iraq; 5 = faulty intelligence about WMDs; 6 = Hussein makes strategic mistakes; 7 = US assembles war coalition; 8 = US invades Iraq.

discovered important evidence that the SUIN or necessary condition proposition is false. The proposition has failed a necessity set-theoretic test.

In a counterfactual chain of sufficient conditions, each subsequent condition comes closer to being necessary as well as sufficient for the outcome (see the discussion of reactive sequences in chapter 11). This is illustrated in figure 5.10 by the fact that the circles for the events become larger over time. At the end of the sequence, the non-actual Gore administration's mobilization of a war coalition is nearly necessary and sufficient for the Iraq War. One could add further content to the causal chain by identifying additional intermediary events between any two conditions separated by a temporal gap. (Harvey's narrative is more sophisticated than this portrayal suggests.) For instance, one could add an additional step at the very end of the sequence—such as a category for the final decision to strike—that brings matters even closer to necessity as well as sufficiency. In addition, some counterfactual links in the chain are more important than others; the most important conditions come close to being necessary as well as sufficient for the next event. In Harvey's narrative, the link between Gore's election and the appointment of a hawkish national security team (sets 1 and 2 in figure 5.10) probably does a lot more explanatory work than the link between the appointment of the team and Iraq's being a central foreign policy concern (sets 2 and 3). In principle, one can diagram the relative importance of counterfactual events in a sufficiency chain by increasing the relative size of the more important counterfactual events (again, see chapter 11).

Each link in the counterfactual chain is a separate sufficiency proposition that could be true or false. Scholars must use set-theoretic tests (at least implicitly) to establish the validity of each link. The credibility of a given link can be examined by exploring the set-membership observations and set-theoretic generalizations that support it. For instance, Harvey supports the claim that a Gore administration would have pursued aggressive multilateralism by drawing on a large number of speeches and statements made by Gore and other likely members of his administration. These speeches and statements show that there was a strong consensus on the threat from Hussein and on the need to act aggressively, in consultation with U.S. allies. Harvey connects this information with implicit generalizations, such as that politicians and policymakers who adopt and maintain clear positions over long periods are likely to sustain those positions throughout their careers. The use of implicit rather than explicit generalizations is not necessarily a problem if the linkage between events is self-evident to the relevant audience (in Harvey's case, these are scholars, policymakers, and members of the educated public). However, if the linkage is not self-evidently true to this audience, a good counterfactual analysis should make explicit the generalizations on which important links in the causal chain depend.[4]

As another example, consider the debate between Jack Goldstone (2006) and Carla Gardina Pestana (2006). In Goldstone's argument, the survival of William of Orange despite being grazed by a bullet in the summer of 1690 is a necessary condition for membership in a series of major historical events, including the Glorious Revolution, the French Revolution, Newtonian science, the Industrial Revolution, and popular democracy in Europe. In her critique of this argument, Gardina Pestana disputes specific linkages in Goldstone's narrative. For instance, she argues that Goldstone's counterfactual analysis depends too heavily on generalizations about the capacity of a single individual—James II—to remake England as he pleased. If one disagrees with Goldstone's implicit generalization about James II's capacities, his counterfactual narrative can unravel: England does not become a semi-Catholic monarchy, France does not dominate Europe, and history is poised to follow a course similar to the one it actually followed.

A final word is in order about forward-looking causal chains that lead to outcomes that are spectacularly different from what happened in the actual world. A well-known example is Pascal's declaration that "had Cleopatra's nose been shorter, the whole face of the world would have changed." While such assertions emphasize the causal importance of contingent events, they depend on deterministic causal chains consisting of fully necessary conditions in the actual world and fully sufficient conditions in the counterfactual world. Upon careful scrutiny, one typically finds that specific links in these chains assume generalizations that cannot sustain this determinism. For instance, contra Pascal, a Cleopatra with a shorter nose may very well have remained a politically influential individual in Roman politics. The goal of counterfactual analysis in the social sciences is not to introduce a change into history and then speculate about what might have happened. Rather, good counterfactual analyses focus on a particular antecedent and a particular outcome, with the goal of carefully assessing a specific proposition.

BACKTRACKING CAUSAL CHAINS

Researchers formulate backtracking causal chains when they propose that certain non-actual events caused the counterfactual antecedent—i.e., they go back in history to construct the causal chain that leads to membership in the counterfactual antecedent. In doing so, they work to introduce only the changes to context that are required for membership in the counterfactual antecedent. If they are able to construct a causal chain that yields membership in the antecedent with only modest changes to the actual world, they conclude that the minimal-rewrite rule applies to the proposition of interest. However, if they cannot generate membership in the antecedent without large disruptions to theoretically important aspects of context, they conclude that the minimal-rewrite rule is violated.

In principle, many alternative explanations could be used to explain the occurrence of any given counterfactual antecedent. For example, with the antecedent *Gore is elected*, one could construct a causal chain in which Bush dies during the campaign and leaves Gore as the only candidate, who then is elected. Of the various possibilities, however, the researcher seeks the explanation that requires the fewest changes to the actual world in order to bring the antecedent into being. Scenarios in which unlikely events (e.g., Bush's unexpected death) generate the counterfactual antecedent are not considered. Instead, the researcher searches for a *contingent event* prior to the counterfactual antecedent that is approximately sufficient for its occurrence. The researcher goes backward in time looking specifically for a contingent historical event that can be changed and then connected to the main counterfactual antecedent via sufficiency links.

Consider Lebow's (2010) discussion of the non-assassination of Franz Ferdinand, which he argues would have blocked the occurrence of World War I. Lebow explicitly discusses possible causal chains that could have brought about this non-assassination. He stresses "how easy it would have been to avert Franz Ferdinand's assassination" with only slight and plausible changes to history (p. 60). For example, if Franz Ferdinand's cavalcade had followed its planned route, it would not have intersected with the location of Gavrilo Princip, the young assassin who happened to be in the right place at the right time to shoot the archduke. Lebow argues that this sufficiency causal chain (cavalcade follows correct route → Princip is not proximate to the cavalcade → Franz Ferdinand is not assassinated) is more plausible than what actually happened. The chain brings us to a counterfactual antecedent (Franz Ferdinand is not assassinated) in a possible world that is virtually identical to the actual world in all other respects.

With miracle counterfactual statements, by contrast, scholars cannot work backward to construct plausible causal chains that produce the proposed antecedent. Consider the miracle counterfactual "If Napoleon had had nuclear weapons, the French Empire would have expanded across the globe." The triviality of the counterfactual is revealed as one causally backtracks and asks about a sequence of events that would have led Napoleon to possess nuclear weapons. We offer one effort to construct such a chain in figure 5.11. The explanation of the counterfactual antecedent requires scientific developments that are nearly impossible scenarios, given the state of knowledge at the time of Napoleon. In turn, these scientific developments require further disrupting counterfactuals for their existence. Each step backward in time introduces a more implausible counterfactual event—creating a "ballooning effect," in which the size of the counterfactual set is completely dwarfed by its negation.

When causal backtracking leads to preposterous scenarios, it is difficult to establish what the world would look like with the counterfactual antecedent in place. One can be certain that the world would be radically different, but exactly how is unclear. In turn, this lack of clarity about conditions at the moment of the counterfactual antecedent makes it difficult or impossible to assess the counterfactual statement. One cannot know whether the counterfactual antecedent is linked to the outcome without knowing the contextual categories in which the world has membership. For instance, if Napoleon had possessed nuclear weapons, then perhaps England would have possessed them, too. And if England had had nuclear weapons, then we might not expect that France would have expanded across the globe; thus, the counterfactual statement would be rendered false. But unless we can know a great deal more about a world in which Napoleon possesses nuclear weapons, we cannot determine the truth of the counterfactual statement one way or the other.

In short, going backward in time to explain a counterfactual antecedent is a tool for elucidating the extent to which the minimal-rewrite rule can be applied. By asking about events that are approximately sufficient for membership in the counterfactual antecedent, one determines how similar the counterfactual world is to the actual world. The utility of small and contingent events as counterfactual antecedents is clear: the world does not need to be radically changed in order to generate membership in a contingent non-actual event.

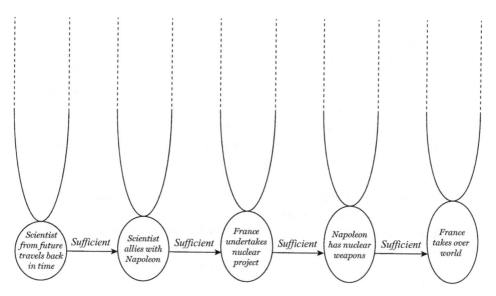

FIGURE 5.11. Backward Projection with a Miracle Counterfactual. Dashed lines indicate an almost infinite set expanding upward.

———

This chapter has sought to provide categories and tools that are useful for constructing good counterfactual statements—i.e., ones that are clear, plausible, and important. To formulate such a counterfactual statement, the researcher must be explicit about the kind of cause (e.g., a necessary, SUIN, or INUS cause) that is proposed to be operating in the actual world. The researcher must be as specific as possible about the features of this actual world cause, as well as the actual world outcome it is proposed to help explain. If one has substantial clarity about the actual world proposition, one can be much clearer about the corresponding counterfactual proposition. To assess the utility of the counterfactual statement, the researcher must determine whether the minimal-rewrite rule applies to it. This consideration may require building a chain of historical counterfactual events that generate the counterfactual antecedent of interest. The plausibility of the counterfactual statement also depends on the ability of the researcher to link, via connecting events, the counterfactual antecedent to the counterfactual outcome.

Good counterfactual statements are invaluable because they allow researchers to evaluate propositions about particular causes of specific outcomes even when only one actual case is considered. The results of a counterfactual analysis can be very important evidence for or against the truth of a proposition within a Bayesian approach (discussed in chapter 7). Researchers can use counterfactual analysis to estimate the extent to which an individual causal factor is necessary and sufficient for a specific outcome in a particular case. The consideration of both cause-varying and context-varying counterfactual cases is crucial to this assessment. Cause-varying counterfactual cases allow for an estimation of the extent to which a particular cause is necessary for an outcome, whereas context-varying counterfactual cases allow for an estimation of the extent to which a particular cause is sufficient for an outcome.

Counterfactual analysis intersects with a wide range of methodological issues in the social sciences, serving as a research tool in its own right and as a foundation for other set-theoretic tools. Some of these tools we have already considered, and others will be explored in subsequent chapters. So far, we have examined the set-theoretic tests that help the analyst evaluate whether one counterfactual event causes another counterfactual event; and we have discussed the regularity model of causality, which is assumed by counterfactual analysis. We shall need to return to counterfactual analysis in later chapters, when we consider the study of sequence analysis, critical events, and path dependence.

6

Sequence Analysis

(coauthored with Erin Kimball Damman and Kendra Koivu)

Set-theoretic sequence analysis is a method of inference that uses the structure of causal chains to reach conclusions about the relative importance of events located at different points in the chain. The methodology resembles in some ways the use of control and mediating variables in statistical research, though its set-theoretic foundations make it vary significantly from statistical analysis in other ways. Set-theoretic sequence analysis uses logical rules to determine the importance of a given causal factor located at a certain point in a causal chain relative to another causal factor located at a different point in the chain. This methodology complements the tools discussed in the prior two chapters. Whereas set-theoretic tests and counterfactual analysis are used to determine whether and the extent to which a factor is necessary and sufficient for an outcome, sequence analysis is used to determine the relative importance of factors that have already been established to be causes of a certain type.

Questions about the relative importance of causes routinely arise in the evaluation of alternative historical episodes. Analysts seek to learn whether causes from one historical period are more important than causes from a different period. Barbara Geddes (2003: 140) nicely poses the issue as a problem: "If two path-dependent arguments set out to explain the same outcome, and one argument concludes that choices made at one historical juncture determined the final outcome while the other identifies a different juncture as critical, how can we tell which is correct?" In the macro social sciences, this problem exists for many famous debates on myriad topics, including historical democratization in Europe (Moore 1966; Downing 1992), rapid economic growth in post–World War II East Asia (Evans 1995; Kohli 2012), national political regimes in Central America (Yashar 1997; Paige 1997), the end of the Cold War (English 2007; Brooks and Wohlforth 2007a, 2007b), military authoritarianism in South America (O'Donnell 1973; Wiarda 1973), the rise of European capitalism (Brenner 1976; Wallerstein 1974), and poor economic performance in postcolonial Africa (Rodney 1972; Bates 1981). In each of these examples, scholars disagree about which historical period contains the most decisive causes for the given outcome.

Similar issues arise with sequential arguments that identify one or more intervening factors that link an initial cause to a final outcome. The problem here is that it is not self-evident whether an intervening causal factor is more important than the initial causal factor that launches the overall sequence. Assume, for example, that Waldner (1999) is correct that the effect of intense elite conflict on poor economic performance in Syria and Turkey during the mid-twentieth century ran through an intervening cause—namely, the absence of a developmental state. Does the existence of this intervening cause (*not–developmental state*) serve to diminish the importance of the initial cause (*intense elite conflict*)? How would we know for these specific cases? Likewise, many scholars agree that the effects of the slave trade on economic development in Africa were mediated by formal European colonialism beginning in the late nineteenth century. To what extent (if any) does recognizing the role of formal European colonialism diminish the causal importance of the prior episode of the slave trade in the explanation of economic crisis in postcolonial Africa?

Set-theoretic sequence analysis explores the relative causal importance of two or more events that are (1) located at different points in time, (2) established to be causes of the outcome of interest, and (3) established to be causally related themselves. For instance, if two causal factors in a sequence are each necessary for the final outcome, sequence analysis can help the researcher determine which one is more important. The method defines *causal importance* using the gold standard of a regularity model of causality: a causal factor becomes more important to the extent that it approximates a necessary *and* sufficient cause (see chapter 3 on causal importance). Sequence analysis is designed to be used with events that have already been established to be approximately necessary and/or sufficient causes of an outcome. It uses logical tools to determine the importance or trivialness of these causal factors *relative to one another*.

Set-theoretic sequence analysis is inspired by the *elaboration model*, originally formulated by Paul Lazarsfeld and his associates at Columbia University for multivariate statistical analysis (see Kendall 1982). Like Lazarsfeld's model, set-theoretic sequence analysis evaluates the importance of an initial cause by considering it in light of a new causal factor that is antecedent or intervening. It asks whether the initial cause retains its importance when the new factor is taken into consideration. However, unlike Lazarsfeld's model, which focuses on variables that are highly correlated with one another, set-theoretic method-ology considers causal factors that have a high level of set-theoretic regularity with one another.

Analyzing Set-Theoretic Causal Chains

Case-study and small-N researchers construct sequences of linked causal events (e.g., $X \rightarrow Z \rightarrow Y$) to explain outcomes. Like historians, these research-ers "explain [outcomes] by tracing the sequence of events that brought them about" (Roberts 1996: 16). This section considers what happens when a case-study researcher elaborates an initial $X \rightarrow Y$ set-theoretic relationship through the introduction of a third factor, either antecedent or intervening. With set-theoretic sequence analysis, the new relationships generated by the third factor can contextualize, diminish, or even make illogical the initial two-factor $X \rightarrow Y$ set-theoretic relationship.

EXTENDING THE ELABORATION MODEL

Lazarsfeld's elaboration model was part of the move in early quantitative social science toward multivariate analysis and the effort to distinguish correlation from causation (Kendall 1982). The central procedure of the model is to elabo-rate an initial bivariate relationship through the introduction of a third, control variable. In some cases, the new relationships created by introducing the third variable confirm or enhance the strength of the original relationship, increasing confidence that it is a causal association. In other cases, elaboration through a third variable weakens and calls into question the initial relationship, leading the researcher to believe that it may be a spurious (i.e., non-causal) relationship.

Although this model was developed for the analysis of variable relation-ships using statistical correlations under the property-possession assumption, it can be extended to case-study explanation using set-theoretic relationships under the spatial-set assumption. The basic application is similar: the analyst begins with an initial $X \rightarrow Y$ relationship and then further evaluates it through the introduction of a third factor, either antecedent or intervening. The key difference is that with set-theoretic analysis, the factors are categories and the relationships are set-membership relations.

As an illustration, consider a relationship in which a case's membership in an initial category X is necessary for its subsequent membership in cat-egory Y. This relationship can be specified as $X -n \rightarrow Y$.[1] One way of using sequence analysis is to introduce an antecedent category—i.e., a third event (Z) that is temporally prior to both X and Y. Set-theoretic sequence analysis leads the researcher to explore the possible logical relationships between Z and X, and between Z and Y. That is, the researcher uses set-theoretic tests and counterfactual analysis to examine the following two unknown relationships:

$$Z -? \rightarrow X -n \rightarrow Y$$
$$\| \text{———}? \text{———} \uparrow$$

Different kinds of set-theoretic relationships may be discovered in this process, resulting in different causal sequences. Set-theoretic analysis evaluates the implications of the new relationships for the relative importance of the original causal factor (X). Depending on the type of relationship that exists between Z and X, and between Z and Y, the importance of the original cause could be diminished or contextualized.

Sequence analysis can also be used with intervening causes. For example, again consider a finding that membership in X is necessary for subsequent membership in Y; that is, $X -n \rightarrow Y$. With an intervening event (Z), the analyst explores the following set-membership relations:

$$X -? \rightarrow Z -? \rightarrow Y$$
$$\| \text{———} n \text{———} \uparrow$$

Depending on the relationships that are discovered between X and Z, and between Z and Y, the initial relationship could, again, be diminished or contextualized.

The causal status of the antecedent and intervening factors used with sequence analysis can correspond to any of the five types of causes specified in chapter 3. In the discussion that follows, however, we focus on necessary causes and sufficient causes. Although scholars often employ INUS causes in case-study and small-N research, INUS causes must be approximately necessary and/or approximately sufficient in order to be *individually* important causes (see also chapter 10 on causal importance). Thus, in this chapter, important individual INUS causes are analyzed as approximately necessary causes and/or approximately sufficient causes. If an individual INUS cause approximates neither a necessary nor a sufficient cause, it cannot be an important cause or a critical event for outcome Y. Minor INUS causes are best analyzed in light of the larger sufficiency combination of which they are a component. This sufficiency combination can be treated as a single factor—an individually sufficient cause—for the purposes of sequence analysis.[2]

CONTEXTUALIZED, DIMINISHED, AND ILLOGICAL RELATIONSHIPS

Let us return to an initial finding about a necessary cause ($X -n \rightarrow Y$). Suppose a researcher considers an antecedent factor and discovers the following relationships:

$$Z-n\to X-n\to Y$$
$$\|\text{———}n\text{———}\uparrow$$

In addition to X being a necessary cause of Y, antecedent Z is a necessary cause of both X and Y, creating a chain of necessary causes. As a concrete example, consider Downing's (1992) argument that, for the states of historical Europe, membership in the category *medieval constitutionalism* was a necessary cause of membership in the category *early democracy*. Downing further suggests that membership in the prior category *Roman Empire* was necessary for membership in both *medieval constitutionalism* and *early democracy*. Thus, Downing's argument follows the form above, where $Z = Roman\ Empire$, $X = medieval\ constitutionalism$, and $Y = early\ democracy$.

Set-theoretic sequence analysis considers how the new relationships introduced by Z affect our understanding of the initial $X-n\to Y$ relationship. For example, in the case of Downing, should we consider *Roman Empire* to be the more important cause of *early democracy*, given that it came first in time? Or should we treat *medieval constitutionalism* as the more important cause of *early democracy*, as Downing does?

By specifying set diagrams that correspond to the events in this causal chain, we can answer this question. Figure 6.1 combines the three set-theoretic relationships ($Z-n\to X$; $X-n\to Y$; and $Z-n\to Y$) into a single causal sequence. The illustration is built from two logical facts: (1) Z must be a superset of both X and Y, because it is necessary for both of these factors; and (2) X must be a superset of Y, because X is necessary for Y. Since both X and Z are necessary for Y, their relative causal importance depends on the extent to which they are also sufficient for Y. As the figure shows, the set for X more closely overlaps with the set for Y, bringing it closer to sufficiency as well as necessity. Given that set X comes closer to sufficiency than Z, we know that it is the more important necessary cause. Hence, *medieval constitutionalism* is the more important cause of *early democracy*, just as Downing suggests.

This example shows how the introduction of a third factor *contextualizes* the initial relationship. The original necessary cause (X) remains the most important cause in the sequence, but we now have additional information about the causes of this cause. Indeed, we can generalize the logic of this example with the following rule:

Rule of Enchained Necessary Causes: In a temporal sequence of linked necessary causes, the relative importance of any given cause increases as its temporal proximity to the outcome increases.

The closer the individual links are to the outcome, the closer they are to being sufficient as well as necessary. One could imagine this rule visually as a sideways funnel that narrows over time as it approaches the target outcome. If one

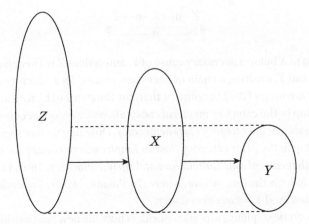

FIGURE 6.1. Set-Theoretic Illustration of Contextualization. $Z =$ *Roman Empire*; $X =$ *medieval constitutionalism*; $Y =$ *early democracy*.

thinks about it in causal terms, the necessary causes become more important over time, such that the final step is nearly sufficient as well as necessary.

It is entirely possible, however, that the introduction of an antecedent factor will *diminish* the relative importance of a more proximate causal factor. More proximate causes are not inevitably more important ones; we can see why in the following example. Let us again assume that the initial relationship involves a necessary cause $(X-\mathrm{n}\rightarrow Y)$. But now imagine that when the antecedent Z is introduced, we discover the following relationships:

$$Z-\mathrm{s}\rightarrow X-\mathrm{n}\rightarrow Y$$
$$\|\text{———}\mathrm{n}\text{———}\uparrow$$

Membership in the antecedent factor Z is necessary for membership in Y, as before, but it is now *sufficient* for membership in X (as opposed to necessary). Imagine that Downing's argument had been that membership in *Roman Empire* was sufficient for membership in *medieval constitutionalism* and necessary for membership in *early democracy*. Would *Roman Empire* then be the more important necessary cause of *early democracy*?

The answer is yes. We can visually understand this result by looking at the set diagram in figure 6.2. While both Z and X are fully necessary causes of Y, Z is the more important one, because Z comes closer to also being sufficient for Y. In this example, then, the initial cause is *diminished* in importance when we introduce the third factor; the more important cause is the more temporally remote factor.

In addition to contextualizing or diminishing an initial relationship, set-theoretic sequence analysis can generate a logical impossibility that requires the analyst to locate the error responsible for the impossible finding. For instance,

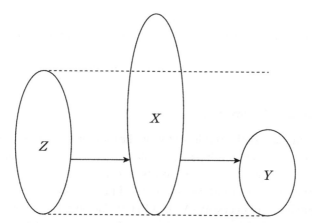

FIGURE 6.2. Set-Theoretic Illustration of Diminishment. $Z =$
Roman Empire; $X =$ medieval constitutionalism; $Y =$ early democracy.

imagine that one starts, again, with the finding that membership in X is necessary for membership in Y, and then discovers the following relationships:

$$Z -n \rightarrow X -n \rightarrow Y$$
$$\| \text{------s------} \uparrow$$

Here the antecedent factor (Z) is necessary for X and sufficient for Y. Yet this overall finding is impossible; it is not a description of relationships that exist in any possible world. If X is necessary for Y, it is logically impossible for Z to be simultaneously necessary for X and sufficient for Y. The finding would require Z to be both a proper subset and a proper superset of X, which defies logic and reality. Since this sequence is not possible, at least one of the three specified relationships must be incorrect. It could be that the original relationship ($X -n \rightarrow Y$) is wrong, though the error could also be with one or both of the other relationships.

Finally, let us introduce a rule for sequences of sufficient causes that parallels the rule above for sequences of necessary causes:

> Rule of Enchained Sufficient Causes: In a temporal sequence of linked sufficient causes, the relative importance of any given cause increases as its temporal proximity to the outcome increases.

With sequences of sufficient causes, each cause comes closer to being necessary as well as sufficient as the sequence moves across time toward the outcome. We encountered this kind of sequence in the illustration of Harvey's (2012) counterfactual chain leading from the election of Al Gore to the non-invasion of Iraq (figure 5.10). One can think of a sufficiency sequence as a sideways funnel, expanding over time to approximate the full space of the target outcome.

Using possible world semantics, one can say that as the sequence proceeds, the possibility that the outcome could be generated by an alternative chain of events diminishes. At the end of the sequence, the temporally most proximate cause is nearly necessary, as well as sufficient, for the outcome.

Inventory and Examples

Table 6.1 summarizes the results of the application of set-theoretic sequence analysis to various relationships. The table considers the 16 possibilities that apply to causal sequences of three events that are characterized by necessity and/or sufficiency relationships. The first column shows whether the initial relationship is one of necessity ($X-n \rightarrow Y$) or sufficiency ($X-s \rightarrow Y$). The second column states whether the third factor, Z, is antecedent ($Z \rightarrow X \rightarrow Y$) or intervening ($X \rightarrow Z \rightarrow Y$). The third column specifies how Z is related to X and Y. The fourth column states the consequence of introducing Z for understanding the role of X in the original $X \rightarrow Y$ relationship: contextualization, diminishment, or logical impossibility. The final column summarizes the explanatory status of Z. The following discussion is organized around the three possible consequences of introducing Z into the initial relationship.

CONTEXTUALIZATION

Sequence analysis *contextualizes* an initial relationship when the new factor (Z) is not more causally important for the outcome (Y) than the original causal factor (X). Different types of contextualization highlight different ways in which the examination of the third factor (Z) enriches our understanding of the initial $X \rightarrow Y$ relationship. We can identify four mutually exclusive subtypes of contextualization: (1) identification of a secondary cause, (2) identification of a partial mechanism, (3) background contextualization, and (4) pathway contextualization.

In some instances of contextualization, the new factor is the same kind of cause with respect to the final outcome as the original factor, but it is less causally important; this result applies to types 1a, 2c, 3d, and 4b in table 6.1. For instance, in the historical context of Western Europe, Luebbert (1991) argues that a prewar alliance between liberals and labor (a Lib-Lab alliance) was sufficient to generate a path that culminated in liberal democracy during the interwar period.[3] Luebbert contextualizes this argument by examining antecedent factors that explain why some European countries were members of *prewar Lib-Lab alliance* and others were not. He finds that the critical antecedent factor is the formation of cohesive middle classes. His argument is that country membership in *historically cohesive middle classes* was sufficient for membership in *prewar Lib-Lab alliance*. Luebbert reasons that

TABLE 6.1. Inventory of Results from Set-Theoretic Sequence Analysis

	Initial $X \to Y$ Relationship	Third Factor (Z)	New Relationships	Result	Status of Z
1a	$X -\text{n} \to Y$	Antecedent	$Z -\text{n} \to X$; $Z -\text{n} \to Y$	*Z contextualizes* the initial relationship.	Secondary cause
1b	$X -\text{n} \to Y$	Antecedent	$Z -\text{n} \to X$; $Z -\text{s} \to Y$	Logically impossible.	—
1c	$X -\text{n} \to Y$	Antecedent	$Z -\text{s} \to X$; $Z -\text{n} \to Y$	*Z diminishes* the initial relationship.	Important cause
1d	$X -\text{n} \to Y$	Antecedent	$Z -\text{s} \to X$; $Z -\text{s} \to Y$	*Z contextualizes* the initial relationship.	Pathway context
2a	$X -\text{n} \to Y$	Intervening	$X -\text{n} \to Z$; $Z -\text{n} \to Y$	*Z diminishes* the initial relationship.	Core mechanism
2b	$X -\text{n} \to Y$	Intervening	$X -\text{n} \to Z$; $Z -\text{s} \to Y$	*Z contextualizes* the initial relationship.	Pathway context
2c	$X -\text{n} \to Y$	Intervening	$X -\text{s} \to Z$; $Z -\text{n} \to Y$	*Z contextualizes* the initial relationship.	Partial mechanism
2d	$X -\text{n} \to Y$	Intervening	$X -\text{s} \to Z$; $Z -\text{s} \to Y$	Logically impossible.	—
3a	$X -\text{s} \to Y$	Antecedent	$Z -\text{n} \to X$; $Z -\text{n} \to Y$	*Z contextualizes* the initial relationship.	Background context
3b	$X -\text{s} \to Y$	Antecedent	$Z -\text{n} \to X$; $Z -\text{s} \to Y$	*Z diminishes* the initial relationship.	Important cause
3c	$X -\text{s} \to Y$	Antecedent	$Z -\text{s} \to X$; $Z -\text{n} \to Y$	Logically impossible.	—
3d	$X -\text{s} \to Y$	Antecedent	$Z -\text{s} \to X$; $Z -\text{s} \to Y$	*Z contextualizes* the initial relationship.	Secondary cause
4a	$X -\text{s} \to Y$	Intervening	$X -\text{n} \to Z$; $Z -\text{n} \to Y$	Logically impossible.	—
4b	$X -\text{s} \to Y$	Intervening	$X -\text{n} \to Z$; $Z -\text{s} \to Y$	*Z contextualizes* the initial relationship.	Partial mechanism
4c	$X -\text{s} \to Y$	Intervening	$X -\text{s} \to Z$; $Z -\text{n} \to Y$	*Z contextualizes* the initial relationship.	Pathway context
4d	$X -\text{s} \to Y$	Intervening	$X -\text{s} \to Z$; $Z -\text{s} \to Y$	*Z diminishes* the initial relationship.	Core mechanism

cohesive middle classes afforded liberals the power and security to safely align with unions and worker organizations. The strong implication is that country membership in *historically cohesive middle classes* was itself enough for membership in the outcome *interwar liberal democracy* in the context of Europe.

When presented set-theoretically, the structure of this part of Luebbert's argument follows type 3d in table 6.1:

$$Z-s\rightarrow X-s\rightarrow Y$$
$$\|\text{------s------}\uparrow$$

where $Z = $ *historically cohesive middle classes*, $X = $ *prewar Lib-Lab alliance*, and $Y = $ *interwar liberal democracy*. Although both Z and X are sufficient causes of Y, the original causal factor, X, is the more important one. Both Z and X are subsets of Y, but X is the larger subset, and thus is closer to being necessary as well as sufficient for the outcome. This result accords nicely with Luebbert's own position, which treats *prewar Lib-Lab alliance* as a crucial cause, while relegating *historically cohesive middle classes* to a contextualizing antecedent cause.

Sequence analysis provides a fairly modest gain in terms of explaining the final outcome when the new factor is a less important cause of the outcome than the original factor (as with types 1a, 2c, 3d, and 4b). If the new causal factor is antecedent and less important than the original causal factor (as in 1a and 3d), we learn about a *secondary cause*—i.e., a cause of a more important cause. By contrast, if the new factor is intervening and less important than the original causal factor (as in 2c and 4b), we learn about a *partial mechanism* through which the original cause operates.

As an example of the identification of a partial mechanism, let us continue with Luebbert's analysis, but focusing now on an intervening cause. Luebbert suggests that the absence of membership in *prewar Lib-Lab alliance* was a necessary cause of both fascism and social democracy.[4] He argues that the absence of case membership in *prewar Lib-Lab alliance* ensured that labor movements were not dominated by moderating middle classes, such that cases acquired membership in the category *strong and independent labor movement*. In turn, membership in *strong and independent labor movement* was necessary for membership in either *interwar fascism* or *interwar social democracy*. This part of Luebbert's argument follows type 2c:

$$\sim X-s\rightarrow Z-n\rightarrow Y$$
$$\|\text{------n------}\uparrow$$

where $X = $ *prewar Lib-Lab alliance*, $Z = $ *strong and independent labor movement*, and $Y = $ *interwar fascism* or *interwar social democracy*. Here, both *not–Lib-Lab alliance* and *strong and independent labor movement* are necessary causes of *fascism* and *social democracy*; however, the original causal factor (*not–Lib-Lab alliance*) is a more important cause. The intervening cause (*strong and independent labor movement*) provides some understanding of the process through which the main cause exerts its sufficiency effect. The intervening cause is a partial mechanism through which *not–Lib-Lab alliance* does productive causal work.

In other instances of contextualization, the new causal factor is not the same kind of cause for the outcome as the original causal factor (types 1d, 2b, 3a, and 4c in table 6.1). Here one can distinguish between *background contextualization* and *pathway contextualization*. Background contextualization occurs when either an antecedent factor (type 3a) or an intervening factor (type 4c) is necessary for the outcome, whereas the original causal factor is sufficient for the outcome. When this is true, the new factor provides an essential context—or background—that must be present for the sufficient cause to exert its effect. Background contextualization is closely related to the scope conditions under which the cause exerts productive effects.

An example of background contextualization is found in Mahoney's *The Legacies of Liberalism* (2001). This work includes the argument that a radical form of state militarization and class polarization during the nineteenth century, what Mahoney calls *radical liberalism,* was sufficient to breed pathways culminating in the outcome *military-authoritarian regime* for Guatemala and El Salvador. The study further argues that, before the liberal reform period, certain conditions—*partially centralized state* and *incipient export economy*—had to be in place in order for liberal leaders to enact these radical reforms. Overall, this part of the argument follows type 3a:

$$Z - n \rightarrow X - s \rightarrow Y$$
$$\| \text{———} n \text{———} \uparrow$$

where $Z = partially\ centralized\ state\ and\ incipient\ export\ economy$, $X = radical\ liberalism$, and $Y = military$-$authoritarian\ regime$. In the argument, while antecedent conditions (Z) provide a contextual backdrop, the main generative causal action happens with *radical liberalism* (X). The antecedent conditions play a permissive background role, one that provides an understanding of how radical liberalism was possible in these countries.

Pathway contextualization, by contrast, happens when either an antecedent factor (1d) or an intervening factor (2b) is sufficient for the outcome, whereas the original factor is necessary for the outcome. In the latter case (2b), the new factor provides one of multiple paths through which the original cause exerts its effect. As an example, let us return once more to Luebbert's argument. We noted that membership in *not–Lib-Lab alliance* is necessary for *fascism* and *social democracy* in interwar Europe. For Luebbert, the most decisive factor separating the fascist cases from the social democratic cases is the interwar alliances made by parties representing farmers. When farmers' parties were allied with workers' parties, countries had membership in *red-green coalition,* a category that was sufficient for membership in *social democracy* (Sweden, Denmark, and Norway followed this path). By contrast, when farmers' parties were allied with urban middle classes, countries were members of *brown-green coalition,* a category that was sufficient for *fascism* (Germany, Italy, and Spain followed this path). When summarized set-theoretically, both of these arguments follow the logic of type 2b:

$$\sim X -n \rightarrow Z_1 -s \rightarrow Y_1$$
$$\parallel\!\!-\!\!-\!\!-\!\!-\!\!-n\!\!-\!\!-\!\!-\!\!-\!\!\uparrow$$

$$\sim X -n \rightarrow Z_2 -s \rightarrow Y_2$$
$$\parallel\!\!-\!\!-\!\!-\!\!-\!\!-n\!\!-\!\!-\!\!-\!\!-\!\!\uparrow$$

where $X = $ *Lib-Lab alliance*, $Z_1 = $ *red-green coalition*, $Z_2 = $ *brown-green coalition*, $Y_1 = $ *social democracy*, and $Y_2 = $ *fascism*. In the arguments, *not–Lib-Lab alliance* is a permissive cause for both *social democracy* and *fascism*. However, the intervening factor (either *red-green coalition* or *brown-green coalition*) highlights the productive causal pathway through which this factor exerts its enabling effect. The historical role of *not–Lib-Lab alliance* in interwar Europe was to permit one of two pathways that culminated in a country's membership in a particular kind of interwar regime. Sequence analysis contextualizes the original finding by showing us these two pathways.

DIMINISHMENT

As opposed to contextualizing a finding, sequence analysis can *diminish* an initial cause by identifying a more important one (see 1c, 2a, 3b, and 4d in table 6.1). For this to happen, the new factor must be the same kind of cause as the original factor, but come closer to being both necessary and sufficient for the outcome. If the new factor is antecedent and is more causally important than the original factor, the more historical cause can be regarded as diminishing the relative importance of the original factor (as in 1c and 3b).

As an example, consider again the debate about the causes of the end of the Cold War between English (2007) and Brooks and Wohlforth (2007a, 2007b; see chapter 5). English argues that ideational factors, such as new thinking, were a necessary cause of the end of the Cold War. Brooks and Wohlforth initially do not disagree that these ideational factors were necessary, but contend that they were relatively trivial. These authors argue that materialist causes, especially long-term economic decline in the Soviet Union, were much more important. To show that English's claims are spurious, they make the following set-theoretic argument (type 1c):

$$Z -s \rightarrow X -n \rightarrow Y$$
$$\parallel\!\!-\!\!-\!\!-\!\!-\!\!-n\!\!-\!\!-\!\!-\!\!-\!\!\uparrow$$

where $Z = $ *Soviet economic decline*, $X = $ *new thinking*, and $Y = $ *end of the Cold War*. Brooks and Wohlforth try to diminish the importance of the causal connection between *new thinking* and *end of the Cold War*. They suggest that while both *Soviet economic decline* and *new thinking* are necessary causes of *end of the Cold War, Soviet economic decline* is the more important one. This is logically true because membership in the set *Soviet economic decline* is closer to being sufficient for membership in *end of the Cold War* than is membership in *new thinking*.

When the new factor is intervening and the original factor is diminished, a *core mechanism* is identified, through which the original factor exerts its effects (as in 2a and 4d). In this case, the original relationship is not spurious; instead, the analyst discovers a category representing the process through which the original causal factor shapes the outcome. Unlike a partial mechanism with contextualization, a core mechanism offers a better explanation for the outcome than the original causal factor.

An example is Waldner's (1999) study of unsuccessful industrialization and economic development in Syria and Turkey during the mid-twentieth century. Waldner argues that membership in *intense elite conflict* was sufficient for membership in *not–successful development*. He then elaborates the argument by considering a key intervening cause: *not–developmental state*. Syria's and Turkey's membership in *intense elite conflict* was sufficient for these cases to lack membership in *developmental state*, which in turn was sufficient for them to lack membership in *successful development*. The overall argument has the form of type 4d:

$$X -\text{s} \rightarrow \sim Z -\text{s} \rightarrow \sim Y$$
$$\| \text{————s————} \uparrow$$

where *X = intense elite conflict, Z = developmental state,* and *Y = successful development.* Here, membership in the original causal factor (*intense elite conflict*) still ensures the absence of membership in *successful development,* but it works through *not–developmental state,* which is an even more important sufficient cause. The implication is that the sufficiency effect of elite conflict on development derives from its prior sufficiency effect on the developmental state. High levels of elite conflict run through this core mechanism to generate unsuccessful development.

Waldner's study is also useful for illustrating how historical explanations work with multiple intermediary steps. Waldner explicitly states that further intervening factors mediate the original relationship. One of them is the *Kaldorian collective dilemma,* which he defines as a set of collective action problems that produce a failure to upgrade productivity, lower costs, and improve goods for existing industries. This factor (*K*) intervenes between *not–developmental state* and *not–successful development* in the following way:

$$X -\text{s} \rightarrow \sim Z -\text{s} \rightarrow K -\text{s} \rightarrow \sim Y$$
$$\| \text{————s————} \uparrow$$

where *X = intense elite conflict, Z = developmental state, K = Kaldorian collective dilemma,* and *Y = successful development. Kaldorian collective dilemma* now becomes the most important mechanism; the sufficiency effects of both *intense elite conflict* and *not–developmental state* run through this new intervening factor. While the importance of the more antecedent factors should not be dismissed, they do their causal work because they generate membership in *Kaldorian collective dilemma*.

LOGICAL IMPOSSIBILITIES

Logical impossibilities can emerge in various ways (types 1b, 2d, 3c, and 4a in table 6.1). In all of the illogical types, the original factor and the new factor are different kinds of causes; logical impossibilities do not arise as long as the factors in the sequence are all necessary causes or all sufficient causes. For an example, let us return briefly to Mahoney's (2001) argument that in the context of Central America, membership in *radical liberalism* was sufficient for subsequent membership in *military-authoritarian regime*. One might counter with the argument that an intervening necessary cause—namely, *not–social reform episode* in the mid-twentieth century—was also a critical event. Imagine, for example, the following alternative explanation:

$$X -\text{n}\rightarrow \sim Z -\text{n}\rightarrow Y$$
$$\parallel\!\!\text{—————s————}\uparrow$$

where $X =$ *radical liberalism of the nineteenth century*, $Z =$ *social reform episode of the 1940s and 1950s*, and $Y =$ *military-authoritarian regime after the 1950s*. The problem here is that this explanation is a logical impossibility (type 4a). *Radical liberalism* (X) cannot be sufficient for *military-authoritarian regime* (Y) unless it is sufficient for all subsequent necessary causes. In this formulation, however, *radical liberalism* is necessary but not sufficient for *not–social reform episode* (Z). The implication is that one or more of the relationships in this model must be incorrectly specified.

In fact, given Yashar's (1997) work on the causes of authoritarianism in Central America, the current consensus view may be that

$$X -\text{s}\rightarrow Z -\text{n}\rightarrow Y$$
$$\parallel\!\!\text{—————s————}\uparrow$$

where $X =$ *radical liberalism of the nineteenth century*, $Z =$ *failed social reform episode of the 1940s and 1950s*, and $Y =$ *military-authoritarian regime after the 1950s*. Membership in *radical liberalism* was approximately sufficient for both the failed social reform episode and the final regime outcome. The failed social reform episode acts as the pathway context through which the effects of the earlier critical event were transmitted.

————

Set-theoretic sequence analysis helps scholars address various problems in case-study and small-N research. When one identifies the causes of a cause, one wishes to know whether these causes are more important than the original cause. Sequence analysis assists researchers in answering this question in a rigorous way. The method distinguishes between antecedent causes that diminish the importance of an original cause and antecedent causes that do not. The ability to distinguish these two possibilities is crucial for understanding what it means to have identified the causes of a cause.

With intervening causes, set-theoretic sequence analysis provides analysts with a framework for conceptualizing different causal roles for the intermediary events in a sequence. The method provides rules for determining whether an intervening event is a core mechanism or a partial mechanism. A core mechanism—a category standing for one or more events through which the initial causal factor does its permissive and productive work—provides a logically satisfying explanation of the enabling and generative process that links the initial cause to the outcome. By contrast, a partial mechanism goes only part of the way toward providing this kind of explanation, inviting more research on the intermediary events that link the cause and the outcome.

The method of sequence analysis offers a tool for structuring scholarly debates about historical causation. Analysts can use this method to determine the specific evidence needed to resolve historical disputes like the ones listed at the beginning of this chapter. Even non-experts can weigh in on these debates, by helping to frame the exact nature of the disagreement and the kinds of evidence that would support each of the opposing sides.

7

Bayesian Analysis
(coauthored with Rodrigo Barrenechea)

Bayesian analysis involves the use of explicit rules to update our beliefs about the likelihood that a proposition is true, given the introduction of new evidence (see Abell 2009; Bennett 2008, 2015; Fairfield 2013; Fairfield and Charman 2017, forthcoming; Humphreys and Jacobs 2015; McKeown 1999; Rohlfing 2013). For instance, consider the proposition that Russian interference was an important cause of Donald Trump's victory in the U.S. presidential election of 2016. Let us assume that we believe that this proposition is just as likely true as false (i.e., it is true with a 50% probability). Let us also assume that we discover set-membership observations showing that Vladimir Putin directly organized a large-scale campaign to support Trump in the months before the election. To what degree should we update our beliefs about the truth of the proposition? Why? How? Bayesian analysis provides explicit answers to these questions; it provides public procedures for *rationally* updating one's beliefs about the likelihood that a given proposition is true in light of new evidence.

A good definition of science includes the use of Bayesian-like principles in the evaluation of evidence. Bayesian analysis is *mandatory* for science, in the sense that any alternative approach to belief updating must be equivalent or run the risk of introducing biases and unnecessary error into conclusions (cf. Cox 1946).[1] Scientific constructivism embraces Bayesian analysis because *all* scientific approaches must embrace Bayesian analysis, or its equivalent, as providing the appropriate rules for using evidence to arrive at conclusions about the truth of propositions.[2]

Bayesian analysis recognizes a basic constructivist point: the scientific assessment of truth unavoidably depends on subjective beliefs. After all, science is concerned with *justified beliefs* about the truth of propositions. The difficulty of precisely specifying one's beliefs fuels debate about the appropriate *way* in which to use Bayesian analysis, but Bayesian analysis itself is not called into question. In the social sciences, the challenge of quantitatively specifying subjective beliefs is significant enough that Bayesianism is often recommended as a heuristic to be used informally, rather than as a set of formal operations to be mathematically implemented (McKeown 1999; Beach and Pedersen 2013). Yet some social scientists argue that researchers should use Bayesianism formally, including by numerically identifying degrees of belief and rigorously applying Bayes' theorem (Abell 2009; Fairfield 2013; Humphreys and Jacobs 2015; Rohlfing 2013; but see also Fairfield and Charman 2017, forthcoming). The set-theoretic approach of this book offers tools that are useful to both those who view Bayesianism as a rule of thumb and those who seek to use the approach quantitatively.

Bayesian analysis shares with scientific constructivism a foundation in set-theoretic logic. Explicitly developing Bayesian analysis from a set-theoretic perspective retains all of the virtues of the approach while making it more user-friendly for case-study and small-N researchers in the social sciences. Exposing the implicit set-theoretic foundations of Bayesian analysis highlights the *logical* mechanics through which small-N and case-study researchers update their beliefs in light of set-membership observations. With a set-theoretic approach to Bayesian analysis, one can see more clearly how researchers shift their beliefs by narrowing or expanding the proportion of all possible worlds that have membership in the category *true proposition*, thus increasing or decreasing the likelihood that the actual world resides in this category.

This chapter begins by examining the connections between set-theoretic analysis and Bayesian analysis. The discussion considers how Bayesian analysis (1) *informs* set-theoretic tests and the use of set-membership observations, and (2) *assumes* and *requires* a set-theoretic approach to science. By placing Bayesian analysis on its set-theoretic foundations, the section presents the epistemological foundation for using set-membership observations in the discovery of truth in scientific constructivism.

The next part of the chapter uses Bayesian principles to explain why some individual set-membership observations are crucial for the assessment of the validity of a proposition, whereas others carry no weight in this assessment. Set-membership observations are distinguished along two dimensions: *consequentialness* and *expectedness*. In turn, these dimensions allow for the definition of different kinds of set-membership observations—including *critical observations*, which are highly consequential but not expected, and *cumulative observations*, which are expected but not highly consequential. The section discusses these different kinds of set-membership observations and the corresponding research strategies and narrative presentations with which they are associated.

The final part of the chapter revisits set-theoretic tests from the perspective of Bayesian analysis. This discussion focuses on (1) the relationship between the consequentialness of an observation and the extent to which a set-membership test approximates the ideals of a deterministic necessity test or a deterministic sufficiency test; and (2) the relationship between the expectedness of a set-membership observation and the difficulty of a set-theoretic test. In general, an easy test references an expected observation, whereas a difficult test references an unexpected one. Thus, to create a difficult necessity test, the analyst designs a test that requires the identification of an *unexpected* observation; to create an easy sufficiency test, the analyst designs a test that requires the identification of an *expected* observation.

A Set-Theoretic Interpretation of Bayesian Analysis

This section uses the tools of set theory to illuminate the assumptions and logic of Bayes' theorem. After presenting an illustration of the theorem under essentialist assumptions, the discussion turns toward a possible worlds understanding of probability and then reintroduces Bayes' theorem in set-theoretic language.

BAYES' THEOREM UNDER THE PROPERTY-POSSESSION ASSUMPTION

With Bayesian analysis as conventionally understood in the social sciences, researchers update their beliefs about the probability that a proposition is true in light of evidence from a case. For example, a researcher may learn a new fact about a specific aspect of a case, such as a statement made by a decision maker, and this fact may change the researcher's beliefs about the validity of the proposition under investigation. Under the property-possession assumption, such facts refer to properties possessed by the case under analysis (cf. Bennett 2015; Fairfield and Charman 2017, forthcoming; Humphreys and Jacobs 2015, forthcoming). With essentialist research, the ability of scholars to learn about the properties of a case is viewed as crucial to carrying out good research.

To apply Bayesian analysis, the researcher estimates three probabilities: (1) the probability representing one's starting belief (or a community's starting belief) that the proposition is true; (2) the probability of observing a specific piece of evidence (i.e., observing some property possessed by a case) if the proposition is true; and (3) the probability of observing the same evidence if the proposition is false. In a common representation of Bayes' theorem, evidence is used with these probabilities to update beliefs as follows:

$$P(H|k) = \frac{p(H)p(k|H)}{p(H)p(k|H) + p(\sim H)p(k|\sim H)},$$

where

> $P(H|k)$ is the updated probability that proposition H is true given evidence k,
>
> $p(H)$ is the prior probability that proposition H is true,
>
> $p(k|H)$ is the likelihood of evidence k if proposition H is true,
>
> $p(\sim H)$ is the prior probability that proposition H is false, and
>
> $p(k|\sim H)$ is the likelihood of evidence k if proposition H is false.

Bennett (2015) uses the example of Tannenwald's (2007) work on the nuclear taboo to illustrate the standard Bayesian approach. The nuclear taboo hypothesis formulated by Tannenwald holds that a normative prohibition against the use of nuclear weapons helps explain the non-use of nuclear weapons since 1945. Bennett suggests, for illustrative purposes, that the prior probability that the nuclear taboo hypothesis is true is 40%. He then considers the probability of observing evidence k if the hypothesis is true and the probability of observing evidence k if the hypothesis is false. Bennett assumes that the probability of observing evidence k if the hypothesis is true is 25% and the probability of observing evidence k if the hypothesis is false is 50%. We can place these numbers into Bayes' equation and arrive at an updated probability that the nuclear taboo hypothesis is true:

$$P(H|k) = \frac{(.40)(.25)}{(.40)(.25)+(.60)(.50)} = \frac{.10}{.10+.30} = \frac{.10}{.40} = .25.$$

In this example, the observation of evidence k has changed the probability that the nuclear taboo hypothesis is true from 40% to 25%. Thus, learning about evidence k substantially decreases confidence in the hypothesis.

A SET-THEORETIC APPROACH

A set-theoretic approach is compatible with Bayesian understandings of probability (see Demey, Kooi, and Sack 2013; Hájek 2012). Broadly speaking, a Bayesian approach falls within the subjective and logical interpretations of probability (Childers 2013; Galavotti 2005). Here, probabilities are *beliefs* about aspects of the world—i.e., they are cognitive phenomena rather than mind-independent properties. The structure of these beliefs is an extension of *logic*; in particular, Bayesianism is an extension of Boolean algebra into a framework intended to quantify states of partial knowledge (Cox 1946; Jaynes 2003; see also Laplace 1814/1952).

The set-theoretic approach uses possible world semantics to understand the beliefs and logic of Bayesian analysis. Possible worlds are the entities that have membership in sets representing events. An analyst's belief about the *proportion* of all possible worlds with membership in a set in which a particular proposition is true allows the analyst to make a quantified probability statement about the likelihood that the proposition is true. Specifically, one derives a probability concerning the truth of a proposition by estimating the proportion of all possible worlds that have membership in a set in which the proposition is true. If one believes that a proposition is true with a 50% probability, it is because one believes that half of all possible worlds have membership in the set in which this proposition is true.[3]

Figure 7.1 is an illustration of probabilities as sets containing possible worlds for the nuclear taboo example. The diagram highlights a core aspect of the set-theoretic approach to Bayesian analysis: probabilities are a reflection of the *relative size* of sets. In the diagram, the actual world is located at some point within the full space of possibilities, which includes all possible worlds. Although we do not know which specific possible world is the one actual world, we do know that 40% of the space is occupied by possible worlds in which the proposition is true (with membership in set H), such that the actual world has a 40% chance of being located in the set in which the proposition is true. To confirm the proposition as true, the analyst does not need to eliminate *all* possible worlds. Instead, one needs to know that no possible worlds have membership in the set in which the proposition is false (set $\sim H$).

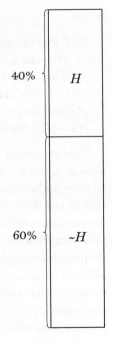

FIGURE 7.1. Set Diagram Illustrating Possible Worlds Approach. H = possible worlds in which the hypothesis is true; $\sim H$ = possible worlds in which the hypothesis is false.

Initial beliefs about the distribution of possible worlds reflect the analyst's knowledge of set-theoretic generalizations and set-membership observations at the outset of research. In the absence of any relevant knowledge, one distributes possible worlds symmetrically between sets H (50%) and $\sim H$ (50%). With some pertinent knowledge, one normally believes that possible worlds are distributed asymmetrically. In the case of the nuclear taboo hypothesis, initial beliefs reflect both the possible worlds generated by a culturalist theory frame (these largely have membership in set H) and the possible worlds generated by rationalist and structuralist theory frames (which largely have membership in set $\sim H$).[4] One's starting beliefs may have most possible worlds situated in $\sim H$, because this set contains most potential states of affairs associated with well-established theories such as rational deterrence theory and neorealism. For instance, most or all possible worlds in which utilitarian calculations of material costs and benefits dictate decisions about the non-use of nuclear weapons fall into set $\sim H$. Likewise, most or all possible worlds in which structural power drives the non-use of nuclear weapons fall into set ~H. By contrast, the possible worlds in which a cultural taboo against the use of nuclear weapons causes their non-use fall into set H.

With the set-theoretic approach, evidence consists of set-membership observations. These observations are used to determine whether the actual world is one of the possible worlds in the set in which the proposition is true. Evidence helps to make this determination by reclassifying possible worlds as non-actual worlds. That is, evidence allows one to conclude that certain states of the world are no longer candidates for being the actual world, because they assume and require the absence of this evidence. In Tannenwald's (2007) study, for example, the existence of transcripts in which U.S. Secretary of Defense Robert McNamara states unequivocally that the use of nuclear weapons in Vietnam is morally inappropriate eliminates possible worlds in which moral considerations did not play a role in the Department of Defense. Insofar as the set in which the nuclear taboo hypothesis is false includes states of the world in which moral considerations are not important, these transcripts reduce the size of that set, and thus lend support to the nuclear taboo hypothesis. This learning process involves *possibility elimination*: one updates one's beliefs because evidence asymmetrically *reduces* the range of possible worlds that can be the actual world.

To further illustrate, figure 7.2 includes a third set, for evidence k. Set k includes all possible worlds in which evidence k is present. With Bayesian analysis, one asks about the extent to which H and ~H have membership in set k.[5] When we assert that there is a 25% probability of observing evidence k if the hypothesis is true, we do so because we believe that 25% of the possible worlds in set H have membership in set k. In the figure, four sets are created by intersecting sets k and ~k with sets H and ~H (the four sets are H & k, H & ~k, ~H & k, and ~H & ~k). Given that the actual world has been found to be a member of set k, the possible worlds that do not have membership in k are no longer candidates for being the actual world. The possible worlds that are members of ~k are now eliminated as being non-actual worlds. The sets of non-actual worlds are called *elimination sets*; they are represented by shaded areas in the figure. The non-shaded areas, which are the subsets of k, are the *remainder sets*: the sets containing the remaining possible worlds that might be the actual world.

As the diagram shows, set-membership observation k has eliminated 75% of all possible worlds in which the proposition is true, leaving behind only 25% of the initially possible worlds where the hypothesis is true. Evidence k has also eliminated 50% of all possible worlds in which the hypothesis is false, leaving behind 50% of the initially possible worlds where the hypothesis is false. The updated probability that the hypothesis is true is determined by the relative size of the remainder sets. The area for the set in which the hypothesis is true (set H) is now only one-third the size of the set in which the hypothesis is false (set ~H). Hence, the updated probability that the hypothesis is true is 25%.

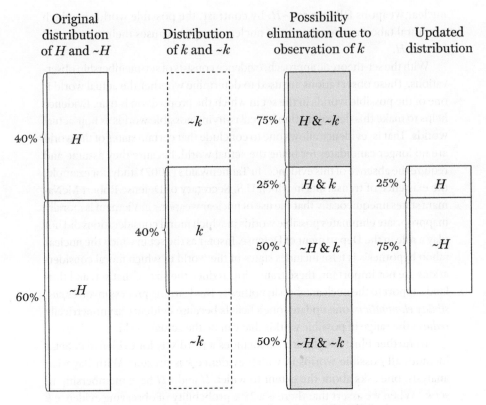

Original
distribution
of *H* and *~H*

Distribution
of *k* and *~k*

Possibility
elimination due to
observation of *k*

Updated
distribution

FIGURE 7.2. Set Diagram Illustrating Belief Updating through Possibility Elimination. *H* = possible worlds in which the hypothesis is true; *~H* = possible worlds in which the hypothesis is false; *k* = evidence *k* is present; *~k* = evidence *k* is not present; & = logical AND; shaded areas = possible worlds that are not the actual world.

The diagram illustrates Bayesian learning by showing how evidence eliminates possible worlds that lack membership in a set in which this evidence is present. The core assumption is simply that the set (either *H* or *~H*) containing the actual world must be a member of the set of possible worlds with the observed evidence *k*. In the example, the elimination of a majority of possible worlds because of evidence *k* is made transparent by comparing the size of the remainder sets to the size of the elimination sets: the remainder sets are smaller. Thus, in addition to adjusting the probability that the hypothesis is true from 40% to 25%, the evidence has focused the analysis on a narrower range of overall possibilities. The outstanding evidence that is needed to pass further judgment on the hypothesis pertains to this reduced range of possible worlds.

The set-theoretic approach allows one to conduct Bayesian analysis without specifying beliefs about probabilities. Instead, one can specify the relative size of sets on the basis of beliefs about the distribution of possible worlds.

Bayesian updating is then accomplished by intersecting sets H and $\sim H$ with set k. The distribution of possible worlds can be expressed with verbal understandings of likelihood, such as "somewhat likely" and "very likely" (cf. Ragin 2000: 158–59). At the same time, it is always possible to attach numbers to the size of sets, such that the set-theoretic approach generates results identical to those in standard Bayesian approaches. However, the verbal expressions and the numbers are not ontologically prior to the sets. Rather, one establishes the verbal expressions and the numerical values on the basis of beliefs about the distribution of possible worlds in sets.

One can also proceed from verbal summaries to numerical probabilities to underlying sets. As an example, consider the famous meteorite-collision theory of the extinction of dinosaurs (Hallam and Wignall 1997; T. Palmer 1999; see also King, Keohane, and Verba 1994; Waldner 2007). The discovery of iridium in a particular layer of the earth's crust in the 1970s substantially increased the probability that the theory is true, at least for many in the relevant scientific community. Figure 7.3 assumes that the prior probability that the meteorite theory is true is "somewhat unlikely," which we can interpret to mean a 40% probability. If the dinosaurs became extinct because of a meteorite collision, how likely is it that iridium would be observed at this layer of the earth's crust? One reasonable answer embraced by many scientists is "very likely," because if a meteorite collision did set into motion the extinction of the dinosaurs, it should have left behind exactly this kind of trace. Hence, one might place $p(k|H)$ for this example at 90%. Likewise, one can ask: If the dinosaurs did *not* become extinct because of a meteorite collision, how likely is it that iridium would be observed at this layer of the earth's crust? Here a reasonable answer might reference the likelihood that this concentration of iridium occurs because of causes unrelated to the dinosaur extinction. On that basis, one might believe that finding this evidence is "fairly unlikely" and place $p(k|\sim H)$ at 25%; that is, there is a 25% chance of observing this iridium if the proposition is false.[6]

In figure 7.3, the effect of observing the iridium on beliefs about the validity of the meteorite-collision theory is illustrated using sets. We see the change in the possible world distribution once we introduce set k and obtain the intersecting sets; the probability of the theory's being true has increased from 40% to about 60%. The evidence has a powerful effect, because only a moderate portion of the possible worlds in which the theory is true are eliminated, whereas most of the worlds in which the theory is false are eliminated. These latter worlds are eliminated because they assume that the iridium is not present (i.e., they lack membership in set k); by contrast, most worlds where the meteorite theory is true do not entail this erroneous assumption (i.e., they are members of set k).

The set-theoretic approach shines light on a basic principle of Bayesian updating: if one finds that the actual world is a member of k, then one must

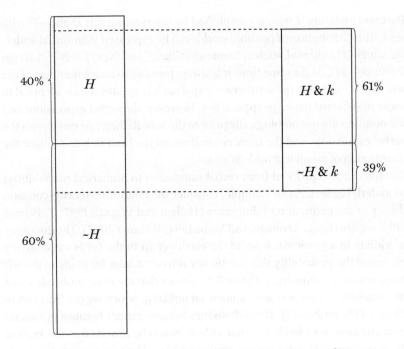

FIGURE 7.3. Illustration of Meteorite-Collision Theory of the Extinction of Dinosaurs. H = possible worlds in which the hypothesis is true; $\sim H$ = possible worlds in which the hypothesis is false; k = evidence k is present; $\sim k$ = evidence k is not present; & = logical AND.

eliminate as impossible all scenarios that assume membership in $\sim k$. Membership in set k is necessary, though not sufficient, for a possible world to be the actual world.

A SET-THEORETIC EXPRESSION OF BAYES' THEOREM

Bayes' theorem itself can be expressed using set-theoretic language. One set-theoretic version of the theorem is

$$H_2 = \frac{H_1(H_1 \in k)}{H_1(H_1 \in k) + \sim H_1(\sim H_1 \in k)},$$

where

H_2 is the updated proportion of possible worlds with membership in the set *valid proposition*,

H_1 is the prior proportion of possible worlds with membership in the set *valid proposition*,

k is the set of possible worlds in which evidence k is present,

$\in$ is the set-membership symbol, and

$\sim$ is the negation symbol.

To illustrate, let us return to the original nuclear taboo example. In this example, H_1 is placed at .40, because that is the initial proportion of possible worlds with membership in set H_1 (*nuclear taboo hypothesis is true*). Likewise, $\sim H$ is placed at .60, because that is the initial proportion of possible worlds with membership in set $\sim H_1$ (*nuclear taboo hypothesis is false*). The expression $(H_1 \in k)$ captures the percentage of possible worlds in set H_1 that are also members of set k (actual world is a member of set k). In the example, 25% of the possible worlds in H_1 have membership in k, and 50% of the possible worlds in $\sim H_1$ have membership in k. When these membership percentages are entered into the set-theoretic version of Bayes' equation, we arrive at the updated proportion of possible worlds that have membership in the set in which the nuclear taboo hypothesis is true:

$$H_2 = \frac{(.40)(.25)}{(.40)(.25)+(.60)(.50)} = \frac{.10}{.10+.30} = \frac{.10}{.40} = .25.$$

As this example shows, Bayesian analysis can be performed without discussing probabilities at all; we can instead discuss the proportion of possible worlds that have membership in sets and their intersections.

Using Evidence

Analysts must decide what kinds of evidence and specific pieces of evidence they will look for when evaluating hypotheses. A set-theoretic approach helps researchers with this challenge by calling attention to both the relative consequentialness of a given piece of evidence and the expectedness of observing that piece of evidence. These distinctions allow for a typology of different kinds of set-membership observations and different modes of narrative presentation.

THE CONSEQUENTIALNESS AND EXPECTEDNESS OF EVIDENCE

In a set-theoretic approach to Bayesian analysis, the *consequentialness* of evidence is defined as the extent to which the evidence changes prior beliefs about the distribution of possible worlds in sets H and $\sim H$. Evidence that is more consequential causes more learning, via belief transformation. The consequentialness (c) of a piece of evidence (k) can be measured by comparing the size of starting sets (H_1) with the size of remainder sets (H_2) after Bayesian updating. A formal measure of consequentialness must also take into consideration the maximum potential belief change that is possible, given the distribution of one's starting beliefs. For example, confirming a proposition when the starting beliefs have the vast majority of all possible worlds in set $\sim H$ is a more radical form of belief transformation than confirming a proposition when the starting beliefs have only half of all possible worlds in set $\sim H$. Analogously, disconfirming a proposition when most possible worlds belong to set H entails a higher level of belief transformation than when most possible worlds already belong to set $\sim H$.

The higher value between H_1 and $\sim H_1$ captures the starting beliefs and the maximum potential belief change that can occur. The set-theoretic formula for consequentialness is then

$$c(k) = |H_1 - H_2| / H_1 \vee \sim H_1.$$

According to standard continuous-set logic, the logical OR in the denominator requires one to take the higher value between H_1 and $\sim H_1$. With this formula, consequentialness ranges from 0 to 1, with 1 being the highest level.[7] As an illustration, consider figure 7.4, which compares the Bayesian learning associated with two pieces of evidence, k_1 and k_2. Here, the consequentialness of k_1 is

$$|.40 - .25| / .60 = .25.$$

Out of a maximum potential consequentialness of 100%, the evidence has shifted beliefs by 25%. The consequentialness of k_2 is identical:

$$|.40 - .25| / .60 = .25.$$

Thus, k_1 and k_2 are equally consequential pieces of evidence.

The *expectedness* of evidence can be defined as the extent to which evidence k is expected to be observed, given one's starting beliefs. Whereas consequentialness concerns belief transformation, expectedness concerns the likelihood—in light of starting beliefs—that the actual world is a member of observation k (regardless of the consequentialness of k).[8] With a set-theoretic approach, expectedness is made visible by observing the extent to which sets H and $\sim H$ are also members of set k. With more-expected evidence, H and $\sim H$ have greater membership in k. More precisely, the set-theoretic formula for expectedness is

$$e(k) = H(H \& k) + \sim H(\sim H \& k).[9]$$

For instance, in figure 7.4, the expectedness of k_1 is

$$.40(.125) + .60(.25) = .20.$$

Thus, prior to the observation of k_1, only 20% of all possible worlds permitted membership in k_1; the observation that the actual world case is a member of k_1 has low expectedness. By contrast, the expectedness of k_2 is

$$.40(.40) + .60(.80) = .64.$$

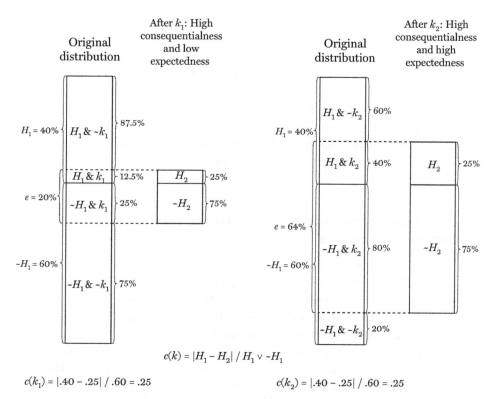

$$c(k) = |H_1 - H_2| / H_1 \vee {\sim} H_1$$

$$c(k_1) = |.40 - .25| / .60 = .25 \qquad\qquad c(k_2) = |.40 - .25| / .60 = .25$$

FIGURE 7.4. Consequentialness and Expectedness. H = possible worlds in which the hypothesis is true; ${\sim}H$ = possible worlds in which the hypothesis is false; k = evidence k is present; ${\sim}k$ = evidence k is not present; & = logical AND; $\vee$ = logical OR.

Prior to the observation of k_2, 64% of all possible worlds permitted membership in k_2; the observation that the actual world is a member of k_2 is fairly expected.

The examples in figure 7.4 show that the consequentialness and expectedness of evidence need not covary. In these examples, the consequentialness of k_1 and k_2 is identical (i.e., .25), but the expectedness of these two pieces of evidence differs quite a lot: .20 for k_1 versus .64 for k_2. The overall relationship between the consequentialness and expectedness of evidence is such that a piece of evidence with low levels of expectedness can have low to high levels of consequentialness, depending on the extent to which sets H and ${\sim}H$ have membership in set k. However, as expectedness approaches the upper limit of 100%, consequentialness decreases, and reaches 0% when the evidence is fully expected.

The researcher may not necessarily specify in advance either the consequentialness or the expectedness of the evidence. Rather, the analyst may recognize these properties only upon the empirically inductive discovery of evidence (cf. Falleti 2006). For example, Skocpol (1992: vii–x) describes how her thinking evolved upon learning that many Americans were receiving substantial public benefits (pensions) as Union veterans of the Civil War. This evidence was surprising to her; she encountered it serendipitously when reading Rubinow's (1913/1969) work on social insurance. The evidence was consequential for her hypotheses about the origins of old-age benefits and social insurance in the United States. In particular, the evidence suggested that these social benefits were launched at a time and through a political process that were different from what Skocpol and many other social scientists had previously believed. Case-study researchers sometimes discover an unexpected but consequential piece of evidence while learning about a case, evidence that substantially changes their beliefs about the validity of a proposition.

TYPES OF SET-MEMBERSHIP OBSERVATIONS AND MODES OF NARRATIVE

The categories of consequentialness and expectedness allow for the classification of different types of set-membership observations: high-priority, low-priority, irrelevant, impossible, critical, and cumulative observations (see figure 7.5). In turn, the use of these observations is associated with particular modes of narrative presentation in case-study research.

High-priority observations are set-membership observations that initially contain many but not all possible worlds as members and that have non-trivial belief-altering effects when discovered. They are called high-priority because when researchers become aware of the *potential* existence of such observations, they will likely target them in their research. They are a good investment of research time: they may well be present, and if they are, they will have important consequences for the validity of the proposition under consideration.

Consider again the debate over the end of the Cold War (discussed in chapter 5). One hypothesis to explain this outcome points to ideational factors—specifically, the intellectual entrepreneurship of Mikhail Gorbachev and other new-thinking reformers (English 2007). An alternative hypothesis holds that longstanding economic decline in the USSR explains both the ideational changes and the Soviet retrenchment (Brooks and Wohlforth 2007b). Through case-study research, English uncovered observations that suggest that Gorbachev and other reformers had an early engagement with new-thinking ideas (in the late 1970s) and that these ideas contributed to the Soviet economic decline. It seems plausible that English targeted these observations for discovery because he believed that they would be present (i.e., they had high expectedness) and that they would substantially decrease the tenability of the economic-decline hypothesis (i.e., they would have high consequentialness). In their rebuttal, Brooks and Wohlforth (2007a) argue that English fails to discuss any observations showing that old thinkers in the government believed that concrete alternatives to retrenchment were possible. They take English's

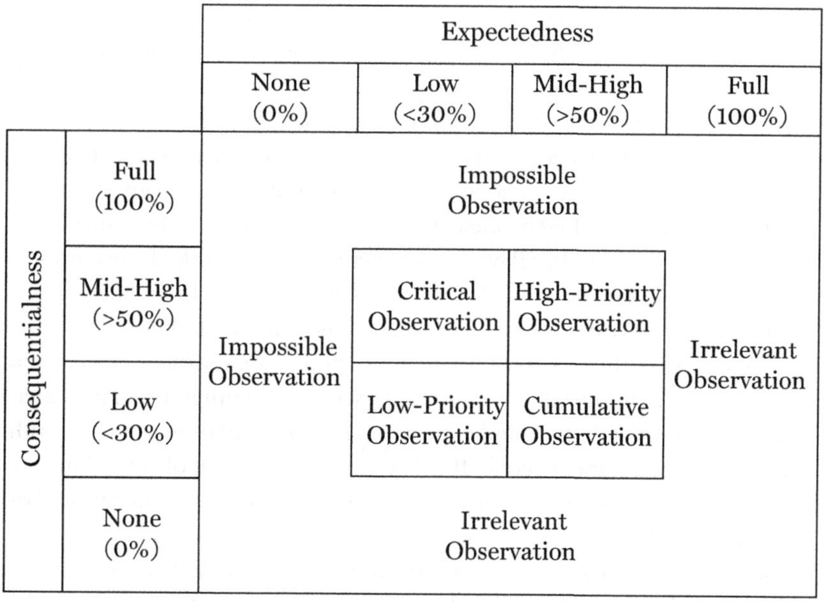

		Expectedness			
		None (0%)	Low (<30%)	Mid-High (>50%)	Full (100%)
Consequentialness	Full (100%)	Impossible Observation			
	Mid-High (>50%)	Impossible Observation	Critical Observation	High-Priority Observation	Irrelevant Observation
	Low (<30%)		Low-Priority Observation	Cumulative Observation	
	None (0%)	Irrelevant Observation			

FIGURE 7.5. Types of Set-Membership Observations

and others' silence about these observations as evidence that such alternatives did not exist.[10] In Brooks and Wohlforth's view, the end of the Cold War may have been the only option, given the material conditions.

At the other end of the spectrum, set-membership observations that are low in both expectedness and consequentialness are *low-priority observations*. These observations are considered likely to be absent, and they will not have much impact even if they are present. When consequentialness reaches zero, in fact, these observations have no value for proposition evaluation.

Irrelevant observations are defined as set-membership observations that cannot have an effect on the relative distribution of possible worlds in sets H and $\sim H$. They include all completely expected observations (i.e., those for which expectedness is 100%), because completely expected observations leave initial sets unaltered and do not change beliefs. Irrelevant observations also include those with some expectedness but whose consequentialness is 0%. Irrelevant observations can eliminate possible worlds, but they do not shift our beliefs about the relative distribution of possible worlds across H and $\sim H$. The idea that some observations are irrelevant is consistent with the broader argument that some pieces of evidence have no probative value and can be safely ignored when assessing hypotheses (Clarke 2002; Mahoney and Goertz 2004).

Within a Bayesian framework, *impossible observations* are those set-membership observations that are completely unexpected (i.e., whose expectedness is 0%) and those that completely eliminate all uncertainty (i.e., whose consequentialness is 100%). Completely unexpected evidence is impossible because it requires the elimination of all possible worlds from both set H and set $\sim H$, meaning that the proposition is neither true nor false, which is logically impossible in a Bayesian framework. Completely consequential evidence is impossible in practice, because it requires one to arrive at a perfect conclusion on the basis of imperfect data. Sometimes the impossible (from the standpoint of initial beliefs) does happen in scientific research (Mahoney and Goertz 2004; Steinhardt 2019). In a Bayesian set-theoretic framework, the occurrence of the impossible exposes the fallaciousness of initial assumptions, likely necessitating a (non-Bayesian) respecification of beliefs and hypotheses.[11]

Finally, two other kinds of set-membership observations—critical and cumulative—are important. They are opposed to each other in terms of their levels of consequentialness and expectedness. A *critical* observation is both consequential and unexpected. The discovery of a critical observation can, by itself, decisively rearrange beliefs about the validity of a proposition. For instance, Rueschemeyer, Stephens, and Stephens (1992) evaluated the unlikely proposition that working-class mobilization was a critical event for democratization in England. They found support for this proposition through the discovery of initially unexpected but decisive observations concerning the role of the working-class Chartist movement and Reform League in pushing forward democracy (pp. 95–97).

A *cumulative* observation has a mid to high level of expectedness, but a low level of consequentialness. A common approach to case-study research involves the gradual accumulation of this kind of evidence in support (or not) of a proposition. The researcher establishes confidence in the proposition through a series of many observations that are not individually consequential but that add up to substantial evidence when taken together. For example, the historian Lauria-Santiago (1999) found cumulative evidence against the proposition that nineteenth-century privatization reforms in El Salvador created a political economy controlled by large landholders. He examined previously unanalyzed land-title documents that repeatedly showed that privatization reforms distributed land parcels as small and medium-sized farms. While no single land document was decisive or unusual, these cumulative observations were, collectively, highly consequential and highly unexpected.

Figure 7.6 depicts a hypothetical series of belief changes brought on by multiple set-membership observations. In this illustration, the observations are fairly expected and consistently supportive of the proposition, with the percentage of possible worlds in which the proposition is true (H) moving from 50% to 67% to 75% to 90%. Each of these observations is independent and thus provides non-redundant evidence in favor of H. In real research, of course, some pieces of evidence may be supportive and others unsupportive, such that the trend is not in a single direction, although one direction may be

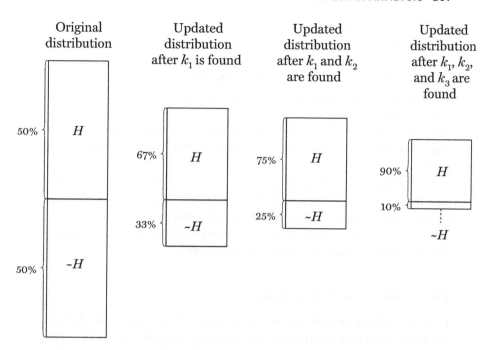

FIGURE 7.6. Illustration of Accumulation of Evidence in Favor of a Hypothesis. H = possible worlds in which the hypothesis is true; $\sim H$ = possible worlds in which the hypothesis is false.

dominant. In addition, a researcher may look at hundreds or even thousands of pieces of evidence, as Lauria-Santiago did; hence, the accumulation of evidence may entail many more steps than the figure suggests.

This discussion suggests two complementary modes of presenting evidence in a case-study narrative. The first is a *cumulative-evidence narrative*, in which the gradual collection of many observations builds support for or against a hypothesis. With this kind of narrative, the researcher uses many observations that are not of great consequence individually, but that collectively add up to being highly consequential. For practical reasons, it is difficult to formally produce a cumulative-evidence narrative for all the observations examined in many qualitative studies (Fairfield and Charman 2017, forthcoming). One would need to specify the changing distribution of possible worlds across hundreds or thousands of observations. It seems more practical to formally consider the overall impact of a *collection* of closely related cumulative observations. This collection is treated as a single piece of evidence, and an analyst diagrams the effect of this collection for the distribution of possible worlds across sets H and $\sim H$.

The second mode of presenting evidence is a *critical-evidence narrative*. Here, one or a small number of consequential pieces of evidence drive conclusions; hence, the narrative is built around a careful discussion of these key pieces. Critical evidence lends itself more naturally to the formal use of set-theoretic Bayesian analysis; a single presentation can be used to specify the consequence of observing the critical evidence. With critical observations, the researcher may consider the effect of prior beliefs on conclusions by examining the evidence across scenarios in which the initial distribution of possible worlds varies (e.g., scenarios in which 25%, 50%, or 75% of possible worlds initially have membership in set H). This approach is useful if researchers seek to persuade analysts whose starting beliefs about the validity of a proposition differ from their own.

In practice, most case-study researchers build cumulative-evidence narratives by drawing on dozens, hundreds, or even thousands of set-membership observations to support their arguments. However, they also use critical-evidence narratives to undercut alternative explanations or to add powerful clinching evidence in favor of their own explanation.

Set-Theoretic Tests Revisited

Bayesian analysis provides a useful way to understand and situate the set-theoretic tests discussed in chapter 4. From this perspective, the set-theoretic tests concern the extent to which observations k and $\sim k$ eliminate possible worlds in sets H and $\sim H$. The tests typically occur when a given observation (k or $\sim k$) retains nearly all of the possible worlds in set H (or $\sim H$) but eliminates many possible worlds in set $\sim H$ (or H).

A deterministic necessity test occurs when all possible worlds in set H require the existence of k; with the observation of $\sim k$, set H becomes the empty set. Approximate necessity tests occur when $\sim k$ eliminates a much higher proportion of the possible worlds in H than in $\sim H$. In the example in figure 7.7, most possible worlds in H (90%) require membership in k. Hence, when it is discovered that the actual world is located in $\sim k$, most of the cases in set H are eliminated, such that one's confidence in the proposition is greatly diminished.

Necessity tests can vary in how difficult they are to pass. To measure the difficulty of a necessity test, one references the expectedness of the observation that is used with the test. With a difficult necessity test, *unexpected* evidence must be present for the proposition to avoid diminution; difficult necessity tests require that set H be a subset of a comparatively small set k. With a difficult necessity test, the observation of k is non-trivial, contingent, and possibly even critical, provided that H does not already contain the vast majority of possible worlds. One can build positive support for a proposition by showing that it can pass difficult necessity tests.

With an easy necessity test, by contrast, *expected* evidence must be present for the proposition to avoid discrediting or falsification. Easy necessity tests require that set H be a subset of a comparatively large set k. With an

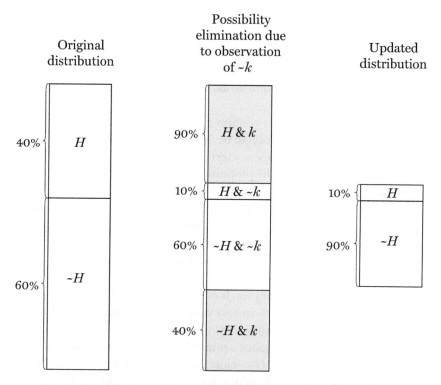

FIGURE 7.7. Illustration of an Approximate Necessity Test. H = possible worlds in which the hypothesis is true; $\sim H$ = possible worlds in which the hypothesis is false; k = evidence k is present; $\sim k$ = evidence k is not present; & = logical AND; shaded areas = possible worlds that are not the actual world.

easy necessity test, finding that the actual world case is a member of $\sim k$ may well be a critical observation (i.e., unexpected and consequential), but this observation may not be targeted, precisely because it is not likely to exist. The observation of k is low-priority (i.e., not expected and not consequential) and thus will not normally be actively sought by the researcher. The implication is that easy necessity tests often occur when researchers *serendipitously* discover a set-membership observation that calls into question a proposition of interest.

As a substantive illustration of a difficult necessity test, consider Chibber's (2003) causal proposition that domestic capitalists blocked successful state-led industrialization in India after independence. A necessity test for this proposition requires evidence that the deliberate efforts by Indian capitalists (e.g., lobbying, personal pleas, slowing down investment) hindered industrial initiatives by the state. Chibber not only presents a great deal of this kind of evidence; he also convinces readers that this kind of evidence is *not expected* in cases such as post-independence India. In other, similar cases, capitalists were unmotivated to oppose the state (e.g., in Korea and Japan), unable to do so because of structural weakness (e.g., in Taiwan), or unsuccessful because the state had the support of a mobilized labor movement (e.g., in France). Chibber strengthens his argument by showing that his necessity test is difficult rather than easy.

A sufficiency test works to confirm a proposition by making it unlikely or impossible for the proposition to be false, as is illustrated in figure 7.8. In its deterministic form, a sufficiency test eliminates all cases in set $\sim H$, leaving only scenarios in which the proposition is true. This kind of test occurs when the actual world is a member of k and all of the possible worlds in $\sim H$ assume and require membership in $\sim k$, meaning that the only remaining possible worlds are members of H. An approximate sufficiency test occurs when the researcher identifies a high-priority or critical observation that strongly supports a proposition. These observations have the effect of reducing $\sim H$ to a small fraction of all possible cases.

The difficulty of a sufficiency test is related to the expectedness of the evidence used with the test. With an easy sufficiency test, *expected* evidence is sufficient (or approximately sufficient) to confirm a proposition. Failing an easy sufficiency test counts against a proposition precisely because evidence k was expected to be present (i.e., most possible worlds are members of set k). By contrast, with a difficult sufficiency test, *unexpected* evidence helps to confirm a proposition. Failing a difficult sufficiency test does not count heavily against a proposition because evidence k was not expected in the first place (i.e., most possible worlds are not members of set k).

A substantive example of a successful sufficiency test (approximating figure 7.8) is Gandhi's (2008) work on the conditions under which dictators establish nominally democratic institutions (e.g., legislatures and parties). She argues that dictators establish these institutions in order to make concessions to domestic groups and thereby thwart rebellions and solicit cooperation. She specifically proposes that a dictator's access to substantial resource wealth should be inversely related to the likelihood of the creation of nominally democratic institutions under dictatorship. Her reasoning is that dictators with access to substantial wealth from natural resources do not need institutions in order to neutralize threats and solicit cooperation. A demanding test of this argument is to observe a sequence of events in which a dictator establishes institutions for the opposition and then withdraws them when natural resources become available. With the case of Kuwait, Gandhi finds this sequential evidence. The Kuwait example is powerful because the possible worlds associated with $\sim H$ cannot easily accommodate this evidence. In set-theoretic terms, very few of the possible worlds associated with set $\sim H$ have membership in set k, leaving behind mostly possible worlds with membership in set H.

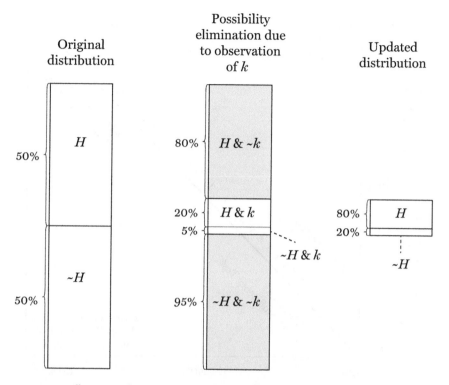

FIGURE 7.8. Illustration of an Approximate Sufficiency Test. H = possible worlds in which the hypothesis is true; $\sim H$ = possible worlds in which the hypothesis is false; k = evidence k is present; $\sim k$ = evidence k is not present; & = logical AND; shaded areas = possible worlds that are not the actual world.

Figure 7.9 situates the set-theoretic tests—necessity tests and sufficiency tests—as locations in a continuous space with dimensions that reflect the magnitude of change that occurs to set H and set $\sim H$ as a result of the observation of evidence k or $\sim k$. The borders of the figure represent impossible observations, or points that are logically contradictory and/or require the elimination of all uncertainty. The diagonal line extending from the lower left corner to the upper right corner indicates the space where irrelevant observations are found, or the zone where observations do not affect the *relative* size of H and $\sim H$. The lower left corner is the space where necessity tests and sufficiency tests generate strong conclusions about propositions. In this lower left zone, a failed necessity test occurs when the observation of $\sim k$ eliminates most cases in set H, while preserving many cases in set $\sim H$. A sufficiency test is the inverse: the observation of k eliminates most cases in set $\sim H$, while preserving many cases in set H.

This classification of set-theoretic tests is like recent probabilistic approaches in that it presents the tests as regions in a continuous two-dimensional space (Humphreys and Jacobs 2015). However, it preserves the orientation of the

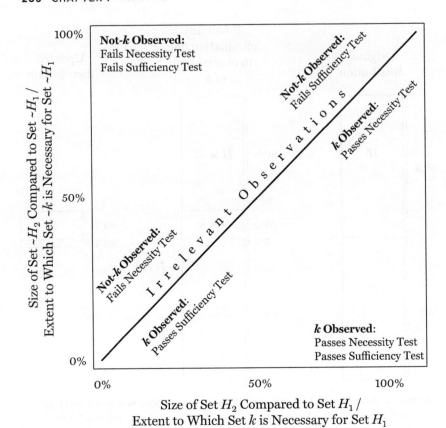

FIGURE 7.9. Set-Theoretic Tests Revisited

approaches that define these tests using necessary and sufficient conditions (Bennett 2008; Collier 2011; Mahoney 2012). In fact, the two dimensions of the figure can be restated precisely in the language of necessary and sufficient conditions: the x-axis refers to the extent to which actual world membership in set k is necessary for membership in set H_1 (and, equivalently, the extent to which actual world membership in $\sim k$ is sufficient for actual world membership in $\sim H_1$). Likewise, the y-axis refers to the extent to which actual world membership in set $\sim k$ is necessary for actual world membership in set $\sim H_1$ (and, equivalently, the extent to which actual world membership in k is sufficient for actual world membership in H_1).

———

Bayesian analysis (or its equivalent) is a fundamental part of scientific epistemology; its application differentiates a scientific approach to estimating certitude from a non-scientific one. It is useful to conceive Bayesian analysis as part of the overarching logical mechanics through which evidence is ideally processed for the purpose of proposition evaluation. Bayesian analysis is appropriate when considering the consequence of *any* evidence introduced to update beliefs about the truth of a proposition (Fairfield and Charman forthcoming; Humphreys and Jacobs forthcoming). Such evidence includes data collected from reading books and documents, interviewing and talking to people, and observing people and situations. It includes findings that are reached through statistical tests, set-theoretic tests, and experimental tests. It includes the conclusions that are derived from comparative analysis, sequence analysis, and counterfactual analysis.

The set-theoretic approach to Bayesian analysis discussed in this chapter shows why and how the observation of evidence can change beliefs about the validity of a proposition. The approach encourages researchers to think visually, with intersecting sets, when assessing evidence. It offers a precise way of distinguishing between consequential evidence and expected evidence. This distinction, in turn, allows for a typology of the kinds of set-membership observations that are used in case-study research, as well as the modes of narrative presentation that are associated with particular kinds of observations. The set-theoretic approach further offers a way of conceptualizing set-theoretic tests that preserves the strengths of previous formulations that use either necessary and sufficient conditions or a probability-based perspective. By doing so, the approach suggests that the distinction between probability analysis and set-theoretic analysis is not a choice between two mutually exclusive alternatives; rather, the former depends ontologically on the latter.

Explanatory Tools

8

Theory Frames and Normative Traditions

Theory frames, which consist of a small number of basic concepts and their relationships, serve as general orientations through which analysts view the substance of social reality. Social scientists use theory frames, often implicitly, in all phases of research: formulating categories and propositions, collecting and interpreting evidence, designing and presenting explanations, and reporting conclusions and summarizing findings. The existence of different theory frames helps arrange scholarly activity into distinct traditions, with competing assumptions, propositions, and accumulated knowledge.

This chapter provides a scientific constructivist approach for understanding and using theory frames. It emphasizes the cognitive foundations of theory frames, as well as their connections to normative traditions. It sees both theory frames and normative traditions as extensions of primitive image schemas and force dynamic models that are basic to human thought. The next chapter considers general categories—*actors, objects, rules, resources, events,* and *processes*—that social scientists use with theory frames to formulate specific propositions, theories, explanations, and narrative accounts. Together, these two chapters offer a way of thinking about social science theory that is grounded in the basic structures of human cognition.

The first section of this chapter conceptualizes theory frames as specialized cognitive structures used for understanding society. Different theory frames differentially "fill in" scripted slots corresponding to the actors, rules, and resources of society. Three basic theory frames in macrosocial research are compared here: rationalist, culturalist, and structuralist theory frames. These frames are grounded in different understandings of the relationships among actors, rules, and resources. The section explores the basic theory frames that characterize particular scholarly works, particular scholars, and even particular disciplines in the social sciences.

The chapter's second section considers the normative side of theory frames. Scientific constructivism rejects a strong version of moral realism, in which normative statements are ontologically objective. This rejection follows necessarily from the constructivist belief that the categories that compose normative propositions—including the evaluative categories—are mind-dependent kinds. Nevertheless, a scientific constructivist approach encourages researchers to analyze these propositions in much the same way as they analyze descriptive and causal propositions. Normative propositions are statements that can be evaluated as true or false in light of accepted scholarly evidence and shared commitments to overarching normative frameworks. Scholars working from the standpoint of different normative traditions may not be able to achieve consensus about the truth of specific propositions. Yet within the value systems of a given normative tradition, they can study normative propositions scientifically and accumulate knowledge about them, using the tools of set-theoretic analysis.

The final section of this chapter considers the affinities between specific theory frames and particular normative traditions. The discussion illustrates how the core assumptions of each theory frame link it to a particular normative tradition: a culturalist theory frame connects to moral relativism, a rationalist theory frame connects to moral utilitarianism, and a structuralist theory frame connects to moral egalitarianism. The connections between specific versions of a theory frame and specialized normative orientations are also analyzed. I propose that particular theory frames are linked to particular normative traditions because they share the same understanding of the relationships among actors, rules, and resources in an idealized model of society.

The Logic of Theory Frames

A *theory frame* is a set of assumptions about orienting concepts and relationships that guide theory construction (Rueschemeyer 2009: 1–2, 12–17). Theory frames are not themselves theories, as conventionally defined,[1] though they do shape the process of theorizing. Theory frames identify the *kinds* of categories and phenomena that merit attention, providing guidelines for their description and analysis. In the social sciences, specific theory frames call attention to certain kinds of actors, certain types of social rules, and certain classes of resources.

To explicate the role of theory frames in social science research, it is useful to begin by considering how cognitive models function in everyday sense-making. From this vantage point, a theory frame can be viewed as a specialized cognitive structure blended from more basic cognitive models and image schemas.

COGNITIVE MODELS AND THEORY FRAMES

Human beings process information about the world using cognitive models (Cienki 2007; Evans 2006; Fillmore 1975; Lakoff 1987; Minsky 1975; Schank and Abelson 1977). *Cognitive models* are stylized scenarios depicting ordinary situations that have a simple structure and follow a recognizable pattern. They are idealized understandings of the entities and activities that compose recurrent happenings in the social world. Particular cognitive models identify a small number of general categories that are structurally and temporally related to one another. The categories function like scripted slots that are executed in specific ways for particular cases.[2] In order to understand any individual category or specific facet of a cognitive model, one must have a grasp of the structure and meaning of the whole model.

Cognitive models characterize the stereotypic actors, rule-bound behaviors, and normal sequences for well-known social events. In contemporary American culture, well-known social events include eating out at a restaurant, walking the dog, grocery shopping, attending a college lecture, getting an oil change, going out to the movies, waiting at the DMV, receiving a manicure, having a nightcap, going to the dentist, preparing for a colonoscopy, and so on. If a friend writes you a text message at 1:23 p.m. saying, "I'm going to be late because my waiter is taking forever to bring the check," the sentence is perfectly comprehensible because we share an understanding of the routines and normal course of affairs that accompany going to a restaurant for lunch.

Cognitive models vary in their complexity. The complexity of a given model is related to the difficulty of learning it. The simplest cognitive models are used by preverbal infants, perhaps during the second six months of life (Mandler 1992; Mandler and Pagán Cánovas 2014). As infants begin to perceive regularities among spatial entities, they create imageries that correspond with these regularities, generating expectations and elementary predictions. Infant minds create cognitive models by integrating two or more image schemas into an enriched structure. This integration can involve the extension of primitive spatial notions to non-spatial elements, such as bodily feelings.[3] Over time, children blend specialized image schemas into ever more complex structures. These structures include the cognitive models required for understanding the meaning of social situations and their constituent parts.

Like the events they depict, cognitive models are located at different levels on a ladder of generality. Cognitive models higher up the ladder are more general than models at a lower level, which are more specific. A set-theoretic way of thinking about the ladder of generality uses superset-subset relations. For example, the cognitive model "eating out at a restaurant" is a subset of the more general model "going out" and a superset of the more specific model "eating out at a fancy restaurant." The ladder of generality also functions as a part-whole hierarchy. For example, the model "eating out at a restaurant" may be one part of the more general model "night out on the town." At the same time, the model "eating out at a restaurant" contains its own specific parts, including the sub-model "getting the check." To understand a cognitive model, one needs to grasp its positioning in both set-theoretic and part-whole hierarchies.

A set-theoretic approach is helpful for studying the ways in which cognitive models generate *prototype effects* for categories (Rosch 1978). Prototype effects occur when individuals view a given case as a partial or problematic member of a category. Consider the category *waiter*, which is dependent on the full enactment of the overall restaurant cognitive model (Schank and Abelson 1977: 42–46). It may be unclear whether an individual is a waiter if important aspects of the restaurant model (e.g., menus, table service, checks) do not apply to his or her employment. With set-theoretic analysis, each relevant aspect of a cognitive model can be viewed as a category in its own right, in which a particular case can be a full member, a partial member, or a non-member. For example, one contextual aspect of the restaurant model is a society in which eating establishments have paid employees who perform specialized work tasks. If this contextual feature is only partially present (e.g., in an eating establishment with only one employee), the restaurant model may not be fully applicable, with the consequence that an individual case may be a partial or a non-ideal-typical member of the category *waiter*.

In the social sciences, image schemas and cognitive models are blended to create the elements that constitute *basic theory frames*. I understand basic theory frames as distinct cognitive structures in their own right. These distinct cognitive structures function as general, specialized, and complex tools that researchers use to make sense of human experience. Basic theory frames are *general* in that they can be applied to a wide range of social situations and behaviors. Social scientists who work with a particular theory frame have great flexibility in the substantive topics and issues they might study. Basic theory frames are *specialized* in the sense that they require much background knowledge for their use. A substantial amount of higher education (e.g., years in graduate school) may be needed to comprehend and proficiently use basic theory frames in the social sciences. Finally, basic theory frames are *complex* in that they combine many underlying cognitive models and image schemas. One cannot fully understand a basic theory frame without first understanding the cognitive models that it presupposes.

We can situate basic theory frames within a hierarchy of cognitive structures ranked from lower to higher levels of complexity and specialization. In the following ranking, basic theory frames are among the more complex and more specialized structures:

—basic image schemas and spatial primitives (e.g., OBJECT, CONTAINER, PATH, MOVE, LINK)
—complex image schemas and force dynamics (object into container, source–path–goal, revolving movement)
—basic cognitive models (grasping an object, eating food, waking up)
—complex cognitive models (carrying out a labor strike, eloping, going through airport security)
—basic theory frames (culturalist, structuralist, and rationalist orientations)
—specialized theory frames (social role theory, structural Marxism, social choice theory)

In this hierarchy, the more complex structures are blended from less complex structures. For example, basic theory frames are blends of basic cognitive models and basic and complex image schemas. The blends form distinct wholes that are psychologically richer than their constituent parts (Fauconnier and Turner 2002; Mandler and Pagán Cánovas 2014).

Scholars use basic theory frames, as well as other cognitive structures, mostly implicitly and unconsciously when making sense of the world in their research. Only upon explicit reflection can they begin to appreciate the full extent to which a given theory frame shapes their research. We do not learn about the ways in which scholars use basic theory frames primarily by examining what they explicitly *say* about theory, but rather by examining the *substantive content* of their works, which reveal the authors' implicit assumptions. We must acknowledge the behind-the-scenes and background role of theory frames in order to understand the logic of social science. Social science is not an inductive art in which scholars perform analyses by starting with a blank slate, lacking assumptions. Rather, social science is a structured practice in which researchers bring to an analysis important assumptions about how a society works. These assumptions have major consequences for the content of their work.

In the study of a particular subject matter, scholars often use the underspecified components of a basic theory frame to build more specialized theoretical orientations. The additional assumptions and categories that scholars add to basic theory frames form the basis of *specialized theory frames*. Whereas basic theory frames are normally left implicit, specialized theory frames are often discussed explicitly. Researchers create them to address the particular puzzles and problems raised by the specific subject matter under study. For instance, as

Rueschemeyer (2009: 13–18) shows, the specialized frames of Barrington Moore (1966) and Theda Skocpol (1979) consist of concepts and relationships concerning the international state system, the state, and socioeconomic classes. These specialized theory frames are closely related: they implicitly share the basic theory frame that I call the structuralist frame. Yet they differ in that Moore's specialized theory frame emphasizes primarily class formation, class conflict, and class coalition building, whereas Skocpol places special emphasis on the state and its relations to other states and societal groups, including classes. Specialized theory frames are close in content to the sets of propositions that constitute theories; when scholars discuss specialized theory frames explicitly, they often do so toward the end of formulating an explicit theory of their subject matter (e.g., a theory of revolution, democracy, or development).

THREE BASIC THEORY FRAMES

In the social sciences, basic theory frames provide stylized understandings of the actors, rules, and resources that characterize societies. Different basic theory frames conceive these categories and their relationships in contrasting ways. Within each frame, however, the conceptions of these categories resonate with one another, allowing us to speak of a *harmonic triad* between the actors, rules, and resources of a particular theory frame (cf. Emirbayer and Mische 1998: 971–72). Just as one note may be dominant within a particular musical triad, so too with a basic theory frame: one of the components—actors, rules, or resources—can be dominant with a particular frame.[4]

Table 8.1 summarizes three basic theory frames used in macrosocial research: culturalist, rationalist, and structuralist theory frames (cf. Lichbach and Zuckerman 1997, 2009). The frames present alternative idealized portraits of society and its components. These frames are *basic* in the sense that they are formulated at a level of generality that is cognitively resonant and easily grasped by social scientists. Above this level, one finds general theoretical categories and relationships. For example, situated at this higher level are classic tensions in social theory, such as agency versus structure, idealism versus materialism, and integration versus disintegration. Below the basic level, one finds specialized theory frames, including specific subtypes of the basic theory frames. For example, social choice theory is a specialized theory frame within the basic rationalist frame; state-centered theory is a specialized theory frame within the basic structuralist frame; and social role theory is a specialized theory frame within the basic culturalist frame.

The three basic theory frames all posit interdependent relationships among actors, resources, and rules. As figure 8.1 illustrates, however, each frame calls special attention to the relationships corresponding to its dominant category. For each frame, one category strikes a dominant note in the triad. Thus, the

TABLE 8.1. A Stylized Typology of Theory Frames

	Culturalist Frame	Rationalist Frame	Structuralist Frame
Dominant Category	Social rules	Actors	Resources
Conception of Actors	Constituted by social norms	Goal-oriented individuals	Constituted by social structures
Conception of Social Rules	Constitutive and regularity codes	Constraints on actors	Elite-controlled instruments
Conception of Resources	Socially constructed entities	Entities with utility for individuals	Constitutive material entities

culturalist theory frame especially emphasizes the ways in which social rules shape actors and resources; the rationalist theory frame stresses the ways in which actors shape social rules and resources; and the structuralist theory frame calls special attention to the ways in which resources shape actors and rules.

Although scholars may use different basic theory frames during the course of their career, or even within a given study, they are usually drawn to, and work within, one particular basic theory frame. For instance, ten well-known scholars whose work exemplifies the culturalist frame are Émile Durkheim, Bronislaw Malinowski, Margaret Mead, Claude Lévi-Strauss, Clifford Geertz, Sherry Ortner, Mary Douglas, James Scott, Joan Scott, and Nancy Scheper-Hughes. Ten well-known scholars who work within the structuralist theory frame are Karl Marx, W. E. B. Du Bois, Sidney Mintz, Immanuel Wallerstein, Theda Skocpol, Evelyne Huber, Michael Burawoy, Erik Olin Wright, Aihwa Ong, and Kathleen Thelen. And ten famous scholars associated with the rationalist theory frame are Adam Smith, James Buchanan, Kenneth Arrow, Gary Becker, Elinor Ostrom, Margaret Levi, Douglass North, Barry Weingast, James Robinson, and Daron Acemoglu. To be sure, not all scholars and scholarly works can be easily associated with a single theory frame. However, I propose that social scientists hold broadly shared beliefs such that, if presented with the typology in table 8.1, they would be able to readily identify which scholars and which works (including their own) belong primarily in which of these three basic theory frames.

The three basic theory frames are not the only way in which one could slice up the different meta-theoretical approaches of social science works. At a higher level of analysis, one could focus on how scholarly works vary in where they stand vis-à-vis basic tensions in social science, such as conflict versus cooperation. At a lower level, one could differentiate a large number of specialized theory frames that characterize particular works focused on particular subject matters. Alternatively, one could propose an entirely different set of dimensions for comparison while still trying to remain at the basic level.

A. Shared Understanding

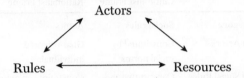

B. Dominant Relationship in Culturalist Theory Frame

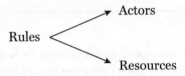

C. Dominant Relationship in Rationalist Theory Frame

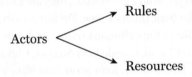

D. Dominant Relationship in Structuralist Theory Frame

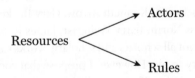

FIGURE 8.1. Dominant Relationships for Basic Theory Frames

However, I argue (below) that the three basic theory frames presented here are deeply rooted in human cognition, through their connection with image schemas and force dynamics. Because of this grounding, these basic theory frames are not part of an arbitrarily designed typology of scholarly works; rather, they reflect the basic cognitive structures that humans use to navigate the world.

Regarding their conceptions of *actors*, the frames differ with respect to these core agents who animate events. A culturalist frame identifies actors on the basis of shared beliefs and norms; a rationalist frame identifies actors on the basis of the goals and preferences of individuals; and a structuralist frame identifies actors on the basis of the position of groups in social structures. Accordingly, culturalists study actors such as sociologists, musicians, and nurses; rationalists study actors such as voters, consumers, and firms; and structuralists study actors such as classes, states, and international organizations. Scholars associated with each of these traditions certainly might study the same kind of actor, but they would ordinarily do so in different ways. For example, when studying a social movement, a culturalist might emphasize the norms that bind the movement together and give it purpose; a rationalist might stress the shared preferences that make it worthwhile for individuals to join the movement; and a structuralist might view the movement as reflecting a socioeconomic division within society.

The three basic theory frames also call attention to different kinds of social *rules*. Cultural theorists stress the importance of informal rules, especially norms that are not consciously perceived. For these scholars, consecutive layers of informal rules serve to constitute norm-based actors and to guide and make meaningful their behavior. By contrast, rationalist scholars call attention to formal rules, especially codified institutional rules that are upheld by public organizations. These scholars stress the regulatory and coordinating effects of institutions, conceiving them as constraints that shape the cost-benefit calculus of self-interested actors with preexisting preferences. Finally, structural theorists emphasize the role of social rules in upholding existing patterns of resource distribution. In this frame, dominant actors control the content of social rules and use them to bolster their power.

Finally, *resources* are conceived in contrasting ways across the frames. With a culturalist frame, analysts focus attention on the shared norms and understandings that underpin resources and make them meaningful and valuable. These researchers view resources as culturally constructed entities whose worth depends on explicit and implicit social understandings. With a rationalist frame, by contrast, analysts view individual preferences as defining what is a resource, understood as an entity (e.g., money, goods, or services) that has utility or value for individuals. These researchers seek to represent individual preferences concerning outcomes related to resources and their distribution. Finally, with a structuralist frame, analysts see resources as material entities that exist independently of the beliefs and preferences of particular individuals. For structuralists, the asymmetrical distribution of resources is constitutive of conflicting collective actors, with the dominant group possessing the resources to shape the norms and culture of a society.

Scholars assess the *validity* of both basic and specialized theory frames on the basis of their *utility* for social research (Rueschemeyer 2009). Specific theory frames are useful to the extent that they suggest new, substantively important, and approximately true propositions. Moreover, they are useful to the extent that they foster novel understandings of problems and solutions, generate good explanations of specific cases, synthesize diverse findings, and support overall programs of knowledge accumulation. Useful theory frames consist of categories and relationships that capture important aspects of experiential reality at a high level of generality. The belief that the content of a useful theory frame corresponds to the content of experiential reality is important for the additional belief that the validity of a theory frame can be derived from its utility in substantive analysis. Useful theory frames deliver valid results because they represent in a general way the entities and structure of society as communities understand and experience it.

THE TRIAD AND FORCE DYNAMICS

The discussion in this section suggests that a meta-cognitive template in which society is composed of actors, rules, and resources holds great importance for social research. The particular assumptions made about the relationships in this model serve as filters through which social scientists make sense of what is happening in the social world, including (as we shall see) what is right and wrong.

Why should the categories *actors*, *rules*, and *resources* and their relationships serve as a foundation for theorizing in the social sciences? An important part of the answer, I propose, is the correspondence between the actor-rule-resource triad and deeply rooted, perhaps innate modes of comprehending reality. The triadic way of conceiving society resonates with the most rudimentary image schemas shared by all people in all cultures. I specifically propose that scholars implicitly recruit the cognitive structures that emerge from physical interaction with the world early in life in order to mentally represent the abstract idea of *society* and its component parts. The argument is that the cognitive structures that help human beings reason about space and force, and thereby navigate the physical world, are repurposed in order to conceptualize society and its parts. This kind of repurposing is essential in order for individuals to make sense of abstract entities that they cannot see or touch (see, e.g., Jackendoff 1983). When scholars seek to understand society, they do not manufacture their conceptualizations out of nothing; they draw on basic cognitive structures that are intuitively grasped by all.

Force dynamics refers to the underlying image schemas concerning force and movement that people use to think and speak about abstract domains (Talmy 1988; Pinker 2007; Wolff 2007; Casasanto 2010; Copley and Harley 2015; Wolff and Thorstad 2017). Although these image schemas are preverbal and nonvisual cognitive structures, they can be comprehended through diagrams that depict a structured space in which entities can move in particular directions with particular degrees of force. A rich literature shows that humans use force dynamics when representing concepts, understanding causation, reasoning about time, and depicting events and processes. I build on this literature in proposing that scholars employ force dynamics when they conceptualize society as an entity made up of interdependent actors, rules, and resources.

Human beings acquire force dynamic comprehension as infants and without any training. In the first six months of life, infants pay attention to the motion of objects on paths moving through space, taking particular notice of containment and blockage (Mandler and Pagán Cánovas 2014). The primitive spatial ideas of OBJECT, SPACE, MOTION, PATH, LOCATION, CONTACT, INTO/OUT OF, and BLOCKED MOTION are what infants are drawn to when encountering the world (Mandler 1992, 2004, 2012). These primitive spatial ideas are also the constituents of force dynamics. The verbs used to designate different kinds of force dynamic patterns correspond to the first image schemas acquired in life (e.g., PUSH, STOP, SUPPORT, PREVENT, RESIST, HINDER, MAINTAIN, ALLOW, OVERCOME) (Mandler and Pagán Cánovas 2014; Gärdenfors 2007; Fauconnier and Turner 2002).

To represent force dynamic patterns, psychologists and cognitive scientists use diagrams that feature entities with tendencies toward motion operating in spaces with forces and counterforces. The example diagrams in figure 8.2 depict an entity with an intrinsic tendency toward rest (the squares) or directed motion (the circles). The structure of the space includes an obstacle (the wall) that can block movement and a potential destination location (the money). The entity encounters forces and counterforces (the arrows) of different strengths (represented by the size of the arrows). Thus, a basic force dynamic model like this one calls attention to (1) an entity with a tendency to either rest or move; (2) the strength of the forces and counterforces acting on the entity; and (3) the structural features of the space, such as obstacles and specific locations.

The actor-rule-resource triad maps closely onto the basic components of force dynamic models. When this triad is cast explicitly in terms of force dynamics, *actors* are the entities that move within the space. Under the analogy, the initial state of an entity toward rest or motion reflects the characteristics—e.g., desires and goals—of the actor (a point highlighted by my use of faces on the entities in figure 8.2). *Rules* correspond to the structure of the space in which the entities move. The space may include physical obstacles and specific destination regions that constrain or enable movement. In addition, rules correspond to background assumptions that are taken for granted, such as the idea that the main entity is a unitary object that possesses a constant identity. Finally, *resources* correspond to the force supporting the entity's movement and any counterforces. Powerful entities move with such force that they can resist or overcome weaker antagonists to reach destination locations.

The appeal of the triadic model is not only a matter of cognitive resonance with deeply seated ideas about entities, forces, and structured spaces. It is also useful for reasons similar to why force dynamic models are useful: it provides foundational ideas for dividing an unconstituted social reality into basic

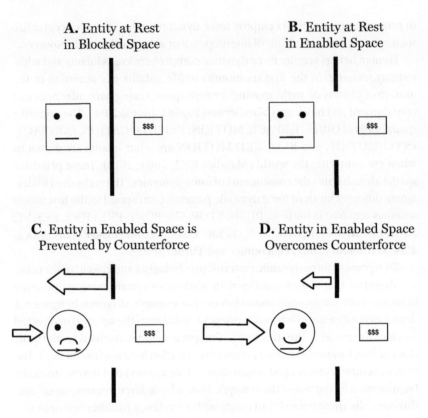

A. Entity at Rest in Blocked Space

B. Entity at Rest in Enabled Space

C. Entity in Enabled Space is Prevented by Counterforce

D. Entity in Enabled Space Overcomes Counterforce

FIGURE 8.2. Illustration of Force Dynamic Patterns

components and relations. Scholars need some starting concepts and relations to ground their understandings of a society; force dynamics provides these starting concepts and relations.

This discussion illustrates the central role of analogical and metaphorical reasoning in the construction of models of society (Bartha 2019; Gentner and Maravilla 2018; Rigney 2001; Swedberg 2014). To make sense of society, scholars draw on ideas from a domain that features elements and relations that are readily and intuitively understood by all people—that is, force dynamics. This well-understood source domain is connected via analogy to an abstract target domain—that is, society. As with analogies in general, the linkage between the source domain (force dynamics) and the target domain (society) depends on the two domains' sharing a system of relations among elements. The source domain provides the model for describing and explaining features of the abstract target domain.

When force dynamics is the source domain, scholars can choose to emphasize certain structural relationships and not others. In line with the discussion

Culturalist Frame
(Cultural Anthropology, 1950s–present;
Political Science, 1950s–1960s;
Sociology, 1950s–1960s; 1990s–present)

Rationalist Frame
(Economics, 1950s–present;
Political Science, 1990s–present)

Structuralist Frame
(Sociology, 1970s–present;
Political Science, 1970s–present)

FIGURE 8.3. Theory Frames and Disciplines in the Social Sciences

in this section, I propose that (1) culturalists emphasize the ways in which society is like a force dynamic pattern in which the structure of the space is of paramount importance; (2) rationalists emphasize the ways in which society is like a force dynamic pattern in which the direction of the entities is of central importance; and (3) structuralists emphasize the ways in which society is like a force dynamic pattern in which the strength of the forces is of foremost importance. These different assumptions offer the starting points for building more specific categories, propositions, and theories that can be used to make sense of myriad topics in the social sciences.

Finally, although the discussion in this section has emphasized the ways in which individual scholars use particular theory frames, it is also possible to see whole disciplines as primarily oriented toward particular theory frames. Figure 8.3 offers a general and suggestive (perhaps provocative) portrait of how the disciplines of cultural anthropology, economics, political science, and sociology can be linked to particular theory frames during the period since the mid-twentieth century. On this view, the discipline of economics is located at the rationalist corner, whereas cultural anthropology is situated at the culturalist corner (archeology falls mostly into the natural sciences). Political science has evolved from systems theory in the 1950s and 1960s (culturalist corner) to materialist Marxism/Weberianism from the 1970s to the present (structuralist corner), adding rational choice theories since the 1990s (rationalist corner). For its part, sociology has always hovered between the culturalist and structuralist corners, with the discipline moving from system/functionalist theory in the 1950s and 1960s to materialist Marxism/Weberianism from the 1970s to the present, and adding a new cultural sociology from the 1990s to the present. Fittingly, sociology as a discipline has never moved toward the rationalist corner, where economics resides.

The Normative Side of Theory Frames

Theory frames have implications for understanding both what *is* and what *ought to be*. In the social sciences, they are used as instruments for the formulation and evaluation of descriptive and causal propositions about the social world. Yet theory frames serve equally as devices for the study of *normative propositions*. Theory frames not only suggest certain ways of answering the questions, "Did event Z occur?" and "Did event X cause event Z?" They also provide direction when answering the question, "Was event Z morally just?" Theory frames act as filters for formulating overall moral visions and for deciding what is right and wrong with respect to the specific events and phenomena under study (Rueschemeyer 2009).

The debate over the degree to which social science is, should, or must be concerned with normative issues has a long history. A scientific constructivist approach to this debate begins with the acknowledgment that societal facts depend on human understandings and collective agreements. Although facts about natural kinds are brute and objective (i.e., their truth does not depend on collective understandings), the same cannot be said of facts about the social world. Societal facts are *ontologically subjective* in the sense that their existence depends on an interaction between human minds and objective reality. Yet within the framework of scientific constructivism, societal facts are *epistemologically objective*: they are true within communities of individuals who share the beliefs and understandings that constitute a semantic context (Hacking 1999: 22; Searle 1995: 7–9; cf. Green and Vervaeke 1997). A conclusion is epistemologically objective when individuals must accept its validity as a requirement for logical consistency with the accepted beliefs of their community. For instance, if we agree that "Jones sincerely promised to pay Begay five dollars," logical coherence in our beliefs requires us to also believe that "Jones *ought* to pay Begay five dollars" (Searle 1964; see also Anscombe 1958). To reject this normative conclusion would force us to give up one or more of our common beliefs. Thus, in our community, the normative statement "Jones ought to pay Begay five dollars" can be derived as an epistemologically objective truth from our non-normative beliefs and our knowledge that Jones sincerely promised to pay Begay five dollars.

Normative statements can be divided into two types according to their epistemological status. The first type consists of normative statements that are epistemologically objective, in the sense that their truth can be derived from existing societal facts within a community. An example is the proposition that slavery in the United States was wrong. If you accept other commonly embraced societal facts in our community (e.g., everyone possesses individual rights), you are logically committed to this proposition as well. The second type of normative statements are epistemologically subjective, in the sense that their truth cannot be established on the basis of shared social knowledge among the members of a semantic community. The proposition that dogs are better than cats is an example. Although I happen to believe that dogs are better than cats, you may disagree, and most likely neither of us can logically derive our belief from societal facts. We probably have to agree to disagree, though a discussion of the matter might usefully expose other normative beliefs and personal tastes about which we disagree.

It may not be clear—or it may be a matter of debate—whether a given statement is epistemologically objective or epistemologically subjective. People and scholars often work to show that their important normative beliefs are epistemologically objective. They marshal evidence and reasoning to support their evaluative claims. They try to show that their important normative views are no mere opinion, but rather the conclusions that one *must* accept provided that one shares certain other reasonable premises.

Scientific constructivism follows a principled middle ground with respect to normative statements. On the one hand, it rejects a strong moral realism (as is found in, e.g., Moore 1922), in which some normative statements are true (or false) in all possible worlds. As a constructivist approach, scientific constructivism does not agree that normative statements are ontologically objective propositions whose truth can be established independently of human beings and human ideas. Instead, the truth of normative statements depends on collective agreement about many issues, including the meaning of the categories that compose normative statements. We need to have some level of agreement about the meaning of *slavery, United States,* and *wrong* before we can assess the truth of the proposition that slavery in the United States was wrong. In this regard, scientific constructivism follows a long line of literature expressing skepticism that specific moral claims can be regarded as necessarily true (see Mackie 1977: chap. 1).

Yet on the other hand, scientific constructivism rejects all arguments—whether relativist (e.g., Rorty 1991) or positivist (e.g., Ayer 1952)—that maintain that normative statements are necessarily arbitrary or meaningless (Harré and Krausz 1996). Scientific constructivism treats normative statements as legitimate and meaningful propositions that can be evaluated on the basis of evidence and reason, at least within specific semantic communities. Scientific constructivism does not sharply distinguish between descriptive and causal propositions, on the one hand, and normative propositions on the other. Thus, it does not assign a radically different epistemological status to the following three statements: (1) labor systems under the Aztec Empire were a form of slavery; (2) population density was an important cause of slavery under the Aztec Empire; and (3) slavery under the Aztec Empire was wrong. Scholars who share a semantic context and a particular normative tradition could work to achieve consensus about whether these statements are true or false. Expert knowledge of the Aztec political and economic systems would help in evaluating their truth, as would good knowledge of relevant generalizations about labor systems and slavery.

Normative statements are distinct from descriptive and causal statements in that they embody evaluative claims and are explicitly linked to our moral beliefs. Our morals seem to be a class of sentiments in which we feel negatively (or positively) toward something and are oriented toward avoidance (or acceptance), cessation (or continuation), and/or withdrawal (or engagement). We seem to use our feelings as information for deciding whether something is right or wrong (Prinz 2014). Our specific categories for emotions, such as anger and sadness, are human kinds that evidence suggests we learn at a young age from those around us (Barrett 2017). Over time, we develop reasonably coherent systems of normative principles—moral compasses—to guide our judgments and behaviors. Our initial attraction or aversion to a particular theory frame can be linked to our preexisting normative system. Theory frames may seem intuitively right or wrong to us in part because of the emotional feelings they stir within us.

Scientific constructivism encourages scholars to assess normative statements dispassionately, on the basis of evidence. If scholars disagree about the truth of a normative statement, they are directed to understand more precisely the contrasting assumptions and beliefs that underpin the disagreement. While in practice they may not always reach agreement concerning the beliefs that drive their different normative conclusions, they should *in principle* be able to locate the sources of their differences. The differences may have to do with the core assumptions of their contrasting general normative systems (e.g., utilitarianism versus egalitarianism). Scholars with different starting assumptions may not be able to engage in productive conversations unless, for the sake of argument, they agree to adopt some shared starting point. By contrast, individuals who do share an overarching normative tradition can work more productively to identify the sources of their different beliefs. This effort can help them understand the underlying beliefs and the perhaps hidden assumptions on which their normative convictions rest.

In short, while scientific constructivism closes the door on the possibility of analyzing normative statements as if they have the ontological status of being true or false, it leaves the door open for the epistemologically objective assessment of normative propositions in the social sciences. It assumes that scholars working within a particular normative tradition can arrive at rational conclusions about the truth of normative statements on the basis of evidence and reason. Scientific constructivism incorporates the goal of *normative inference* into the social sciences, alongside descriptive inference and causal inference.

The Logic of Normative Traditions

This section discusses three general normative traditions: relativism, utilitarianism, and egalitarianism. The goal of the discussion is not to provide a comprehensive overview of these rich traditions; only cursory descriptions of them are offered here. Rather, the goal is to explore how normative traditions are rooted in specific understandings of the actor-rule-resource triad, which in turn links particular normative traditions to particular theory frames. I argue that the relativist, utilitarian, and egalitarian normative traditions are linked to, respectively, the culturalist, rationalist, and structuralist theory frames. These connections exist because normative traditions and theory frames share specific ways of configuring the actor-rule-resource triad. The need for analytical consistency helps explain why scholars usually adopt theory frames and normative traditions that are built from the same understanding of the actor-rule-resource triad.[5]

The discussion in this section provides new categories for classifying and understanding the normative frameworks that are used in the social sciences. To date, few systematic efforts have been made at identifying and analyzing the different normative orientations actually used by social science researchers in their work. As a result, we lack a shared vocabulary for discussing and comparing the moral assumptions of individual social researchers, such as Edward Said, Talcott Parsons, Elinor Ostrom, Jon Elster, Patricia Hill Collins, and Theda Skocpol. This section provides an initial framework for understanding and comparing the normative orientations of not only individual scholars, but also larger research fields and even whole academic disciplines. The framework offered here is tentative and subject to refinement. I see this discussion as presenting a needed but still imperfect delineation of the moral approaches used in the social sciences.[6]

Figure 8.4 provides a guide to the discussion. The figure uses the triadic model to illustrate the differences among the three overarching moral traditions, as well as the two more specialized orientations associated with each tradition. The first column shows the core assumption of each framework—that is, which component of the interdependent actor-rule-resource triad is dominant. The second column shows, for each specialized orientation within an overarching framework, the additional assumption about the relationship between the non-dominant components of the triad. For example, moral relativism is associated with culture/power and interpretive/functionalist orientations that agree about the centrality of rules but disagree about whether resources mainly shape actors or the reverse. The final column presents a ranking by relative importance of the components in the triad for all six specialized orientations.

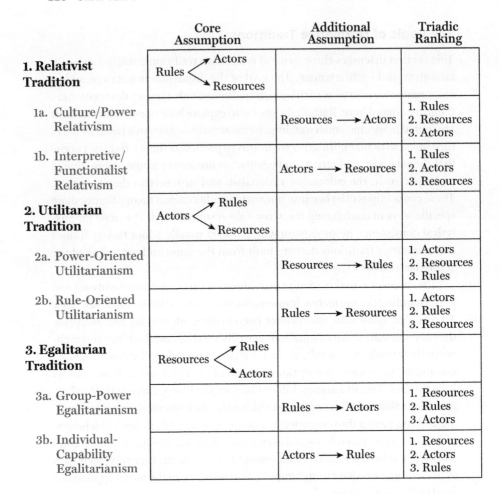

	Core Assumption	Additional Assumption	Triadic Ranking
1. Relativist Tradition	Rules < Actors / Resources		
1a. Culture/Power Relativism		Resources → Actors	1. Rules 2. Resources 3. Actors
1b. Interpretive/ Functionalist Relativism		Actors → Resources	1. Rules 2. Actors 3. Resources
2. Utilitarian Tradition	Actors < Rules / Resources		
2a. Power-Oriented Utilitarianism		Resources → Rules	1. Actors 2. Resources 3. Rules
2b. Rule-Oriented Utilitarianism		Rules → Resources	1. Actors 2. Rules 3. Resources
3. Egalitarian Tradition	Resources < Rules / Actors		
3a. Group-Power Egalitarianism		Rules → Actors	1. Resources 2. Rules 3. Actors
3b. Individual- Capability Egalitarianism		Actors → Rules	1. Resources 2. Actors 3. Rules

FIGURE 8.4. Normative Traditions and Specialized Orientations

THE RELATIVIST TRADITION

The assumption that social rules are at the foundation of experienced reality fits neatly with the normative tradition known as *moral relativism* (Mackie 1977; Harman 1996; Gowans 2018; cf. Durkheim 1893/1964; Nietzsche 1886/1966). Under moral relativism, all societal rules—including all moral codes—are cultural inventions. While individuals may believe that their society's moral codes are universally applicable, they cannot logically support this argument: no universal standards or ultimate principles exist from which to create a normative orientation that necessarily applies to all human societies. For instance, the normative proposition that murder is wrong may be true and quite meaningful relative to the ethical codes of some societies (e.g., modern societies) but false and still quite meaningful relative to the ethical standards of other societies (e.g., hunting and gathering societies). The problem is that no ground-floor principle exists to support any of these consequential ethical codes. Scholars lack the principle or the objective measure to establish the legitimacy of an ethical system as true across all possible societies (Lyotard 1979; Rorty 1979).

Within a relativist framework, social scientists can descriptively study the moral codes and normative standards that exist within and across societies (Fassin 2008). Moral relativism is consistent with interpretive research that strips away surface phenomena to demystify and expose buried or concealed modes of human understanding. Relativism is also consistent with research that examines how actors and organizations impose their moral programs and value-laden ideologies onto subject populations (see, e.g., Scott 1998; Steinmetz 1999; Butler 1990; Escobar 1995). However, moral relativism prohibits researchers from upholding any particular moral framework as the singularly appropriate ethical system for evaluating societies. In fact, an important aspect of interpretive research is moral self-reflection, in which researchers question the role of their own values in shaping the research findings (Caduff 2011).

In the social sciences, moral relativists generally work within a culturalist theory frame that assumes that social rules profoundly shape the properties of actors and the distribution of resources within a society. However, they differ in the specific aspects of culture that they choose to highlight. Some moral relativists are interested in identifying and interpreting the social rules that give meaning to human experience and that function as the societal glue that holds communities together. Other moral relativists are interested in the ways in which nexuses of power are used to impose cultural values and practices onto subject populations, who may resist such imposition in the effort to maintain cultural integrity and authenticity.

A *culture/power normative orientation* emphasizes the role of resources in the constitution of actors (i.e., resources → actors), rather than the reverse. This orientation specifically recognizes the role of resources in constituting asymmetrical groups with opposing identities and interests. Scholars working within this orientation study how resource-rich actors impose self-serving ethical standards and norms on less powerful actors (cf. Fanon 1963/2004; Foucault 1975/1995; Said 1978; Esteva 1992). Depending on the particular cultural categories under study, a culture/power orientation may look at nations, regions, ethnoracial groups, gender groups, socioeconomic groups, professional groups, and status groups. In each case, the animating consideration is the imposition of a moral code (e.g., "colonialism is necessary") by a dominant group (e.g., colonial authorities) on a subordinate group (e.g., native populations) (Mamdani 1996). Culture/power scholars criticize the "gaze" through which the dominant group pejoratively comprehends and conceptualizes the subordinate group. Substantive research from a culture/power perspective often calls attention to the hypocrisy of the dominant group in creating and upholding a moral code as if it were a universal and legitimate set of norms, rather than a coercive device for advancing its own self-serving goals (e.g., Block and Somers 2014; Go 2011; Steinmetz 2007). By the same token, these researchers give agency to subordinate groups, presenting their stories and experienced reality through narrative accounts that capture otherwise hidden voices (e.g., Wolf 1982; Abu-Lughod 1993; Bourgois 2003; De León 2015).

An *interpretive/functionalist normative orientation*, in contrast, downplays the role of resources in constituting actors, emphasizing the opposite relationship (actors → resources). With this version of relativism, the focus is on the ways in which social rules help create order and meaning for individuals living within particular communities and societies. The rules and institutions of a society prevent anarchy by allowing actors to share consequential beliefs about appropriate behavior and just conventions for distributing resources. For interpretive/functionalist scholars, the function of social rules and institutions— including moral and ethical codes—is to coordinate meaningful behavior and to harmonize individual conceptions of reality so that a community or society is characterized by stable and predictable patterns in the constitution and allocation of resources (cf. Davis and Moore 1945; Parsons 1951; Radcliffe-Brown 1952; Lévi-Strauss 1949/1969; Douglas 1966; Johnson 1966; Huntington 1968; Geertz 1973). With an interpretive/functionalist approach, no universal standards of right and wrong exist with which to judge societies. Certain types of societies may be evolutionarily more successful than others (e.g., chiefdoms versus bands; sovereign states versus city-states), but these "winning" societies are not normatively superior to their competitors. The point of such analysis is not to impose a normative program on the societies and communities under study; rather, the point is to reveal and make legible the hidden codes, logics, and practices that constitute these societies and communities. To do this, a certain degree of moral neutrality and moral distancing is necessary (Geertz 1974).

THE UTILITARIAN TRADITION

The normative tradition known as *moral utilitarianism* (or *moral consequentialism*) is linked to the rationalist theory frame through the assumption that actors are the dominant component of the actor-rule-resource triad. Utilitarianism holds that the morally just outcome is the one that yields the greatest amount of good for the greatest number of people (Bentham 1789/1907; Mill 1861/1998; Popper 1945/2013; cf. Hobbes 1651/2012; Locke 1690/1980).[7] This general principle is underspecified, and scholars within this tradition have differentiated more specific principles of morality (e.g., rule versus act utilitarianism; total net versus average net utilitarianism; foreseeable versus unforeseeable utilitarianism) (Sinnott-Armstrong 2015). The common thread that unites these different strands is a focus on the net consequences of different possible outcomes, given the preferences of the actors under study. Utilitarianism endorses as morally just those past or possible outcomes that maximize the net good, even if these outcomes require individuals to defy the dominant ethical codes of society. Likewise, utilitarianism endorses the use of power by an elite to create an inequality-enhancing institution so long as that institution serves to maximize the net good. In utilitarianism, the preferences of individuals drive assessments of net consequences. Individual preferences are taken at face value as preexisting "givens"; questions about the origins of preferences are not typically addressed in this tradition (Sen and Williams 1982).

Utilitarian scholars sometimes focus on specific societies defined by particular distributions of preferences (Wright 2013). Because individuals in one society may have preferences distinct from those of individuals in another society, the outcomes that are normatively just may vary across societies. In one society, polygamy may be morally appropriate because it maximizes the net good; in another society, monogamy may be morally appropriate for the same reason. Despite specific societal differences, however, human beings share certain preferences across all, or nearly all, possible societies (cf. Nozick 1974; Singer 1981; Greene 2013). These common preferences allow utilitarians to generalize about universally good and universally bad outcomes. For example, nearly all people in all societies prefer life over death, health over sickness, safety over danger, knowledge over ignorance, happiness over misery, and freedom over bondage. On all of these dimensions, human societies have improved rapidly over the last 200 years, such that some utilitarians celebrate the progress of humankind under enlightenment principles (Pinker 2018). Indeed, some utilitarians suggest that the ability of human beings to gradually solve collective action problems (Olson 1965) and to create social arrangements that move away from zero-sum conflict toward positive-sum cooperation is the hallmark of human achievement (North 1981; Ostrom 1990; Wright 2000).

Utilitarianism is an actor-centric approach, in which the preferences of individuals ultimately determine what is morally just. Nevertheless, scholars adopt differing views regarding the relationship between rules and resources. *Power-oriented utilitarians* work from the assumption that resources primarily shape rules (resources → rules). These scholars assume that power differentials among groups of individuals affect the content of the rules of society (Elster 1985; Przeworski 1985; Levi 1988; Knight 1992; Acemoglu and Robinson 2008). Crucially, these scholars believe that social structures have constitutive effects, creating group actors with particular interests and identities. Thus, instead of focusing on atomistic individuals, power-oriented utilitarians analyze categorical groups defined by shared preferences, such as elites and masses or capitalists and workers.[8] They approach questions of justice and morality through a focus on the net consequences of outcomes for individuals, as filtered through power-laden social structures that constitute asymmetrical social groups. In general, outcomes that support the interests of subordinate actors are morally desirable, because they maximize the greatest good for the greatest number. Questions about the morality of actions that challenge the social structures themselves raise complicated normative issues related to probabilities of success and the short-run and long-run preferences of group members in societies stratified by power differentials. These questions must be worked through by focusing on the net utility of the actions, given the preferences of individuals who reside in these societies.

By contrast, *rule-oriented utilitarians* emphasize the ways in which rules shape resources (rules → resources). These scholars focus on atomistic and self-interested individuals and the consequences of their choices about rule construction for the net good of society. They often explicitly consider how individuals can design social rules in ways that promote the public interest, including through solutions to collective action problems that stand in the way of human well-being (e.g., Hardin 1968; Buchanan 1975; Axelrod 1984; Ostrom 1990, 2009; North 1990; Skyrms 2014). Institutions are morally just insofar as they shape available choices and opportunity costs in ways that result in favorable net consequences. The institutions and their sustaining resources reflect the preferences of self-interested individuals. This kind of rule-oriented utilitarianism is consistent with Rawlsian veil-of-ignorance thought experiments that ask one to imagine designing a social contract without knowledge of one's identity and position in the resulting society (Rawls 1971/1999; Freeman 2019; see also Kant 1781/1998). Rule-oriented utilitarians point out that individuals in this "original position" would prefer societies in which institutional arrangements are in place that reduce uncertainty and predictably coordinate behavior.

THE EGALITARIAN TRADITION

Finally, the normative tradition known as *moral egalitarianism* places resources front and center within the actor-rule-resource triad. This tradition holds that equality in the distribution of resources—and specifically, certain kinds of resources (e.g., opportunities, political rights, wealth, welfare)—is inherently desirable (Cohen 1995; Dworkin 2000; MacKinnon 2001; Roemer 1996; cf. Marx and Engels 1848/2012). Equality is a normative ideal to be achieved and a necessary condition for justice; it has intrinsic value as an end in its own right and is a prerequisite for moral rightfulness more generally. Moral egalitarianism differs from relativism by virtue of this commitment to an equality principle that holds across all possible worlds. It differs from utilitarianism by placing a concern with equality above a concern with the maximization of utility. With moral egalitarianism, a behavior can be morally just even though it does not serve to enhance the net good of society when measured by individual subjective preferences.

Scholars in the egalitarian tradition generally work within structuralist approaches that see resource distribution as constitutive of justice, and categories such as power, exploitation, and liberation as essential to analysis. However, egalitarians differ with respect to questions concerning the relative importance of actors and rules. *Group-power egalitarians* emphasize the role of rules in constituting actors (rules → actors) much more than the reverse. This emphasis leads them to focus on categorical groups rather than individuals. The identity groups that fall along a given structural axis stand in a zero-sum relationship, in which the power of the dominant group depends on the exploitation of the subordinate group. In their normative analyses, group-power egalitarians often emphasize one specific categorical division within a society. In turn, this division is associated with a particular kind of critical analysis, and perhaps a specific set of liberation goals. For instance, economic divisions are linked to critical class analysis (Marx and Engels 1848/2012; Burawoy 1982; Poulantzas 1975; Wright 1997), racial divisions are linked to critical race analysis (Du Bois 1995; Morris 1984; Bonilla-Silva 2006; Feagin 2009; Itzigsohn and Brown 2020), and gender divisions are linked to critical gender analysis (Fraser 1989; Ortner and Whitehead 1981; Ridgeway and Correll 2004; Scott 1999). Over the last three decades, group-power egalitarians have explored the ways in which multiple categorical divisions intersect and reinforce one another; these scholars adopt a perspective that is both critical and intersectional (Acker 2006; Collins 2019; McCall 2005; Pattillo 2013).[9] Group-power egalitarians may view as normatively desirable those behaviors and events that promote greater resource equality among the opposing categorical groups. Yet they ultimately seek to erode the exploitative nature of the categorical division itself, including the identity roles associated with the division. For group-power egalitarians, the real solution is structural transformation to destroy the oppressive aspects of the categorical identities themselves.

Other egalitarians focus more on the role of individuals in shaping rules (actors → rules) while still assuming that resources are the primary mover in the actor-rule-resource triad. These *individual-capability egalitarians* start with atomistic individuals rather than categorical groups, and they explore the ways in which individuals shape rules to promote equality. This approach specifically focuses on the degree to which individuals have sufficient capabilities to enjoy a flourishing life and to do and be what they have reason to want to do and be (Nussbaum 1992, 1999, 2000, 2011; Sen 1992, 1999, 2002, 2009; Crocker 2008; Robeyns 2016).[10] These scholars examine whether resources are distributed in ways that provide equality in individual capabilities, rather than equality in outcomes in individual lives. Individual-capability egalitarians may identify universal capabilities that are considered necessary for the survival and basic functioning of all human beings. Providing access to surplus resources (e.g., food, shelter, security) that ensure these basic capabilities is always just. Yet the approach assigns individuals much freedom in deciding exactly how to use their capabilities to pursue their own particular good lives. While the approach recognizes the possibility of false consciousness (i.e., misinformed beliefs propagated by powerful actors), it generally takes individual desires as legitimate and appropriate. Prevailing societal rules are problematic not mainly because they cause individuals to seek an unworthy life, but because they deny individuals the capacity to realize their worthy desires and the worthwhile life that they seek.

COMPARING ORIENTATIONS

The six moral orientations discussed above are similar to and different from one another in complex ways. My approach here has been to group them into three traditions on the basis of their understanding of the *most important* component in the actor-rule-resource triad. An alternative approach to comparison is to group the orientations on the basis of their understanding of the *least important* component in the triad. From this perspective, similarities exist between (1) group-power egalitarianism and culture/power relativism, (2) interpretive/functionalist relativism and rule-oriented utilitarianism, and (3) power-oriented utilitarianism and individual-capability egalitarianism. Let us consider these three pairings in turn.

First, group-power egalitarians (e.g., Karl Marx, Patricia Hill Collins, Michael Burawoy, Nancy Fraser) share important assumptions with scholars working from a culture/power relativist perspective (e.g., Michel Foucault, Edward Said, Judith Butler, Nancy Scheper-Hughes). In particular, both group-power egalitarians and culture/power relativists emphasize the ways in which resources shape actors. This shared assumption allows them to focus on asymmetrical collective actors as the primary units of analysis. The assumption also leads them to assign power an important place in the analysis. One important difference between them, however, is that group-power egalitarians ground their critical analysis in a set of moral principles, whereas culture/power relativists are critical of any totalizing meta-narrative. Group-power egalitarians work toward revolutionary structural transformation to achieve specific societal visions (e.g., socialism, matriarchy, truly equal citizenship). By contrast, culture/power relativists work toward structural transformation to liberate individuals from any and all belief systems that act as modes of domination.

Second, interesting similarities exist between scholars working from the interpretive/functionalist orientation of moral relativism (e.g., Émile Durkheim, Clifford Geertz, Mary Douglas, Marshall Sahlins) and scholars who embrace the rule-oriented strand of utilitarianism (e.g., Jeremy Bentham, Steven Pinker, Douglass North, Elinor Ostrom). All of these scholars share the belief that actors have the capacity to make meaningful choices; the identities and interests of actors are not simply a reflection of the distribution of material resources within society. Accordingly, interpretive/functionalists and rule-oriented utilitarians do not focus on domination and exploitation when making moral judgments and normative assessments. Instead, they treat cultural and ethical systems as background environments in which actors must operate as agents and make choices—including moral choices about the distribution of resources—that they and others perceive to be meaningful and consequential. Interpretive/functionalist scholars focus on the rule context within which actor choices occur; they eschew questions about the moral standing of either the choices or the rules that shape those choices. For their part, rule-oriented utilitarians are concerned with the net utility of the choices of autonomous individuals, perhaps drawing attention to those critical decisions that play an important role in promoting or hindering human progress and societal development. A key difference between the interpretive/functionalists and the rule-oriented utilitarians is that the latter believe they have an objective yardstick for assessing societal progress over time, whereas the former reject the possibility of a common standard and seek understanding while maintaining normative distance.

Third, affinities exist between scholars working from the moral standpoint of power-oriented utilitarianism (e.g., Adam Przeworski, Margaret Levi, Daron Acemoglu, James Robinson) and those working from the moral approach of individual-capability egalitarianism (e.g., Amartya Sen, Martha Nussbaum, Ingrid Robeyns, Michael Woolcock). These scholars see justice as linked to the fulfillment of the preferences of individuals or collectivities of individuals defined by shared preferences. Injustice arises because resources are concentrated in elite hands, leading individuals to lack adequate capabilities to realize their preferences. In these orientations, resource distribution and power are used to explain injustice and the possibility of emancipation. For individual-capability egalitarians, equality in the distribution of resources is a prerequisite for, and a component of, a just society. Power-oriented utilitarians may agree about the value of equality, but only insofar as equality maximizes the net good within society. Individual-capability egalitarians assume that individuals share objective interests as human beings; by contrast, power-oriented utilitarians remain focused on the subjective interests of individuals.

———

To conclude this discussion, let us return to the idea that whole scholarly communities tend to adopt theory frames and normative traditions that are

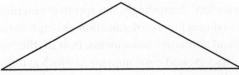

Relativist Tradition
(Cultural Anthropology, 1950s–present;
Political Science, 1950s–1960s;
Sociology, 1950s–1960s; 1990s–present)

Utilitarian Tradition
(Economics, 1950s–present;
Political Science, 1990s–present)

Egalitarian Tradition
(Sociology, 1970s–present;
Political Science, 1970s–present)

FIGURE 8.5. Normative Traditions and Disciplines in the Social Sciences

consistent with one another. As figure 8.5 shows, we can view the social science disciplines as primarily connected to particular moral traditions, just as we earlier viewed them as linked to particular theory frames. Figure 8.5 reproduces figure 8.3 except that it replaces the names of the theory frames with the names of the normative traditions. Economics and contemporary political science are now linked to utilitarianism; cultural anthropology and cultural sociology (1990s to the present) are connected to relativism; and structural sociology and structural political science are tied to egalitarianism. As before, I exclude human-oriented disciplines that fall significantly into the natural sciences, such as archeology, psychology, and cognitive science. I also do not attempt to situate any disciplines within the humanities.

The placement of the social science disciplines in figures 8.3 and 8.5 raises a larger set of issues concerning why individual scholars choose to work within particular academic disciplines. I am not prepared to fully explore these issues here, but I do wish to note that some scholars can be drawn to, or drawn away from, a particular discipline depending on whether it accords with their personal values. For example, a structuralist with firm egalitarian values may be alienated from the discipline of economics in part because it works within a rationalist and utilitarian framework. By the same token, a rationalist with utilitarian values may be put off by the transformative agenda supported by many scholars working within the discipline of sociology. While normative beliefs play a role in selecting scholars into particular disciplines within the social sciences, it is also true that scholars are socialized into the values of particular disciplines during their years as undergraduate and graduate students.

Scientific constructivism does not endorse any particular theory frame or normative tradition. Instead, it provides tools and methods for building and assessing theories, explanations, and propositions associated with different frames and traditions. Under a scientific constructivist approach, the *validity* of a theory frame depends on its *usefulness* for substantive research goals, such as explaining outcomes in particular cases or developing generalizations about the causes of events. Scholars must build the case for a given theory frame and its affiliated normative tradition by using accepted evidence, explicitly stated assumptions, and logical principles in order to answer important questions, solve substantive problems, and accumulate stable knowledge. In short, social scientists can best argue for their favored theory frame and/or moral tradition by showing that its assumptions yield successful social scientific research.

The next chapter continues to discuss theory in the social sciences, but it focuses on general categories to be used when building explanations of social phenomena. These general categories include, but are not limited to, the three components of the triad: actors, rules, and resources.

9

Categories for Constructing Theories and Explanations

This chapter considers several categories that serve as building blocks for constructing theories and explanations in social science research. The categories include the idea of an *event* and its constituents, i.e., *actors* and *objects*. The categories also include *social rules, social resources,* and *social power,* three interconnected ideas that social scientists use to make sense of human behavior. In addition, the chapter explores a number of temporal ideas, including *time* and *process*. The discussion of these various categories assumes that social scientists must creatively and imaginatively formulate explanations of the social world. Underlying this chapter is the premise that good understandings of key theoretical ideas can help scholars better make sense of what has happened, why it happened, and what it means that it happened.

Theory-building categories such as *actor, rule, resource, event,* and *process* are versatile tools that can be used by scholars who embrace different theory frames and who support different normative programs. The categories can be used in the analysis of many different substantive topics and to study many possible research questions, and they can serve as tools for identifying research topics and research questions in the first place. They can be used for constructing the content of exactly what takes place in the social world; as tools to structure narrative presentations and descriptive accounts; and in the formulation of normative propositions and value-based assessments of social happenings. The categories can be used to construct the occurrences that scholars seek to explain, the factors that might cause those occurrences, and the reasons why those factors might cause those occurrences.

This chapter is divided into four sections that explore the following categories: (1) *event*, *actor*, and *object*; (2) *rule*, *institution*, and *structure*; (3) *resource* and *power*; and (4) *time*, *process*, and *change*. Each section can be read on its own, and it is not essential to read the sections in any particular order. For each section, I focus on the definitions of the categories and their positionings within larger semantic fields. I devote much attention to the subtypes of the categories that scholars use to construct specific, detailed understandings of experienced reality. I also discuss the implicit assumptions that scholars accept as true when they use the categories. This effort requires exploring the background cognitive structures on which meanings depend. My goal throughout is to promote shared understandings of the categories and to stimulate ideas for their creative use in substantive research.

Events, Actors, and Objects

Events serve as temporal and substantive anchors for organizing the presentation of case-study research. Choices about which events to emphasize, how to describe their content, and how to situate them in relation to one another are among the most important decisions to be made when periodizing and presenting case narratives. Barrington Moore's (1966) seminal comparative-historical work on democracy and dictatorship features general events, such as *the commercialization of agriculture*, that appear as specific events in particular cases, such as *the enclosure movement* in England. Howard Becker's (1953) famous study "Becoming a Marihuana User" generalizes about marijuana-use events (e.g., "the new user may not get high the first time") from multiple individual experiences of marijuana use (e.g., "I didn't get high the first time"). Theda Skocpol's (1979) magisterial work *States and Social Revolutions* offers narratives in which general events common to all social revolutions (e.g., *lower-class revolts*) are analyzed as event sequences distinctive to individual cases (e.g., *the bread riots of 1789 in France*). In each of these studies, general and particular events are used to build the main categories of analysis, formulate the core theoretical propositions, and structure the narrative presentation.

A crucial component of presenting an event is constructing the actors and objects that compose the substantive content of the event. Scholars must choose the kinds of actors to emphasize, as well as the interactions among these actors and their specific decisions and actions that merit attention. Likewise, scholars must choose the kinds of non-animate objects that need to be emphasized as components of an event. Although they cannot make these decisions through a mechanical application of rules, they do follow certain heuristics when making choices. This section seeks to identify these heuristics and offer tools to inform the imaginative construction of events in social science research.

TEMPORAL SLICES OF CONSTRUCTED REALITY

A researcher constructs an event by identifying the social processes and states of affairs (e.g., basic changes in class and state structures) that mark a period in the history of a case (e.g., 1789–99 in France). The category is given a label (e.g., *the French Revolution*) that signifies the event. The category for an event is a structured whole whose parts include actors, objects, social rules, and resources.[1] The nature of these parts and the relationships among them—including temporal relationships—define the substance of the event (cf. Mandler 1984: 14, 76).

The prototypical event is marked by a period of time with crisp boundaries and by a principle of unity (Harré and Secord 1972: 10–13; Mandler 1984; cf. Sewell 1996). Insofar as the idea of a beginning and an end does not apply, a state of affairs has weak or no membership in the category *event*. For the same reason, many objects and actors—such as books and armies—are not regarded as good examples of events (Casati and Varzi 1999: 169–71; 2015: 3). These entities may help define the substantive content of an event, but they are not usually seen as events themselves. Thus, books and armies may feature heavily in seminar meetings and wars, respectively, but only the latter categories are regarded as members of *event*. Likewise, while specific processes are defined by a unifying principle, they lack membership in the category *event* because they do not have clear beginning and ending points. For instance, we feel uncomfortable labeling processes such as modernization, aging, and secularization as events because they lack crisp temporal boundaries.

Actual events include as their members at least one actual case.[2] Events with exactly one actual case as a member are *particular events*; events with more than one actual case as members are *general events*. If our cases are countries (itself a general category), *the French Revolution* is a particular event, because France is the only actual case member. By contrast, *social revolution* is a general event. General events include particular events as their members: the category *social revolution* includes the category *the French Revolution* as one of its members. Particular events can be situated within a part-whole hierarchy in which any particular event has more-specific events as its parts. More-specific events are temporal-spatial slices of the overarching event. For instance, *the storming of the Bastille* is a specific event that is a part of *the French Revolution*. Within *the storming of the Bastille*, one could slice out events that are even more specific, which in turn are composed of events that are yet more specific, and so on.

The categories for particular events contain multiple possible cases as members, only one of which is an actual case. The possible cases include different ways in which the actual case may have occurred. For instance, the actual case *France 1789–99* may or may not have membership in the category *country with powerful bourgeois dominant class*; historians seem to debate this issue. Likewise, this case may or may not have membership in the category *country with rising industrial economy*; again, this issue is debated. As a result, the category *France 1789–99* includes as its members possible cases in which (1) *France 1789–99* is a member of both *powerful bourgeois dominant class* and *rising industrial economy*, (2) *France 1789–99* is a member of neither of these categories, and (3) *France 1789–99* is a member of one but not both of these categories. Only one *actual case* is a member of *France 1789–99*; but with our present knowledge and understanding, many *possible cases* are members of this category, and we do not know which one of these possible cases is the actual case.

The level of detail featured in the narrative presentation of a case study is closely related to the generality of the events described in the narrative (cf. Mandler 2004). The analyst must choose the appropriate level of generality at which to cast the main explanation. In her causal analysis of the French Revolution, for example, Skocpol (1979: 60–64) emphasizes the event *international pressure in France* as an important causal factor. Her narrative reveals that this event has many sub-events as parts. For example, the War of the League of Augsburg (1688–97) and the War of the Spanish Succession (1701–14) are sub-events of *international pressure in France*. In addition, *international pressure in France* is itself a part of an even more overarching event in Skocpol's causal argument—namely, *state breakdown*. Her narrative moves fluidly across events at different levels of generality, identifying key causal factors at higher levels and showing how these overarching causes consist of sub-events and sub-causes that capture nuances in French history (Mahoney 1999: 1164–68).

In small-N studies, researchers arrive at *different but systematically related answers* to questions about the causes of a general event and the causes of particular events that are individual members of that general event. For example, a researcher studying the cases of France, Russia, and China might ask (1) what caused social revolutions (a general event) in these countries; and (2) what caused the French Revolution, what caused the Russian Revolution, and what caused the Chinese Revolution. The answer to the question about the general event features general causes; the answers to the questions about the particular events feature particular causes. Particular causes are systematically related to general causes as both parts of wholes and subsets of larger sets. When researchers spell out these relationships, they show how particular events are parts of more general explanations. For example, a particular cause of the Chinese Revolution is the Nanchang Uprising in August 1927, whereas a particular cause of the Russian Revolution is the seizure of land by Russian peasants south and southeast of Moscow in 1917. Given that these events are distinctive to the cases of China and Russia, respectively, it is correct to say that the causes of the Chinese and Russian revolutions are different. At the same time, however, these distinctive events are *members of* the general category *peasant uprising,* which is a *part of* the general category *peasant revolution,* which is a general cause of *social revolution* in France, Russia, and China alike (Skocpol 1979).[3] Small-N researchers try to attend to both the general and the particular. They work to show how particular events fit within general events by illustrating how the former are subsets and/or parts of the latter.

BUILDING THE ACTORS AND OBJECTS OF EVENTS

The substantive content of an event may be meaningful to us for practical, analytical, or normative reasons. We mark milestone events in our lives associated with, for example, birth, graduation, friendship, employment, residential location, home ownership, children, illness, divorce, and retirement. Political scientists distinguish, for example, independence, state consolidation, revolution, war, and democratic transition as general events that countries can experience. The substantive content of all of these events is circumscribed in part by the kind of case under analysis: individuals, but usually not countries, can be members of the events *marriage* and *retirement*; countries, but usually not individuals, can be members of the events *independence* and *democratic breakdown.* The kind of case under study—such as physicians, families, movements, countries, or world systems—places limits on the kinds of events that can be the focus of attention (Soifer 2018).

In the social sciences, the substantive content of an event consists mainly of actors and objects, as well as the social rules and resources that constitute and structure those actors and objects. Researchers identify types of *actors* using categories (e.g., *petit bourgeoisie, indigenous people, rural women, dominant class, refugee, hegemon*) that are analytically useful and collectively recognized by a relevant scholarly or public community. The categories impose boundaries around individuals who are similar and different with respect to their membership in many other categories (cf. Kashima et al. 2005; Lamont and Molnár 2002). The types of actors under study may reflect the theoretical or normative interests of the researcher; the categories may be useful for particular descriptive or explanatory tasks. For some events, whether particular or general, a single person is the main actor. For other events, the main actor is a group of human beings. Types of collective actors include organizations, movements, socioeconomic classes, governments, cities, countries, empires, interstate systems, and more. The choice of which actors to emphasize significantly shapes the main substantive content and overall presentation of the event.

Across the social sciences, researchers understand actors to be *intentional agents.* They normally view actors as *rational* in the thin sense that their behavior is motivated by their beliefs and desires (Elster 1986b; Taylor 1988; Wendt 1999: 113–30). Researchers adopt this *intentional stance* as a way of making sense of the internal processes that propel an actor's behavior (Dennett 1987: 48–49; Elster 1983). In addition to beliefs and desires, analysts may also include emotions and feelings, such as anger or fear, as part of their understanding of actor intentionality (Elster 1999; Rueschemeyer 2009; Searle 1995: 8). Social scientists use the intentional stance when defining the specific actors under study (e.g., *financial capitalists, tenant farmers, informal-sector workers*); they call attention to the actor's possession of particular interests and specific motivating beliefs. Likewise, social scientists explain the behavior of these actors using the intentional stance: they assume that actors would have behaved differently given different beliefs and desires. In some fields, scholars formalize the intentional stance using mathematical tools such as game-theoretic models of decision-making (Nash 1997; von Neumann and Morgenstern 1944; Arrow 1983). But the core idea that actors are guided by their beliefs and desires need not commit researchers to an explicit or implicit rational choice approach to social analysis. For instance, culturalists and structuralists commonly treat actors as intentional agents; they assume that the positions of actors within social structures or cultural communities constitute their interests or values, which in turn explain their behaviors.

In our everyday life, we use the intentional stance as a folk theory of human psychology; it is the main basis for our interpretations, explanations, and predictions of the behavior of the people around us. Our possibly innate ability to view other people as intentional actors allows for a we-attitude and a shared intentionality, which in turn help to explain our ability to cooperate in collective projects, use language, construct human kinds, and establish culture (Gilbert 1987, 1992; Bloom 1996; Tomasello et al. 2005; see also Smith 1759/2002; Durkheim 1912/1961). An important component of what it means to be human is to adopt the intentional stance as the basis for understanding the behavior of oneself and others.

The main scientific alternative to the intentional stance is the view that human behavior involves the unconscious implementation of habits, skills, and dispositions that are physically encoded in human brains and bodies (Bourdieu 1977, 1984, 1990; Turner 1994, 2002; cf. Skinner 1953). On this view, human behavior is the enactment of practices that human beings are physically and mentally "equipped" (e.g., trained, disciplined, habituated, wired, programmed) to carry out. Behavior only appears to be consistent with rules because actors are disposed to behave in rule-like ways. After the fact, individuals may understand their behavior as driven by their preexisting beliefs, desires, and conscious will (Libet 1985; Wegner 2018; Chater 2018). Yet these post hoc understandings are themselves the enactment of human dispositions and skills; they do not reflect real mental states that actually motivate behavior. On this view, categories such as *beliefs, desires,* and *emotions* are not natural kinds; they do not correspond to entities that exist anywhere in nature.

Whether or not the intentional stance proves irrelevant to the natural scientific explanation of behavior remains to be seen (Churchland 1981; Stich 1983; Nagel 1986; Turner 1994, 2002; Varela, Thompson, and Rosch 2016). For the social sciences, however, the intentional stance is an indispensable tool for describing experiential reality. Human reality *as it is experienced* consists of behaviors that are motivated by inner beliefs and desires. To be sure, social scientists must avoid essentializing the intentional stance; they must not treat the beliefs and desires of the actors they study as if they exist as natural kinds. They must analyze beliefs and desires as they do all other human kinds: they are categories that correspond to conceptual spaces in human minds and refer to mostly uncomprehended natural kinds.[4] From this constructivist perspective, social scientists can unproblematically use the intentional stance as the basis for building theories of human behavior.

Another common practice in the social sciences is to treat actors as *unitary actors*. When analyzing individuals, social scientists do not usually consider the illusion of the self (but see Mead 1934; Schutz 1970; Elster 1986a; Metzinger 2009; Hood 2012). The competing brain modules, impulses, and desires of a given person are not often analyzed as separate actors themselves. Rather, the person is treated as a coherent entity with coherent goals and ideas. With collective actors, likewise, the norm is to treat the actor as an intentional agent that purposively carries out behaviors. States, movements, classes, and other collective actors are anthropomorphized in the social sciences (Coleman 1982: chap. 1; Geser 1992; Sheehy 2006; Wendt 1999: 195–96). Yet depending on the level of detail of the narrative, the analyst may well pull apart collective actors into constitutive parts—i.e., into the sub-actors that compose the whole. For instance, state-centric theorists often analyze militaries, agencies, legislatures, or even individual people when formulating narratives (McDonnell 2017, 2020). The specification of the sub-actors need not undercut the assumption that one is analyzing unitary actors; the sub-actors are treated as unitary actors themselves. While the level of generality at which the analyst adopts the assumption of a unitary actor can shift in the course of the analysis, the assumption is still applied to each specific actor under study.

A constructivist approach nicely accommodates this conceptual slicing and dicing of actors at different levels of generality. The approach recognizes that the membership boundaries of actors do not reflect natural or objective divisions (Lamont and Molnár 2002). How one carves out actors is a creative process that cannot be mechanically read out of the data or algorithmically generated from the facts of a case. Category construction is shaped by the researcher's analytic goals, overall understandings of the subject matter, theoretical orientation, normative values, and personal experience as a member of one or more relevant cultures.

In addition to actors, *non-animate objects* are part of the substance of events. In comparison to the events in which they are situated, objects tend to be more squarely located in space and less squarely located in time (Casati and Varzi 1999: 169–71; 2015: 3). Some objects are self-sustaining entities that have an identity independent of all human cognitions. Such partial natural kinds include aspects of the landscape (e.g., rivers, mountains, grasslands); natural resources (coal, diamonds, timber); and ecologies suitable for various human purposes (plant-gathering, fishing, animal domestication). In most social science research, the cases in which events occur are geographical spaces, such as cities, counties, countries, and continents. Social revolutions occur within the geographical spaces corresponding to states: the French Revolution occurred in the specific space of France. Bounded units of land more generally are emphasized in events—as resources that help constitute actors (e.g., landed elites), as locations linked to cultural orientations (rural values), and as valued objects that motivate behavior (land revolts).

Many objects are entities that depend on human cognitions for their existence and identity. These objects include the technologies and artifacts that individuals use to interact with the social and natural worlds (cf. Hackett et al. 2008). Some examples are shelters and buildings, transportation and communication devices, and tools for leisure and productive activities. Human-dependent objects figure prominently in events, either as the foci of actors' attention or as part of the background context in which behavior occurs. The role of objects in defining context can be seen in the fact that technological and scientific innovations often define periods in world-historical time. For example, the advent of settled agriculture, the use of iron tools, and the splitting of the atom mark new epochs in world history. Although human beings essentialize artifacts and technologies by implicitly understanding them as entities created by designers to serve certain human purposes (see chapter 1), this mode of artifact essentialism is not necessarily an illusion: technologies and artifacts are in fact often designed and produced to help people interact with the natural world in predictable and useful ways. Technologies and artifacts reflect the profound ability of human beings to successfully understand and control the natural world.

Like actors, objects can be partitioned into sets that are more general (e.g., books) or more specific (social science books), including sets with only one actual case member (the particular book you are now reading). Objects are structured wholes that can be disaggregated into the parts that compose them; for example, a (physical) book has pages and a cover. When case-study researchers write narratives of events, they must make choices about the level of generality at which to situate objects. These choices are closely related to their decisions about the categories used to describe the actors who engage with objects.

This discussion illustrates some of the mechanics of event construction with a set-theoretic approach. The actors and objects that animate events are constructed with categories that are related to one another in systematic ways (i.e., by superset-subset and part-whole relations). Set-theoretic analysts are always both "lumpers" and "splitters" (Hexter 1979: 241–43): they conduct analysis by grouping sets into supersets (lumping) and dividing sets into subsets (splitting). Nevertheless, analysts vary in the level of generality of the categories at which they cast their main descriptions and explanations—making some of them worthy of the name "lumpers" and others worthy of the name "splitters."

Social Rules

Scholars from different theoretical and epistemological traditions— structuralists and culturalists, rational choice theorists and symbolic interactionists, Durkheimians and Marxists, positivists and postmodernists—build theories of human behavior by identifying social rules. They use social rules to interpret the meaning of behaviors to the actors who take part in those behaviors, and to specify the actions that count as certain forms of behavior and the entities that count as certain types of actors and objects. They draw on social rules to explain why actors carry out certain kinds of behavior and why these have certain kinds of consequences. The assumption that social rules directly or indirectly shape human behavior is an important feature of nearly all theories of human behavior.

CHARACTERISTICS OF SOCIAL RULES

Social rules (or simply *rules*) are instructions for constituting and regulating human behavior (cf. von Wright 1971: 151–53; Harré 1974: 162–65; Ostrom 1986; Searle 1995: 25–27; Elder-Vass 2012: chap. 4). They have the following generic forms:

X counts as behavior Y in context C.
In context C, do behavior Y or receive sanction S.

Social rules are logical statements that connect human kind categories designating situations (C, as above), particular actions (X), general actions (Y), and sanctions for non-compliance (S). By virtue of their logical form, social rules can be represented symbolically as set-theoretic expressions. Elucidating the content of these set-theoretic expressions amounts to discovering the codes that enable and constrain meaningful human behavior.

The extent to which individuals recognize social rules varies. Sometimes people follow rules explicitly and self-consciously, as when they struggle to assemble furniture using instructions. More commonly, human behavior does not involve the conscious enactment of rules or any self-aware rule-following. Most rules exist in an unrecognized and perhaps even unrecognizable form. Individuals who behave in accordance with social rules usually have no immediate awareness of the rules they are following.

Given that rules often go unrecognized, scholars must explain how they can still enable and constrain human behavior. Scholars normally assume that human beings *unconsciously* follow most social rules (Durkheim 1895/1982; Mead 1934; Goffman 1969; Geertz 1973; Harré 1974; Chomsky 1975; Ostrom 1986; Schmidt 2008). Social scientists may believe that rules are stored and enacted in the neural and synaptic hardware of the brain. However, because humans lack any direct access to their brain's hardware, most of this rule enactment occurs behind the scenes—beyond the purview of our conscious awareness.[5] Only after the fact can individuals be made aware of their unconscious rule-following. For example, they can become aware of otherwise unrecognized social rules through breaching experiments, in which an experimenter forces a subject to violate an otherwise hidden rule in order to expose it (Garfinkel 1967). Likewise, through immersion in a cultural community, interpretive and ethnographic researchers can help individuals identify the implicit rules that are unconsciously followed within that community (Geertz 1973).

Under a scientific constructivist approach, specific social rules (e.g., "be quiet in the dentist's waiting room") exist as shared knowledge in the minds of the actors to whom these rules apply (e.g., individuals in a dentist's waiting room). This shared knowledge is located in the individuals' brains, but scientists seem to be far away from understanding exactly how brains store and use this kind of information.[6] Fortunately, knowledge of the natural kind entities and processes to which social rules refer is not needed for successful social science research. With scientific constructivism, the meaning of a social rule—including the meaning of the categories that compose the rule (e.g., *the dentist's waiting room* and *quiet*)—depends on collective human understandings. The brain materials and neural arrangements that ground these collective understandings are largely irrelevant to the substance of the social analysis.

What *is* relevant and important for the social sciences are the collective understandings on which social rules depend. Rules must be meaningful to not only the social scientists who study them (and their audiences), but also, at least implicitly, to the actors under study whose behavior is covered by them. With scientific constructivist research, social rules are ontologically dependent on both (1) the collective and explicit understandings of social researchers and their audiences, and (2) the collective, mostly implicit understandings of the actors to whom the social rules apply. The content of social science research focuses on the second kind of collective understandings (among actors) as a basis for arriving at the first kind of collective understandings (among authors and their audiences). Because the audiences for social science works may include the very actors under study, researchers can cause these actors to become aware of the previously unconscious rules that they follow (Bourdieu 1977, 1984, 1989; Giddens 1979, 1984).

Rules and behaviors are distinct entities, a fact that may become obvious when the rules are not followed (e.g., when someone has a loud phone conversation in the dentist's waiting room). The degree to which individuals have membership in the set *compliant with social rule X* is related to the extent to which they have membership in the set *aware of social rule X* (Berger and Luckmann 1966; Zucker 1983; Jepperson 1991; Powell 1991). At one extreme, actors may be well aware of a rule, have good ideas about its role in social order, and actively seek to support it or destroy it. With recognized rules, compliance can be problematic, and rule maintenance may be far from automatic. At the other extreme, a rule may be unrecognized or unrecognizable. Unrecognized rules are protected from direct efforts to modify or overturn them. The fact that many social rules exist without recognition can be viewed as a bias for the status quo in human reality. Humans are less likely to change rules that they do not even recognize as existing. This status quo bias helps explain the path-dependent nature of most of human culture and experienced reality (see chapter 11 on path dependence).

Social rules are efficacious in part because they carry sanctions; they are *punitive codes* that entail a punishment for non-compliance: "In context C, do behavior Y or receive sanction S" (see Levi 1988; Ostrom 1990; Stryker 1994; Rueschemeyer 2009). The sanction can range from the tacit disapproval of others to the infliction of painful death. The rule entails an instruction for behavior by the sanctioners as well: "If behavior Y is not carried out in context C, then impose sanction S." The extent of the enforcement of sanctions varies in practice, with significant implications for behavior. Behavior is more likely to fall into the compliant category when sanctions fall into the strongly enforced category. For this reason, important social rules are likely to be supported by enforceable sanctions. We can often estimate the practical importance of a rule by the extent to which individuals and groups dedicate resources to monitoring compliance and ensuring enforcement and implementation of sanctions.

Recognized social rules are subject to variable interpretation (Stryker 1994; Thelen 2003, 2004). The human kind categories referenced in a social rule are not defined by inherent properties; their meaning depends on intersubjective understandings. The content of this meaning is subject to opinion, debate, and contestation. Even when formally codified, rules and their guiding expectations embody ambiguity. Rules cannot be specified with sufficient precision to fully clarify the categories they reference and the contexts of their enactment. Actors can dispute whether specific cases are instances of the context specified in the rule, and they can contend that the complexities of a given situation defy the categories identified in the rule or confound the spirit of the rule.[7]

Social rules exist alongside one another in a complex web of interrelated set-theoretic instructions (cf. Geertz 1973; Searle 1995; Pierson and Skocpol 2002; Sewell 2005; Reed 2008; Elder-Vass 2012). To understand and explain behavior, researchers must take into account the multiplicity of rules that are relevant to the situation under study. Social rules may reinforce one another to greater or lesser degrees, directing behavior in coherent ways. Rules may also cluster together to define coherent social roles (e.g., teacher, parent, or friend) and their corresponding role sequences (Harré and Secord 1972). These social rules and role sequences may clash with one another. At a meeting, social rules governing politeness toward the speaker may clash with rules governing the length of speaking time; the individual in the role of chair of the meeting may face the dilemma of whether to cut off the speaker. The uncertainty produced by clashes among competing roles may generate non-compliance with the rules associated with one of the roles. These same uncertainties may foster the formation of new rules: actors may design novel codes for covering ambiguities and conflicts among the existing rules and roles.

TYPES OF RULES

Social rules exist in a hierarchy in which some rules depend on other rules for their meaning (Sewell 2005). The *depth* of a rule corresponds to the extent to which the rule is (1) necessary for the meaning of other rules, and (2) dependent on other rules for its own meaning. *Deep rules* make possible many other rules but do not require many other rules themselves. The deepest rules tend to be taken for granted, used unconsciously, and nearly impossible to change. Logic is perhaps the deepest of all rules, providing the infrastructure for all other rule-making—including mathematics, which is also a system of deep rules. Linguistic structures are another set of deep rules that are crucial to human beings' construction of reality. Their instantiation is typically unconscious (especially when they are learned in early childhood), allowing for non-reflective communication and free-flowing conscious thought. Essentialism is also a set of deep rules that silently structure conscious thought and language. Because essentialist principles are so deeply grounded, they are quite difficult to recognize, much less treat as optional provisions that do not need to be instantiated. A principal challenge taken up in this book is the design of procedures to avoid the instantiation of this deep rule set.

Surface-level rules depend on many other rules for their meaning but provide a foundation for relatively few additional rules. Examples include tax laws, property laws, voting laws, baseball rules, dress codes, conversation norms, and restaurant tipping norms. These rules are visible, subject to contestation, and vulnerable to change. The interdependence of rules means that the analysis of a surface rule can lead to analysis of the deeper rules that make the surface rule possible. Even simple actions, such as a blink or a wink, can be analyzed in light of multiple layers of rules (Geertz 1973; Reed 2008; von Wright 1971). Analysts inevitably face challenges regarding how many of these layers to peel back when making sense of a given action. For most actions, analysts must assume that their audience has significant knowledge of the underlying social rules; the vast majority of these rules go unanalyzed and unmentioned.

Some social rules are *codified*—i.e., explicitly identified and recorded, typically in writing. Penal codes, constitutions, and codes of conduct are examples of codified systems of rules. *Non-codified* social rules, by contrast, are not explicitly elaborated through writing or other recorded means. *Norms* are mostly non-codified rules; they are implicit expectations about how people ought to behave (Rueschemeyer 2009: 64; see also Gibbs 1965; Gross and Hyde 2017: 364–72; Hechter and Opp 2001; Parsons 1937: 75). The vast majority of social rules that govern human behavior are not codified. All codified rules themselves depend on a huge range of implicit rules for their meaning. Durkheim (1893/1964) famously pointed out the non-contractual bases of contracts: the commonly understood but not formally specified norms about how to conduct oneself and run a society on which all contracts depend.

Rules may be distinguished according to the kind of actor involved in their creation, interpretation, and enforcement (Helmke and Levitsky 2004: 727). With *official rules*, the authorities overseeing the rules are regarded or portrayed as legitimate within the community that is subject to the rules. By contrast, *unofficial rules* are established, interpreted, and enforced outside of authoritative channels and beyond the purview of the authorities. I prefer to use the term *formal rules* to refer to rules that are both codified and official; *informal rules* are a residual category that contains any rules that are not codified, not official, or neither codified nor official.

A *social institution* (or simply *institution*) is a system of enduring rules that affect the distribution of significant resources (cf. Hall and Taylor 1996: 938; Immergut 1998; Jepperson 1991: 145; Knight 1992: 2–3; North 1990: 3; Pierson 2004: 104; Powell 1991: 197; Rueschemeyer 2009: 204; Thelen and Steinmo 1992: 2). This definition distinguishes institutions from isolated rules, from rules that are frequently changed, and from rules that do not have important distributional consequences. Examples of social institutions include marriage, friendship, corporate ownership, imprisonment, graduation, citizenship, sovereignty, nationhood, slavery, and communism. Examples of non-institutional rules include an individual provision of a constitution (which is not a system of rules), placing a salad fork to the outside of a regular fork when setting a dinner table (which does not distribute significant resources), and the French Constitution of 1791 (which was not enduring). Social scientists tend to analyze social institutions rather than non-institutional rules, though some scholarship focuses on the latter. In most contexts, the categories *rule* and *institution* can be used interchangeably without causing analytical confusion; it is also acceptable to refer to *institutional rules.*

Under this definition, institutions are systems of rules, not actors; institutions do not carry out actions. They are thus distinguished from organizations and other collective actors such as corporations, socioeconomic classes, movements, ethnic groups, and states. Institutions are also distinguished from individuals with role identities, such as aunts, professors, vendors, capitalists, spiritual leaders, and doormen. Organizations, collective actors, and individuals with role identities are often the main actors in the narratives of events. These actors are constituted, enabled, and constrained by social institutions, but they are not social institutions themselves.

I prefer to use the concept *social structure* (or simply *structure*) to refer to a social institution that distributes resources in ways that constitute mutually dependent role identities and that regulate behavior among the actors with the constituted identities (cf. Bhaskar 1979/1998: 42–44; Wendt 1999: 224–28). For example, a traditional agrarian structure includes a system of formal and informal rules governing property and interpersonal relations; this rule system constitutes and regulates peasants and landlords. In most societies, a family structure includes norms that define and regulate the roles of grandparent, parent, child, and grandchild. The social structure of a college or university features professors and students with corresponding roles and relations. Social structures often create asymmetrical, binary identity roles that assume and require one another (e.g., mother-child, doctor-patient, teacher-student, ruler-ruled, state-society).

Social rules can also be distinguished according to their constitutive versus regulatory effects (von Wright 1971; Searle 1995; Wendt 1998). *Constitutive rules* designate an entity as having membership in a category corresponding to a type of actor, object, behavior, event, process, and so on. They have the following logical form: X is sufficient for Y in context Z. For instance, if the category of interest is *working class* (Y), the analyst identifies the conditions (X) that are sufficient for an entity to be a member of this category. For members of a given society, the constituting conditions that make an entity a certain kind of thing—such as a peasant, plow, chore, harvest, or drought—are usually implicit and only unconsciously known.

In the social sciences, interpretive researchers are centrally concerned with the *context* that enables an entity to be a certain kind of actor, object, behavior, or process (Rabinow and Sullivan 1987; Schmidt 2008; Yanow and Schwartz-Shea 2015; Bevir and Blakely 2018).[8] For instance, consider the sentence "The working class in the East Midlands of England fought for its democratic inclusion." The sentence references an actor (the working class), an object (the East

Midlands), a behavior (fought), and a process (democratic inclusion). Each of these components depends on a background context that makes it possible for an entity to be a working class, the East Midlands, the act of having fought, and the process of democratic inclusion. The East Midlands can exist because the country of England exists, which in turn is possible because of rules allowing for sovereign countries. The context that enables the existence of any actor, object, or behavior may be clarified by defining the category corresponding to the actor, object, or behavior (e.g., by defining *the East Midlands*). However, a definition of a category is not equivalent to the permissive social context that makes the category possible. Most of the context that allows for the existence of an object, such as the East Midlands, must remain implicit. This permissive context is usually made explicit only when it is necessary in order to enhance intersubjective understanding about the meaning of an entity. If intersubjective agreement already exists, or is obtained satisfactorily with a good definition, no further clarification of the enabling context is ordinarily pursued.

Regulatory rules coordinate behavior by prescribing appropriate actions and imposing penalties for non-compliance (Durkheim 1893/1964; von Wright 1971). They have the following basic form: in context C, do behavior Y or receive sanction S. Regulatory rules include all of the obligatory codes of society that guide the behavior of actors (individual or collective) by threatening some form of punishment. Criminal laws are a classic example, because they consist of formal provisions with well-specified sanctions. But regulatory rules also encompass all unwritten norms that tacitly direct behavior and sanction non-compliance. Most norms are, precisely, informal regulatory rules.

We often explain behavior in part by identifying the regulatory rules that govern it. If an individual's behavior is consistent with a regulatory rule, we may conclude that the rule was a cause of the behavior. For instance, to explain why a driver stops at a stop sign, we will probably reference traffic laws as a central causal factor. We may conclude, perhaps based on counterfactual analysis, that these laws were a necessary condition for the observed behavior. Of course, the laws by themselves are not the full story; they are not sufficient for the behavior. We might also reference the goals of the driver (e.g., to avoid an accident) and perhaps even the machinery of the car (e.g., working brakes). But the traffic laws are essential and non-trivial in explaining the behavior. Although this example illustrates a formal rule, the idea that regulatory rules cause behavior applies equally well to informal rules of all kinds.

Regulatory rules are not equivalent to incentives for non-compulsory behavior. Incentives for non-compulsory behavior have the following logical form: in context C choose to do optional behavior Y, and receive benefit B. These instructions correspond to enticements designed to encourage certain kinds of sought-after behavior. For example, a grocery store may provide a discount for bringing your own grocery bags. Crucially, however, the implementation side of this reward system requires a regulatory rule that obligates the reward distributor to provide the benefit as stipulated. A punitive social rule helps ensure the distribution of the reward. If the grocery-store checker refuses to give you the discount as required, you may call the manager, you may frown, or you may just let it go—but you are *expected* to impose a sanction. If I am behind you in line, I am under some obligation to share the resentment while the checker puts the groceries into your own bags. The general point is that incentives designed to induce certain kinds of voluntary behavior require regulatory rules to ensure the enactment of the incentive.

Social rules are the substance of human civilizations, and their identification is essential for the work of social science. The regulatory side of social rules inhibits certain kinds of behavior through the application of sanctions, while the constitutive side of social rules makes possible meaningful behavior in the first place. All human institutions and all coordinated human behavior depend on the constitutive effects of social rules. Without social rules, complex human behaviors and human civilization would not exist.

Resources and Power

Social scientists use the concepts *resources* and *power* to describe and explain the capacities, interests, and behaviors of actors. They study resources and power to understand why actors stand in conflictual relations with one another and why one actor may dominate over another. Scholars recognize that resources and power drive the construction and maintenance of social institutions, as well as the occurrence and internal dynamics of events. This section considers the categories *resources* and *power* from a scientific constructivist perspective, putting them into dialogue with the categories *actor* and *rule*.

SOCIAL RESOURCES

Social resources (or simply *resources*) are entities that supply actors with the capacity to formulate, pursue, and achieve desires (cf. Dowding 1991: 61; Giddens 1979: 93–94; 1984: 33; Morriss 2002: xli–xlv, 138–44). Many, though not all, of the resources of interest to social scientists are human kinds (e.g., money, knowledge, allies). The referents of a resource are ultimately natural kinds (e.g., paper money is constituted mostly by carbon, hydrogen, and oxygen), but the natural kind composition of a resource is usually irrelevant to its definition and status as a resource. Most resources depend on human minds for their existence; they are resources only insofar as individuals collectively agree that they have value or utility beyond their natural kind composition.

The definition of resources as entities that enable actors to formulate, pursue, and achieve desires presupposes and complements an intentionalist view of actors.[9] Resources are specifically linked to the ability, capacity, or potential of actors to realize their desires. Actors fulfill their desires when they are sufficiently motivated to do so and when they have adequate and appropriate resources. The category *desire* is defined broadly, to include a wide range of goals and impulses that motivate or propel actor behavior (Wendt 1999: 116–30). The desires of an actor include unconscious fundamental needs, some of which are rooted in human biology, and specific preferences and goals, whether large or small, long-term or immediate.

Resources help translate the general desires of actors, including their most basic human needs, into specific preferences. The basic needs of human beings arguably include physical security, stable expectations about the social world, association with others, self-esteem, and growth and development (Wendt 1999: 131–32; see also Nussbaum 2000, 2011). Our access to resources—along with the particular social rules in which we find ourselves embedded—shapes the ways in which we translate these fundamental desires into more specific ones. We may all share the same need for shelter, but we will differ in the content of our specific desires for shelter because we have differential access to resources. A low-income person and a millionaire may both spend much time and energy on securing a home that meets their aspirations, but those aspirations will differ quite a lot.

Resources are not always more "concrete," "material," or "physical" than social rules (cf. Giddens 1979; Sewell 1992). Notably, resources such as knowledge and information may not have a material expression beyond encodings in brains or silicon chips. Many resources are abstract objects that do not exist in any directly perceivable form (e.g., ideas, emotional states, collective understandings). As with all human kinds, the identification of an entity as a resource is subject to spatial and temporal variation. Resources are material and ideational in the same way that other human kinds are material and ideational: they refer to uncomprehended natural kinds and depend ontologically on the machinery of human brains for their existence as certain kinds of things.

Social rules and resources are intimately connected (Bourdieu 1990; Giddens 1979; Ostrom 1990; Sewell 1992; Stryker 1994). Actors engage rules to try to gain resources, and they use resources to try to change rules. Rules are essential for the existence and efficacy of many resources. Rules assign value and status to objects and actors, thereby helping actors fulfill their desires. Rules also establish the context in which actors pursue their desires, shaping what can and cannot count as a resource at any given time and place. Conversely, the distribution of resources is centrally involved in the creation and maintenance of social rules. In explaining why different rules characterize different societies, the historical and contemporary allocation of resources figures as a prominent consideration. Differences in resource allocations shape the kinds of rules that are present in a given society and the kinds of actors who exist to defend, oppose, follow, and ignore those rules.

Resources can be divided into two types on the basis of how they are constituted, which in turn has implications for how they can be transformed. *Collectively dependent resources* require the collective recognition of a community of actors in order to have efficacy (cf. Berger and Luckmann 1966). These resources are valuable only insofar as actors treat them as valuable. Notable examples include money, artwork, and high-status social roles. Without collective recognition, money (in whatever physical or virtual form), artwork (in whatever medium), and high-status roles (such as professor or group leader) lose their value as *social* resources. But when collectively recognized, these entities and roles are useful for the pursuit of a range of goals, large and small, within a society.

Self-efficacious resources are valuable to individuals and groups regardless of whether they are collectively recognized as valuable within a community. Their status as resources to an individual does not depend on shared beliefs. These resources (many of which are partial natural kinds) include some inanimate objects, such as shelter, food, and tools. They also include some actor characteristics, such as strength, dexterity, and knowledge. While food and strength (for example) exist as *categories* by virtue of social construction and collective consensus, their efficacy as *entities* for fulfilling certain desires of an individual, such as relieving hunger or moving a heavy object, does not require collective recognition by others.

A given resource may be both self-efficacious and collectively dependent. For instance, a particular silver dollar coin can be used as a tool to help pry open a cabinet; in this sense, the coin is a self-efficacious resource. But that same coin's value as money depends on collective recognition. Likewise, a given piece of art may bring aesthetic pleasure to an individual independently of the reactions of others. But for the artwork to have monetary value in a market, or to bestow social status on its creator and owner, it must be deemed valuable by others.

Unlike self-efficacious resources, collectively dependent resources *are* subject to struggles over their meaning. With a collectively dependent resource, actors may work to contest (or bolster) the consensus that makes the resource efficacious. A professor enjoys the social status associated with this role only as long as the role is recognized as prestigious. Dollar bills count as money only so long as we have agreement about that matter. Land can be private property only insofar as we recognize individual possession. Repeated patterns of behavior may have the effect of naturalizing collectively dependent resources. Simply by using money, for example, we recreate and reinforce the behaviors and beliefs sustaining this resource (Searle 1995: chap. 5; cf. Simmel

1907/1978). At one extreme, we may unconsciously enact and reproduce the rules underpinning collectively dependent resources. At the other extreme, we may need regulatory rules and substantial resources to generate the collective acceptance required for the existence of a given resource (Knight 1992: 139–45). A resource such as the ownership of property does not produce collective acceptance by itself; it needs to be upheld by laws and backed up with considerable resources of other kinds. Laws and money are needed to create organizations that ensure the protection of private property (i.e., the police) and assist with the resolution of disputes (i.e., the courts). Without these costly organizational actors, the collective recognition required for private property ownership would break down (North 1981).

SOCIAL POWER

Social power (or simply *power*) refers to the resource-derived capacities of actors (Morriss 2002; Dowding 1991, 2006; cf. Weber 1978). If resources are conceptualized as the entities that supply actors with capacity (or capability), then power can be viewed as that capacity (or capability). Under this definition, *power* and *the exercise of power* are separate categories. An actor can possess power without actually using it (Morriss 2002; Searle 2015). Likewise, under this definition, *power* and *influence* are separate categories (cf. Lasswell and Kaplan 1950; Dahl 1957; Connolly 1974). *Power* is a dispositional category that refers to a capacity to *effect an outcome* (i.e., to bring about an outcome); *influence* is a result of the exercise of power in which one thing *affects* (i.e., alters, shapes, impinges, or changes) another thing. In many domains, a great deal of *power* is a necessary condition for *influence*. When this is true, the category *influential actor* is a subset of the category *powerful actor*.

This definition of *power* as actor capability presupposes the intentional stance toward actors. Actors choose to exercise their power (or not) on the basis of their beliefs and desires.[10] Power *enables* outcomes, but it still requires some kind of activation—perhaps *willful activation*—for its potentiality to be realized. The category *power* is normally used with an essentialist orientation; we understand power to be a property *possessed* by actors. Just as the intentional stance naturalizes the beliefs and desires of actors, the category *power* naturalizes the capabilities and potentialities of actors. Under essentialism, it is routinely believed that actors possess different levels of power.

A constructivist social science avoids this essentialism and recognizes that *power* is dependent on human understandings. The very category *power*—like *resource*—is a social construction that does not literally exist in nature. Actors do not literally possess the power to effect outcomes in the way that copper possesses the power to conduct electricity (cf. Harré and Madden 1975; Harré 2002). *Natural power* refers to the natural capacities of natural kinds; *social power* refers to the constructed capacities of constructed actors.[11] Whereas the exercise of natural power does not involve intentionality, the exercise of social power presupposes actor interests and choices.

In set-theoretic constructivist research, analysts focus on the membership and partial membership of cases in categories such as *powerful actor* and *powerless actor*. Particular individuals or groups are members, partial members, or non-members of these categories. The natural kinds that constitute the individuals or groups that are potential members of a particular category need not be consistent and stable; we do not know or understand these natural kinds. The meanings of *powerful actor* and *powerless actor* exist as conceptual spaces in the minds of researchers and other language users. Researchers come to understand these meanings from various sources, including their participation in communities in which powerful actors are part of the experienced reality.

The definition of power as capability makes the idea of *power to* more basic than the idea of *power over* (Ball 1993; Morriss 2002; cf. Wartenberg 1990). Cases of *power over* are a subset of cases of *power to*. For instance, one kind of *power to* is the capacity of actor *A* to cause actor *B* to do what *A* wants *B* to do when *B* otherwise would not (Weber 1978; Dahl 1957). Another kind of *power to* is the capacity of actor *A* to cause actor *B* to want what *A* wants even though *B* otherwise would not (Lukes 1974; Gaventa 1980). In both cases, the effect enabled by actor *A*'s *power to* is its *power over* actor *B*. The problem with focusing exclusively on the idea of *power over* is that it leaves out capacities that do not involve conflicts of interest between actors (cf. Benton 1981). It excludes, by definition, all consideration of capabilities that do not involve the domination, manipulation, or control of an opponent.

The notions of *power to* and *power over* are grounded in different image schemas. The idea of *power to* derives from primitive force dynamics and intuitive physics, in which more massive objects have more power (McCloskey 1983; Talmy 1988). A large, heavy object has the capacity to exert greater force than a small, light object. Objects in force dynamics are easily extended metaphorically to constructed actors, such that powerful actors can be thought of as massive objects and weak actors as small ones. In this spatial imagery, intentionality is viewed metaphorically as acceleration and speed. When actors choose to use their power, they are like objects with a given mass shifting from a state of rest to a state of motion with a certain force.

For its part, the idea of *power over* is rooted in an imagery of vertical spatial position, where *up* is authority and control, and *down* is subordination and lack of control (Lakoff and Johnson 1980; Schubert 2005). An actor's vertical position substitutes for physical size. The *power over* image has an experiential basis in which physical size corresponds to physical strength, and one actor's having power over another is metaphorically like emerging on top in a physical conflict. The physical-mass metaphor associated with *power to* remains basic in this imagery. Actors who occupy top vertical positions do so because they are big, strong, and capable of exerting great force.

The power of an actor varies across social domains, and an actor's capacity to produce an outcome varies across outcomes. In the social sciences, scholars commonly distinguish types of actor power according to the domains in which, and the outcomes for which, the power is relevant. In Mann's (1986) seminal framework, four kinds of macrosocial power are delineated: ideological, economic, military, and political. These kinds of power correspond to the capabilities that a collective actor possesses within a given institutionalized arena. They also correspond more generally to the kinds of resources that dictate outcomes in certain arenas of social life. Many other typologies of power exist in the social science literature (e.g., Lukes 1974; Isaac 1987b; Dowding 2019; Barnett and Duvall 2005; Searle 2015; Weber 1978). The typologies are often rooted in the construction of different kinds of actors, such as *religious authorities, corporate leaders, military commanders, landed elites,* and *political officials.* Power typologies highlight different kinds of social resources as the basis for different kinds of actor power and different kinds of powerful actors themselves.

Possible world semantics is useful for analyzing the counterfactuals embedded in assertions about actor power. To assert that an actor has the power to effect outcome Y is to assert that there is a possible world in which the actor actually exercises its power to effect outcome Y. Asserting that an actor has the capacity to effect Y is equivalent to asserting that it is *possible* to effect Y. If it is *possible* for an actor to effect Y, then there is a possible world in which the actor *does* effect Y. If there is no possible world in which the actor effects Y, then the actor does not have the power to effect Y.

If actor A has the power to effect outcome Y but does not do so, *why* does actor A not do so? The intentional stance identifies the beliefs and desires of actor A as immediate causes of the non-exercise of power. Actor A *chooses* not to effect Y because of A's beliefs and desires. In other worlds that are non-actual, the beliefs and desires of actor A are different, and A uses its power to effect Y. The counterfactual issue is not whether *any* possible world exists in which actor A effects Y; one can imagine a world different from our own in which A effects Y. The important question for counterfactual analysis is whether actor A effects Y in a world identical to our own except that the beliefs and desires of actor A are different.

This kind of counterfactual question informs our understandings of responsibility and obligation. Lord Salisbury once declared, "Those who have the absolute power of preventing lamentable events and, knowing what is taking place, refuse to exercise that power, are responsible for what happens" (quoted in Morriss 2002: 39; see also Connolly 1974). Undergirding this kind of declaration is the intentional stance and its formula for explaining behavior: beliefs and desires plus capabilities equal behavior. In the Lord Salisbury example, actors who have the capability to prevent a "lamentable" outcome are under an obligation to do so; less powerful actors do not carry the burden of this obligation. Yet these less powerful actors do carry the burdens of their general powerlessness: their lack of capability may place them at the mercy of the powerful when faced with tragedies that could be prevented.

RESOURCES, RULES, AND ACTORS

Social theories conceptualize resources and rules as mutually implicating entities (see chapter 8 on the actor-rule-resource triad). On the one hand, it is common to view the distribution of power across actors as centrally involved in the creation, change, and dismantlement of social rules. Theories in which power is highlighted see important rules as the outcome of distributional conflict among opposing categorical actors with different levels and kinds of resources (Marx and Engels 1848/2012; Gaventa 1980; Knight 1992). On the other hand, the rule-governed distribution of resources affects the ability of actors to realize their desires. Rules themselves are resources, because of their enabling and constraining effects. Rules can distribute resources in ways that *enable* certain kinds of behavior, which in turn allows actors to fulfill certain desires. The creation of a law that defines marriage as a union of two people regardless of their sex provides rights that newly enable some people to fulfill their desire to be married. Rules can also distribute resources in ways that *constrain* behavior by prohibiting or otherwise penalizing certain actions, which also fulfills some actors' desires. A law that defines marriage as exclusively a union between a man and a woman is a resource for actors who want to weaken the movement for LGBTQ rights.

Rules *unevenly* distribute resources across actors with different desires and different preexisting endowments of resources. Many rules are created precisely to distribute resources to individuals or groups identified as having particular traits or who already have certain other resources (e.g., knowledge, skill, wealth). The reward systems built into economic institutions such as job markets are an example: the intended function of job markets is to select and reward individuals who are regarded as possessing certain desired characteristics. Even rules that seem to be neutral, such as the codes that guide everyday appropriate behavior, have distributional consequences. To take one example, consider the rules that constitute and regulate standard American speech. These rules do not result in a neutral medium of exchange (cf. Sewell 2005: 147–48). Rather, they favor individuals who have access to personal or collective resources that allow them to be skilled users of the language as prescribed by this rule system. We appreciate the distributional consequences when we realize that "correct" pronunciation and grammar can be associated with one's standing in the community as an educated, or "refined," human being.

Rules create conflicting interests among the actors differentially affected by them. These conflicts, which are a potential engine of change, are contained within all important rule systems (Mahoney and Thelen 2010). A conflict will remain latent if the rule in question is an unrecognized feature of social reality. Conflicts may also remain latent because of asymmetries in actor power: disadvantaged actors may acquiesce in a status quo that seems inescapable. Many institutions tend toward stability because they disproportionately distribute resources to actors who are already powerful, reinforcing their position and better enabling them to uphold the arrangements from which they already benefit. This reinforcement of power is one reason that abrupt institutional change, as opposed to gradual change, is hard to bring about.

The uneven distributional effects of rules are centrally involved in the constitution of collective actors. Individuals are commonly advantaged (or disadvantaged) by multiple institutions that reinforce one another. A position of privilege (or lack of privilege) within these institutional complexes provides individuals with a shared basis for subjective identification and coordinated action as a group. Some collective actors become politically active in conjunction with their self-perceptions as disadvantaged in the flow of resources from institutional complexes. Individuals may see themselves as members of groups based on race, ethnicity, class, gender, or sexual orientation that occupy a subordinate position with respect to institutional resources. Even if individuals do not self-identify in these ways, social analysts may nevertheless view them as collective actors, on the basis of their locations in the posited social structures.

In summary, the approach presented here conceives resources as existing in a mutually constitutive relationship with the beliefs and desires of actors. On the one hand, beliefs and desires help constitute resources by identifying what is regarded as valuable within a society. Social resources such as money and private property depend on human understandings for their existence. On the other hand, resources help constitute beliefs and desires. Access to resources (e.g., money and private property) provides access to social experiences (e.g., schooling and friendship groups) that shape the content of beliefs and desires. These beliefs and desires may, in turn, serve to legitimate the shared understandings on which resources depend.

Temporality

Assumptions concerning the category *time* are important, built-in components of all social science theories and explanations. One cannot construct a theory or formulate an explanation without making some assumptions about the duration, timing, ordering, and/or speed of social phenomena. Although temporal commitments are often left implicit, much can be gained by making them explicit. Scholars can build more precise, interesting, and useful theories and explanations if they explicitly consider the temporal dimensions of their research.

In the social sciences, researchers cannot simply describe the temporal features of a preexisting objective reality. There is no singularly correct way to specify the time-based aspects of the phenomena under study. Rather, they must work to *construct* the temporal dimensions of their research. They must imaginatively explore what is gained and what is lost by looking at a social phenomenon from one temporal perspective rather than another. Their research questions and goals must drive considerations about the most appropriate and useful temporal perspectives (cf. Pierson 2004: 80–81).

This section offers tools for conceptualizing some of the more important ways in which temporality enters into social science analysis. The discussion is organized around two main distinctions. The first is *punctuated change* versus *gradual change*, which is the axis of important debates in the social sciences. This distinction provides a basis for identifying different kinds of change. The second distinction, concerning the difference between *process* and *event*, provides a basis for identifying different kinds of explanations in the social sciences.

PUNCTUATED VERSUS GRADUAL CHANGE

Debates concerning punctuated versus gradual change are commonplace across the sciences. In biology, most famously, the issue animates the controversy over whether the pace of evolution generally is incremental or punctuated (Gould and Eldredge 1977; Dawkins 1986). In geology and paleontology, gradualists and catastrophists disagree over the speed of specific events, such as the extinction of dinosaurs (e.g., Hallam and Wignall 1997). In the philosophy of science, scholars debate whether the advance of knowledge itself is gradual or punctuated (e.g., Kuhn 1970; Toulmin 1972). In the social sciences, similar controversies arise in discussions about whether institutional change is punctuated with critical junctures and abrupt shifts or whether such change is a gradual and slow-moving process (Thelen 1999, 2004; Streeck and Thelen 2005; Pierson 2004; Mahoney and Thelen 2010).

A simple but helpful way of distinguishing types of institutional change focuses on two dimensions: the *size* and *duration* of a change (cf. Aminzade 1992; Pierson 2004; Grzymala-Busse 2011). Figure 9.1 presents a typology of the four kinds of change based on the cross-tabulation of the two dimensions. In the social sciences, the research question and the kind of change under study may evolve in tandem with one another as the analyst learns about a given topic.

In this typology, *abrupt change* is defined as a *large* transformation that takes place over a *short* duration. *Punctuated change* occurs specifically when

Duration of Change

		Short	Long
Size of Change	Large	Abrupt or Punctuated Change	Transformative Gradual Change
	Small	Minor Shift	Minor Gradual Change

FIGURE 9.1. Typology of Institutional Change

an abrupt change is preceded and followed by long stretches of time without considerable change. Critical event analysis, while not requiring abrupt change, is nevertheless well suited for analyzing it. Critical event analysis (see chapter 10) identifies bounded episodes that punctuate historical sequences with causally important occurrences.

By contrast, a *minor shift* takes place when a short-duration occurrence yields a *small* amount of change. As defined here, minor shifts are one-off occurrences that do not cumulate over time or become part of a larger phenomenon of change; they are stand-alone episodes. These shifts are generally not a focus of analytic attention or a central part of institutional analysis.

Transformative gradual change occurs when a *large* change takes place over a *long* period of time. A transformative gradual change may be a single process in which a phenomenon of interest changes incrementally. Alternatively, it may be a series of small, discrete changes that gradually accumulate to produce a large change. With this latter subtype, the analyst treats the whole series of individual changes as representing a coherent phenomenon of gradual change (Thelen 2004).

By contrast, *minor gradual change* occurs when a long process or a long series of events produces only a *small* change. Minor gradual change also divides into two subtypes. One is a single long process that produces only a small amount of change. For instance, a state-led process of nation building may feature ambitious programs that, in the end, bring about only a small change. The other subtype is a long series of discrete events that mostly cancel each other out. For instance, a series of radical policy initiatives and subsequent reversals may add up to only a minor gradual change.

In the social sciences, scholars disagree about the frequency of punctuated (or abrupt) change versus transformative gradual change. The nature of the debate depends on whether the change dimension or the duration dimension is at the forefront. When the change dimension is emphasized, the debate concerns the amount of change that actually occurs during a given period. The animating question is, "Was the amount of change large or small during the episode under study?" This kind of debate arises when scholars disagree about the extent of stability versus change that characterizes a given event. Even events such as revolutions and regime breakdowns can fuel disputes among analysts about the magnitude of the transformation. Disagreement can stem from many sources: scholars can view a particular event at different levels of analysis; they may be concerned with different consequences of the event; they may disagree about the defining categories that constitute the event; or they may have different understandings of the status quo arrangement that preceded the event. It is generally worth asking what is gained and what is lost by viewing a phenomenon as representing a large change versus a small change. If scholars are convinced that a given event or process entails a large change (or a small one), they can often still discover new insights by taking the opposite perspective and constructing the event or process under the assumption that it is, instead, a small change (or a large one).

The other way of framing the debate emphasizes the duration dimension. Here the animating question is, "How quickly did a case (a system, organization, country, person) change from one state to another?" The punctuated-change answer to this question is, "The change happened during a brief period." By contrast, the gradual-change answer is, "The change occurred as part of a long process or a long series of incremental steps." From the perspective of scientific constructivism, changes in cases do not have the ontological quality of lasting a specific amount of time. Nevertheless, an analyst cannot meaningfully assign to an occurrence a duration that violates broad understandings of that occurrence. For instance, one cannot intelligibly assert that the change in Mexico from *Spanish colonial territory* to *sovereign country* occurred over a period of eight centuries. Yet scholars can meaningfully discuss whether this change occurred gradually over decades, or rapidly over a matter of years, or even months and days.

In thinking about the duration of a particular change, a useful approach is to identify the permissible boundaries of its duration, which specify how long and how short the change can be cast without misconstruing its meaning. In some cases, a change must be construed as quite long (or short) in order to preserve its meaning as understood within a given semantic context. Often, however, the permissible range of duration varies quite a lot. Scholars can explore the analytical advantages and disadvantages of viewing the change with different durations. For instance, it is useful to think about the transition in Mexico from colonial territory to sovereign country as a long process for some analytical purposes, and as an abrupt shift for others.

Scholars who emphasize gradual change sometimes call attention to what is lost when analytic commitments lead academic communities to focus mainly on changes that are abrupt and punctuated (Thelen 1999, 2004; Streeck and Thelen 2005; Pierson 2004; Mahoney and Thelen 2010). They worry that the effort to identify sudden changes and decisive turning points directs too much attention away from elements of stability and the gradual aspects of change. Likewise, they worry that certain theoretical orientations, such as rational choice theory, require analysts to view a given phenomenon from only a short-run temporal perspective. Their point is that the scholarly community stands to gain valuable insights by viewing changes through a gradualist lens and conceiving shifts as unfolding over long periods of time.

EVENTS AND PROCESSES AS CAUSES AND OUTCOMES

This section discusses the construction of causal factors and outcomes as events, processes, and combinations of the two (cf. Abbott 2001: chap. 6; Aminzade 1992; Grzymala-Busse 2011; Pierson 2004: chap. 3; Sewell 2005: chaps. 3, 7, 8). The social world is not objectively organized into predefined social events and processes; social scientists must creatively construct the events and processes of their analyses. Many phenomena can be legitimately cast as either an event or a process. For example, one can speak of the process of industrialization in eighteenth- and nineteenth-century England, and one can speak of the Industrial Revolution as an event in England from approximately 1730 to 1870. Likewise, we can understand the French Revolution both as a well-bounded event from 1789 to 1799 and as a process of many complex changes that started in the mid-eighteenth century and ended in the mid-nineteenth century. Events can launch processes, intersect with processes, and conclude processes. Processes can begin and end with events, and they may be interrupted by events. Processes consist in part of different events, and events consist in part of different processes. For instance, the process of industrialization in England contained important events corresponding to specific technological and manufacturing breakthroughs; and the Industrial Revolution in England consisted in part of general processes of technological advancement and mechanized mass production in factories.

The distinction between event and process is linked to the category *time*. Time lacks an obvious literal definition; it is usually defined using metonymy and metaphor (Lakoff and Johnson 1999; Moore 2006; see also Evans 2013). Psychologically, our experience of events drives our experience of time, rather than the other way around. We often conceive time metonymically as successive iterations of a given kind of event. Because we experience events as continuous, directional, and irreversible, we also experience time as continuous, directional, and irreversible. When we look closely at a period of time, we find that it consists of specific events. When we pull back and take a broader temporal perspective, we often see processes. Cognitive scientists assert that events are more basic than processes; the latter ultimately reduce to the former (Lakoff 1987; Evans 2013).[12] For their part, events reduce (cognitively

Type of Outcome

		Discrete Event	Ongoing Process
Type of Cause	Ongoing Process	Threshold and Conjunctural Effects	Constant and Cumulative Effects
	Discrete Event	Necessity and Sufficiency Effects	Self-Reproducing and Feedback Effects

FIGURE 9.2. Typology of Causal Effects

speaking) to sub-events, as well as to the actors, objects, rules, and resources that constitute them.

Our understanding of time is spatial in nature. We use spatial metaphors to think about time (Lakoff and Johnson 1980; Lakoff 1987; Evans 2013). Two basic metaphors are TIME IS A LOCATION IN SPACE and TIME IS AN OBJECT IN SPACE. In the social sciences, the former metaphor informs our use of the category *event*, whereas the latter metaphor informs our use of the category *process*. *Event* can be viewed metaphorically as a particular segment on a one-dimensional line. Social scientists use this metaphor when they mark off specific events on a timeline. By contrast, *process* is understood metaphorically as a continuous flow that moves across a space. Social scientists tend to see events as *contained in time* and processes as *flowing across time*.

With institutional analysis, a given cause or outcome can be conceived either as an event or as a process. The choice is highly consequential. Depending on whether the cause or outcome is conceptualized as an event or a process, its explanation features one of four kinds of causal effects, as identified in figure 9.2 (cf. Aminzade 1992; Pierson 2004; Grzymala-Busse 2011). This typology provides category names for each kind of effect: threshold and conjunctural effects; constant and cumulative effects; self-reproducing and feedback effects; and necessity and sufficiency effects.

First, *threshold and conjunctural effects* are in operation when an ongoing process causes a discrete event. This causal pattern characterizes critical mass arguments: small changes cumulate in a process that eventually reaches a tipping point, at which time a discrete outcome occurs. A nice example is Goldstone's (1991) theory of revolutions, which proposes that slow-moving demographic changes accumulate over time and yield the sudden event of revolution. Granovetter's (1978: 1423–24) original analysis of threshold effects suggests that this causal pattern may also characterize inventions, riots, strikes, and voting choices. Pierson (2004: 83–87) notes that scholars have used threshold analysis for explaining the origins of specific events such as the U.S. civil rights movement, social democratic hegemony in Scandinavia, and critical realignments in U.S. politics. For instance, McAdam (1982) shows how the Montgomery bus boycott was caused by the long-term decline of cotton, which gradually fueled northern migration, which in turn fueled the growth of Black churches and political organizations, which were essential for the outcome of the boycott (see also Morris 1984).

Conjunctural effects also fall into the category in which a process causes an event (Aminzade 1992: 466–67; Pierson 2004: 55–58). A *conjuncture* is the coming together—the temporal and spatial intersection—of two or more independent processes. The result of the intersection can be a specific event that is located at a specific time. A good example is Skocpol's (1979) explanation of social revolutions, which she views as sudden events resulting from the intersection of a process of state collapse and a process of peasant revolt.

Second, *constant and cumulative effects* characterize explanations in which both causes and outcomes are processes, rather than events. With constant effects, a given causal process remains stably in operation, repeatedly generating an ongoing process as its outcome. Continuity in the outcome process can be observed as long as the causal process remains in operation. Stinchcombe (1968: 101) offers the following example:

> If we ask why cotton this year will be produced in the same areas that produced cotton last year, we find a series of causes of cotton production that stay fairly constant: the angle of the sun, the supply of water, the cotton plant's physiology, the approximately constant amount of clothes people wear, the cost advantage of cotton over wool and synthetics, the cheapness of [African American] labor in the South and Mexican labor in the Southwest, and the like.

Stinchcombe suggests how a series of constant causes all contribute to generate a stable process in which cotton is produced in the same areas year after year.

Cumulative effects also fall into the category in which both causes and outcomes are processes. With cumulative effects, the causal process is a gradually changing and consistently directed phenomenon that gives rise to another process of interest (Pierson 2004: 82–83). For example, Putnam (2000) explains the gradual decay of social capital in the United States as a product of the gradual spread of television and the slow removal of pre-television generations from the population. Cumulative effects also occur in reciprocal causal relationships among processes such as changes in population size, literacy rates, life expectancy, income, and educational attainment. For instance, the process of increasing literacy could be explained as a product of the process of increasing income, and vice versa.

Third, *self-reproducing and feedback effects* mark patterns of causation in which an event launches a coherent, self-contained process. A good example is the causal pattern that I call *self-reinforcing path dependence* (see chapter 11).

With this pattern, a critical event causes a process that is marked by a repro-ductive logic—specifically, an increasing-returns process (Arthur 1994; Pier-son 2004). Once initiated, this process contains the seeds of its own self-reproduction. This overall pattern of causation corresponds to Stinchcombe's (1968) understanding of *historicist causation*, in which an event starts a process that persists long after the end of the event.

In the social sciences, the analysis of feedback effects often breaks down into two separate components: (1) the identification of the event or events that originally caused the feedback process, and (2) the feedback process itself. It is useful to distinguish three kinds of feedback processes: continuous, self-amplifying, and self-eroding (Falleti and Mahoney 2015: 220–22). A *continuous process* is caused by an event and then persists in a stable form over time. For example, the decision to get married or to become a U.S. citizen causes a change in marital or citizenship status that remains stable over time. With a *self-amplifying process*, an initial event establishes a process marked by the expansion, augmentation, or strengthening of a starting pattern or occurrence. For example, many analyses of path dependence from economics consider how a contingent event sets into motion a pattern characterized by exponential growth in the mar-ket share of a particular technology. With a *self-eroding process*, an initial event sets into motion a process in which the initial configuration or unifying principle is gradually diminished, weakened, or decreased. For instance, an employer's decision to maintain the minimum wage at a certain level initiates a gradual ero-sion of the employees' purchasing power. As with other temporal distinctions, this threefold typology of feedback effects is analytical rather than ontological. The distinction is intended to help scholars conceptualize the various long-run processual effects that an event can bring into being.

Finally, *necessity and sufficiency effects* apply to patterns in which one event causes another event. This kind of causality falls within the regularity model of causality discussed in chapter 3, and it is further elaborated in the next chapter, on critical events. Necessity and sufficiency effects have a special status in that they are assumed by and required for the other three kinds of causal effects. For instance, threshold and conjunctural effects are premised on the idea that a process reaches a point at which it is approximately sufficient for a discrete event; constant effects likewise assume that a first process is approximately sufficient for a second process. Self-reproducing and feedback effects consist of sequences of events in which one event is approximately necessary and/or suf-ficient for the next event in the sequence (see chapter 11 on path dependence).

The foundational status of necessity and sufficiency effects is related to the cognitive dependence of processes on events. Researchers who study pro-cesses break them apart into constitutive events for the purposes of causal analysis. They conceptualize the process as a sequence of discrete events that are linked through necessity and/or sufficiency effects. With sequence analysis, social scientists view social reality as consisting simultaneously of static entities *in time* (i.e., each event in the sequence is located squarely in time) and dynamic entities moving *across time* (i.e., the sequence as a whole moves across time). The tension between these two views of time has not been lost on social theorists (see Bourdieu 1989; Emirbayer 1997), nor has the fact that social science approaches to causation end up focusing on static entities in time (Manicas 1981; Skocpol 1994; Sewell 1996). The cognitive primacy of events may explain why scholars have found it so difficult to pursue causal analysis from a perspective in which temporally unbounded entities are the focus of attention (cf. Abbott 2016).

———

This chapter has discussed categories that social scientists can use to formulate propositions and theories, develop explanations, build narrative presentations, and understand social reality more generally. I specifically focused on the categories *actor, object, rule, institution, structure, resource, power, event, process,* and *time.* My approach has been to discuss the *meaning* of these theory-building categories within the semantic context of the contemporary social sciences. I have also focused on developing subtypes of the categories and situating the categories alongside other related categories. The goal throughout has been to provide useful tools for substantive research that is both constructivist and scientific.

Under scientific constructivism, social scientists can use theory-building categories in substantive research to generate new understandings of social reality itself. The categories contain insights for constructing social reality by naming and defining phenomena, by creating metaphors and generating analogies, by building typologies and making generalizations, and by proposing tentative relationships and explanations (Swedberg 2017). Yet scientific constructivism does not afford social scientists the freedom to build theory and create social reality just as they please. They must do so in ways that are consistent with an already constructed experiential reality—with the understandings of the social world that they and their intended audiences share. This experiential reality both contains the raw material for creative theory construction and establishes the boundaries for what analysts can and cannot intelligibly build.

The next two chapters return to the logic of sequences in the social sciences. Attention focuses on both the beginning of a sequence (chapter 10) and the intermediary events of a sequence that lead to an outcome (chapter 11). Each of these components of analysis poses interesting challenges and opportunities for social scientists.

10

Critical Event Analysis

(coauthored with Laura García-Montoya)

Critical event analysis is the implicit analytic framework that people use when asked to explain the major choices in their lives. For example, if asked why we selected a certain career path or specific life partner, we typically call attention to a small number of salient events that we understand to be important causes. These events may be important because we believe that they helped set into motion a subsequent chain of occurrences that led to the outcome. They may also be important because we believe that if the events were counterfactually taken away (or changed), the outcome of interest would not have occurred. The events on which we focus are usually contingent occurrences that could have turned out differently. Thinking about these contingent events leads naturally to consideration of the alternative trajectories our lives might have followed.

In the social sciences, case-study analysts also focus much attention on critical events—sometimes referred to as watersheds, turning points, or critical junctures—when explaining outcomes of interest. These analysts suggest that, during relatively well-defined periods, cases experience occurrences that are highly consequential for their subsequent development. Table 10.1 presents ten examples of critical events from comparative-historical studies in political science and sociology. As the table suggests, the range of cases and topics to which critical event analysis might be applied is quite wide. A cursory look at the table also suggests that critical event analysis is easier to carry out if one already knows something about the historical case and events under consideration.

TABLE 10.1. Examples of Critical Events in Case-Study Research

	Case	Critical Event	Outcome	Importance
Chibber (2003)	South Korea	Export-led industrialization (ELI) strategy (1964–65)	Enduring developmental state	High necessity/ moderate sufficiency
Goldstone (1998b)	England	Invention of Newcomen pumping machine (1712)	Industrial Revolution (mid-18th to early 20th century)	High necessity/ moderate sufficiency
Isaac et al. (1994)	United States	Assassination of Martin Luther King Jr. (1968)	Relief explosion via AFDC expansion (1968–1970s)	High necessity/ moderate sufficiency
Karl (1997)	Venezuela	Oil booms (1973 and 1979)	State disorganization and regime decay (1980s–1990s)	Moderate necessity/ high sufficiency
Kurtz (2013)	Uruguay	Battle's "rain of programs" (1903–7 and 1911–15)	State effectiveness (1930s–)	Moderate necessity/ high sufficiency
Lebow (2010)	States system	Assassination of Franz Ferdinand (1914)	World War I	High necessity/ moderate sufficiency
Mahoney (2001)	Honduras	Aborted liberalism (1876–83)	Traditional dictatorship (1932–82)	High necessity/high sufficiency
Riedl (2014)	Ghana	Strategy of incorporation (1981–85)	Stable, institutionalized party system	Moderate necessity/ high sufficiency
Slater (2010)	Malaysia	Urban strike wave (1945–48)	Elite cohesion and political stability (1969–)	High necessity/high sufficiency
Thelen (2004)	Germany	Handicraft Protection Law of 1897	High-skill, plant-based apprenticeship economy	High necessity/ moderate sufficiency

Note: Many of the studies in this table examine critical events across multiple cases. For the sake of illustration, however, we summarize only one case from each study.

Critical events are defined as contingent events that are causally important for a specific outcome in a particular case. The following passage from Robert Frost's poem "The Road Not Taken" illustrates the features of this definition:

> Two roads diverged in a wood, and I—
> I took the one less traveled by,
> And that has made all the difference.

The traveler faces a choice between two clear alternatives, and the decision to take the road less traveled is a contingent event. The event is extremely important; in fact, it makes all the difference.

The centrality of *causal importance* for Frost's poem can be seen if we change the words of the last line as follows: "And that has made a small difference." Clearly, this change dramatically weakens the traveler's bold assertion and the allure of the poem. If one formulates the last sentence as a probabilistic cause, it becomes even weaker: "And that has probably made a small difference."

The centrality of *contingency* in the passage can be seen if we change the second line to: "I took the one usually traveled by." Without the contingency, one wonders why following the usual path made such a big difference, and why the traveler bothers to call attention to the divergence of roads at all. If we completely eliminate contingency, such that only one road exists in the wood, the poem no longer makes sense.

Critical event analysis is attractive to social scientists in part because it promises a parsimonious explanation of a puzzling outcome. A single cause does much of the explanatory lifting. Beyond explanatory austerity, critical event analysis is appealing because the critical event is not "predetermined." With critical event analysis, the counterfactual question of what would have happened—what could have happened—is spotlighted and given center stage. The idea that things could have turned out differently captures the imagination and stimulates counterfactual explorations.

To be sure, critical event analysis is not always an appropriate explanatory framework. Outcomes are often the result of gradual processes that unfold over long periods of time. With gradualist explanations, no single event is of decisive causal importance; a process of many small events pushing in a consistent direction drives the outcome. For instance, consider a poem titled "The Roads Consistently Followed":

Repeatedly roads diverged in a wood, and I—
I consistently followed the road to the left,
And that has made all the difference.

While this gradualist version of Frost's poem is not as intriguing as the original, it is certainly possible that it better characterizes the trajectory of most cases and phenomena of interest in the social sciences (cf. Thelen 1999, 2003, 2004). In the social sciences today, the frequency of punctuated change versus gradual change (see chapter 9) remains an open question. Another open question concerns which *kinds* of puzzling outcomes are best explained by critical events, as opposed to gradual processes of change.

This chapter considers the definitional and methodological issues that arise in critical event analysis. We argue that causal importance is defined by the necessity effects and sufficiency effects that an event exerts on an outcome. A *causally important event* is one that is either highly necessary or highly sufficient (or both) for an outcome of interest; in addition, a causally important event cannot have either a low level of necessity or a low level of sufficiency for the outcome of interest. A *contingent event* is one that is not expected to occur but that does occur. This chapter will show how causal importance and contingency are closely linked in the explanation of outcomes. After discussing these methodological issues, we will consider how to apply the critical event framework in substantive research and explore its implicit use in the field of comparative-historical analysis.

The Necessity and Sufficiency Effects of Events

This section introduces two kinds of effects that an event can exert on an outcome: necessity effects and sufficiency effects (cf. Hall 2004; Soifer 2012). This distinction provides the foundation for the definition of *causally important event* that is developed later in the chapter. In this section, attention focuses on how the study of necessity effects and the study of sufficiency effects require the use of different kinds of counterfactuals. The discussion also underscores the different cognitive foundations of the two kinds of causal effects.

NECESSITY EFFECTS

One way in which events exert causal effects on other events is by making certain outcomes possible that otherwise would be impossible (Abend forthcoming). We call these causal aspects of events their *necessity effects*. The necessity effects of an event correspond to the ways in which the event enables or permits an outcome. An event makes possible an outcome by *influencing the context and circumstances* in which the event operates and the outcome occurs. The necessity effects of an event do not generate a direct pathway to an outcome; they do not directly produce the outcome. Rather, they *allow* productive causal forces to unfold and generate the outcome without being derailed or blocked. The necessity effects of an event cause direct changes not to the main outcome, but to the context and circumstances of the case. An event exerts necessity effects by helping produce a permissive setting—that is, by removing blockages and dislodging obstacles that stand in the way of the operation of a productive causal force.

To study necessity effects, scholars use counterfactual analysis in which the causal event of interest is changed or negated (Goertz and Levy 2007a). The standard rules of counterfactual analysis apply to the study of necessity effects—including the minimal-rewrite rule, which requires that the negation of the event be achieved by means of the smallest possible changes to the actual world (Tetlock and Belkin 1996a: 7–8, 23–25; Levy 2008: 634–38; cf. Lewis 1979). The minimal-rewrite rule is easily violated when drawn-out, multifaceted events are the antecedent conditions that are negated or changed in a counterfactual analysis. For example, one might propose *Spanish colonialism* as a critical event for an episode of postcolonial civil violence in Nicaragua. However, the logical complement of this event–i.e., *not–Spanish colonialism*—is a vague category that lacks substantive content. If the negation of an event is not clear, the difference-making effects of the positive event are also not clear. To understand what would have happened without the event, the analyst must identify the specific alternatives to the event that motivate the counterfactual (Garfinkel 1981).

The idea that events can exert necessity effects is rooted in basic notions of causation that are learned as early as the first six months of life (Mandler 1992; Mandler and Pagán Cánovas 2014; cf. Lakoff and Johnson 1980; Lakoff 1987). The primitive spatial categories BLOCK and UNBLOCK seem especially important in grounding the pattern of causation that corresponds to necessity effects. Necessity effects invoke an image schema featuring the removal of an obstacle that is blocking the movement of an entity headed toward a location in space. The force that removes the obstacle plays a causal role for the outcome of the entity's reaching its destination. This imagery is central to force dynamic patterns corresponding to PREVENT and LET (Talmy 1988). These patterns assume that an entity has a certain destination that may or may not be realized, depending on whether or not a permissive context exists.

SUFFICIENCY EFFECTS

Events may cause outcomes by playing a productive and generative role in actively bringing about the outcomes (cf. Lewis 2000; McDermott 2002). We call these causal aspects of events their *sufficiency effects*. Here, one understands events to produce outcomes by setting into motion a chain of subsequent events that culminates in the outcome of interest. The sufficiency effect of the initial event runs through, and exists because of, this causal chain, which ultimately reaches and makes contact with the outcome. The logical relationship between the initial event and the final outcome is one of sufficiency, not necessity and counterfactual dependence. A well-defined event specifies those aspects of the event that are hypothesized to generate an outcome by virtue of an intermediary causal chain of events.[1]

Whereas the necessity effects of an event are consistent with a counterfactual model of causation, the sufficiency effects of an event are the focus of a regularity model of causation (Psillos 2002, 2009). A regularity model requires the following components for causality between event X and event Y: (1) X precedes Y in time, (2) X is directly or indirectly necessary and/or sufficient for Y across all relevant possible worlds, and (3) X is spatiotemporally linked to Y (see chapter 3). This understanding of causality does not insist on counterfactual dependence; it insists only that X be systematically and spatiotemporally related to Y across all relevant possible worlds. Scholars who study sufficiency effects are concerned with the causal chain that connects event X and event Y.

They are specifically interested in understanding how and why an initial event can launch a causal process that culminates in the outcome of interest. The sufficiency effects of a critical event capture its capacity to unleash a causal chain that ensures the outcome.[2]

The idea of sufficiency effects is rooted in primitive spatial ideas and basic image schemas learned in infancy (Mandler 1992; Mandler and Pagán Cánovas 2014; cf. Lakoff and Johnson 1980; Lakoff 1987). The core categories that ground sufficiency effects include ANIMATE MOVE, START PATH, LINK, PATH TO, and CONTACT. Critical event analysis is especially concerned with ANIMATE MOVE and START PATH. These ideas can be blended with notions such as PUSH and FORCED MOVEMENT. With this enriched structure, we can view the sufficiency effects of a critical event as acting like a force that pushes an object in a certain direction or along a certain path to eventually make spatiotemporal contact with a final location.

AN ILLUSTRATION

The causal analysis of a potential critical event requires the analyst to *identify* and *distinguish* its necessity effects and its sufficiency effects. All non-trivial causal events exert both kinds of effects to some degree. However, the *extent to which* they exert each kind of effect can vary. To illustrate, let us consider the proposition that the election of George W. Bush in 2000 was a critical event for the U.S. invasion of Iraq in 2003 (see Harvey 2012). How does the analyst identify the extent of necessity effects and sufficiency effects of *the election of Bush* for *the Iraq invasion*?

As a first step, the analyst can use existing theory and knowledge to identify those aspects of *the election of Bush* that might be causally important. For example, the analyst might initially call attention to three causally relevant categories of which Bush is a member: (1) *Republican Party affiliation*, (2) *hawkish foreign policy orientation*, and (3) *personal animosity toward Saddam Hussein*. The identification of these categories clarifies useful alternatives to the event, such as the election of a president who is a member of the categories *Democratic, dovish*, and/or *not personally hostile to Hussein*. The exercise underscores that appropriate alternatives would be to substitute another individual who is elected president, as opposed to scenarios in which Bush is still in power but a member of the set *not-elected* (e.g., in which Bush comes to power via a military coup). Thus, the relevant counterfactuals are instances of *the election of not-Bush*, as opposed to all instantiations of *not–the election of Bush* (see Garfinkel 1981 on "contrast spaces").

To examine the necessity effects of *the election of Bush*, the analyst considers counterfactuals that have the following form: if event X had not occurred, then outcome Y would not have occurred. Figure 10.1 illustrates this counterfactual

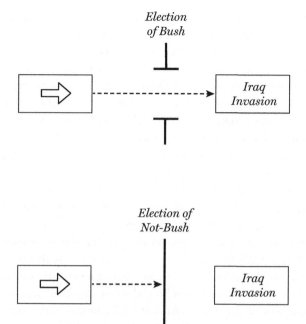

FIGURE 10.1. Illustration of Necessity Effects

logic for the Bush–Iraq invasion example. The figure is a force dynamic diagram that calls attention to the generic structure of necessity effects. It illustrates how *the election of Bush* creates an opening (or removes a blockage) for the occurrence of *the Iraq invasion*. The diagram assumes that a productive force (represented by the arrow) already exists to generate the invasion. The effect of *the election of Bush* is to allow this force to carry out its productive work. Bush's election may have permitted the invasion by, for instance, providing a context in which actors and organizations that sought intervention could operate as productive forces. The Bush administration dismissed the findings of United Nations inspectors, tacitly encouraged the U.S. public to believe that Hussein was linked to the 9/11 attacks, and elevated proponents of a military solution over those who favored diplomacy. These actions may have created an opening for pro-invasion forces to initiate the invasion.

To determine the extent to which *the election of Bush* was necessary for *the Iraq invasion*, the analyst investigates whether *the election of not-Bush* would have blocked the invasion. This investigation is carried out through the construction of a *cause-varying counterfactual* (see chapter 5) in which another individual is elected president. The analyst might begin by considering *the election of Al Gore in 2000*, which is the most plausible and obvious instantiation of *the election of not-Bush*. Other possible cases exist: John McCain could have won the Republican primary, been elected president in 2000, and invaded Iraq. However, the Gore counterfactual is by far the most plausible alternative. If one wants to show that *the election of Bush* was necessary for *the Iraq invasion*, the following counterfactual should be true: If Al Gore had been elected president in 2000, the United States would not have invaded Iraq. Interestingly, Harvey (2012) argues, with persuasive evidence, that this counterfactual is probably not correct: a Gore administration probably *would* have invaded Iraq. If so, *the election of Bush* had, at best, only modest necessity effects.

For analysis of the sufficiency effects, by contrast, the analyst identifies the causal chain that leads from *the election of Bush* to *the Iraq invasion*. A simple version of this chain might include the following steps: *the election of Bush* → *the administration's early obsession with and tacit support for an invasion* → *Bush's encouragement of dubious arguments for intervention* → *Bush's attempt to build domestic and international coalitions for an invasion* → *Iraq invasion*. The relevant counterfactuals for the analysis of sufficiency effects do not involve changing *the election of Bush*. Rather, the analyst formulates *context-varying counterfactuals* (see chapter 5) that keep the first step intact and instead alter specific aspects of circumstance and context. These counterfactual cases help the investigator learn whether X can produce Y in different contexts. If the cause is fully sufficient for the outcome, it should always be followed by the outcome despite theoretically relevant changes to context.

Figure 10.2 illustrates the generic structure of sufficiency effects using a force dynamic model with two scenarios. In the first (top) scenario, *the election of Bush* produces a sequence that leads to and makes contact with *the Iraq invasion*. The sequence includes two events that act as intervening mechanisms: event M_1 (*Bush encourages dubious arguments in favor of an invasion*) and event M_2 (*Bush wins domestic and international support for an invasion*). These events are proposed links in the causal chain that connects *the election of Bush* to *the Iraq invasion*. This scenario also includes a permissive context (context C) that enables *the Iraq invasion* by allowing M_1 to connect with M_2. For example, context C might refer to the setting that followed from Saddam Hussein's decision to not fully cooperate with weapons inspectors in Iraq, a strategic blunder that led U.S. allies to suspect that Iraq probably possessed weapons of mass destruction.

The scenario in the lower half of the figure is a context-varying counterfactual that does not follow the full sequence starting with *the election of Bush* and ending with *the Iraq invasion*. Here, the counterfactual change is introduced to the permissive context that allowed M_1 to generate M_2; the new context (i.e., not–context C) acts as an obstacle and prevents event M_1 from producing event M_2. In this counterfactual scenario, event M_2 never occurs, which in turn prevents the occurrence of *the Iraq invasion*, even though *the election of Bush* is still in place. The scenario shows how *the election of Bush* is not sufficient to produce *the Iraq invasion* in a possible world in which Hussein behaves more rationally.

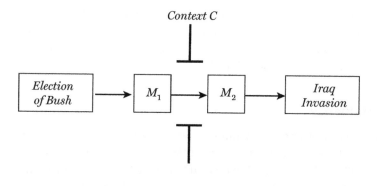

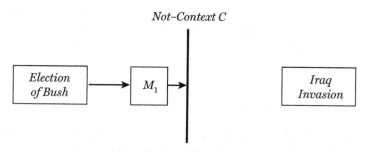

FIGURE 10.2. Illustration of Sufficiency Effects. M_1 = *Bush encourages dubious arguments in favor of an invasion*; M_2 = *Bush wins domestic and international support for an invasion.*

The extent of sufficiency effects of *the election of Bush* is assessed by asking whether unusual circumstances or an atypical context were needed to sustain the chain of events leading to *the Iraq invasion.* The analyst explores what would have happened without contingent or unusual features being in place. For instance, faulty intelligence reports regarding the presence of weapons of mass destruction in Iraq are an important part of the context of the causal chain. The analyst can ask whether this faulty intelligence was a contingent oddity. If so, the analyst may conclude that *the election of Bush* would not have led to *the Iraq invasion* if not for accidentally inaccurate intelligence reports. Yet if one concludes that the faulty intelligence reports were not a contingent or accidental occurrence, but rather an expected outcome of Bush's election, then one must leave them in place when assessing the sufficiency effects of *the election of Bush.*

Critical events, then, cause outcomes through their necessity effects and sufficiency effects. When formulating and evaluating propositions about the necessity effects of an event, the challenge is to identify how the event shapes aspects of context and circumstance to allow productive forces to operate. Here the focus is on cause-varying counterfactuals, in which non-actual alternatives to the causal event are put into place while holding context constant. By contrast, when formulating and evaluating propositions about the sufficiency effects of an event, the analyst constructs a causal chain that links the event to the outcome. Here the focus is on context-varying counterfactuals, in which specific contingent aspects of context are altered but the main causal event is held constant, as in the actual world.

Contingency

The literature on critical junctures sometimes defines these junctures as characterized by contingency (Bernhard 2015; Capoccia 2015; Capoccia and Keleman 2007; Mahoney 2001; Roberts 2014; Soifer 2012). Likewise, the literature on path dependence often identifies the event that launches a self-reinforcing sequence as unpredictable or contingent (see chapter 11). This section offers a definition of contingency intended to accommodate the different ways in which scholars use this term. It discusses why critical events must be contingent events when the goal of analysis is the explanation of puzzling outcomes in particular cases.

DEFINING CONTINGENCY

Social scientists lack a uniform vocabulary for discussing contingency. In the economic history literature, economists use the expression "small events" to refer to the occurrences that trigger path dependence (e.g., Arthur 1994; David 1985; North 1990). Small events are characterized by "chance" and "randomness"; the ideal-typical small event is randomly generated and of low probability. A contingent event is an occurrence that would not occur on many or most historical reruns that begin with the same initial conditions. In the literature on critical junctures, scholars emphasize agency, subjective discretion, and deliberate choice when discussing contingency (Capoccia 2015; Mahoney 2001). A contingent event is unpredictable in light of macroscopic causal variables; it falls outside the scope of the theories that are used to explain self-reinforcing sequences. Social scientists who work on unsettled times and moments of transition stress the ways in which the weakening of structural constraints allows micro events and individual and group decisions to carry unusual weight in shaping outcomes (Katznelson 2003; Linz 1978; O'Donnell and Schmitter 1986; Swidler 1986). Relatedly, social scientists associate contingency with "exogenous shocks" that emanate from outside of a system and suddenly and unpredictably reshuffle its elements, with long-lasting consequences (Berman 1998; Gourevitch 1986).

Despite their differences, these formulations have in common the following idea: *an event is contingent when it is not expected to occur but does occur.* The source of the expectations may vary, ranging from the predictions of theoretical traditions to the values of known causal factors to preexisting likelihood functions to commonsense intuitions. In each case, nevertheless, the contingent event is not well anticipated by the relevant model, theory, function, or belief system. In this sense, events are contingent vis-à-vis our expectations; our expectations help *make* events contingent. If a given scholar adopts a new set of expectations, the status of a given event can move from contingent to not contingent (or vice versa). The argument that scholarly beliefs help construct the contingency of events is consistent with the overall approach of this book; by contrast, the argument fits uncomfortably within an essentialist approach.

Different kinds of contingency can be delineated on the basis of the nature and source of one's expectations. Some scholars might insist that only events that are unexpected vis-à-vis *all* approximately valid theories of reality should count as contingent. They might be convinced that one should treat contingency as an objective fact about the world in much the same way that some quantum physicists assume randomness is inherent to reality. At the other extreme, many scholars find it useful to treat an event as contingent if it is unexpected vis-à-vis one particular theory that is designed to explain the outcome of interest. Economists treat events as contingent if they are not well predicted by neoclassical theory (Arthur 1994). Intermediate approaches between these two extremes are also possible. One might treat an event as contingent if it is not expected by social science theories in general, even though it might be anticipated by natural science theories. Critical event analysis does not mandate any particular approach regarding how broadly one should cast the net when formulating expectations. However, critical event analysis does require that analysts be clear and consistent about the nature of their expectations.

MEASURING CONTINGENCY

For measurement purposes, it is useful to differentiate two ways in which expectations can help generate contingent events. One mode involves the occurrence of an event that is *not probable* given expectations derived from knowledge of causal factors associated with relevant theories. At the extreme, a contingent event directly contradicts the predictions of relevant theories. For instance, the actual world may be a member of event X even though conditions that are usually sufficient for membership in $\sim X$ are present; or the actual world may be a member of event X even though conditions that are usually necessary for membership in X are absent. A less extreme version of this kind of contingency is when membership in an outcome category appears unlikely given our expectations. Scholars may regard outcomes that could just as easily have not occurred (in light of relevant theories) as contingent events. For instance, one might regard the outcome of a specific coin flip (heads or tails) as a contingent event.

A set-theoretic approach to measuring this type of contingency examines the distribution of possible worlds across the event and its logical complement. For an event X, contingency is measured as follows:

$$\text{Contingency of event } X = \% \text{ of possible worlds in } \sim X. \qquad (10.1)$$

With this measure, one might say that a contingent event occurs when the actual world is located in set X but many or most possible worlds are located in set $\sim X$. Possible worlds are located in $\sim X$ to the degree that our theoretically informed expectations predict membership in $\sim X$ at the time of the occurrence of X. To estimate the distribution of possible worlds across X and $\sim X$, the analyst may use the counterfactual tools discussed in chapter 5.

A second way in which expectations help generate contingency is when an event of interest falls outside of the scope of relevant theories and thus is not anticipated. Systematic causal factors neither predict nor fail to predict the event; they simply do not consider or anticipate its possibility, leaving the event as a random occurrence. An example is an *exogenous shock*: an event that suddenly and unexpectedly disrupts or overturns a normal context or system, perhaps creating an atypical and rare set of circumstances. Examples of such shocks in small-N research include wars, natural disasters, and interventions that shift a broad range of contextual features within the case. By definition, an exogenous shock is an unexpected occurrence from the perspective of endogenous causal factors. The shock need not be truly random; it need only be random vis-à-vis the orientation that defines systematic causes in a given study. The nature of these systematic causes varies across disciplines and theoretical frameworks. For instance, a social scientist might reasonably regard the earthquake of 1972 near Managua as an exogenous shock that was an important cause of the Nicaraguan Revolution in 1979. While this earthquake was not a truly random occurrence, it is appropriately constructed as a random event from the standpoint of social science theories of revolution.

This kind of *out-of-scope contingency* also encompasses small-scale and idiosyncratic events that escape the discerning power of theories. These events may be specific happenings—such as the death of a particular individual or the outcome of a specific battle—that are too microscopic or too idiosyncratic to a case to fall within the scope of relevant theoretical frameworks. For instance, analysts seem to generally agree about specific historical factors that caused the initial adoption of the QWERTY keyboard (i.e., type-bar jamming in early typewriters), but these factors are contingent because they are too historically specific to be accommodated within neoclassical economics or other general theories (for a dissenting view, see Liebowitz and Margolis 1990).

The measure in equation (10.1) also applies to out-of-scope contingency. However, the problem is that with out-of-scope contingency, the researcher does not have a theoretically informed basis for situating possible cases. If the researcher is truly ignorant about the distribution, a standard solution is to evenly distribute possible cases across X and $\sim X$. Hence, in a situation of complete uncertainty, the occurrence of X and $\sim X$ are equally likely. Equation (10.1) is still appropriate in this situation, though it is more useful if one has some basis to formulate expectations about the occurrence of event X.

THE RULE OF CAUSAL CONTINGENCY

For a contingent outcome Y, any *individually important* causal event X will also be contingent. One can think about the relationship in the following way: in order to explain membership in the sparsely occupied category Y, any factor X cannot be causally important if it is a heavily occupied category, because it will have weak coverage vis-à-vis Y. If event X plays a major causal role for contingent outcome Y, the occurrence of X must also be contingent.

If we generalize this idea, we arrive at the following rule.

Rule of Causal Contingency: The level of contingency of an individually important cause always approximates the level of contingency of the outcome it explains.

Contingency is built into critical event analysis insofar as this mode of analysis seeks to explain outcomes that were not expected to occur. However, for an outcome that *was* expected to occur, an individually important causal factor will not be contingent. Contingent events are, at best, minor causes of non-contingent outcomes.

Another way to think about this rule is by considering individually sufficient and individually necessary causes (see figure 10.3). A sufficient cause of Y must always be more contingent than Y itself, because a sufficient cause (represented by X_3 in the figure) is a subset of its outcome. A critical event cannot be sufficient for an outcome unless the proportion of cases in the negation set for the critical event is higher than the proportion of cases in the negation set for the outcome. With a necessary cause, by contrast, the causal factor (X_2 in the figure) will always be less contingent than the outcome. If the outcome is only borderline contingent, a necessary cause of that outcome may not be contingent. However, if the outcome is clearly contingent, any *important* necessary cause will also be contingent, albeit slightly less contingent than the outcome for which it is necessary.

The Rule of Causal Contingency allows one to use knowledge of the contingency of an outcome to determine whether a critical event must also be contingent. For instance, consider the ten examples of causally important events in table 10.1. Insofar as the outcomes under analysis in these studies are contingent events, then the proposed causal events *must* also be contingent if they are in fact individually important causes. Alternatively, if the outcomes

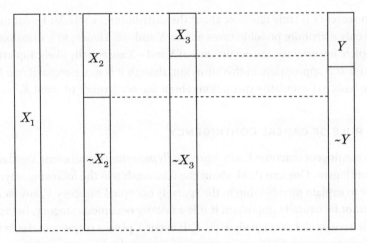

FIGURE 10.3. Illustration of the Rule of Causal Contingency. X_1 is necessary but neither important nor contingent; X_2 is necessary, contingent, and important; X_3 is sufficient, contingent, and important.

under analysis are well explained by relevant theories, then the proposed causal events *cannot* be contingent if they are important causes. We classify the causal events in these studies as contingent because the authors are explaining outcomes that are puzzling.

Causal Importance

With a regularity model of causation, a maximally important cause is an event that is both necessary and sufficient for an outcome. An event that is causally important—though not a maximally important cause—must approach this gold standard. This section develops tools for analysts to use in estimating the degree to which an event approximates the gold standard of causality. These tools employ separate kinds of counterfactual analysis for estimating necessity effects and sufficiency effects. The section sets benchmarks for an event to qualify as causally important. Specifically, an event must have (1) a high degree of either necessity or sufficiency, and (2) at least a moderate degree of both necessity and sufficiency.

ESTIMATING NECESSITY AND SUFFICIENCY WITH POSSIBLE CASES

Set-theoretic methodologists have developed formulas for calculating the extent to which a condition is consistent with necessity and with sufficiency (e.g., Ragin 2008: chap. 3; Schneider and Wagemann 2012: chap. 5). With dichotomous sets, cases are coded 1 for membership and 0 for nonmembership. The formulas for necessity and sufficiency are then as follows:

% Necessary $(X \rightarrow Y) =$ Number of cases where $X=1$ and
$$Y=1 \text{ / Number of cases where } Y=1; \qquad (10.2)$$

% Sufficient $(X \rightarrow Y) =$ Number of cases where $X=1$ and
$$Y=1 \text{ / Number of cases where } X=1. \qquad (10.3)$$

With continuous sets, simple modifications are needed to accommodate partial set membership (Zadeh 1965; Ragin 2008: 52–53). But the underlying rule remains the same: one calculates the percentage of cases consistent with necessity and the percentage consistent with sufficiency. For both dichotomous sets and continuous sets, this measure is called *consistency* in the set-theoretic literature (Ragin 2000, 2008; Rihoux and Ragin 2009; Schneider and Wagemann 2012).

Equations (10.2) and (10.3) are easy to use if one knows the membership values of all cases for X and Y in a well-defined population. With small-N research, however, determining these values is a difficult conceptual exercise, because one is dealing almost entirely with non-actual cases. The scores for the one actual case normally are consistent with both necessity and sufficiency (i.e., $X=1$ and $Y=1$). To use the equations, therefore, the analyst must estimate the distribution of the larger population of possible cases.

To estimate this distribution, the analyst considers only those possible cases that are analytically relevant *and* that carry at least moderate weight. *Analytically relevant possible cases* introduce changes either to the main event X under study (i.e., particular instantiations of $\sim X$) or to individually contingent aspects of the context in which X operates. Analysts construct these types of possible cases with theoretical considerations in mind and with the goal of maximizing leverage for understanding the causal effects of X. Possible cases that vary event X introduce specific alternatives to X in order to spotlight the potential necessity effects of X. These counterfactual cases fall within the appropriate contrast space of event X (Garfinkel 1981), allowing the analyst to sharpen the focus on the ways in which X produces contextual conditions that make the outcome possible. Possible cases that vary a contingent aspect of context (while holding X constant) target the sufficiency effects of event X. To identify which specific aspects of context to change, the analyst uses relevant theories that suggest the importance of specific background conditions in allowing the outcome. The analyst then constructs cases in which changes are introduced to contingent aspects of context that are normally treated as background events and processes, in order to explore whether event X is still sufficient for the outcome.

At least moderately weighted cases are possible cases that are relatively proximate to the actual world; the weight assigned to a given case corresponds to its proximity to the actual world. The idea of weighting an individual case makes sense because any particular possible case is really a *group* of possible cases that are identical in theoretically relevant characteristics but that differ from one another in trivial respects. For example, the possible case *Al Gore is elected president* includes one version in which the weather is sunny during his first press conference and another version in which it is not. If a particular case is proximate to the actual world, as with the Al Gore example, it represents a large group of cases with trivial differences that add up to a high proportion of all possible cases. The size of this overall group corresponds to the proximity of the particular case to the actual world.

Because the possible cases used in the analysis of necessity effects and sufficiency effects differ fundamentally, the investigator examines separately these two sets of relevant and at least moderately weighted possible cases. For each set, the analyst identifies and distinguishes consistent cases and inconsistent cases. *Consistent cases* are those in which $X = 0$ and $Y = 0$ for the evaluation of necessity, and $X = 1$ and $Y = 1$ for the evaluation of sufficiency. *Inconsistent cases* are those in which $X = 0$ and $Y = 1$ for the evaluation of necessity, and $X = 1$ and $Y = 0$ for the evaluation of sufficiency. In practice, analysts must estimate whether a given case is *more likely* consistent or *more likely* inconsistent.[3] The degree to which X is necessary or is sufficient for Y depends on the total weight of the consistent cases relative to the total weight of the inconsistent cases. Not uncommonly, a single heavily weighted case drives the overall balance of consistent versus inconsistent cases.

As a more concrete illustration, consider again the proposition that membership in *the election of Bush* was a critical event for membership in *the invasion of Iraq*. To estimate the necessity effect of this event, the analyst creates cases with different versions of ~X, that is, different cases of *the election of not-Bush*. All of these cases must be at least moderately weighted. The analyst might ask whether, among this group, any case exists that is likely consistent with the counterfactual. One might argue that it seems plausible, and even quite likely, that if Bill Bradley (a dovish Democrat with no special animosity toward Saddam Hussein) had won the primary and the general election, the United States would not have invaded Iraq. This case lends support to the proposition that Bush's election was necessary for the invasion. But other, more heavily weighted cases are not consistent with this hypothesis. For example, it seems plausible to believe that if John McCain (a hawkish Republican) had won the Republican primary and the general election, the United States still would have invaded Iraq. Most importantly, Harvey's (2012) analysis finds that the Iraq invasion is more plausible than not in a world in which Al Gore is elected president instead of Bush. The potential inconsistency of this plausible and proximate case is quite damaging for the proposition that membership in *the election of Bush* was necessary for membership in *the invasion of Iraq*.

For the evaluation of sufficiency effects, the analyst constructs possible cases in which X remains the same as in the actual world but in which changes are introduced to events or processes that are part of the background context.

Not all aspects of context need be considered for change. Rather, the analyst alters only individual events or processes that are (1) contingent, (2) potential difference-makers, and (3) theoretically relevant. The requirement of contingency overlaps with the requirement that all counterfactual cases carry at least moderate weight, which ensures that only changes to context that are proximate to the actual world are considered. Conditions that are not contingent, such as (in the Iraq invasion example) the United States' having an electoral democracy and presidential system, are left in place. The second requirement—that the event be a potential difference-maker—focuses the counterfactual analysis around conditions whose absence or negation could have changed or negated the outcome. These counterfactual changes allow the analyst to explore whether event X was sufficient for outcome Y even in a world in which a potential necessary condition for the outcome was absent.

The third requirement stipulates that the analyst allow theory to guide decisions about which specific contextual conditions to change when estimating sufficiency effects. For example, structural realist theories emphasize the importance of military capabilities in explaining wars (Waltz 1979; Levy and Thompson 2010). These theories might lead the analyst to consider background events related to the military power of Iraq. One such condition that may have been essential for the outcome of war is the inaccurate assessment by the U.S. Department of Defense concerning the probability that Iraq possessed weapons of mass destruction. Would the United States have invaded if it had had better intelligence on this question? Another potential difference-maker suggested by structural realism is Saddam Hussein's strategy of allowing the international community to believe that Iraq possessed weapons of mass destruction. Would the United States have invaded if Hussein had more accurately represented Iraq's military capabilities? A third background event that may have been essential is Secretary of State Colin Powell's 2003 presentation to the United Nations Security Council suggesting that the Iraqi government had operational links to terrorist organizations, including Al-Qaeda. Would the United States have invaded without Powell's presentation to the UN?

Of these three counterfactuals, one might argue that the first scenario requires a large historical revision and thus must be excluded from consideration (or only lightly weighted). The argument is that the intelligence failure was not accidental or contingent, but rather an expected outcome of Bush's election (e.g., the administration actively caused this intelligence failure). The other two counterfactual scenarios are more easily viewed as contingent from the perspective of structural realist theories of war. The second one, concerning Hussein's strategic blunder, carries substantial weight, because individual actors do not normally misrepresent their capabilities in ways that are detrimental to their survival. The third counterfactual also carries substantial weight, given that so many experts were surprised that Powell went along with the administration's assertion that Hussein was linked to terrorists and was an imminent national security threat. Here is not the place to substantively assess these two counterfactuals. However, insofar as one can present evidence showing that the Bush administration would have invaded under either counterfactual situation, one can conclude that *the election of Bush* exerts at least moderate sufficiency effects for *the invasion of Iraq*.

SUBSTANTIVE IMPORTANCE AND SUBSTANTIVE RELEVANCE

The relative importance of any cause is a function of its necessity effects and its sufficiency effects. A cause becomes more important as it comes closer to being both necessary and sufficient for the outcome of interest. A necessary and sufficient cause is the exclusive enabler and producer of the outcome across all analytically relevant cases. With such a cause, the minimal and complete Boolean solution set is $Y = X$.

A core issue for critical event analysis concerns the exact thresholds of necessity and sufficiency required for an event to have causal importance and thus be considered a critical event. How necessary and how sufficient must a cause be to achieve causal importance? To address this issue, we distinguish between two aspects of a causal relationship: substantive importance and substantive relevance. To qualify as a critical event, an event must meet specified thresholds on each of these dimensions.[4]

A relationship is characterized by *substantive importance* to the extent that membership in a category fully enables and/or fully produces membership in a different category. Accordingly, to estimate substantive importance, the analyst considers the extent to which a condition is necessary *or* sufficient for an outcome. We propose that to qualify as a causally important event, a condition must come reasonably close to 100% (e.g., 90%) on *either* the necessity dimension *or* the sufficiency dimension. Thus, all critical events are either approximately necessary or approximately sufficient (or both) for the outcome under study.

Substantive relevance concerns the extent to which membership in a category is relevant, as opposed to trivial, for membership in another category. A causal factor is relevant for an outcome to the extent that membership in a category has at least some role in both enabling and producing membership in another category. The criterion of relevance excludes from causal importance all trivial necessary conditions, which are necessary conditions that are nearly always present across all possible cases; and it excludes all trivial sufficient conditions, which are sufficient conditions that are virtually never present across all possible cases. To measure substantive relevance, one determines the extent to which a condition is necessary *and* sufficient for an outcome. We propose that to qualify as a causally important event, a condition must have at least an intermediate value (e.g., at least 50%) for *both* the necessity *and* the sufficiency dimensions. This threshold has the effect of ensuring that no trivial conditions are included as causally important events.

After estimating the necessity and sufficiency effects of a condition, the analyst uses Boolean rules to measure the condition's substantive importance and substantive relevance. Measuring substantive importance requires using the logical OR to determine the extent to which a condition is necessary *or* sufficient for an outcome. With the logical OR, the analyst takes the *higher value* between the condition's necessity and sufficiency effects as its value for substantive importance. The equation is simply

$$\text{Substantive Importance } (X \rightarrow Y) = \max([\% \text{ Necessary } (X \rightarrow Y)], [\% \text{ Sufficient } (X \rightarrow Y)]). \tag{10.4}$$

We propose that all causally important events must have a high value on substantive importance, such as 90% or higher. This rule ensures that a critical event either enables an outcome to the point that counterfactual dependence nearly applies, *or* produces an outcome to the point that the event is followed by the outcome across most reasonable contexts.

Substantive relevance is considered in order to ensure that no trivial condition is classified as a causally important event. With substantive relevance, the analyst uses the logical AND in measuring the extent to which a condition is necessary *and* sufficient for the outcome. With the logical AND, the analyst takes the *lower value* between the condition's necessity and sufficiency effects as its value for substantive relevance. The equation is simply

$$\text{Substantive Relevance } (X \rightarrow Y) = \min([\% \text{ Necessary } (X \rightarrow Y)], [\% \text{ Sufficient } (X \rightarrow Y)]). \tag{10.5}$$

Imposing a threshold of at least 50% for substantive relevance serves to weed out trivial conditions. With this threshold, an individual factor cannot be a critical event if the outcome is overdetermined or if the event is part of a standard context or typical set of circumstances that are normally present.

In large-N research, the analyst may be able to make a precise numerical estimate of the extent to which event X is necessary and is sufficient for outcome Y. In case-study and small-N research, by contrast, such precise numerical estimates are rarely, if ever, possible. Case-study and small-N researchers must make general estimates about the extent to which event X is necessary and is sufficient for outcome Y. These estimates must make sense given the evidence and the belief systems shared by the researcher and the audience. The analyst uses theory and evidence in the effort to arrive at conclusions that are epistemologically valid within a given semantic context.

Case-study and small-N researchers can use evidence and theory to score events on an ordinal scale—such as high, moderate, and low—for their necessity and sufficiency effects. When an ordinal scale is used, the number of gradations may have to be quite small, perhaps three or four categories. Beyond this range, scholars may lack the discriminating power to make estimates that are meaningful to them and their audiences. With an ordinal scale, the threshold for a critical event can be set such that an event (1) must have the highest level for either necessity or sufficiency (or both), and (2) cannot have the lowest level for either necessity or sufficiency. For instance, the coding of events in table 10.1 (at the beginning of this chapter) uses a three-point scale in which an event is scored as high, moderate, or low for the dimensions of necessity and sufficiency. These are critical events because the authors present evidence that, we believe, suggests the events exert either high necessity *or* high sufficiency effects (or both), and because the evidence shows that the events exert at least moderate necessity *and* moderate sufficiency effects.

TYPES OF IMPORTANT INUS CAUSES

The definition of causal importance presented above allows for critical events that are neither fully necessary nor fully sufficient for the outcome of interest; critical events are, instead, important INUS causes for the outcome. Here we consider the three main kinds of INUS causes that meet the standard of causal importance required for critical events.

The first type is an INUS cause that is almost necessary (e.g., 95%) but only moderately sufficient (e.g., 55%) for an outcome. Let us call this kind of INUS cause an *approximately necessary cause*. Like a necessary cause, an approximately necessary cause permits a counterfactual statement, though not a deterministic one. If X is an approximately necessary cause of Y, and if X had not occurred (or had occurred differently), then Y *probably* would not have occurred (or would have occurred differently). Although an approximately necessary cause permits a probabilistic counterfactual statement, the cause does not offer a nearly complete explanation of Y. By definition, this kind of cause is only moderately sufficient for Y. Additional causal factors are needed to explain the production of the outcome of interest.

Second, let us call an important INUS cause that is almost sufficient (e.g., 95%) but only moderately necessary (e.g., 55%) for an outcome an *approximately sufficient cause*. Like a sufficient cause, an approximately sufficient cause does not require the identification of other important causal factors to provide a satisfactory explanation of the outcome. In identifying an approximately sufficient cause, the analyst has formulated an explanation that offers a nearly complete account of one of the ways in which the outcome is produced across all possible cases. However, an approximately sufficient cause does not lend itself to a strong counterfactual statement. One cannot say that in the absence of a particular approximately sufficient cause, a particular outcome probably would have been absent. Instead, with an approximately sufficient cause, the outcome may well be overdetermined, such that it may have occurred even without the approximately sufficient cause. In some but not all possible cases, the outcome occurs in the absence of the approximately sufficient cause.

Finally, let us call an important INUS condition that is almost necessary and almost sufficient for an outcome an *approximately necessary and sufficient cause*. This kind of cause has the virtues of both approximately necessary and approximately sufficient causes. Thus, like an approximately necessary cause, it allows for a probabilistic counterfactual statement: if X had not occurred, then Y probably would not have occurred. Likewise, it is similar to an approximately sufficient cause in that it allows for a probabilistic regularity statement: once X occurred, Y was very likely to occur. An approximately necessary and sufficient cause comes close to the gold standard of set-theoretic causality.

Illustrations of Critical Events

Table 10.1 lists ten studies that identify and examine critical events for substantively important token outcomes. For each study, the table summarizes why the event meets the criteria of a critical event. A three-point ordinal scale (high, moderate, low) is used to characterize the degree of necessity and sufficiency for each event. The following discussion focuses on two of the ten studies.

Let us first consider the case of Ghana in Rachel Riedl's book *Authoritarian Origins of Democratic Party Systems in Africa* (2014). Riedl seeks to explain Ghana's trajectory of political change in the democratic era, starting with the founding democratic election of the incumbent military leader, J. J. Rawlings, in 1992 and culminating with high party system institutionalization. The causal logic of this sequence is of interest in itself, but the concern here is with the historical causes of the sequence. Why did Ghana experience a controlled democratic transition in which a coherent and genuinely competitive party system emerged?

In answering this question, Riedl highlights a critical event: the choice by Ghanaian leaders under the previous authoritarian regime (1981–85) to adopt what Riedl calls a *strategy of incorporation*. She argues that postcolonial leaders in Ghana faced a choice concerning how to establish a political order: with a strategy of incorporation, a strategy of state substitution, or a revolutionary strategy. Riedl argues that the choice of a specific option "could not have been predicted ex ante" (p. 10). She finds that the decision turned on the agency of Rawlings, who sought to use his political organization to unify the country through grassroots mobilization and citizen participation. Riedl (p. 109) is explicit that this choice was "contingent" in part because it involved the beliefs and agency of a particular leader and in part because it was driven by situationally specific factors in Ghana. She makes it clear that structural conditions and other general causal factors left the critical choice underdetermined.

Although Riedl does not discuss necessary and sufficient conditions, the application of the critical event framework suggests that this event was highly sufficient and moderately necessary for the controlled democratic transition. On the sufficiency side, Riedl traces the process through which a strategy of incorporation generated local elite support, which was self-reinforcing over the medium to long run. In turn, local elite support, regardless of contextual contingencies, ensured that the democratic transition would unfold in a political environment in which the authoritarian government enjoyed substantial support and the opposition was weak and divided. Riedl shows that a strategy of incorporation produced a similar sequence and outcome in Senegal, an otherwise different case. Hence, once Rawlings began pursuing the strategy of incorporation in the early 1980s, Ghana was on a pathway very likely to end with a controlled democratic transition, short of major changes to non-contingent aspects of context.

On the necessity side, the logic of Riedl's argument suggests that if Rawlings or other leaders had pursued a strategy of state substitution, Ghana would not have had its controlled transition. However, if Ghana had followed a path of revolution, the country probably would have still experienced a controlled transition. The text does not discuss which of these two counterfactual alternatives—a state substitution strategy or a revolutionary strategy—requires a more radical rewrite of Ghana's actual history. But either counterfactual scenario was possible, and the key point is that Ghana could have experienced the same outcome of a controlled democratic transition if the country had followed a revolutionary strategy as its path to postcolonial stability.

In sum, the selection of a strategy of incorporation more or less ensured a controlled democratic transition in Ghana, given the non-contingent circumstances in place (high sufficiency). However, Ghana may have still arrived at this outcome even without the selection of this strategy (moderate necessity).

A quite different example is Richard Ned Lebow's (2010) argument that the assassination of Archduke Franz Ferdinand of Austria (and his wife, Sophie) was an important cause of the continental war in the summer of 1914, which in turn was an important cause of World War I and many other major outcomes in world history. Lebow is explicit that the assassination was both contingent and necessary for the continental war. With respect to contingency, he emphasizes "how easy it would have been to avert Franz Ferdinand's assassination" with only slight and plausible changes to history (p. 60). For example, if Ferdinand's cavalcade had followed its planned route, the assassination probably would not have occurred. With respect to necessity, Lebow explicitly analyzes possible cases in which the assassination does not occur. He concludes that without the assassination, "there would have been no war in the summer of 1914" (p. 87).

With respect to sufficiency, Lebow argues that the assassination played an important and independent causal role for the continental war. Specifically, the event exerted sufficiency effects by changing the way in which leaders viewed ongoing events, causing them to be more risk-taking in their behavior (p. 96). Estimating the full extent of the assassination's sufficiency effects requires the examination of analytically relevant non-actual cases in which the assassination occurs but contingent aspects of context are changed. Lebow indirectly explores these possible cases by considering counterfactual cases in which the assassination occurs but earlier contingent events do not take place. This approach allows him to ask whether the assassination would have led to the war if Russia had not been so threatened or if Austro-Serb hostility had not been at maximum intensity. Lebow finds that, for the war to occur, many contingent aspects of background context had to be in place; relatively proximate cases exist in which the assassination occurs but is not followed by the continental war. Thus, while the assassination exerted non-trivial productive effects for the war, it did not come close to making the war inevitable.

In sum, the assassination of Franz Ferdinand was, according to Lebow, essential for the war in the summer of 1914 (high necessity). However, the occurrence of the assassination did not ensure that this war would take place (moderate sufficiency).

The studies by Riedl and Lebow identify critical events with different causal effects. Both events are contingent and causally important, but the nature of their causal importance is different. In Riedl's argument, the early pursuit of stabilization via incorporation in Ghana had productive and generative properties that nearly ensured a particular path of political development. By contrast, in Lebow's argument, the assassination had primarily enabling and permissive properties, allowing other causes to do their productive work.

Critical events that are marked by high sufficiency and moderate necessity are often linked to self-reinforcing path dependence (see chapter 11 on kinds of sequences in path dependence). Here, a critical event yields an initial outcome that is amplified and perhaps stabilized over time, via an increasing-returns process. Once the sequence is launched, the initial outcome is reinforced even in the absence of the critical event that generated it (Stinchcombe 1968). The productive properties of high-sufficiency critical events can generate histori-cal lock-in: an initial event triggers a self-perpetuating outcome from which escape is difficult.

By contrast, critical events that have high necessity and moderate suffi-ciency are linked to reactive path dependence. Here, a critical event launches a chain of disparate events, each one being a reaction to the previous event and causally important for the next one. The sequence concludes with the main outcome of interest. Reactive path dependence is featured in studies that show how an initial small or unpredictable event (e.g., an assassination or a specific choice) is essential for an important outcome down the line that seems unrelated to the initial event. These arguments invite counterfactual considerations of how history could have turned out differently with a small change at the beginning of the sequence.

To date, scholars have not distinguished critical events that produce self-reinforcing sequences through their sufficiency effects from critical events that set into motion reactive sequences through their necessity effects. Nor have they explored critical event analyses that combine these two modes of explanation. One reason for these omissions is that scholars have not explicitly discussed issues of necessity and sufficiency in their work on critical events. An important payoff of employing the set-theoretic approach is that it requires authors to be specific about the hypothesized necessity and sufficiency effects of their critical events, steering the analysis toward clearer, more precise, and more interesting propositions and findings.

––––––

Defined by both causal importance and contingency, critical events are break-points in the history of a case that direct the case toward an outcome of interest. This outcome may be the start of a process with its own self-contained reproductive logic; alternatively, the outcome may be a discrete event that is connected to the critical event via an intermediary chain of events. Either way, the critical event is a historical occurrence that exerts its causal effect over time—potentially a long period of time.

An occurrence that is a critical event for a particular outcome is never 100% sufficient for that outcome; non-actual cases always exist in which the same initial occurrence takes place but the outcome of interest does not. One potential reason for the absence of the outcome of interest in these non-actual cases is a breakdown in the causal chain that connects the initial occurrence and the outcome. The non-actual cases veer off the path of the actual world at some point along the way—i.e., at some point after the initial occurrence but before the final outcome. What is a critical event in the actual world is not a critical event in these non-actual cases, because the outcome of interest does not occur.

An important implication follows: events sometimes occur in the actual world that are not critical events even though they are critical events in most other possible worlds. These events exert the same effects for the outcome of interest in the actual world as in all other possible worlds (e.g., 90% sufficient and 70% necessary). However, because of a broken link in the causal chain that connects the event to the outcome of interest, the outcome does not take place in the actual world. This kind of actual world event can be called an *almost-critical* event: an event that is a critical event in most possible worlds but not in the actual world, because the outcome of interest does not take place in the actual world. An almost-critical event may go unnoticed in the annals of history; the historical record does not usually call attention to contingent events that "should have" or "normally would have" been important causes of particular outcomes of interest if not for the occurrence of atypical breakdowns in the chains leading to these outcomes. Just as roads not followed lead one to ask what might have been, almost-critical events lead one to consider what should have been.

The idea of an event that would have been a critical event but for a broken link in the typical causal chain leading to the outcome suggests that analysts must devote special attention to the intermediary events that compose this chain. When the chain itself is viewed as a process, it becomes the path on which a case travels from an initial event to an outcome of interest. The next chapter focuses on these paths.

11

Path Dependence Analysis

Path dependence as a mode of analysis is associated with one of the most basic cognitive structures that human beings use to make sense of the world: the idea of a *path*. The utility of this image schema for social science explanation can be illustrated using three set-theoretic metaphors concerning location. First, the path schema suggests the metaphor STATES ARE LOCATIONS, in the sense that a state of affairs is a bounded location in space—i.e., states of affairs are sets. Second, the path schema suggests the metaphor CHANGES ARE MOVEMENTS, in the sense that entities move into and out of these bounded locations in space—i.e., changes are movements into and out of sets. Third, the path schema suggests the metaphor CAUSATION IS FORCED MOVEMENT, in the sense that an entity is forced to move from one bounded location to another—i.e., causation is forced movement from one set to another set (cf. Lakoff and Johnson 1999: 178–80).

The idea of path dependence resonates with many scholars (and people in general) because it accords with our shared *source-path-goal schema*. This complex image schema incorporates the ideas of a beginning point and an end point, along with a spatial understanding of time (Lakoff and Johnson 1999: chap. 10). Saslaw (1996: 220) describes the source-path-goal schema as follows:

> The [source-path-goal] schema has a grounding in bodily experience; when we move anywhere there is a place from which we start out, a sequence of contiguous locations connecting the starting and ending points, and a direction. Thus, the structural elements of the schema include: (1) a source or starting point, (2) a destination or end point (or goal), (3) a path or sequence of contiguous locations connecting the source and

the destination, and (4) a direction toward the destination. The basic logic of the schema is that in proceeding from a source to a destination along a path, one must go through all intermediate points on the path; moreover, the further along the path you are, the more time has passed since starting.

These four structural elements correspond to essential components of path-dependent analysis in the social sciences. Work on path dependence involves the study of how and why a case follows one specific path from among a range of possibilities. The explanation of why the case starts down a particular path in the first place is crucial to the analysis. Likewise, path-dependent analysis is centrally concerned with the sequence of contiguous events that compose the path and that connect a starting point with a final outcome. The causal steps or processes that define the direction of the path and the causal logic of the sequence are of great importance in this mode of analysis.

In the social sciences, path dependence is defined by both an initial critical event *and* the ensuing process that the critical event sets into motion—including, often, a final outcome. On the front end of the sequence, the requirement that a critical event set things into motion ensures that outcomes cannot be explained adequately on the basis of conditions immediately prior to the critical event (cf. Arthur 1994: 17; Haydu 1998: 352; Goldstone 1998a: 834–35). Rather, *ex ante* conditions—often called *initial conditions* or *antecedent conditions*—do not effectively anticipate the final outcome (cf. Slater and Simmons 2010).[1] "Path dependence is a property of a system such that the outcome over a period of time is not determined by any particular set of initial conditions. Rather, a system that exhibits path dependency is one in which outcomes are related stochastically to initial conditions" (Goldstone 1998a: 834). Path-dependent sequences feature theoretically puzzling outcomes that are not well explained by the conditions that existed prior to the occurrence of the critical event that launches the sequence.

With path dependence, sequences are *highly sensitive to early events* (see Schelling 1978: 15; Gleick 1987: 8). As Paul Pierson (2004: 71) writes, "early parts of a sequence matter much more than later parts, an event that happens 'too late' may have no impact, though it might have been of great consequence if the timing had been different."[2] Whereas initial conditions do not anticipate the outcome, the critical event that starts the sequence moves a case decisively toward the outcome. The requirement that the sequence begin with a critical event differentiates path dependence from the more general idea that "the past matters," or "the future is dependent on the past." With a contingent event at the front end, unpredictability (in which outcomes cannot be foreseen *ex ante*) rapidly shifts to predictability (in which each event or episode in a sequence enables and/or produces the next event or episode). The explanatory focus is on the critical event, since it represents a shift point in expectations about the likelihood of the final outcome.

This chapter is divided into two sections that discuss the two dominant kinds of sequences analyzed in research on path dependence: self-reinforcing sequences and reactive sequences. *Self-reinforcing sequences* are characterized by the formation and long-term reproduction of a given social rule, institution, or other entity. Here, the "path" of path dependence consists of episodes in the life of the entity under analysis. Self-reinforcing sequences do not involve total stasis and stability immediately following a critical event. Rather, they are marked by *increasing-returns processes*, at least during the early phases of the sequence (cf. Helpman and Krugman 1985; Romer 1986; Arthur 1994; Pierson 2004). With increasing returns, the dominance of a particular institution (or other entity) increases relative to alternatives, such that it becomes more and more difficult for alternative options to prevail. Historical lock-in can result even when the original adoption of the institution, or other entity, contradicts the predictions of the theory frame that is used to explain the increasing-returns process.

Self-reinforcing path dependence yields outcomes that are perplexing in light of the analyst's theory frame. The economists who originally popularized the notion of path dependence worked within a rationalist theory frame and assumed that utilitarian cost-benefit analysis explains increasing-returns processes. For these scholars, path dependence is intriguing because an increasing-returns process yields an enduring institutional result that is less "efficient" than one or more alternative institutional options that were available prior to the initiating critical event. Social scientists who work within other theory frames (e.g., culturalist and structuralist frames) point to alternative, non-utilitarian logics that drive reproductive processes and generate outcomes that defy the predictions of their theory frames.

Reactive sequences are chains of temporally ordered and causally connected events (cf. Abbott 1983; Griffin 1992; Sewell 1996). These sequences are reactive in the sense that each event within the sequence is a direct reaction to a temporally prior event. With reactive sequences, the final event is the outcome under investigation, and thus the overall chain of events can be seen as a path leading to the outcome. For a reactive sequence to follow a specifically path-dependent trajectory, as opposed to representing only a sequence of causally connected events, the initial event that sets the chain into motion must be a critical event. This requirement ensures that initial conditions prior to the critical event do not anticipate the final outcome.

With a reactive sequence, the logic of the causal chain is not one of increasing returns. Rather, the path of a reactive sequence consists of a series of *discrete events* that are causally linked. These events are temporally separated and have distinct substantive content. Indeed, a reactive sequence is often marked by backlash events that reverse, rather than reinforce, a prior episode. The causal logic of a reactive sequence is such that each event is approximately neces- sary and/or approximately sufficient for the next event in the chain. Necessity bonds and/or sufficiency bonds move the sequence along over time, providing the explanation of how and why an initial event causes a final outcome that may be quite temporally and substantively removed.

Self-Reinforcing Sequences

Self-reinforcing path dependence follows Stinchcombe's (1968) mode of *his- toricist explanation* (see also Nagel 1979: 25–26). Historicist explanation identi- fies two types of causes: "The first is the particular circumstances which caused a tradition to be started. The second is the general process by which social patterns reproduce themselves" (Stinchcombe 1968: 103). With a historicist explanation, the causal factors responsible for the genesis of an institution are different from the causal factors responsible for the reproduction of the institution. Unlike periods of institutional genesis, which are contingent vis- à-vis the theory frame of interest, institutional reproduction is explained by causal factors associated with the theory frame. This dichotomy underlies what can be called *the paradox of path dependence*: institutional continuity is well explained by a theoretical framework that cannot explain the adoption of the institution in the first place.

THE LOGIC OF INSTITUTIONAL REPRODUCTION

With self-reinforcing path dependence, a critical event X causes an initial out- come Y_1, which I shall treat as the adoption of a particular institutional arrange- ment from a set of alternatives. Before the occurrence of event X, outcome Y_1 was not well anticipated by the theory frame of interest; both X and Y_1 are contingent events in light of initial conditions and the predictions of the theory frame. Outcome Y_1 is then reproduced over many episodes, yielding a stable sequence: $Y_2, Y_3, \ldots Y_n$. The reproduction of the outcome over time can be understood to mean that the core social rules characterizing the institution remain in place. The institution is marked by various other changes over time, such that Y_1 is not identical to Y_2. However, the continuity of certain key social rules allows observers to conclude that the institution persists over time.

Increasing-returns processes describe the diminishing possibility of adopt- ing alternatives that were available at the beginning of the sequence. Prior to the critical event, institutions A, B, and Y, for example, were all equal possibili- ties. However, the initial selection of institution Y gives it an advantage, and its reproduction increasingly closes the door (though perhaps always leaving it open a crack) to the possibility of choosing alternative A or B. Increasing returns at the beginning of a self-reinforcing sequence thus has the effect of locking in institution Y and locking out institutions A and B. At some point, the extent to which Y is ensured from one period to the next may reach an equilibrium. At that time, the self-reinforcement of Y occurs without increasing returns. Increasing-returns processes usually characterize the early parts of a self-reinforcing sequence, when a given outcome solidifies its position vis-à-vis the historically available alternatives.

In a self-reinforcing sequence, each episode in the reproduction of outcome Y is an important cause of the subsequent episode. Thus, Y_1 is itself an important cause—i.e., a non-trivial and approximately necessary and/or sufficient cause—of Y_2. This kind of sequence features a reproductive feedback loop running from outcome Y back onto Y. Reproductive feedback loops explain how institutions, objects, and other entities maintain their identities over time (see Deutsch and Garbacz 2018). The challenge of analysis is to identify the nature of the reproductive loop itself. What aspects of an outcome allow or force the outcome to perpetuate itself over time? As we shall see, scholars using different theory frames answer this question in different ways.

Figure 11.1 illustrates a path-dependent sequence in which *necessity bonds* (or *links*) characterize the self-reproducing logic. In this example, event X is an important necessary cause of Y_1. Both X and Y_1 are contingent events vis-à-vis initial conditions and the theory frame of interest, which can be seen in the figure by their small sizes relative to their negations (i.e., X relative to $\sim X$ and Y_1 relative to $\sim Y_1$). This self-reinforcing sequence is marked by causal links that are 100% necessary for subsequent links. Each causal link is counterfactually dependent on all prior causal links; equivalently, each prior episode of Y is essential for all subsequent episodes of Y. Without Y_1, we would not see Y_2, Y_3, and so on.

Figure 11.2 illustrates a path-dependent sequence in which *sufficiency links* characterize the self-reproducing logic. In this example, event X is an important sufficient cause of institution Y_1. The existence of the institution ensures its reproduction over time. Thus, regardless of variations in context and circumstance, the existence of Y_1 ensures the existence of Y_2, which ensures the existence of Y_3, and so on. In the example, Y_1, all by itself, deterministically produces Y_2 and all subsequent versions of Y. However, the final outcome can occur without X or any of the other prior steps. In a chain of sufficient but not necessary links, each event is slightly overdetermined throughout the sequence. Thus, Y_2, Y_3, and so on occasionally occur in possible worlds that lack Y_1. A small percentage of possible worlds exist in which we end up with Y for any given episode, even though it did not exist in the previous episode.

In both figures 11.1 and 11.2, the distribution of possible worlds across a set and its negation (e.g., Y_2 and $\sim Y_2$) corresponds to the expectations generated

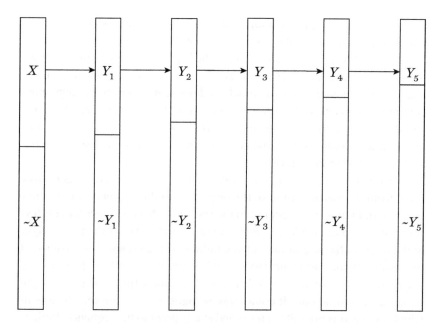

FIGURE 11.1. Self-Reinforcing Sequence: Necessity Bonds

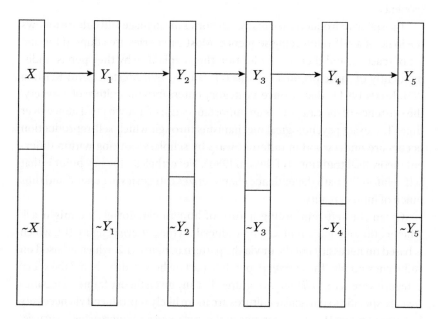

FIGURE 11.2. Self-Reinforcing Sequence: Sufficiency Bonds

by the investigator's theory frame and antecedent conditions. In figure 11.1, outcome Y becomes less likely over time from the vantage point of the theory frame when it is applied to conditions at the beginning of the sequence. With this chain of necessary causes, each causal link in the sequence becomes more and more contingent in light of initial conditions; analogously, the outcome's continuation becomes more surprising over time. Viewed over time, the actual world category Y follows a funnel of causality in which the area of the funnel contracts, coming closer and closer to the size of Y in the last step in the sequence (cf. Mahoney and Snyder 1999).

With figure 11.2, by contrast, outcome Y becomes less contingent over time; from the vantage point of the beginning of the sequence and the relevant theory frame, the existence of the institution becomes increasingly less surprising. One can explain Y_3 better than Y_2, and Y_4 better than Y_3, in light of the relevant frame and the initial conditions. The *eventual* occurrence of the institution may be unsurprising, but its occurrence *early* in the sequence is contingent and surprising. With sufficiency links, the persistence of the outcome is ensured once it comes into being. However, the specific way in which it persists is not fully determined at any point in the sequence. Rather, the particular pathway through which the outcome is generated becomes more defined as time passes. Thus, the funnel of causality for Y in figure 11.2 expands in size over time, increasingly approaching the area of Y in the final step in the sequence.

The stable reproduction of many categories in language and culture follows the logic of a self-reinforcing sequence. Most categories are adopted for one set of reasons, and their very adoption then explains why they persist independently of those original reasons (cf. James 1890; Merton 1948; Krishna 1971; Kukla 1994). That is, once a category enters into the culture of a society, the existence of the category is an important cause of its own persistence over time. The exact psychological mechanisms through which self-reproduction occurs are understood in different ways by scholars working within different theoretical traditions (cf. Jussim 1986). Nevertheless, the key point is that self-reinforcing path dependence characterizes categories in general and thus much of human reality.

Given the self-reinforcing nature of human categories, we might ask whether they are more typically reproduced via the pattern in figure 11.1, which is based on necessity bonds, or via the pattern in figure 11.2, which is based on sufficiency bonds. The answer depends in part on how widely shared the social categories are across *all* human cultures. For any given theory frame, categories that are specific to particular cultures are more likely reproduced via necessity links, as in figure 11.1. The existence of these categories is increasingly surprising over time, relative to initial expectations. By contrast, categories that are widely shared across cultures are more likely to follow the sufficiency pattern of figure 11.2. With these relatively universal categories, we expect cultures to eventually converge on their use, such that their adoption is increasingly likely over time.

THE PARADOX OF PATH DEPENDENCE

The paradox of path dependence arises when a researcher finds that (1) the *initial adoption* of an institution contradicts the predictions of the theory frame being employed, and (2) the *reproduction* of the institution is well explained by that theory frame. For example, in economic history, analysts show how certain economic outcomes are "inefficient," thereby contradicting the predictions of neoclassical theory. Yet these same analysts rely fully on neoclassical theory and efficiency arguments to explain the *reproduction* of these inefficient outcomes once they unexpectedly come into being.

Path-dependent arguments often call attention to options that were possible at the time of initial conditions (i.e., before the critical event) but that are no longer viable alternatives. For instance, although David (1985) believes that the Dvorak keyboard format was more efficient than the QWERTY format, he does not believe it would be rational for contemporary economic actors to replace QWERTY with the Dvorak format, given the heavy costs of technology reversal. Likewise, when Piore and Sabel (1984: chap. 2) argue that mass production is an inefficient outcome, they are comparing mass production to a possibility that existed in the nineteenth century—namely, craft production. Piore and Sabel do not believe it would be efficient to abandon mass production for craft production at this point in history. The contradiction of theory inherent in path-dependent self-reinforcing sequences, then, applies with respect to options that were available at the time of initial conditions, rather than to currently available options.

The paradox of path dependence operates relative to the particular theory frame that explains the self-reinforcement of an outcome over time. For most economists, this theory frame is, broadly speaking, rational choice theory, which can be understood to encompass neoclassical economics. Relative to rational choice theory, the persistence of inefficient outcomes in major arenas of the economy is puzzling, because the operation of rational actors competing to maximize profits in an open market should serve to weed out inefficiency, especially if the inefficiency is well recognized and superior alternatives are known and readily available. However, long-run market inefficiency may not be puzzling relative to alternative theory frames, such as the culturalist and structuralist theory frames. In this regard, we must recall that events, sequences, and outcomes do not have the quality of being inherently puzzling or surprising independently of analysts' beliefs. Path dependence and its paradox of self-reinforcement depend on the theoretical orientation of the researcher or the research community.

TYPES OF SELF-REINFORCING PATH DEPENDENCE

As is summarized in table 11.1, the three theory frames discussed in chapter 8—the rationalist, culturalist, and structuralist frames—suggest different modes of institutional reproduction. Each frame proposes a distinctive reason why path-dependent institutions are theoretically intriguing. Likewise, each frame suggests a different means and process of reversing self-reinforcing processes.

In the field of economic history, analysts employ a *rationalist theory frame* to explain self-reinforcing processes (Camic 1979; Coleman 1990; Collins 1994: chap. 2). Under this frame, actors rationally choose to reproduce institutions—including perhaps suboptimal ones—because any potential benefits of transformation are outweighed by the costs. For example, in the case of technologies, major barriers to transformation are imposed by research and development commitments, complementary investments, and consumer acceptance (Arthur 1994). Similarly, with organizational institutions, factors such as information dissemination, organizational interdependencies, and user proficiency may work to lock in prevailing arrangements (Powell 1991). North (1990: 94) generalizes the rational choice logic of institutional reproduction in terms of the benefits of learning effects, coordination effects, and adaptive expectations, as well as the costs imposed by irretrievable investments.

In this literature, the logic of increasing returns has been used to explain the persistence of many inefficient technologies, including some related to typewriter keyboards, automobiles, video recorders, electricity supplies, nuclear power plants, railroad gauges, pesticides, televisions, pollution-control systems, and computer programming languages (Mahoney 2000). Perhaps the most famous example is the development and persistence of the QWERTY keyboard layout (David 1985). The origins of QWERTY are clearly addressed in the standard account: actors initially adopted this layout because it helped solve problems related to type-bar jamming on early typewriters. The adoption of QWERTY falls into the set of contingent events, because it is outside the explanatory scope of neoclassical theory. The main cause—the need for a solution to type-bar jamming—is idiosyncratic to this case. QWERTY continued to dominate even after the jamming problem had been solved. Because of irretrievable costs, coordination effects, and adaptive expectations, QWERTY persisted long after the causes responsible for its original adoption had disappeared.

TABLE 11.1. Typology of Path-Dependent Frameworks of Institutional Reproduction

	Rationalist Frame	Culturalist Frame	Structuralist Frame
Mechanism of Reproduction	Institution is reproduced through the rational cost-benefit assessments of actors.	Institution is reproduced because actors believe it is morally just or appropriate.	Institution is reproduced because it is supported by an elite group of actors.
Potential Characteristics of Institution	Institution may be less efficient than previously available alternatives.	Institution may be less consistent with values of actors than previously available alternatives.	Institution may empower an elite group that was previously subordinate.
Mechanism of Change	Increased competitive pressures; learning processes.	Changes in the values or subjective beliefs of actors.	Weakening of elites and strengthening of subordinate groups.

With a *culturalist theory frame*, by contrast, institutional reproduction is grounded in actors' subjective orientations and beliefs about what is appropriate or morally correct (Dowling and Pfeffer 1975; Griswold 2012; Scott 1991; Stryker 1994). Institutional reproduction occurs when actors view an institution as legitimate and thus voluntarily opt for its reproduction. Beliefs in the appropriateness of an institution may range from active moral approval to passive acquiescence in the face of an overwhelming status quo. Whatever the degree of support, culturalist explanations assume that the decision of actors to reproduce an institution derives from their own understandings about the right thing to do rather than from a meticulous cost-benefit analysis or from resource-derived actor power. These understandings, in turn, are embedded in larger systems of meaning and overarching norms. An adequate explanation of institutional replacement requires referencing the overarching culture in which the institution is embedded. The institution's rules are but one component of a larger system of interlocking and interdependent meanings.

From the perspective of this frame, a given institution may be contingently selected and then reinforced through processes that increase legitimacy and appropriateness, even if other previously available institutions would have been more legitimate and appropriate within the larger cultural system. Increasing-legitimation processes are marked by a positive feedback cycle, in which an initial precedent for what is appropriate or "normal" forms a basis for making future decisions about what is appropriate or normal. A cycle of self-reinforcement occurs: the institution that is initially favored sets a standard for normalcy; the institution is reproduced because it is seen as normal and appropriate; and the reproduction of the institution reinforces its appropriateness even if it clashes with larger cultural norms.

An example of this cycle is found in Karen Orren's *Belated Feudalism: Labor, the Law, and Liberal Development in the United States* (1991). The central institution that Orren examines is the law of master and servant that characterized labor legislation in the United States from the beginning of the republic until well into the twentieth century. Orren argues that this law defied the liberal principle of sovereign individuality by prescribing enforceable obligations on employees as a status right. Surprisingly, the law was carried over from medieval Europe into the United States, contradicting the predictions of theories that assume liberal labor legislation should have prevailed. Once the legislation was adopted, however, it persisted for more than 150 years. To explain this remarkable persistence, Orren emphasizes the role of American courts in upholding and legitimating the law. In her view, judges enforced the law because they believed it was appropriate. Specifically, "the judges believed that what was at stake was no less than the moral order of things," and hence they upheld the law (p. 114). Over time, with each ruling in defense of the legislation, a new precedent was established that reinforced the appropriateness of the master-servant employment legislation in the liberal United States.

Culturalist explanations locate institutional transformation with changes in actors' subjective evaluations and moral codes concerning appropriateness. These shifts drive overt and covert challenges to what is taken to be acceptable and normal. Depending on the specific institution in question, changes in subjective orientations and declines in legitimacy may be linked to structural isomorphism with rationalized myths (Meyer and Rowan 1977), declines in institutional efficacy and stability (Linz 1978: 19), or the introduction of new ideas by political leaders (Fagen 1969).[3] Regardless of the particular cause of declining legitimacy, the fundamental mechanism of change is a breakdown in the beliefs required for the reproduction of an institution. With a culturalist frame, institutional transformation ultimately results from changes in actors' subjective beliefs and orientations, not from changes in the power distribution among actors or changes in the revealed preferences of rational actors.

Finally, with a *structuralist theory frame*, scholars emphasize power dynamics to explain institutional persistence and continuity. For structuralists, institutions distribute resources unevenly, creating categorical groups with conflicting interests vis-à-vis institutional reproduction (Knight 1992; Weber 1978: chap. 2; Rueschemeyer 1986; Mahoney and Thelen 2010). An institution can persist even when most individuals or groups prefer to change it, provided that an elite which benefits from the existing arrangement has sufficient resources to promote its reproduction.

In path-dependent analyses that use a structuralist frame, the genesis of an institution is not a predictable outgrowth of preexisting power arrangements associated with initial conditions. Once the institution develops, however, it is reinforced through predictable power dynamics: the institution empowers a certain group at the expense of other groups; the advantaged group uses its additional power to fortify the institution; the fortification of the institution increases the power of the advantaged group; and the advantaged group uses its enhanced power to pursue additional institutional fortification. This sequence of empowerment can take place even if the collectivity that benefits from the institution was initially subordinate to an alternative collective actor that favored the adoption of a different institution.

William G. Roy's *Socializing Capital: The Rise of the Large Industrial Corporation in America* (1997) offers a structuralist and path-dependent explanation of the United States' transformation after the 1840s from an economy with state-supported corporations to an economy dominated by large private corporations. Roy argues that the rise of the large private corporation economy depended on a series of nearly simultaneous events: the depression of 1837, the decision of states to invest in canal corporations, the spread of railroads, and the rise of Jacksonian anti-statism (pp. 72–74, 280–81). A change in any of these events—including the *timing* of the events—could have tipped the balance in favor of the large public enterprise. Although the United States was not certain to enter the category *economy dominated by large private corporations*, the prevailing power dynamics increasingly secured the country's membership in this outcome during the mid-nineteenth century. Most importantly, Roy argues that a new corporate class segment benefited from private corporations and worked to reproduce this outcome. It did so even though, at an earlier point, "the winners [i.e., the corporate leaders] were not always at the top of the social pyramid" (p. 260). Hence, private corporations helped constitute and empower U.S. corporate leaders, rather than the other way around. Once the economic elite coalesced, it worked to reinforce and ensure the dominance of the institution first responsible for its position at the top of the socioeconomic hierarchy.

Structuralist accounts assume that institutional reproduction creates a perhaps latent conflict between collective actors that are advantaged versus those that are disadvantaged by the persistence of an institution. The presence of this conflict means that a dynamic of potential change is built into institutions, even as a dynamic of self-reinforcement also characterizes them. Social structures may reproduce themselves until they reach a critical threshold, after which time self-reinforcement gives way to the inherently conflictual aspects of the institution, and eventually to institutional change (cf. Eisenstadt 1964). For example, some analysts stress that the reproduction of elite-supported institutions can eventually disadvantage subordinate groups to the point that these groups successfully challenge the prevailing arrangements (e.g., Burawoy 1985: 85–86). Likewise, some theorists hypothesize that the very process through which an institution empowers an elite group eventually becomes a source of divisions within this elite group, which in turn facilitates a transformation of existing arrangements (e.g., Rueschemeyer and Evans 1985; Evans 1995: 229–30). These logics underpin structural theories that envision a sequence of stages, or phases, through which cases travel over time. Each stage exhibits institutional stability, but it eventually breaks down, giving way to a new stage marked by its own emergent axis of categorical group division. Perhaps the most famous example of this kind of change is Marx's vision of societal evolution, in which a given mode of production carries the seeds of its own transformation, ensuring that class conflict moves societies along a predestined sequence of modes of production.

Reactive Sequences

Reactive sequences are chains of temporally ordered and causally connected events. In a reactive sequence, each event is both a reaction to antecedent events and a cause of subsequent events. With path dependence, the event that launches the sequence is a *critical event* for the final outcome. Slight alterations to this critical event can produce large downstream changes. Chaos theorists popularized this idea of sensitive dependence on initial conditions with the famous example of the butterfly effect—"the notion that a butterfly stirring in the air today in Peking can transform storm systems next month in New York" (Gleick 1987: 8).

Reactive sequences differ significantly from self-reinforcing sequences. Whereas self-reinforcing sequences are characterized by reproductive logics, reactive sequences are marked by transformative logics. In a reactive sequence, the initial critical event triggers subsequent developments not by reinforcing a given pattern, but by setting into motion a chain of tightly linked reactions. As Pierson (1998: 21) suggests, "initial disturbances are crucial not because they generate positive feedback, but because they trigger a powerful response . . . action and reaction move the system in a new direction, but not one that reinforces the first move."

THE FRONT END

In historical analysis, it is not always self-evident how one should identify the starting point of a sequence. It is common for an investigator to keep reaching back in time to identify the causes of other causes in the sequence. This infinite-regress problem is especially acute with reactive sequences, because they have no obvious starting point—unlike self-reinforcing sequences, which begin with the establishment of an institution or other outcome that then endures over time

In a path-dependent analysis, however, the initial event that sets a sequence into motion is both contingent and causally important (i.e., it is a critical event). From the perspective of theory, such an event can appear as a highly consequential interruption in the historical flow of a case. As Sewell (1996) suggests, sequential analysis often begins by focusing on unpredictable events—what he calls "initial ruptures"—that mark a "surprising break" with theoretical expectations. By focusing on such breakpoints, analysts of reactive sequences avoid the problem of infinite historical regress. They begin the analysis with an event that upsets ongoing conditions. The critical event itself is not well explained by these conditions, and it stands out as a breakpoint that cuts through the seamless tapestry of history.

Initial contingency is responsible for many of the theoretically intriguing aspects of reactive sequences. With critical events that are approximately necessary conditions, the analyst is able to show how a final outcome seemingly unrelated to the initial contingent event would likely not have occurred in the absence of the initial low-probability event. With critical events that are approximately sufficient conditions, the analyst shows how a final outcome was nearly destined to occur once the seemingly unrelated and contingent event took place. Two types of contingent events are thus associated with two types of path-dependent explanation: (1) an important outcome is almost fully dependent on a temporally remote and highly improbable historical event, and (2) an important outcome was almost destined to occur once a temporally remote and highly improbable historical event occurred.

The critical event that triggers the reactive sequence may itself be the intersection point of two or more prior sequences. The point in time at which two independent sequences intersect—that is, the *conjuncture*—will often not be predictable in advance (Skocpol 1979: 320; Braudel 1980; Abbott 1992: 438–39; Aminzade 1992: 466–67; Quadagno and Knapp 1992: 499; Sewell 1996: 862). Likewise, the specific event generated by the intersection of the sequences may be outside the resolving power of prevailing theories. Hence, conjunctures are often unanticipated, contingent occurrences (Zuckerman 1997: 289; Mandelbaum 1987: 156–57; Boudon 1986: 175).

THE CAUSAL CHAIN

With a reactive sequence, the analyst connects an initially contingent event to a final outcome by constructing a chain of intermediary events. The number and nature of the intermediary events are shaped by the need to have tight linkages, in which one event is causally important for the next. The analyst does not need to identify a causal chain in which no temporal gaps exist between events. Nor does the analyst need to identify as many intermediary events as possible. Rather, the goal of the analysis is to describe a causal chain in which each step clearly enables and/or produces the next step from the vantage point of the theory frame of interest.

Some path-dependent reactive sequences are marked by bonds that are understood to closely approximate necessity. Consider the following proverb:

> For want of a nail, the shoe was lost;
> For want of the shoe, the horse was lost;
> For want of the horse, the rider was lost;
> For want of the rider, the battle was lost;
> For want of the battle, the kingdom was lost;
> And all from the want of a horseshoe nail.

In this sequence, the opening contingent event is the absence of the horseshoe nail, which is understood to be accidental and ultimately necessary for the downfall of the kingdom. The most straightforward way to interpret the proverb is as a sequence of necessity links. This interpretation allows for a counterfactual rendering of each link in the chain—i.e., the negation of any one event would serve to negate the next event. It also allows for the counterfactual assertion in the last line, which seems to say that all steps in the sequence, including the final outcome, depend on the opening accidental event.

A possible world and set-theoretic approach invites the analyst to develop necessity bonds by considering the closest possible inconsistent case for each link in the chain. For example, consider the link between the lost rider and the lost battle, which is one of the least convincing claims at face value. Why should we suppose that an entire battle was lost simply because a single horse and rider went down? We need more information and context to evaluate the plausibility of this link. A set-theoretic approach encourages us to consider the most plausible alternatives to the rider's being lost. Why would the survival of the rider (if we assume "lost" means "killed") have caused the battle to turn out differently? What would have happened if the horse had been injured but not killed? Was the rider especially skilled, or perhaps a leader of the kingdom with membership in a category such as *king* or *queen*? Either the rider or the battle must have had membership in some unusual categories; otherwise, the assertion seems dubious. A set-theoretic approach encourages researchers to carefully establish bonds of necessity through the close examination of the case at hand and through consideration of relevant counterfactuals and proximate possible world scenarios.

Chains of approximately sufficient links are also compatible with reactive sequences. With these sequences, the initial critical event nearly ensures that the outcome will occur. However, the outcome could have happened even without the critical event. As the sequence progresses over time, each causal factor comes closer and closer to being necessary as well as sufficient. This sequence is commonly found in "destined pathway" explanations in which a contingent historical cause initiates a path that is, from the beginning, destined to end in the outcome of interest. As the path proceeds, the explanation becomes more and more complete; by the end of the sequence, the researcher has arrived at a nearly comprehensive historical explanation of the outcome (Fulbrook and Skocpol 1984).

Stinchcombe (1968: 101) points out that "we very often observe social phenomena that stay the same from year to year. Often the best prediction we can make is that 'this year will be just like last year.'" These kinds of predictions are often successful because the existence of a social phenomenon in a given year is *approximately sufficient* for its existence in the next year. Stinchcombe offers many examples of path dependence via sufficiency links, including this one:

> The countries which are now Protestant are countries whose kings were Protestant after the wars following the Reformation. Where the Protestants were militarily defeated, or where the king was never converted, Catholicism continued to be institutionalized . . . Conversely, where the Protestants won, Protestantism was institutionalized (p. 108).

Most Europeans who are Protestant hold their beliefs because of potentially contingent events that occurred in the sixteenth century. Once this religion took hold, however, it was locked in via the logic of sufficiency, shaping the beliefs of millions of Europeans for hundreds of years and continuing today.

Historical narrative is an especially useful method for describing and making sense of the multiple steps in a reactive sequence (e.g., Reisch 1991; Mahoney 1999). Narrative permits a sequential presentation in which the investigator isolates particular links within the overall causal chain. With narrative, the analyst can provide "a scene by scene description of the particular causal path" through which the initial breakpoint leads to a final outcome (Reisch 1991: 17). Furthermore, the step-by-step approach of narrative allows the analyst to use counterfactual analysis for specific links in the chain. The narrative can help the investigator identify what Aminzade (1992: 463) calls "key choice points" in the sequence—i.e., "forks in the road . . . marked by the presence of alternative possible paths." These choice points facilitate the exploration of hypothetical "paths not taken" and alternative futures that could have occurred if particular events in the reactive sequence had been different.

The narrative presentation of a reactive sequence is informed by implicit and explicit theoretical assumptions. Some of the individual links in the causal chain draw on folk theories of human psychology. These theories are strong generalizations or even nearly law-like statements—often nested in a hierarchy—that are regarded as obviously true within a given cultural community. For example, a folk generalization that informs many narratives is the intentional stance, i.e., the idea that individuals carry out actions on the basis of their beliefs and desires. This generalization allows for other generalizations, such as the idea that individuals who face unpleasant conditions seek to change these conditions, or that individuals who are threatened seek to preserve their status and resources. As Homans (1967) suggests, analysts largely take for granted these law-like generalizations that underpin many connections in a narrative account (see also Roberts 1996; Goldstone 1998a). The purpose of a narrative presentation is not to expose and make explicit all of the implicit generalizations that are assumed to operate in an enchained sequence. Rather, the purpose is to highlight the salient and tightly coupled events in the causal chain leading to the outcome.

Other links in a causal chain may depend on generalizations associated with particular theory frames. These links may receive more attention and discussion precisely because they cannot be taken for granted. For instance, consider the assertion that a particular union strike led factory owners to advertise for new employees. For scholars working within some theoretical orientations, this causal connection may seem obvious and trivial. Yet scholars associated with other traditions may seek insight about the generalization(s) that underpin this linkage. Those working within the rationalist, culturalist, and structuralist traditions may also differ in their understandings of *why* certain events are linked together in enchained sequences. For instance, a structuralist might see the linkage above as an effort by the capitalist class to undermine a show of working-class solidarity that threatens their structural position. By contrast, a rationalist might see the linkage as a financially prudent decision by profit-maximizing owners who must operate in a competitive market.

SUBSTANTIVE ILLUSTRATIONS

Substantive analyses of reactive sequences that are path-dependent often focus on rare outcomes, deviant cases, and instances of "exceptionalism." Deviant-case studies "analyze cases in which an outcome that had been predicted by theory did not occur" (Emigh 1997: 649). Deviant cases often deviate from the expectations of a theory because a critical event redirects their developmental trajectory down an atypical path. For example, students of "American exceptionalism" have emphasized historical accidents, random events, and small differences in starting conditions to explain the absence of socialism in the United States (Temin 1991; Voss 1993; Eidlin 2018). In the rare cases where socialist organizations are present in the United States, scholars have relied on particularistic historical factors to explain these unusual occurrences (e.g., Lipset, Trow, and Coleman 1956; Kimeldorf 1988). Other examples of outcomes studied in path-dependent analyses include the absence of a European-style welfare state in the United States, sustained high growth in South Korea and Taiwan, delayed industrialization in Italy, the establishment of democracy in Costa Rica, the establishment of democracy in India, prosperity in Botswana, the agriculture revolution in Europe, the decline of China by the late fifteenth century, agrarian capitalism in England, and the development of a world

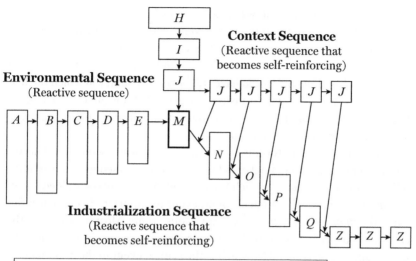

Context Sequence
(Reactive sequence that
becomes self-reinforcing)

Environmental Sequence
(Reactive sequence)

Industrialization Sequence
(Reactive sequence that
becomes self-reinforcing)

Key:
A: Limited forest area, abundant coal near sea, and cold climate.
B: Long-term heavy reliance on coal for heat.
C: Surface coal is exhausted.
D: Effort to dig for deeper coal.
E: Ground water fills mine shafts.

H: Limited monarchy.
I: Limited Anglican authority and toleration.
J: Liberal culture.

M: Development of first steam engine.

N: Improvement of steam engine.
O: Reduction in coal prices.
P: Reduction in price of iron and steel.
Q: Development of railways and ships.

Z: Mass distribution of industrial production and goods.

FIGURE 11.3. Goldstone's (1998b) Explanation of the Industrial Revolution in England

capitalist system in Europe (Skocpol 1992; Evans 1995; Emigh 1997; Paige 1997; Lange 2009; Tudor 2013; Diamond 1997; Pomeranz 2001; Brenner 1976; Wallerstein 1974).

Jack Goldstone's (1998b) work on the origins of the Industrial Revolution offers a nice example of sequential analysis in case-study explanation (see figure 11.3). In this work, the *environmental sequence* (events *A–E* in the figure) is a series of reactions marked by counterfactual bonds, in which each event is necessary for all subsequent events. Goldstone's presentation of the environmental sequence follows the logic of the horseshoe proverb, in which each event is dependent on the prior event. Although Goldstone does not invoke possible world semantics, his presentation invites one to imagine an England in which coal was not central to heating homes. It invites one to ask whether such an England would have still been the country in which the first steam engine was invented. Goldstone suggests that it is difficult to imagine England's developing the first steam engine if the need for removing water from mine shafts had not come up.

The *context sequence* (events $H-J$) begins as a reactive sequence of necessary conditions that yield England's liberal culture. This sequence turns into a self-reinforcing sequence in which England's liberal culture is sustained (event J).[4] The endurance of this background event is important because it influences the *industrialization sequence* at various points. Most importantly, the context sequence intersects with the environmental sequence to produce the first steam engine (event M), which is the critical event in the argument. In 1712, in a successful effort to produce a machine for pumping water to clear the deep-shaft mines, Thomas Newcomen created a bulky, noisy apparatus that made steam from the water and coal found at the mouth of the mines. According to Goldstone, "it was just chance that England had been using coal for so many centuries, and now needed a way to pump clear deep mines that held exactly the fuel needed for the clumsy Newcomen pumping machine" (p. 273). Indeed, in Goldstone's view, the unlikely events that led to the steam engine were a "perhaps one-in-a-million conjuncture" (p. 271).

Once the steam engine was developed, it triggered a predictable sequence of reactions in which further innovations and improvements followed. The early steps in the industrialization sequence (events $M-Z$) feature a sufficiency logic: the inefficient Newcomen steam engine itself was enough, in context J, to trigger improvements by subsequent inventors, such as James Watt (event N). These more efficient steam engines dramatically improved the extraction of coal, which in context J ensured a reduction in coal prices (event O). In turn,

> cheap coal made possible cheaper iron and steel. Cheap coal plus cheap iron made possible the construction of railways and ships built of iron, fueled by coal, and powered by engines producing steam. Railways and ships made possible mass national and international distribution of metal tools, textiles, and other products that could be more cheaply made with steam-powered metal-reinforced machinery [events O, P, Q, and Z] (p. 275).

These later steps (events $O-Z$) follow a necessity logic, as revealed by Goldstone's use of the expression "made possible" in this passage. The industrialization sequence (events $M-Z$) begins as a reactive sequence with both sufficiency and necessity components. As the diagram shows, the whole sequence operates within the context of England's liberal culture (event J). Goldstone regards this cultural context as permissive for the unfolding of each step in the industrialization sequence.

In sum, according to Goldstone, "there was nothing necessary or inevitable" about England's breakthrough to modern industrialism (p. 275). Rather, this outcome was dependent on the development of steam power—a contingent event that grew out of a highly improbable concurrence of prior events and that triggered a rather deterministic sequence of reactions. Set-theoretic analysis helps to clarify the logic of such arguments; a set diagram in particular is useful for specifying the components and structure of this kind of narrative argument.

———

This chapter has provided a new, set-theoretic approach for the analysis of path dependence in macro-oriented social science. The approach provides theory-building tools by employing basic cognitive structures in order to represent and explain the historical trajectories of cases. Specifically, the approach uses the source-path-goal image schema that is learned in infancy as part of comprehending objects in motion. The set-theoretic approach repurposes this universal, abstract, and implicit sense-making cognitive structure in order to formulate substantively grounded accounts of the distinctive pathways that particular cases follow to arrive at particular outcomes. These substantive accounts resonate with social scientists (and others) because they are rooted in an image schema that all humans use to comprehend the world around them.

The framework developed here identifies two types of path-dependent sequences: self-reinforcing sequences and reactive sequences. Self-reinforcing sequences are marked by a critical event that produces a given social rule, institution, or other entity, which is then reproduced over time, often through an increasing-returns process during the early stages. By contrast, reactive sequences feature dynamics of reaction and counterreaction, in which an initial event triggers a different and perhaps contradictory event, instead of a process of expansion, continuation, or reproduction. What unites these two types is the fact that they begin with critical events that subsequently enable and/or generate sequences marked by tight causal linkages. With path dependence, the events or episodes that compose the enchained sequence are connected by bonds of approximate necessity and/or sufficiency. The overall sequence either constitutes (in the case of self-reinforcing sequences) or culminates in (with reactive sequences) the final outcome of interest.

Finally, the constructivist approach of this book obviates a problem associated with path dependence that arises in essentialist work. The problem is that in essentialist social science, the identification of path dependence is not objective; rather, it depends on the beliefs and expectations of a researcher or research community. For instance, the identification of an event at the front end of a sequence as contingent depends on beliefs and expectations, as does the identification of an outcome as puzzling. Whereas the presence of human subjectivity is troubling for essentialist social science, it is not for constructivist social science. From a constructivist perspective, all of the categories used in the analysis of path dependence, like social science analysis more generally, depend on shared assumptions and beliefs. The study of path dependence is no more or less dependent on human subjectivity than other kinds of analysis. Constructivism liberates path dependence by showing how this kind of analysis does not require any special assumptions about belief dependence beyond those that are required for any mode of social science analysis.

Conclusion

In this book, I have presented theoretical and methodological tools for the pursuit of scientific constructivist research in the social sciences. Perhaps the book's most basic and important idea is the value of analyzing social science categories as sets in which other categories can have membership, including degrees of partial membership. I have offered a wide range of tools for implementing this kind of analysis—which is simple to propose, but not always easy to carry out. Some of these set-theoretic tools have been previously well developed in the literature; others are new methods, including new procedures for working with theory frames and normative principles. The overall toolkit presented here aims to serve as a guide for the pursuit of scientific constructivist research in the future.

The use of set-theoretic analysis as outlined in this book places social science on a constructivist foundation. Because set-theoretic analysis is not inherently a constructivist approach, the book reconfigures this kind of analysis for the study of mind-dependent categories. It does so by reconceptualizing the meaning of the category *set*. Whereas a set is conventionally defined as a collection of entities that share one or more properties, a set is defined here as a bounded location in space in which other sets can have membership, including partial membership. The standard definition of a set assumes that entities possess similarities and differences prior to their set membership. By contrast, this book assumes that set membership is ultimately what makes entities similar or different.

The shift to constructivism is complete when we understand social science categories as conceptual spaces in the mind's representational apparatus. Conceived in this way, social science categories are sets that have a grounding in the machinery of human brains and that are ontologically dependent on human minds. Social science categories refer to entities that are composed of natural kinds, but they lack a one-to-one correspondence with those natural kinds at any level of generality. It is fruitless to define a social science category in terms of the heterogeneous natural kinds that constitute each member of the category.

My argument concerning the need for a constructivist social science builds on decades of research in psychology, cognitive science, philosophy, cognitive linguistics, and neuroscience—research that calls into question the essentialist orientation that currently guides mainstream social science. Under essentialism, the objects and entities around us are implicitly or explicitly understood to possess hidden properties that endow them with identities and natures. These properties may be understood as socially acquired traits, but they are nonetheless believed to function as the stable core of categories. An essentialist approach is so basic to how we think and speak that it is hard to grasp that the approach is simply an illusion. Yet the science on this matter is clear: instances of a category do not actually possess similar inner essences or properties that make them members of the category. Our categories can work quite well even if they do not pick out any natural kinds. The tension between what the evidence from science tells us and what we experience to be true means that constructivist social scientists must live with a certain degree of conflict. It also means that they will always lose the debate with their essentialist colleagues if intuition is the basis for adjudicating truth.

This book endorses *science* as the appropriate way to learn about both the natural world and the social world. Science involves the systematic use of logic and evidence to derive conclusions about the truth of propositions; it provides a sound epistemology for discovering the entities, properties, and processes that constitute both objective and experiential reality. For the natural world, scientists quite appropriately seek to learn about and describe reality as it exists independently of human minds. Their use of logic allows for objectivity in the process of reasoning about truth; their use of mathematics provides indispensable tools for describing the structure of reality.

For the social world, social scientists are equally concerned with the epistemologically objective truth of propositions. However, social science categories do not map a mind-independent external reality; they emerge from an interaction between the mind and external reality. Stability in the meanings of social science categories, and thus stability in the truth of propositions involving social science categories, depends on continuity in shared understandings and background beliefs. Precisely because this continuity is common within communities, social scientists can evaluate propositions scientifically; they can use evidence and truth-preserving methodologies to describe the structure of social reality as communities experience that reality over sometimes considerable periods of time. Social scientists can explain, in ways that are approximately true within particular semantic contexts, how processes work and why outcomes occur. They can use theoretical tools and human imagination to build good and even ingenious explanations, and they can employ methodological tools to rationally assess the validity of those explanations. Scientists who study the social world can generate findings that help individuals and communities more effectively engage with their experienced reality, including by promoting continuity and change in desired ways.

Social science thus works as a *science* because human reality features substantial stability in the collective beliefs and semantic understandings on which categories depend. We can assume the unproblematic reproduction of much of social reality, and even the more contested aspects of social reality often exhibit enormous stability. This continuity is so taken for granted that we communicate about our categories as if they literally pick out mind-independent entities existing naturally in the external world.

The human disposition to unconsciously and automatically essentialize human kinds helps to explain the stability of categories. If we perceive social reality through an unconscious essentialist lens, as we ordinarily do, it is difficult for us to see that nearly all of social reality is dependent on implicit collective understandings. Essentialism disguises the constructed nature of social reality by presenting it to us as naturally existing objects, properties, and processes. In doing so, essentialism stabilizes the rules and institutions that constitute our experienced reality. If we were to lose the capacity to engage in essentialism, the collective beliefs on which societies depend would surely falter, and the societies themselves would cease to exist. Essentialism is, in this sense, a necessary and quite functional illusion for the development and persistence of human civilization. We need essentialism in order to sustain the collective beliefs on which our experienced reality depends.

———

The illusion of essentialism may be functional for human society, but the mandate of science is to expose psychological illusions rather than reproduce them. In that spirit, I have proposed and developed a scientific constructivist approach intended to avoid essentialist biases in the production of social science knowledge. Specifically, I have called for a set-theoretic social science, in which analysts study relationships among categories—conceptualized as sets in the mind for use in the classification of heterogeneous entities as members of a given category. I have argued against the practice of conducting social science research under the assumption that variables track objective properties in the world.

The proposal that analysts give up on essentialism as the ontology for social science is asking a great deal. I believe that if we social constructivists are going to insist on a non-essentialist approach to the scientific study of society, we owe our skeptical colleagues an account of exactly how such an approach can be carried out in practice. Inspired by this conviction, I have in this book not only sought to explain why social science must abandon essentialism and embrace constructivism and all of its implications. I have also sought to provide specific methodological and theoretical tools for conducting research under scientific constructivist assumptions.

GLOSSARY

The following glossary provides a short definition for many of the specialized terms that appear in this book. The definitions correspond to the meaning of the terms as they are used in the context of the book.

abstract object: A posited entity that lacks a spatiotemporal existence. See also *unobservable object.*

accidental property: A characteristic of a *natural kind* that is not essential to its constitution at any level of generality. See also *essential property*; *incidental property.*

actor: An individual or group whose behavior is understood to be guided by beliefs and desires. See also *intentional stance.*

actual case: A *case* that contains the *actual world* as one of its members.

actual causality: See *token causality.*

actual event: An *event* that contains at least one *actual case* as a member.

actual world: The specific *world* in which we reside.

almost-critical event: An event that is a *critical event* in most *possible worlds* but not in the *actual world.*

approximately necessary and sufficient condition: An *INUS condition* that is nearly a *necessary and sufficient condition.*

approximately necessary condition: An *INUS condition* that is nearly a *necessary condition.*

approximately sufficient condition: An *INUS condition* that is nearly a *sufficient condition.*

approximately true proposition: A statement that is believed to be a *true proposition* with a very high degree of *certitude.*

artifact essentialism: A mode of *essentialism* in which the essences of *objects* are related to their presumed design history.

Bayesian analysis: A logical approach for updating beliefs about whether a *proposition* is a *true proposition* in light of *evidence.*

case: A *category* for the main *unit of analysis* in a given study. See also *actual case*; *non-actual case*; *possible case.*

case study: The intensive analysis of a single *actual case.*

category: A relationship between (1) a *conceptual space* in the mind that is used in the classification of entities, and (2) the classified entities themselves.

causal importance: The extent to which a *cause* approximates a *necessary and sufficient condition.*

causal inference: A belief about *causality* derived from *logic* and *evidence.*

causal power: The dynamic disposition of a *natural kind.*

causality: The relationship between a *cause* and its effect.

causation: See *causality.*

cause: An antecedent and non-spurious *necessary, sufficient, necessary and sufficient, INUS,* or *SUIN condition* for an outcome.

cause, maximally important: An antecedent and non-spurious *necessary and sufficient condition* for an outcome.

certainty: See *certitude*.

certitude: The extent to which one believes that another belief is true.

cognitive model: A stylized depiction of the entities and relationships that compose recurrent social situations. See also *script*.

collectively dependent resource: A *resource* whose value to *actors* depends on social recognition and collective understandings.

complexity: The length of the shortest algorithm in a system of logic for specifying a *rule* or system of rules.

concept: See *category*.

conceptual space: A bounded region in the hyperspace of the mind corresponding to a *category*.

consequentialness: The extent to which *evidence* changes initial beliefs about the *truth* of a *proposition* in *Bayesian analysis*.

constitutive rule: Instructions specifying what is required for an entity to be a certain kind of entity.

constructivism: An ontological approach that treats *categories* as mind-dependent entities that exist by virtue of collective understanding. See also *human kind*; *radical constructivism*; *scientific constructivism*.

context: Background *categories* that are not the main categories of analysis.

contingency: The extent to which the occurrence of a phenomenon is not anticipated by one or more *theories*.

contingent event: An *event* that was not expected to occur.

contingent proposition: A *proposition* that is true in at least one *possible world* that could be the *actual world*, and false in at least one possible world that could be the actual world. See also *false proposition*; *true proposition*.

continuous-set analysis: A mode of *set-theoretic analysis* in which a *set* can have partial membership in another set. See also *dichotomous-set analysis*.

continuous-set measurement: The assessment of the extent to which one *category* is a member of another category.

counterfactual statement: A subjunctive conditional statement in which the antecedent condition is a *non-actual event*.

crisp-set analysis: See *dichotomous-set analysis*.

critical event: An *event* that is *contingent* and *causally important* for an outcome in a particular *case*. See also *almost-critical event*.

critical observation: A *set-membership observation* that has a high level of *consequentialness* and a low level of *expectedness*. See also *Bayesian analysis*.

critical realism: An ontological approach that holds that social mechanisms exist as real entities with *causal powers*. See also *realism*.

critical-evidence narrative: A *narrative* that is structured around at least one *critical observation*.

cumulative observation: A *set-membership observation* that has a low level of *consequentialness* and a high level of *expectedness*. See also *Bayesian analysis*.

cumulative-evidence narrative: A *narrative* that is structured around several *cumulative observations*.

deduction: See *empirical deduction*; *logical deduction*.

deep rule: A *rule* that is necessary for the meaning of many other rules but is not dependent on many other rules for its own meaning.

descriptive inference: A belief about the *truth* of a descriptive *proposition* derived from *logic* and *evidence*.

deterministic relationship: An association between *categories* in which membership in one category is fully necessary and/or fully sufficient for membership in another category.

dichotomous-set analysis: A mode of *set-theoretic analysis* in which set membership is measured dichotomously. See also *continuous-set analysis*.

dispositional mechanism: An *essential property* of a *natural kind* that endows it with a *causal power*. See also *intervening mechanism*; *theoretical mechanism*.

elaboration model: The statistical analysis of a bivariate relationship through the introduction of a control variable, either intervening or antecedent. See also *sequence elaboration*.

empirical deduction: The formulation of *propositions* and *theories* prior to the analysis of *evidence*. See also *logical deduction*.

empirical induction: The formulation of *propositions* and *theories* from the analysis of *evidence*. See also *logical induction*.

essential property: An inner characteristic that is possessed by and constitutive of the members of a given kind. See also *accidental property*; *incidental property*.

essentialism: A cognitive orientation in which entities are understood to possess inner essences and true natures independently of human beings. See also *artifact essentialism*; *innate essentialism*; *social essentialism*.

event: A *category* that designates a temporally bounded episode composed of *actors* and *objects* and structured by *rules* and *resources*.

evidence: Sensory input from the *actual world* that is processed by the mind and used in the evaluation of *propositions* and *theories*. See also *set-membership observation*.

expectedness: The extent to which *evidence* is expected to be observed, given initial beliefs, in *Bayesian analysis*.

experiential reality: The *categories* that are experienced as real entities, properties, and processes within particular communities. See also *objective reality*.

fact: See *societal fact*.

false proposition: A *proposition* that is false in the *actual world*. See also *contingent proposition*.

force dynamics: The use of spatial entities, forces, and movements to describe and comprehend language and *reality*. See also *image schema*.

formal rule: An explicitly codified *rule* that is upheld by a legitimate authority.

fuzzy-set analysis: See *continuous-set analysis*.

gradual change: A change that occurs over a long period of time. See also *punctuated change*.

human kind: A mind-dependent collection of entities that are similar by virtue of shared beliefs. See also *natural kind*; *partial natural kind*.

hypothesis: See *proposition*.

ideal type: A *non-actual case* that is the best example of a *category*. See also *prototype*.

illogical relationship: An association among *categories* that violates a principle of first-order logic.

image schema: An easily understood, recurring pattern with which the mind builds more complex cognitive structures.

impossible observation: An *observation* that is 100% certain or 100% unexpected in *Bayesian analysis*.

impossible world: An imaginary spatiotemporal domain in which at least one transcendental truth is false.

incidental property: A characteristic of an instance of a *natural kind* that distinguishes the instance from other instances of the same kind. See also *accidental property*; *essential property*.

induction: See *empirical induction*; *logical induction*.

informal rule: A *rule* that is not codified and/or not upheld by a legitimate authority. See also *norm*.

innate essentialism: A mode of *essentialism* in which the essences of individuals and other life forms are related to their inherited biological properties.

institution: A system of enduring *social rules* that affects the distribution of important *resources*.

intentional stance: The view that the beliefs and desires of an *actor* motivate its behavior.

intervening mechanism: An intermediary step in a causal chain of three or more *events*. See also *dispositional mechanism*; *theoretical mechanism*.

INUS condition: A *category* for which membership is Insufficient but Necessary for membership in another category, for which membership is Unnecessary but Sufficient for a target category. See also *approximately necessary condition*; *approximately sufficient condition*; *approximately necessary and sufficient condition*.

irrelevant observation: A *set-membership observation* that does not alter beliefs concerning the *truth* of a *proposition*.

ladder of generality: A group of *categories* that are systematically related to one another as a *set-theoretic hierarchy* or a *part-whole hierarchy*.

level of analysis: The generality of a *category* relative to other categories within a *semantic field*.

logic: A system of necessarily true statements that can be expressed in a formal language and that provides the basis for sound reasoning.

logical deduction: A type of reasoning in which the *truth* of the premises of an argument is sufficient for the truth of the conclusion of the argument. See also *empirical deduction*.

logical importance: The higher value between the extent to which a condition is necessary for another condition and the extent to which a condition is sufficient for another condition. See also *logical relevance*.

logical induction: A type of reasoning in which the *truth* of the premises of an argument is not sufficient for the truth of the conclusion of the argument. See also *empirical induction*.

logical relevance: The lower value between the extent to which a condition is necessary for another condition and the extent to which a condition is sufficient for another condition. See also *logical importance*.

maximally true proposition: The *ideal type* of the category *true proposition*.

mechanism: See *dispositional mechanism*; *intervening mechanism*; *theoretical mechanism*.

mereology: The study of part-whole relationships.

metaphor: The semantic extension of a term from one domain (a source domain) to another domain (a target domain).

minimal-rewrite rule: The principle that the most useful *counterfactual statements* have non-actual antecedents that are similar to the *actual world*.

moral realism: The thesis that *normative statements* are objectively true or false.

narrative: A description of a *case* centered around *events, processes, actors, objects, rules,* and *resources*.

natural kind: A collection of entities that exist independently of human minds, share *essential properties*, possess specific *causal powers*, and are a part of *objective reality*. See also *human kind*; *partial natural kind*.

natural science: The application of *science* to the study of *partial natural kinds* and *natural kinds*.

naturalization: The practice of treating *human kinds* as if they are *natural kinds*. See also *reification*.

necessary and sufficient condition: A *category* in which (1) units must have membership to be a member of another category (the target category); and (2) all units with membership are also members of the target category. See also *approximately necessary and sufficient condition*.

necessary condition: A *category* in which units must have membership in order to be a member of another category (the target category). See also *approximately necessary condition*.

necessary condition counterfactual: A *counterfactual statement* that is derived from a *proposition* in which the true antecedent is believed to be a *necessary condition* for an outcome.

necessity test: A *set-theoretic test* in which a *set-membership observation* is necessary for the *truth* of a *contingent proposition*. See also *sufficiency test*.

non-actual case: A *case* that contains only *non-actual worlds* as members.

non-actual event: An *event* that contains only *non-actual cases* as members.

non-actual world: A *possible world* in which we do not reside. See also *actual world*.

norm: A shared expectation encoded in human brains about how people ought to behave.

normative inference: A belief about the *truth* of a *normative statement* derived from *logic* and *evidence*.

normative statement: An evaluative or value-laden statement.

normative tradition: An overarching system of normative beliefs rooted in general principles and assumptions.

object: A non-sentient entity.

objective fact, epistemologically: A *true proposition* within a particular *semantic context*. See also *societal fact*; *experiential reality*.

objective fact, ontologically: A *true proposition* in all *possible worlds*.

objective reality: The totality of all *natural kinds* in all *possible worlds*. See also *experiential reality*.

observation: Sensory input from the actual world that is comprehended using *conceptual spaces*. See also *set-membership observation*.

overdetermination: A relationship in which two or more *sufficient conditions* or *sufficiency combinations* are present for an outcome in a particular *case*.

part-whole hierarchy: A hierarchy in which entities at higher levels are composed of entities at lower levels.

partial natural kind: A collection of entities that has significant but not complete membership in the category *natural kind*.

path dependence: A causal process in which a *critical event* sets into motion a *self-reinforcing sequence* or a *reactive sequence*.

possible case: A *case* in which the *actual world* could be, or could have been, a member.

possible world: A *world* in which no transcendental truths are false.

possible world semantics: The use of references to *possible worlds* to understand and employ systems of *logic*, including modal logic and *Bayesian analysis*.

power: The *resource*-derived capabilities of an *actor*.

process: A *category* that designates a pattern of change that is marked by a unifying principle and that occurs over a loosely bounded period of time. See also *event*; *gradual change*.

property set: A collection of distinct elements that all share one or more properties.

property-possession assumption: The belief that the instances of a *category* possess shared *essential properties*.

proposition: A descriptive, causal, or normative statement about a *possible world* that is either true or false.

prototype: A point within a *conceptual space* associated with the idealized best example of a *category*.

punctuated change: A large transformation that takes place over a short duration and that is preceded and followed by periods of stability. See also *gradual change*.

qualitative comparative analysis (QCA): A set-theoretic methodology that uses Boolean algebra to express *category* relationships and generate solution sets.

radical constructivism: A type of *constructivism* that rejects the idea that *science* can be used to establish the approximate truth of *propositions*. See also *scientific constructivism*.

reactive sequence: A chain of discrete, temporally ordered, and causally connected *events* that culminate in an outcome of interest.

real world: A *world* in which no transcendental truths are false.

realism: An ontological approach that holds that a structured *world* exists independently of all human beings. See also *critical realism*.

reality: See *experiential reality; objective reality.*

regularity: A relationship in which a *category* or a combination of categories is a *sufficient condition* for a subsequent target category.

regularity model of causality: An approach in which *causality* exists between *events* if three conditions are met: (1) temporal succession, (2) spatiotemporal contiguity, and (3) constant conjunction.

regulatory rule: Behavioral instructions that prescribe appropriate actions and specify sanctions for non-compliance.

reification: The explicit or implicit belief that *human kinds* are mind-independent entities with an identity and disposition.

resource: An entity that is valuable to *actors* for the formation, pursuit, and achievement of goals. See also *collectively dependent resource; self-efficacious resource.*

rule: An algorithmic procedure that can be expressed in a formal language. See also *social rule.*

Rule of Causal Contingency: The principle that the level of *contingency* of a causally important individual *category* approximates the level of contingency of the target category it explains.

science: An epistemological approach in which one systematically uses *logic* and *evidence* to evaluate the truth of *contingent propositions* about the *actual world*. See also *natural science; social science.*

scientific constructivism: An approach that combines *constructivism* and *science* for the study of *human kinds.*

script: A stylized depiction of everyday situations as interconnected slots and requirements for filling the slots. See also *cognitive model.*

self-efficacious resource: A *resource* whose value to *actors* does not depend on social recognition and collective understandings.

self-reinforcing sequence: Causally connected temporal stages in which an initial outcome is repeated, amplified, and/or stabilized over time.

semantic context: A setting in which a community of individuals share beliefs about the meaning of a wide range of *categories.*

semantic field: A group of related *categories* that create a *set-theoretic hierarchy* or a *part-whole hierarchy.*

sequence elaboration: The *set-theoretic analysis* of a relationship between two *events* in light of a third event, either intervening or antecedent. See also *elaboration model.*

set: A bounded location in space in which entities can have membership. See also *property set.*

set-membership observation: An *observation* that grounds a belief held with very high *certitude* that the *actual world* has membership in a specific *category*. See also *evidence; societal fact.*

set-theoretic analysis: A scientific approach in which *categories* are analyzed as *sets.*

set-theoretic generalization: A relationship among two or more *categories* that is expressed set-theoretically.

set-theoretic hierarchy: A system of hereditary *sets* in which lower levels are proper members of higher levels.

set-theoretic test: The logical assessment of a *contingent proposition* using a *set-membership observation* and a *set-theoretic generalization*. See also *necessity test; sufficiency test.*

small-N analysis: The study of approximately 2 to 20 *cases.*

social essentialism: A mode of *essentialism* in which the essences of entities are believed to be socially and historically acquired.

social role: A system of *rules* that constitute an identity.

social rule: Algorithmic instructions for constituting and regulating behavior. See also *constitutive rule; deep rule; formal rule; informal rule; regulatory rule; surface-level rule.*

social science: The application of *science* to the study of *human kinds.*

societal fact: A shared belief held with very high *certitude* within a society that a *proposition* is true. See also *objective fact*; *set-membership observation*.

spatial set: A *set* in which entities with membership do not share any *essential properties*. See also *property set*.

spatial-set assumption: The belief that the instances of a *category* are similar by virtue of their membership in a *set* located in the mind.

spectral property: An *essential property* of a *natural kind* that exhibits a range of quantitative variation across particular instances of the kind. See also *variable*.

structure: An *institution* that constitutes and regulates asymmetrical *social roles*.

subjective, ontologically: The state of being dependent on the human mind for existence.

sufficiency combination: Two or more non-sufficient conditions that are jointly sufficient for another condition.

sufficiency test: A *set-theoretic test* in which a *set-membership observation* is sufficient for the truth of a *proposition*. See also *necessity test*.

sufficient condition: A *category* in which all units with membership are also members of another category (the target category). See also *approximately sufficient condition*.

SUIN condition: A *category* for which membership is Sufficient but Unnecessary for membership in another category, for which membership is Insufficient but Necessary for a target category.

SUIN condition counterfactual: A *counterfactual statement* that is derived from a *proposition* in which the true antecedent is believed to be a *SUIN condition* for an outcome.

surface-level rule: A *rule* that is dependent on many other rules for its own meaning but that is not necessary for the meaning of many other rules.

theoretical mechanism: A general *category* that subsumes relationships among other categories. See also *dispositional mechanism*; *intervening mechanism*.

theorizing: The process of formulating assumptions, *categories*, and *propositions* to explain phenomena.

theory: A group of related assumptions, *categories*, and *propositions* used in the explanation of phenomena.

theory frame: The background *categories* and assumptions that scholars use to understand society and its basic components.

token causality: A causal relationship that applies to a particular *case*, known as a token. See also *type causality*.

true proposition: A statement that is an accurate characterization of *experiential reality* or *objective reality*. See also *approximately true proposition*.

truth: A *true proposition* or the quality of being a true proposition.

type causality: A causal relationship among general *categories* that is instantiated by particular *cases*. See also *token causality*.

unit of analysis: The *natural kinds* that are understood to be a coherent entity with membership in a *category* designating a specific kind of spatiotemporal entity. See also *case*; *world*.

universal: A *property set* of particulars (i.e., an immanent universal); alternatively, a *set* that exists as an *abstract object* independently of any particulars (i.e., a transcendent universal).

unobservable object: A posited entity to which human beings have no sensory access at a given time. See also *abstract object*.

variable: A systematic conceptualization of similarities and differences in a property possessed by *cases*.

within-case analysis: The detailed analysis of aspects of a particular *case*.

world: A closed, maximal spatiotemporal domain that includes all entities, and only entities, that have a causal, spatial, and/or temporal relationship with one another.

NOTES

Introduction

1. The phrase "carve nature at its joints" is from Plato's *Phaedrus*, sections 265d–266a. This metaphor implies that analysts can divide up the world according to its natural divisions, in a manner similar to how a skilled butcher cuts up animals according to their anatomical structure. The term *one-to-one correspondence* refers to mathematical bijection, in which each element of one set is paired with exactly one element of the other set. I also use the term to include surjection, in which each element of one set is paired with one element of another set.

Chapter 1: Scientific Constructivism

1. This spatiotemporal stability does not prohibit variation among the *accidental properties* of natural kinds; only the essential properties of these kinds are stable across time and space. Accidental properties are characteristics of an entity that are not essential to its constitution at any level of generality (Copi 1954; Robertson 2009). An *incidental property* is a characteristic that is essential to an individual instance of a natural kind but not to the natural kind in general (Ellis 2001: 76–78).

2. The main alternative to platonism is mathematical fictionalism, a view that is defended in different ways and to different degrees in Balaguer (1998), Field (2016), Lakoff and Núñez (2000), Livio (2009), and Leng (2010), as well as throughout Wittgenstein's philosophy (1922/1972, 1953/2001, 1956/1978). The set-theoretic realism embraced in this book is indebted to Gödel (1947), who proved that no logical system can capture *all* the truths of mathematics (the first incompleteness theorem) and that no logical system for mathematics can, on its own, be *proved* to be fully consistent (the second incompleteness theorem). Notwithstanding Gödel's theorems, the applicability of logic to science knows few bounds (Warner 1989; Nagel 1997: chaps. 4–5; Hanna 2006).

3. Some philosophers—e.g., Clark and Chalmers (1998), Wilson (2004), and Clark (2008)—argue that the mind can be partially located outside of the brain and indeed the entire human body. For my purposes here, however, I follow the convention of treating minds and brains as coextensive entities, with the former existing virtually inside the latter. See Rupert (2009) for a good critique of the extended-mind theory.

4. The exception is psychological kinds (e.g., mental states such as happiness), which can be viewed as human kinds whose specific instances are brain states.

5. Spatiotemporal instability has long complicated efforts to treat biological species as natural kinds (LaPorte 2004). Many analysts propose that biological species are defined by clusters of traits that tend to cohere together (Boyd 1991; Browning 1978; Dupré 1981; Hacking 1991; Mellor 1977; Millikan 1999; Wilson, Barker, and Brigandt 2007). Another approach is to view biological species as having partial membership in the set of natural kinds (cf. Keil 1989; Grandy 2007).

I favor the latter approach and support the idea that classes of entities can have varying degrees of membership in the set of natural kinds (cf. Lewis 1984: 227–28).

6. The category *natural kind* is a human kind category. Without human beings, the category would not exist, though the entities that are natural kinds would still exist and operate just as their properties require them to operate. For somewhat different views on whether the category *life* is a natural kind, see Cleland (2013) and Dupré (1993). See also Wendt (2015: chap. 7).

7. Churchland (1985) uses the label *practical kinds* for partial natural kinds. By contrast, other philosophers and scientists feel comfortable viewing partial natural kinds as full-blown natural kinds (see LaPorte 2004: chap. 1 for the relevant literature). I view natural kinds as an ideal type, and thus I understand categories such as *tiger, mountain*, and *planet* as partial natural kinds.

8. The question of whether we can ever identify full-blown natural kinds is linked to the broader issue of whether we can conceive of things in a way that does not depend on our human sensory make-up (Locke 1690/1975; Bradley 1897; McGinn 1983, 1999; Nagel 1986). Humans may not be equipped to fully identify, describe, and comprehend natural kinds.

9. Categories in the middle of the continuum have an ambiguous status with respect to whether they should be located in the natural sciences or the social sciences. Examples of ambiguous categories include mental disorders (e.g., *generalized anxiety disorder, depression, schizophrenia*), emotions (*happiness, sadness, fright*), and ancestral background (e.g., as defined by DNA testing).

10. I am by no means a linguist, but the built-in essentialist bias of the English language seems to be linked to the verb *to be*, as well as to possession verbs, such as *to have*. Because I write and consciously think in English, many passages in this book suggest the property-possession assumption. Spanish uses two versions of *to be*, though both still imply possession (temporary or permanent). What seems to be needed are versions of *to be* and possession verbs for two ontological states: (1) states of being that are culturally and historically dependent; and (2) states of being that exist across all spatiotemporal domains. I do not know which, if any, languages have such versions of these verbs.

11. As Locke (1690/1980: 293) put it, "Essence may be taken for the very being of anything, whereby it is what it is. And thus the real internal, but generally . . . unknown constitution of things, whereon their discoverable qualities depend, may be called their essence." In the context of this book, I am especially interested in the "entitativity" or "reification" side of essentialism—i.e., the understanding of a category as a coherent whole and a distinct entity in the world (Haslam, Rothschild, and Ernst 2004).

12. Here I do not discuss *arbitrary kinds*—i.e., categories in which the members are *not* assumed to share any hidden properties that endow them with a meaningful identity and that support generalizations (Lakoff 1987; Haward et al. 2018). Examples of such kinds include objects between 6.23 and 7.11 meters in length; tigers born on odd-numbered days; and teachers who occasionally sleep on the right side of the bed. Arbitrary kinds do not group together members to form a generally useful category; they do not allow for important inductive inferences or provide deep insight into the workings of the social world. As Gelman (2003: 53) suggests, categories at very high levels of generality (e.g., *thing*) and very low levels of generality (e.g., *red stapler* vs. *black stapler*) are often arbitrary kinds, and their arbitrary features are not essentialized (see also Coley, Medin, and Atran 1997). Categories at the "basic level" (Lakoff 1987) are essentialized within particular cultures.

13. Many constructivist scholars arrive at constructivism through a critique of materialism—i.e., a critique of the thesis that physical entities constitute social reality. These constructivist scholars emphasize the role of ideas in constituting social structures and social life. In this formulation, a constructivist solution is linked mainly to idealism (Wendt 1999: chap. 1). By contrast, I arrive at constructivism through a critique of essentialism, understood as a general cognitive bias that all humans share. Correspondingly, I understand constructivism first and

foremost as involving a solution to these essentialist biases. In this book, I do not delve into questions about whether natural kinds are constituted by physical material (see Wendt 2015). However, my ontology does include the existence of space and time, which are constitutive of cases and worlds.

14. In the United States, people often understand racial categories (e.g., *African American*) as biological, inevitable, distinct, and permanently fixed identities. An inherent essentialist view of race encourages racist generalizations about individuals (Bonilla-Silva 1997; Hirschfeld 1996; Mandalaywala, Amodio, and Rhodes 2018). Similar remarks can be made about categories related to gender (Diesendruck et al. 2013; Taylor, Rhodes, and Gelman 2009; Waxman 2010), ethnicity and caste (Gil-White 2001), and mental disorders (Haslam and Ernst 2002; Hacking 1995a, 1995b). The connection between essentialism and discrimination is more complicated for sexual orientation categories (Haslam and Levy 2006).

15. Empiricists go so far as to reject the idea that observations and evidence are mind-dependent at all (Popper 1934/1968). By contrast, in his famous work on concepts, Sartori hints that the attributes of concepts may be mind-dependent all the way down. However, he consciously decides to remain agnostic on the matter and proceeds under the assumption that concepts coherently track objective reality (1975: 20, 33; 1984: 24–25).

16. Within the realist traditions of the social sciences, the *critical realist* school of philosophy goes the furthest in acknowledging the constructed aspects of human reality (Bhaskar 1975, 1979/1998; Collier 1994; Gorski 2013; Somers 1998; Archer 1995; Steinmetz 1998; Sayer 2000; Smith 2010; Elder-Vass 2012). Nevertheless, their whole program depends on the claim that mechanisms exist on the plane of the real and that their powers operate in the world independently of any particular individual, including investigators themselves. By contrast, scientific constructivism argues that human kinds are dependent on human minds at all levels of explanation and analysis (Bourdieu 1989; I. Reed 2008, 2011; von Wright 1971). The categories that critical realists identify as social structures and mechanisms are no exception.

17. Indeed, our psychological orientations may have been shaped by natural selection to hide the truth, in order to promote adaptive behavior (Cosmides 1989; Hoffman, Singh, and Prakash 2015; Hoffman 2019).

18. Balkenius and Gärdenfors (2016) propose that conceptual spaces are grounded in and emerge naturally from underlying *neural spaces* in the brain. They suggest that "spatial coding is implicit in most neural mechanisms" (p. 4), and they see neural spaces and conceptual spaces as corresponding to two different levels of representation (symbols exist at a third level of representation). Their model does not assume that the mind is entirely a symbol-processing machine; human reasoning, they argue, involves something more than manipulating symbols (e.g., spatial and analogical reasoning), even though symbol manipulation is important to human reason (see Marcus 2001; O'Brien and Opie 2006; Berent and Marcus 2019).

19. For opposing views in this reductionism debate, compare Crane and Mellor (1990) to Churchland (1986).

20. Other scholars suggest that categories be represented as star-shaped sets, rather than convex sets (Hernández-Conde 2017; Bechberger and Kühnberger 2019).

21. For understanding the cognitive mechanisms that underpin consciousness, I benefited from Graziano's (2019) attention schema theory.

22. Some of these qualities may approximate natural kinds, in which case the entity in fact at least partially possesses the quality. The question of exactly which qualities of objects approximate natural kinds, as opposed to human kinds, has preoccupied philosophers for centuries. Locke (1690/1980) argued that color is a secondary quality (i.e., a human kind) created by the mind, whereas shape is a primary quality (i.e., a natural kind) that does not depend on the mind. For a thoughtful, more contemporary discussion, see McGinn (1983).

23. Image schemas cannot be fully reduced to either propositional subject-predicate structures or mental pictures and diagrams (Johnson 1987; Lakoff 1987; Mandler 2004; but see Vervaeke and Green 1997); they are preverbal and independent of language. However, in practice, researchers must use propositions and diagrams to describe image schemas. Cross-cultural diversity in the use of spatial-relations concepts (see Dodge and Lakoff 2005) suggests that the only universal image schemas may be the most general notions of space and location. For a useful summary of the "primitives" used to build image schemas, see Mandler and Pagán Cánovas (2014: 518).

24. A metaphor depends on some initial alignment across domains (Jackendoff 1983, 1992, 2002; Pinker 2007). However, the metaphor carries additional meaning that goes beyond this similarity (Gentner et al. 2001).

25. Rejecting logic vitiates all science, including any distinction between true and false (Holt 2018). Scholars who reject logic owe us an account of how communication is possible and why science works.

26. The containment image schema is more basic than all, or nearly all, other image schemas, perhaps emerging neurologically from the sense of touch during the prenatal period. Another basic schema is OBJECT, roughly understood as bounded matter (see Santibáñez 2002; Szwedek 2017). Interestingly, the obvious visual representation for an object is a set (i.e., a closed shape standing for the boundedness of matter). Objects and containers may imply and require each other. Evidence suggests that the primitive ideas MOTION and LOCATION IN SPACE are also among the first conceptual tools that infants use to make sense of the world (Mandler 2004; Mandler and Pagán Cánovas 2014).

27. If one wishes to occupy the "view from nowhere" (Nagel 1974, 1986)—i.e., a neutral, fully objective, and non-human-centric view of reality—one might begin by trying to think about the world in a way that does not depend on the containment and object image schemas.

28. As previously mentioned, the nature of the brain processing that leads to category representations is not well understood. The process may or may not be rule-governed in a way that can be expressed algorithmically, algebraically, or set-theoretically.

29. I distinguish between *continuous-set analysis* and *dichotomous-set analysis*; this distinction calls attention to the kind of measurement used with set-theoretic analysis. Another way of distinguishing the two approaches calls attention to the nature of set boundaries: *permeable-set analysis* versus *crisp-set analysis*. As labels, both *continuous* and *permeable* are preferable to *fuzzy*, which is a misleading adjective for describing both set-theoretic measurement and set-membership relationships.

30. Methods designed to study type-2 fuzzy sets are used in the analysis of differences in prototype proximity among two or more cases that are full members (or full non-members) of a category (see Zadeh 1972; Arfi 2010).

31. Simple diagrams cannot, of course, always be used to model set-theoretic operations; two-dimensional illustrations quickly run into problems with complex categories and associations. The relationship between logical reasoning, human thought, and diagrams has been studied for decades. For various entries into this literature, see Allwein and Barwise (1996), Baron (1969), Edwards (2004), and Shin, Lemon, and Mumma (2018). Software tools for interacting with multiple-set Euler and Venn diagrams are now updated at a dizzying pace.

Chapter 2: Foundations of Set-Theoretic Analysis

1. The set-theoretic approach assumes that all entities are sets; urelements do not exist as distinct non-set entities. This approach is thus vulnerable to Russell's paradox. That is, the approach leads us to assume a universal set that contains all sets, which generates a contradiction. I am aware that the universal set cannot itself be a set. I find efforts in mathematics to reclassify the

universal set as a "proper class" or "category of all sets" to be unsatisfactory. For my purposes here, I follow the solution of Zermelo-Fraenkel set theory and focus only on pure sets (i.e., hereditary sets), obviating the need to believe in or assume a universal set. Yet I do find the idea of a unique transcendental set to be intuitively—almost spiritually—appealing.

2. There is a Latin American story—at least I am telling it as a Latin American story—about a social scientist who, having been told that all experienced reality is constituted by spatial sets that are in turn constituted by spatial sets, asked (perhaps she was really a philosopher; it is the way they behave), what constitutes the spatial sets? More spatial sets. And those sets? Ah, *amiga*, after that it is spatial sets all the way down. (My apologies to Clifford Geertz [1973: 28–29].)

3. The prototypes of categories are the potentially idealized best examples of the category, rather than typical examples. For instance, a typical chair has full membership in the category *chair* but probably does not match the prototype of this category. In fact, a typical chair need not match the prototype of the category *typical chair*, though it probably does match the prototype of the category *this particular typical chair*.

4. The distinction between set membership and proximity to the prototype of a set helps make sense of compound categories such as *pet fish* (see Smith and Osherson 1984). Although a pet fish is a member of both *pet* and *fish*, the prototypical pet fish is not the prototypical member of either one of these sets.

5. A spatial set is the kind of entity that could be used to make progress on the hard problem of consciousness (Chalmers 2010: 25–27). Sets have both a phenomenal aspect and a physical aspect. Our conscious experience is one aspect of a set; the other aspect is embodied in the hardware of the human brain. Hence, sets seem promising for linking the material composition of our brains to the subjective experience of our consciousness. Obviously, the idea that sets are the "extra ingredient" needed to explain consciousness is speculative, to say the least.

6. When variables are treated as sets, the members of the set are the possible values that the variable can assume. For instance, if the variable *eye color* is treated as a set, the members of this set are the different possible kinds of eye colors (e.g., blue, brown, green). Likewise, if *level of democracy* is treated as a set, the members of the set are the different possible levels of democracy (e.g., high, intermediate, low). The point is worth making because it illustrates that variables themselves rely on a set-membership logic.

7. Set-theoretic analysts do study quantitatively the extent to which cases are members of sets. However, these quantitative values do not correspond to properties possessed by the cases; rather, they reflect membership relations among constructed categories. The relational analysis of constructed categories differs fundamentally from the study of relationships among properties possessed by cases (see Bourdieu 1989, 1990; Emirbayer 1997; Fuchs 2001).

8. According to mainstream contemporary cosmological physics, the actual world is a spherical region of space from which light has had time to reach us during the roughly 14 billion years since the Big Bang. Alternatively, from the perspective of quantum mechanics, the actual world is our location in Hilbert space (Tegmark 2014: chaps. 6–8).

9. Strictly speaking, the propositions are *world in which Osama bin Laden died in 2011* and *world in which Venezuela was wealthier than Colombia in the late nineteenth century*. For ease of presentation, I omit the words "world in which" from the category labels.

10. Because our current physical laws for large objects are different from our physical laws for particles, it is not clear that we know the fundamental laws of physics. The best candidates for these laws include string theory (Greene 2004, 2011) and quantum loop theory (Smolin 2001, 2006).

11. At the highest level of spatial aggregation, a possible world corresponds to an individual universe within infinite space. The total number of *unique* possible universes is finite (though still larger than a googolplex). The total number of *all* universes is infinite. The frequency at which a given universe appears can vary quite a bit (Tegmark 2014).

12. Modal realism is the view that possible worlds are real worlds, and it is elaborated and defended spiritedly in Lewis (1986a). Modal realism is consistent with a "many worlds" interpretation of quantum mechanics, which I regard as the most plausible understanding of subatomic processes currently on offer (see Becker 2018; Carroll 2019; DeWitt and Graham 1973). Physicists increasingly favor the many worlds interpretation over the Copenhagen interpretation (Tegmark 2014: 226–30). Modal realism is also consistent with the cosmological theory of quantum mechanics, external inflationary theory, string theory, and quantum loop theory. I mention these mainstream theories to reassure or remind readers that modal realism is not an extravagant viewpoint from the perspective of theoretical physics.

13. Classical possibilism assigns actual things and merely possible things a different ontological status. This ontological differentiation is built around a distinction between "being" and "existence" (see Linsky and Zalta 1991). By contrast, modal realism assigns actual things and possible things the same ontological status; it rejects the distinction between being and existence. With modal realism, the difference between the actual and the possible is only relational; it depends on the spatiotemporal world in which the speaker happens to be located. What is an actual world for a speaker located in one closed spatiotemporal domain is a non-actual possible world for a speaker located in a different closed spatiotemporal domain (and vice versa). Speakers privilege as the actual world the one in which they happen to reside (Lewis 1990).

14. The *totality of everything* consists of both a structured reality, which corresponds to all possible arrangements of all natural kinds (cf. Wittgenstein 1922/1972 on the idea of "substance"), and an unreality, which corresponds to all nonsense and meaninglessness. Possible worlds are a way of dividing up all of reality into distinct spatiotemporal domains; impossible worlds are a manner of speaking as if one could divide unreality into separate spatiotemporal domains.

15. In fact, when possible worlds are treated as real entities, one can plausibly derive the rules of modal logic from the rules of classical, first-order logic (Lewis 1986a, 1986b).

16. Part-whole relations, such as are illustrated in the hierarchy in figure 2.5, are the subject of the field of mereology, which has a complicated and unresolved relationship with set theory (Varzi 2016; see also Goodman 1951; Lewis 1973; Markman and Seibert 1976). A variety of part-whole relations exist, only some of which can be defined in an ontologically rigorous way (Keet and Artale 2008). In this book, I focus on ontologically rigorous part-whole relations that can be expressed set-theoretically. Consider, as an illustration, the canonical confounding example of hand-musician-orchestra. Normally, this example is understood as a non-transitive meronymic part-whole relationship. Thus, a musician is a part of an orchestra, and a hand is a part of a musician, but a hand is not a part of an orchestra (Odell 1998). From a set-theoretic perspective, however, the set *orchestra* is a subset of *entities with musicians*, which is a subset of *entities with hands*. It follows that *orchestra* is logically a subset of *entities with hands*.

17. With a part-whole (or mereological) approach, a case is a spatiotemporal part of a world with distinguishing substantive content (cf. Gerring 2017: 27; Seawright and Collier 2010: 315). See also Ragin (1992: 9).

18. Micro-oriented social science often focuses on individuals, a partial natural kind. As a result, micro-level social science research may be centrally concerned with both partial natural kinds and human kinds. Psychology is a good example of a field that straddles the line between the natural sciences and the social sciences in the categories it examines. Some work in demography also straddles this line.

19. With a part-whole approach, an actual case is defined as a constructed spatiotemporal part of the actual world.

20. With a part-whole approach, a non-actual case is defined as a constructed spatiotemporal part of a non-actual possible world.

21. The concept of set-membership observation is similar to the idea of *basic information* in Popper (1934/1968) and Hempel's (1980) terminology; *societal fact* in Mandelbaum's (1955) work; *evidence* in Bayesian analysis (see chapter 7; Williamson 2000); *within-case observation* and *causal-process observation* in qualitative methodology (Campbell 1975; Collier, Brady, and Seawright 2010); and *social fact* in Searle's (1995) constructivist philosophy.

22. I prefer the label *societal fact* (Mandelbaum 1955) to *fact* for describing set-membership observations. *Societal fact* suggests a dependence on the beliefs of the members of a society. Unlike objective facts (e.g., $2 + 2 = 4$), societal facts are true statements within particular societies.

23. Cascading belief disruption can occur if a proposition that is intrinsically justified to the highest degree is discovered to be false. This disruption can be a threat to the ontological security of self, which seeks stability in the categories and rules that compose experiential reality (Giddens 1984, 1991). Human beings are biased toward believing truths whose falsity would have these disruptive consequences. This point is worth making given that the argument of this book asks social scientists to let go of essentialist beliefs.

24. In this book, I do not explore the rhetorical strategies that analysts use to convince their audience that a finding is valid (see Collins 1981; Knorr Cetina 1999; Potter 1996; Pinch and Bijker 1989). These "fact-making practices" include appealing to direct sensory experience, scholarly and authoritative consensus, the reliability of a source of evidence, and common sense.

25. In the broadest sense, this book follows a *correspondence theory of truth*. With a correspondence theory, propositions are the potential truth members and facts are the truth makers. In the natural sciences, facts approximately describe aspects of objective reality. In the social sciences, however, facts consist of constructed categories that capture an interaction between the mind and objective reality. In the social sciences, truths correspond in part to the shared beliefs on which facts are ontologically dependent. The philosophical literature on correspondence theories of truth and their alternatives is vast in scope and depth (see Glanzberg 2018a, 2018b for accessible entries into this literature). For related work on *verisimilitude*, which strongly informs the discussion in this section, see Popper (1963, 1976) and the literature discussed in Oddie (1981) and Niiniluoto (1998).

Chapter 3: Set-Theoretic Methodology

1. When I refer to a *necessary condition*, I mean a condition that is necessary but not sufficient. When I refer to a *sufficient condition*, I mean a condition that is sufficient but not necessary.

2. I define *explanation* as the identification of a dependency relation between categories (cf. Kim 1974; Kitcher 1989). I use the word *explanation* for both constitutive and causal analysis (cf. Wendt 1998; I. Reed 2011). The categories in a constitutive explanation are not separated in time; the categories in a causal explanation are temporally separated. I realize that some social scientists prefer to reserve the word *explanation* for causal analysis only.

3. In this book, I use terminology such as "*X* is necessary for *Y*." A more precise formulation of this statement is "membership in *X* is necessary for membership in *Y*."

4. Within a set-theoretic framework, no other possibilities for set-membership relations exist beyond these five types, unless one considers conditions that are necessary and/or sufficient for INUS and SUIN conditions. In Mackie's (1980) formulation, combinations of conditions are analyzed in relation to an outcome; individual conditions are analyzed in terms of their relation to these combinations. An individual condition could be a necessary, sufficient, or necessary and sufficient component of the combination. Likewise, the combination itself could be necessary, sufficient, or necessary and sufficient for the outcome. We can thus code any individual condition first according to its logical status as a component of the combination, and second according to the logical status of the combination of which it is a part. This generates nine relationships, in which the first code is the factor's status for the combination and the second code is the combination's status

for the outcome: (1) necessary–necessary, (2) necessary–sufficient, (3) necessary–necessary and sufficient, (4) sufficient–necessary, (5) sufficient–sufficient, (6) sufficient–necessary and sufficient, (7) necessary and sufficient–necessary, (8) necessary and sufficient–sufficient, and (9) necessary and sufficient–necessary and sufficient. Of these nine, an INUS condition corresponds with type 2, while a SUIN condition corresponds with type 4. The other seven possibilities, however, can be reduced to individually necessary and/or sufficient conditions. Types 1, 3, and 7 are logically the same thing as a necessary condition. Types 5, 6, and 8 are logically the same thing as a sufficient condition. Type 9 is logically the same thing as a necessary and sufficient condition.

5. Although this book is concerned with token causality, the definition of causality proposed here can be used in the analysis of either token causality (also known as single-case or actual causality) or type causality (also known as general-case or property-level causality).

6. Most of these studies have a counterfactual understanding of causation as their starting point (e.g., Lewis 1973; Woodward 2003; Halpern and Pearl 2005; Halpern and Hitchcock 2010; Halpern 2016). An important work on token causality from a regularity perspective is Baumgartner (2013). In the social sciences, qualitative comparative analysis (QCA) is usually associated with type causality (see, e.g., Ragin 1987, 2000, 2008), but it can be linked to token causation (see Beach and Rohlfing forthcoming; Rihoux and Ragin 2009; Rohlfing 2012; Schneider and Rohlfing 2013, forthcoming; Schneider and Wagemann 2012). Other contemporary works on token causation include McDermott (2002), Menzies (2004), Glymour and Wimberly (2007), Wright (2011), and Paul and Hall (2013).

7. To explain the difficulty of making valid causal inferences in the social sciences, non-constructivist analysts suggest various other reasons as well. One reason concerns the presumed greater complexity of the social world compared to the natural world, including the need to study intentional agents who have free will. Another reason is that social science variables exhibit inherent probabilistic effects similar to those in quantum physics. I do not believe that these reasons are well founded in evidence (see Wegner 2018 on free will; and Waldner 2017 on quantum randomness).

8. Regularity models are often associated with Hume, though he arguably also endorsed a process/disposition view of causality for natural kinds. I follow Hume quite closely insofar as he favored a regularity model for human kinds and a causal power model for natural kinds. On the debate over whether Hume actually advocated a causal power model, compare Strawson (1989) and Psillos (2002).

9. The idea that two entities can make direct spatiotemporal contact raises the set of philosophical problems known as Zeno's paradoxes. For a fascinating discussion from the standpoint of physics, see Lange (2002).

10. A debate exists in the philosophical literature about whether solution sets must be fully minimized, or minimized in such a way as to achieve the best balance between simplicity and strength (see Psillos 2002: 147–54). A version of this debate also appears in the QCA literature (e.g., Thiem 2017; Schneider 2018).

11. Ideally, the solution set for a given outcome identifies *all* conditions and combinations of conditions that are sufficient for the outcome, such that if these conditions and combinations were aggregated into a single factor, this factor would be both necessary and sufficient for the outcome.

12. Defining a cause as a necessary and sufficient condition still may not solve all problems of causality that have been identified by philosophers. For an overview of these various problems, see Yablo (2004). As Menzies (2011: 186–87) points out, most of these problems are related to issues of preemption (see also Hall 2004; Paul and Hall 2013; Schaffer 2000; Woodward 2003).

13. These circumstances are sometimes called *scope conditions*. Scope conditions are one or more factors that must be present for a relationship to operate as theorized (see Walker and Cohen

1985; Goertz and Mahoney 2012: chap. 16). In the social sciences, scope conditions are closely related to the cognitive models that must be applicable for a relationship to operate as theorized.

14. If ideal types function like white holes, then trivial necessary conditions function like black holes, absorbing all cases as members.

15. INUS conditions are linked together as sufficiency combinations via the logical AND. For example, the individual conditions in the following equation are INUS conditions: $(A \& B)$ $\vee (C \& D) \rightarrow Y$. One calculates the value of a case in each sufficiency combination by using the minimum value of that case among the INUS conditions that make up the combination. One then takes the maximum value among the two combinations as the overall value for the case.

16. The data and categories are from Mahoney (2003).

17. In continuous-set analysis, the formula for calculating the "coverage," or "importance," of a necessary condition is mathematically identical to the formula used to calculate the extent to which the condition achieves sufficiency. In other words, the coverage of a necessary condition measures the extent to which the condition approximates a sufficient condition. Likewise, the coverage of a sufficient condition measures the extent to which the condition approximates a necessary condition. With a necessary condition, it is worth noting, one must also consider its "relevance," which is summarized in QCA with the relevance of necessity (RON) measure (Schneider and Wagemann 2012).

Chapter 4: Set-Theoretic Tests

1. These tests are set-theoretic versions of what qualitative methodologists call *process-tracing tests* (Van Evera 1997: 31–32; Bennett 2010: 208–11; Collier 2011). Set-theoretic tests repurpose process-tracing tests for set-theoretic analysis.

2. As discussed in chapter 2, the precise degree of certitude associated with set-membership observations and set-membership generalizations can also vary. The focus in this chapter is on the uncertainty introduced by the use of non-deterministic generalizations (e.g., nearly all Xs are Ys).

3. This set-theoretic test follows the logic of contraposition. One can also carry out a sufficiency test by asking whether the case is a member of any category—or combination of categories—that is known to be *sufficient* for membership in the target category. If so, the case is a member of the target category.

4. Philosophers sometimes note that present traces overdetermine the existence of a past event, by which they mean that several present-day traces are each individually sufficient to infer the existence of a past event (Lewis 1986b; Cleland 2002). The present overdetermines the past. This feature of the direction of time explains why we are much better at predicting and explaining the past than the future.

5. If X is necessary for Y, it must also be necessary for all intervening mechanisms that are sufficient for Y, including combinations of conditions that are sufficient for Y. Logically speaking, X cannot be necessary for Y unless it is necessary for all intervening conditions that are sufficient for Y.

6. One can always question the generalizations used with set-theoretic tests, including the extent to which they approximate the deterministic ideals of full necessity or full sufficiency. The strength/validity of a set-theoretic test depends on the strength/validity of the generalization used with the test.

7. Some methodologists believe that case-study and small-N research is primarily an inductive mode of analysis whose utility resides with theory generation. These analysts may believe that small-N research is a weak mode for assessing the validity of theories because of an insufficient number of cases to carry out statistical tests (Campbell 1975; Lijphart 1971; Goldthorpe 1997; Fearon and Laitin 2008; cf. Gerring 2017).

8. The empirically inductive nature of case-study and small-N research might be seen as contrasting with quantitative research, in which investigators are sometimes encouraged to design a statistical model before analyzing data. In practice, though, various refinements to statistical models in light of the data routinely occur in quantitative research (Collier, Brady, and Seawright 2010: 171–72). In addition, case-study and small-N researchers draw on different set-membership observations when formulating propositions versus testing propositions (Rueschemeyer 2003). Under Bayesian assumptions, the timing of the discovery of evidence makes no difference for the strength of an inference.

Chapter 5: Counterfactual Analysis

1. However, one can estimate the extent to which X is sufficient for Y by counterfactually altering contingent aspects of context.

2. This ceteris paribus clause may not be possible in practice (as noted above for a sufficient condition counterfactual).

3. By contrast, with sufficient condition counterfactuals, the counterfactual causal chain is connected via *necessity* links. One can think about this relationship in the following way: (1) to assert that X is necessary for Y is also to assert that $\sim X$ is sufficient for $\sim Y$; and (2) to assert that X is sufficient for Y is also to assert that $\sim X$ is necessary for $\sim Y$. Some of the philosophical implications of this relationship come up in Lewis's (1979) discussion of the arrow of time.

4. Critics may seek out "weak links" in a causal chain, but counterfactual arguments do not necessarily collapse if one link is found to be faulty. The analyst must repair the link and redesign the counterfactual chain, but the new steps may lead to membership in the same outcome.

Chapter 6: Sequence Analysis

1. Let us assume that this initial relationship was discovered and evaluated using set-theoretic tests and counterfactual analysis (see chapters 4 and 5).

2. Likewise, a complete combination of SUIN causes can be treated as a necessary cause.

3. Since Lib-Lab alliances required the broad context of Europe, this factor is, strictly speaking, an INUS cause.

4. This cause requires the context of Europe to operate and is bound to that scope.

Chapter 7: Bayesian Analysis

1. For a good review of the literature on this argument, see Van Horn (2003).

2. To embrace Bayesian analysis, and science more generally, is a normative commitment (see Sher 2013). Among other things, the endorsement of Bayesian analysis involves an advocacy for true and justified belief.

3. Because the distribution of possible worlds is used to derive probabilities, a probability, or likelihood, is not attached to any individual possible world. The distribution of possible worlds explains probabilities rather than the other way around (cf. Childers 2013: chap. 5). Insofar as a particular possible world seems much more likely than another, it is because that possible world has many near duplicates (or is easily duplicated), such that its associated group greatly outnumbers the other world and its associated group (see also chapter 10).

4. On the methodological issues that multiple rival hypotheses raise for Bayesian analysis in general, compare Fairfield and Charman (forthcoming) with Zaks (2017).

5. The partial membership of one set (e.g., H) in another set (e.g., k) is the focus of continuous-set analysis (see, e.g., Zadeh 1965). However, Bayesian analysis is built on dichotomous sets: each

possible world has either full membership or no membership in a given set. For example, each possible world is a member of either set H or set $\sim H$. The dichotomous orientation of Bayesian analysis results from the assumption that a hypothesis is either true or false, and hence must be either true or false in all possible worlds. If one were to relax this assumption, allowing hypotheses to be partly true and partly false, then continuous-set analysis would be an appropriate method-ological choice. However, the use of partial membership functions and continuous-set analysis would require a basic reworking of Bayes' theorem that I do not undertake in this book. See also Van Horn (2003: 4–5).

6. These estimates of the likelihood of finding this evidence (the iridium in the earth's crust) if the proposition is true and if the proposition is false may be too conservative. Fairfield and Char-man (2017, forthcoming) advocate using a logarithmic (nonlinear) scale for assigning probabilities, an approach that allows evidence to more dramatically shift prior beliefs.

7. It bears noting that consequentialness is different from the likelihood ratio used in standard Bayesian analysis. The set-theoretic formula that generates the likelihood ratio is $H \& k \, / \sim H \& k$.

8. Evidence k and evidence $\sim k$ must be formulated as mutually exclusive set-membership observations that can be independently discovered. The failure to observe evidence k is not equivalent to the observation of $\sim k$. (On missing evidence, see Gonzalez-Ocantos and LaPorte forthcoming.)

9. Expectedness is the denominator of the set-theoretic expression of Bayes' theorem.

10. "Scholars have looked long and hard for evidence of alternatives to retrenchment . . . If any researcher has the motive and background to uncover significant evidence of this kind, it is Robert English. Yet he did not do so" (Brooks and Wohlforth 2007a: 273).

11. "When new evidence suggests new theories, a non-Bayesian shift in the belief function may take place" (Earman 1992: 100). See Bennett (2008: 714) for a discussion of the areas in which Bayesian analysis is not compatible with belief updating. In this book, I treat theory development as the expansion of possible worlds that were not previously conceived. Thus, whereas the dis-covery of new evidence can *reduce* the range of possible worlds, the creation of new theory can *expand* the range of possible worlds.

Chapter 8: Theory Frames and Normative Traditions

1. To be sure, no single definition of *theory* is shared by all (Sayer 2000: chap. 2; Abend 2008). I use the following definition, which I regard as conventional: a theory is a set of related categories and propositions that are used in the explanation of phenomena (Swedberg 2017: 14; cf. Merton 1945; Stinchcombe 1968; Camic and Gross 1998).

2. A cognitive model overlaps closely with what Schank and Abelson (1977: 41) call a *script*: "A script is made up of slots and requirements about what can fill those slots. The structure is an interconnected whole, and what is in one slot affects what can be in another. Scripts handle stylized everyday situations."

3. A child's understandings of distinct emotions come much later (at, e.g., age four to five). See Mandler and Pagán Cánovas (2014) and Barrett (2017).

4. In this chapter, I do not consider the role of objects in social science theory frames. How-ever, it is worth noting that a geographic theory frame places non-animate objects front and center in its imagery. With a geographic frame, features of the "natural" landscape and environment sound the dominant note. Because these features are often partial natural kinds, a geographic theory frame engages, and falls partly into, the natural sciences.

5. The normative traditions considered in this section do not cover the full range of moral frameworks in the social sciences. Notably, the discussion does not consider any normative tradi-tion in which non-sentient objects are the center of attention. An object-centered theory frame

can be connected to *environmental ethics*, which rejects the anthropocentrism found in most other orientations and focuses on the intrinsic value of non-human entities (Brennan 2014). Environmental ethics falls at the intersection of the social sciences and the natural sciences. Likewise, the discussion does not consider any normative tradition in which living entities other than humans and animals, such as trees or microbes, are assigned substantial normative weight. *Multispecies ethnography* embraces a normative program that focuses on the fates of a host of other organisms besides human beings (Kirksey and Helmreich 2010).

6. Although scholars have not devoted much attention to the different normative orientations that animate substantive research in the social sciences, they have considered at great length the appropriate role of morals in social science more generally. For some classic statements from different disciplines, see D'Andrade (1995), Gouldner (1962), Hirschman (2013), Scheper-Hughes (1995), Taylor (1985), and Weber (1949). In addition, the whole subfield of political theory within political science is explicitly concerned with normative issues.

7. Although this summary slogan ("the greatest good for the greatest number") is common, it is actually somewhat misleading. An action that maximizes the greatest good for the greatest number does not necessarily maximize the *net* good for the group in question and thus does not, strictly speaking, follow the principle of utility. On the history of utilitarianism, including this slogan, see Driver (2014).

8. *Categorical groups* are collections of individuals who occupy similar positions within social structures and who consciously or unconsciously share a social identity (Tilly 1998: 6).

9. Set-theoretic work from an intersectional perspective also now exists (Ragin and Fiss 2017).

10. Closely related to the capability orientation is a *relational-equality orientation*, which proposes that resources should be distributed to allow all individuals to relate to one another as equals, enjoying the same status and effective power (Anderson 1999; Walzer 1983; cf. Marx 1972). This orientation sees the good society as one in which all citizens have the capacity to function as dignified people in all human interactions, as full participants in civil society, as valuable workers in a cooperative economic system, and as coequal members of a democratic state—conditions that define a society with *truly equal citizenship*.

Chapter 9: Categories for Constructing Theories and Explanations

1. Structured wholes can be analyzed as sets because the idea of a *whole* presupposes the notion of a *set*. However, the extent to which part-whole relations can be analyzed set-theoretically is still an unresolved issue (Koslicki 2008: chap. 8; see also Markman and Seibert 1976).

2. *Non-actual events* include only non-actual cases as members. *Impossible events* include only impossible cases as members. Mereologically speaking, impossible events are parts of impossible cases, which are parts of impossible worlds.

3. These relationships can be formulated entirely in set-theoretic terms. For example, the actual case of China is a member of the observation *Nanchang Uprising*, which is a subset of *peasant uprising*, which is a superset of *peasant revolution*, which is a cause of *social revolution* in France, Russia, and China.

4. In this book, I follow the constructivist literature and refer to "shared beliefs" to describe the brain encodings (i.e., conceptual spaces) on which human kinds depend for their existence (see chapter 1).

5. An alternative view holds that social rules are not encoded in human brains, even though social rules predict and describe behavior. On this view, human beings do not unconsciously enact rules, because the brain does not function like a rule-processing machine in the first place (Searle 1995: chap. 6; Turner 2002). Social rules only *indirectly* explain the content of human

behavior. In particular, they affect behavior by promoting the development of certain kinds of dispositions, habits, and abilities, and this *habitus* separately causes individuals to behave in a way that is consistent with social rules (cf. Bourdieu 1977, 1989, 1990; Wittgenstein 1953/2001).

6. At present, scientists do not even agree on whether brains carry out rule-guided procedures that can be modeled using algebraic language (see Berent and Marcus 2019).

7. The *complexity* of the social rules that govern a situation, group, or society can vary. One way to measure the degree of complexity of a rule is by the length of the shortest possible algorithm in a system of logic that specifies the rule (cf. Kolmogorov complexity; see Li and Vitányi 1997). Rules that are more complex require longer algorithms. By this standard, the overall complexity of a society is defined as the total length of all of the algorithms that specify its social rules (or perhaps its dominant social rules). Insofar as we believe that societies generally have become more complex over time, we perhaps do so because we believe societal rules have become more complex. A rough indicator of the complexity of a situation is the amount of time required to explain the norms of the situation to someone who is unfamiliar with them: it usually takes longer to explain the norms of more complex situations.

8. The relationship between interpretation and scientific explanation has been debated for decades (e.g., Abel 1948, 1975; Wax 1967). In contemporary social science, one part of the debate focuses on the extent to which interpretive analysis is consistent with modern causal identification approaches (Lawler and Waldner forthcoming). Another part of the debate is concerned with the scientific question of whether people follow rules at all (e.g., Turner 2002). Beyond these concerns, scholars continue to discuss the political implications of interpretive analysis (e.g., Fay 1975; Jackson 2020).

9. Again, this intentional model of human psychology may prove irrelevant to scientific models of cognition at some point in the future (Stich 1983). The argument of this book is not that human beings literally are intentional agents propelled by their beliefs and desires. The question of whether the psychological properties of individuals, such as their beliefs and desires, are partial natural kinds is much debated (see chapter 1).

10. To be sure, some capabilities are exercised unconsciously and involuntarily. Sometimes we cannot help exercising our abilities. For example, if someone unexpectedly shouts a command at you in a language you understand, you have no choice but to understand the meaning of that command.

11. Under this definition, the category *power* applies to actors and not social rules; social rules cannot be members of the category *powerful actor* (cf. Foucault 1982; Isaac 1987a, 1987b). Instead, social rules can be members of *influential and consequential entities*, and they can shape whether particular actors are members of *powerful actor* (see Hacking 1981).

12. This distinction between events and processes has interesting parallels to the distinction between particles and fields in the natural sciences. Particles are point-like entities located at specific times and places; fields are diffuse entities located across space and time (cf. Carroll 2019: 44). In the social sciences, by contrast, the category *field* is often used to describe a social order, a context, or a set of background conditions (e.g., Bourdieu 1984; Martin 2003; Fligstein and McAdam 2012).

Chapter 10: Critical Event Analysis

1. The sufficiency effects of a particular event are understood to generate a *distinctive process* that culminates in the outcome of interest. The appeal to a distinctive process is important because it helps the analyst address issues of overdetermination, when two or more events are each sufficient for the outcome. While two sufficient events will yield the same outcome, they will do so via different causal chains, through empirically distinct paths. For instance, in the well-known

firing squad example of overdetermination (e.g., Schaffer 2003), the spatial pathway of each bullet is distinct, allowing one to distinguish and assess each individually sufficient cause.

2. An event may also exert sufficiency effects on an outcome by blocking other productive causes, thereby lessening the extent to which the outcome is overdetermined. The capacity to block other productive forces is important for distinguishing the relative importance of two or more individually sufficient conditions. The most important sufficient conditions are those that exert effects such that they do not allow other sufficient conditions to operate, ensuring that they are the exclusive factors that produce outcomes. For instance, a member of a firing squad who kills all other members of the squad just before killing the victim would play a more important causal role in the victim's death than if he had allowed the other members to simultaneously kill the victim.

3. As previously mentioned, a case that is at least moderately weighted represents a large group of cases with trivial differences. Among this group, a certain proportion of cases may be consistent and a certain proportion inconsistent.

4. The categories of substantive importance and substantive relevance are derived from the measures of, respectively, consistency and coverage in the QCA literature (e.g., Ragin 2008; Schneider and Wagemann 2012).

Chapter 11: Path Dependence Analysis

1. Nevertheless, early-warning signals may precede the start of the critical event that launches the path-dependent sequence (cf. Scheffer et al. 2009).

2. More generally, with path dependence, "the order of events makes a difference" (Abbott 1983: 129); "*when* things happen within a sequence affects *how* they happen" (Tilly 1984: 14, his emphasis).

3. The concept of *legitimacy* is often divided into different kinds. The most famous example is surely Max Weber's (1978) three ideal types of legitimacy—charismatic, traditional, and rational-legal.

4. Goldstone's analysis does not explore the causal processes underpinning the reproduction of England's liberal culture. In the figure, therefore, the size of the repeating sets for event *J* is arbitrary relative to the size of the other sets in the diagram.

REFERENCES

Abbott, Andrew. 1983. "Sequences of Social Events: Concepts and Methods for the Analysis of Order in Social Processes." *Historical Methods* 16: 129–47.

———. 1992. "From Causes to Events: Notes on Narrative Positivism." *Sociological Methods and Research* 20: 428–55.

———. 2001. *Time Matters: On Theory and Method.* Chicago: University of Chicago Press.

———. 2016. *Processual Sociology.* Chicago: University of Chicago Press.

Abel, Theodore. 1948. "The Operation Called Verstehen." *American Journal of Sociology* 54: 211–18.

———. 1975. "Verstehen I and Verstehen II." *Theory and Decision* 6: 99–102.

Abell, Peter. 2009. "A Case for Cases: Comparative Narratives in Sociological Research." *Sociological Methods and Research* 38: 38–70.

Abend, Gabriel. 2008. "Two Main Problems in the Sociology of Morality." *Theory and Society* 37: 87–125.

———. Forthcoming. "Making Things Possible." *Sociological Methods and Research.*

Abu-Lughod, Lila. 1993. *Writing Women's Worlds: Bedouin Stories.* Berkeley: University of California Press.

Acemoglu, Daron, and James Robinson. 2008. "Persistence of Power, Elites, and Institutions." *American Economic Review* 98: 267–93.

Acker, Joan. 2006. "Inequality Regimes: Gender, Class, and Race in Organizations." *Gender and Society* 20: 441–64.

Ahn, Woo-kyoung, Charles W. Kalish, Susan A. Gelman, Douglas L. Medin, Christian Luhmann, Scott Atran, John D. Coley, and Patrick Shafto. 2001. "Why Essences Are Essential in the Psychology of Concepts." *Cognition* 82: 59–69.

Ahn, Woo-kyoung, Charles W. Kalish, Douglas L. Medin, and Susan A. Gelman. 1995. "The Role of Covariation versus Mechanism Information in Causal Attribution." *Cognition* 54: 299–352.

Allwein, Gerard, and Jon Barwise, eds. 1996. *Logical Reasoning with Diagrams.* New York: Oxford University Press.

Aminzade, Ronald. 1992. "Historical Sociology and Time." *Sociological Methods and Research* 20: 456–80.

Anderson, Elizabeth S. 1999. "What Is the Point of Equality?" *Ethics* 109: 287–337.

Anscombe, G. E. M. 1958. "On Brute Facts." *Analysis* 18: 69–72.

———. 1971. *Causality and Determination.* Cambridge: Cambridge University Press.

Arabatzis, Theodore. 2006. *Representing Electrons: A Biographical Approach to Theoretical Entities.* Chicago: University of Chicago Press.

Archer, Margaret S. 1995. *Realist Social Theory: The Morphogenetic Approach.* Cambridge: Cambridge University Press.

Arfi, Badredine. 2010. *Linguistic Fuzzy Set Methods in Social Sciences.* Berlin: Springer.

Armstrong, David M. 1983. *What Is a Law of Nature?* Cambridge: Cambridge University Press.

———. 1989. *Universals: An Opinionated Introduction.* Boulder, CO: Westview Press.

———. 1997. *A World of States of Affairs.* Cambridge: Cambridge University Press.

Aronowitz, Robert A. 1991. "Lyme Disease: The Social Construction of a New Disease and Its Social Consequences." *Milbank Quarterly* 69: 79–112.

Aronson, Jerrold L. 1990. "Verisimilitude and Type Hierarchies." *Philosophical Topics* 18: 5–28.

Arrow, Kenneth J. 1983. *Collected Papers of Kenneth J. Arrow: General Equilibrium*. Cambridge, MA: Harvard University Press.

Arthur, W. Brian. 1994. *Increasing Returns and Path Dependence in the Economy*. Ann Arbor: University of Michigan Press.

Atran, Scott. 1998. "Folk Biology and the Anthropology of Science: Cognitive Universals and Cultural Particulars." *Behavioral and Brain Sciences* 21: 547–609.

Atran, Scott, and Douglas Medin. 2008. *The Native Mind and the Cultural Construction of Nature*. Cambridge, MA: MIT Press.

Axelrod, Robert. 1984. *The Evolution of Cooperation*. New York: Basic Books.

Ayer, Alfred Jules. 1952. *Language, Truth and Logic*. New York: Dover.

Ayers, Michael R. 1981. "Locke versus Aristotle on Natural Kinds." *Journal of Philosophy* 78: 247–72.

Bagaria, Joan. 2019. "Set Theory." *Stanford Encyclopedia of Philosophy*, Fall edition.

Balaguer, Mark. 1998. *Platonism and Anti-Platonism in Mathematics*. Oxford: Oxford University Press.

Balkenius, Christian, and Peter Gärdenfors. 2016. "Spaces in the Brain: From Neurons to Meanings." *Frontiers in Psychology* 7: 1–12.

Ball, Terrence. 1993. "Power." Pp. 548–57 in *A Companion to Contemporary Political Philosophy*, edited by Robert E. Goodin and Philip Pettit. Oxford: Blackwell.

Barbier, Jacques A. 1980. *Reform and Politics in Bourbon Chile, 1755–1796*. Ottawa: University of Ottawa Press.

Barnes, Barry. 1974. *Scientific Knowledge and Sociological Theory*. London: Routledge.

Barnett, Michael, and Raymond Duvall. 2005. "Power in Global Governance." Pp. 1–32 in *Power in Global Governance*, edited by Michael Barnett and Raymond Duvall. Cambridge: Cambridge University Press.

Baron, Margaret E. 1969. "A Note on the Historical Development of Logic Diagrams: Leibniz, Euler and Venn." *Mathematical Gazette* 53: 113–25.

Barrenechea, Rodrigo, and Isabel Castillo. 2019. "The Many Roads to Rome: Family Resemblance Concepts in the Social Sciences." *Quality and Quantity* 53: 107–30.

Barrett, Lisa Feldman. 2006. "Are Emotions Natural Kinds?" *Perspectives on Psychological Science* 1: 28–58.

———. 2017. *How Emotions Are Made: The Secret Life of the Brain*. Boston: Houghton Mifflin Harcourt.

Barsalou, Lawrence W. 1983. "Ad Hoc Categories." *Memory and Cognition* 11: 211–27.

———. 1999. "Perceptual Symbol Systems" (with comments). *Behavioral and Brain Sciences* 22: 577–660.

———. 2004. "Abstraction as a Dynamic Construal in Perceptual Symbol Systems." Pp. 389–431 in *Building Object Categories*, edited by L. Gershkoff-Stowe and D. Rakison. Mahwah, NJ: Lawrence Erlbaum.

———. 2016. "Situated Conceptualization: Theory and Application." Pp. 11–37 in *Foundations of Embodied Cognition: Perceptual and Emotional Embodiment*, edited by Yann Coelle and Martin H. Fisher. London: Routledge.

Bartha, Paul. 2019. "Analogy and Analogical Reasoning." *Stanford Encyclopedia of Philosophy*, Spring edition.

Bates, Robert. 1981. *States and Markets in Tropical Africa: The Political Basis of Agricultural Policies*. Berkeley: University of California Press.

Baumgartner, Michael. 2008. "Regularity Theories Reassessed." *Philosophia* 36: 327–54.

———. 2013. "A Regularity Theoretic Approach to Actual Causation." *Erkenntnis* 78: 85–109.

Beach, Derek, and Rasmus Brun Pedersen. 2013. *Process-Tracing Methods: Foundations and Guidelines*. Ann Arbor: University of Michigan.

Beach, Derek, and Ingo Rohlfing. Forthcoming. "Integrating Cross-Case Analyses and Process Tracing in Set-Theoretic Research: Strategies and Parameters of Debate." *Sociological Methods and Research*.

Bechberger, Lucas, and Kai-Uwe Kühnberger. 2019. "Formalized Conceptual Spaces with a Geometric Representation of Correlations." Pp. 29–58 in *Conceptual Spaces: Elaborations and Applications*, edited by Mauri Kaipainen, Frank Zenker, Antti Hautamäki, and Peter Gärdenfors. Cham, Switzerland: Springer.

Becker, Adam. 2018. *What Is Real? The Unfinished Quest for the Meaning of Quantum Physics*. New York: Basic Books.

Becker, Howard. 1953. "Becoming a Marihuana User." *American Journal of Sociology* 59: 235–42.

Beebee, Helen, Christopher Hitchcock, and Peter Menzies, eds. 2009. *The Oxford Handbook of Causation*. Oxford: Oxford University Press.

Bennett, Andrew. 2008. "Process Tracing: A Bayesian Perspective." Pp. 702–21 in Box-Steffensmeier, Brady, and Collier, *Oxford Handbook of Political Methodology*.

———. 2010. "Process Tracing and Causal Inference." Pp. 207–36 in Brady and Collier, *Rethinking Social Inquiry*.

———. 2015. "Appendix: Disciplining Our Conjectures: Systematizing Process Tracing with Bayesian Analysis." Pp. 276–98 in Bennett and Checkel, *Process Tracing*.

Bennett, Andrew, and Jeffrey T. Checkel, eds. 2015. *Process Tracing: From Metaphor to Analytic Tool*. Cambridge: Cambridge University Press.

Bentham, Jeremy. 1789/1907. *An Introduction to the Principles of Morals and Legislation*. Oxford: Clarendon Press.

Benton, T. 1981. "'Objective' Interests and the Sociology of Power." *Sociology* 15: 161–84.

Berent, Iris, and Gary Marcus. 2019. "No Integration without Structured Representations: Response to Pater." *Language* 95: e75–e86.

Berger, Peter L., and Thomas Luckmann. 1966. *The Social Construction of Reality: A Treatise in the Sociology of Knowledge*. New York: Doubleday.

Berman, Sheri. 1998. "Path Dependency and Political Action: Reexamining Responses to the Depression." *Comparative Politics* 30: 379–400.

Bernhard, Michael. 2015. "Chronic Instability and the Limits of Path Dependence." *Perspectives on Politics* 13: 976–91.

Bevir, Mark, and Jason Blakely. 2018. *Interpretive Social Science: An Anti-Naturalist Approach*. Oxford: Oxford University Press.

Bhaskar, Roy. 1975. *A Realist Theory of Science*. Leeds, UK: Leeds Books.

———. 1979/1998. *The Possibility of Naturalism: A Philosophical Critique of the Contemporary Human Sciences*. 3rd ed. London: Routledge.

Blalock, Hubert M. 1982. *Conceptualization and Measurement in the Social Sciences*. Beverly Hills, CA: Sage.

Block, Fred, and Margaret R. Somers. 2014. *The Power of Market Fundamentalism: Karl Polanyi's Critique*. Cambridge, MA: Harvard University Press.

Bloom, Paul. 1996. "Intention, History, and Artifact Concepts." *Cognition* 60: 1–29.

———. 1998. "Theories of Artifact Categorization." *Cognition* 66: 87–93.

———. 2000. *How Children Learn the Meanings of Words*. Cambridge, MA: MIT Press.

———. 2010. *How Pleasure Works: The New Science of Why We Like What We Like*. New York: Random House.

Bollen, Kenneth A. 2002. "Latent Variables in Psychology and the Social Sciences." *Annual Review of Psychology* 53: 605–34.

Bonilla-Silva, Eduardo. 1997. "Rethinking Racism: Toward a Structural Interpretation." *American Sociological Review* 62: 465–80.

———. 2006. *Racism without Racists: Color-Blind Racism and the Persistence of Racial Inequality in the United States*. Lanham, MD: Rowman and Littlefield.

Bostrom, Nick. 2003. "Are We Living in a Computer Simulation?" *Philosophical Quarterly* 53: 243–55.

Boudon, Raymond. 1986. *Theories of Social Change: A Critical Appraisal*. Berkeley: University of California Press.

Bourdieu, Pierre. 1977. *Outline of a Theory of Practice*. Cambridge: Cambridge University Press.

———. 1984. *Distinction: A Social Critique of the Judgment of Taste*. Cambridge, MA: Harvard University Press.

———. 1989. "Social Space and Symbolic Power." *Sociological Theory* 7: 14–25.

———. 1990. *The Logic of Practice*. Stanford, CA: Stanford University Press.

———. 1991. *Language and Symbolic Power*. Malden, MA: Polity Press.

Bourgois, Philippe. 2003. *In Search of Respect: Selling Crack in El Barrio*. 2nd ed. Cambridge: Cambridge University Press.

Bowman, Kirk, Fabrice Lehoucq, and James Mahoney. 2005. "Measuring Political Democracy: Case Expertise, Data Adequacy, and Central America." *Comparative Political Studies* 38: 939–70.

Box-Steffensmeier, Janet M., Henry E. Brady, and David Collier, eds. 2008. *The Oxford Handbook of Political Methodology*. Oxford: Oxford University Press.

Boyd, Richard. 1990. "Realism, Approximate Truth, and Philosophical Method." Pp. 355–91 in *Scientific Theories*, edited by C. Wade Savage. Minneapolis: University of Minnesota Press.

———. 1991. "Realism, Anti-Foundationalism and the Enthusiasm for Natural Kinds." *Philosophical Studies* 61: 127–48.

———. 2010. "Homeostasis, Higher Taxa, and Monophyly." *Philosophy of Science* 77: 686–701.

Bradley, Francis H. 1897. *Appearance and Reality*. Oxford: Clarendon Press.

Bradley, Raymond, and Norman Swartz. 1979. *Possible Worlds: An Introduction to Logic and Its Philosophy*. Indianapolis, IN: Hackett.

Brady, Henry E., and David Collier, eds. 2010. *Rethinking Social Inquiry: Diverse Tools, Shared Standards*. 2nd ed. Lanham, MD: Rowman and Littlefield.

Braudel, Fernand. 1980. *On History*. Chicago: University of Chicago Press.

Braumoeller, Bear F., and Gary Goertz. 2000. "The Methodology of Necessary Conditions." *American Journal of Political Science* 44: 844–58.

———. 2002. "Watching Your Posterior." *Political Analysis* 10: 198–203.

Brennan, Andrew. 2014. *Thinking about Nature: An Investigation of Nature, Value, and Ecology*. London: Routledge.

Brenner, Robert. 1976. "Agrarian Class Structure and Economic Development in Pre-industrial Europe." *Past and Present* 70: 30–75.

Briggs, Charles L., and Clara Mantini-Briggs. 2003. *Stories in the Time of Cholera: Racial Profiling during a Medical Emergency*. Berkeley: University of California Press.

Brooks, Clem, and Jeff Manza. 2007. *Why Welfare States Persist: The Importance of Public Opinion in Democracies*. Chicago: University of Chicago Press.

Brooks, Stephen G., and William C. Wohlforth. 2007a. "New versus Old Thinking in Qualitative Research." Pp. 261–80 in Goertz and Levy, *Explaining War and Peace*.

———. 2007b. "Power, Globalization, and the End of the Cold War: Reevaluating a Landmark Case for Ideas." Pp. 195–236 in Goertz and Levy, *Explaining War and Peace*.

Brown, Phil. 1995. "Naming and Framing: The Social Construction of Diagnosis and Illness." *Journal of Health and Social Behavior*, extra issue, 34–52.

Brown, Roger. 1958. "How Shall a Thing Be Called?" *Psychological Review* 65: 14–21.

———. 1965. *Social Psychology*. New York: Free Press.

Browning, Douglas. 1978. "Presidential Address: Believing in Natural Kinds." *Southwestern Journal of Philosophy* 9 (1): 135–48.

Brubaker, Rogers, Mara Loveman, and Peter Stamatov. 2004. "Ethnicity as Cognition." *Theory and Society* 33: 31–64.

Buchanan, James M. 1975. *The Limits of Liberty: Between Anarchy and Leviathan*. Chicago: University of Chicago Press.

Bunge, Mario. 1959. *Causality: The Place of Causal Principle in Modern Science*. Cambridge, MA: Harvard University Press.

———. 1997. "Mechanisms and Explanation." *Philosophy of the Social Sciences* 27: 410–65.

Burawoy, Michael. 1982. *Manufacturing Consent: Changes in the Labor Process under Monopoly Capitalism*. Chicago: University of Chicago Press.

———. 1985. *The Politics of Production: Factory Regimes under Capitalism and Socialism*. London: Verso.

Butler, Judith. 1990. *Gender Trouble: Feminism and the Subversion of Identity*. London: Routledge.

Caduff, Carlo. 2011. "Anthropology's Ethics: Moral Positionalism, Cultural Relativism, and Critical Analysis." *Anthropological Theory* 11: 465–80.

Camic, Charles. 1979. "The Utilitarians Revisited." *American Journal of Sociology* 85: 516–50.

Camic, Charles, and Neil Gross. 1998. "Contemporary Developments in Sociological Theory: Current Projects and Conditions of Possibility." *Annual Review of Sociology* 24: 453–76.

Campbell, Donald T. 1958. "Common Fate, Similarity, and Other Indices of the Status of Aggregates of Persons as Social Entities." *Behavioral Science* 3: 14–25.

———. 1975. "'Degrees of Freedom' and the Case Study." *Comparative Political Studies* 8: 178–93.

Campbell, Donald T., and Julian C. Stanley. 1963. *Experimental and Quasi-Experimental Designs for Research*. Chicago: Rand McNally.

Campbell, Mildred. 1942. *The English Yeoman under Elizabeth and the Early Stuarts*. New Haven, CT: Yale University Press.

Campbell, N. R. 1920. *Physics: The Elements*. New York: Cambridge University Press.

Cantor, Georg. 1915. *Contributions to the Founding of the Theory of Transfinite Numbers*. Translated by Philip E. B. Jourdain. Chicago: Open Court.

Capoccia, Giovanni. 2015. "Critical Junctures and Institutional Change." Pp. 147–79 in Mahoney and Thelen, *Advances in Comparative-Historical Analysis*.

Capoccia, Giovanni, and R. D. Keleman. 2007. "The Study of Critical Junctures: Theory, Narrative, and Counterfactuals in Institutional Analysis." *World Politics* 59: 341–69.

Carey, Susan. 2009. *The Origin of Concepts*. Oxford: Oxford University Press.

Carroll, John W. 1991. "Property-Level Causation?" *Philosophical Studies* 63: 245–70.

———. 2009. "Anti-Reductionism." Pp. 279–98 in Beebee, Hitchcock, and Menzies, *Oxford Handbook of Causation*.

Carroll, Sean. 2017. "Why Boltzmann Brains Are Bad." Manuscript, Walter Burke Institute for Theoretical Physics, California Institute of Technology, Pasadena, CA, February 6.

———. 2019. *Something Deeply Hidden: Quantum Worlds and the Emergence of Spacetime*. New York: Penguin.

Cartwright, Nancy. 1989. *Nature's Capacities and Their Measurement*. Oxford: Clarendon.

———. 2004. "Causation: One Word, Many Things." *Philosophy of Science* 71: 805–19.

Casasanto, Daniel. 2010. "Space for Thinking." Pp. 453–78 in *Cognition and Space: The State of the Art and New Directions*, edited by Vyvyan Evans and Paul Chilton. London: Equinox.

Casati, Roberto, and Achille C. Varzi. 1999. *Parts and Places: The Structures of Spatial Representation*. Cambridge, MA: MIT Press.

Casati, Roberto, and Achille C. Varzi. 2015. "Events." *The Stanford Encyclopedia of Philosophy*, Spring edition.

Cavieres, Eduardo. 1996. *El comercio chileno en la economía colonial*. Valparaíso, Chile: Ediciones Universitarias de Valparaíso.

Chalmers, David J. 2010. *The Character of Consciousness*. Oxford: Oxford University Press.

Chater, Nick. 2018. *The Mind Is Flat: The Illusion of Mental Depth and the Impoverished Mind*. London: Random House.

Chibber, Vivek. 2003. *Locked in Place: State-Building and Late Industrialization in India*. Princeton, NJ: Princeton University Press.

Childers, Timothy. 2013. *Philosophy and Probability*. Oxford: Oxford University Press.

Chisholm, Roderick M. 1996. *A Realistic Theory of Categories: An Essay on Ontology*. Cambridge: Cambridge University Press.

Chomsky, Noam. 1975. *Reflections on Language*. New York: Pantheon.

Churchland, Patricia. 1986. *Neurophilosophy*. Cambridge, MA: MIT Press.

Churchland, Paul M. 1981. "Eliminative Materialism and the Propositional Attitudes." *Journal of Philosophy* 78: 67–90.

———. 1985. "Conceptual Progress and Word/World Relations: In Search of the Essence of Natural Kinds." *Canadian Journal of Philosophy* 15: 1–17.

———. 1988. "Perceptual Plasticity and Theoretical Neutrality: A Reply to Jerry Fodor." *Philosophy of Science* 55: 167–87.

———. 1989. *A Neurocomputational Perspective: The Nature of Mind and the Structure of Science*. Cambridge, MA: MIT Press.

———. 1998. "Conceptual Similarity across Sensory and Neural Diversity: The Fodor/Lepore Challenge Answered." *Journal of Philosophy* 95: 5–32.

———. 2012. *Plato's Camera: How the Physical Brain Captures a Landscape of Abstract Universals*. Cambridge, MA: MIT Press.

Cienki, Alan. 2007. "Frames, Idealized Cognitive Models, and Domains." Pp. 170–87 in *The Oxford Handbook of Cognitive Linguistics*, edited by Dirk Geeraerts and Hubert Cuyckens. Oxford: Oxford University Press.

Cimpian, Andrel, and Erika Salomon. 2014. "The Inherence Heuristic: An Intuitive Means of Making Sense of the World, and a Potential Precursor to Psychological Essentialism." *Behavioral and Brain Sciences* 37: 461–527.

Clark, Andy. 2008. *Supersizing the Mind: Embodiment, Action, and Cognitive Extension*. Oxford: Oxford University Press.

———. 2013. "Whatever Next? Predictive Brains, Situated Agents, and the Future of Cognitive Science" (with comments). *Behavioral and Brain Sciences* 36: 181–253.

———. 2016. *Surfing Uncertainty: Prediction, Action, and the Embodied Mind*. Oxford: Oxford University Press.

Clark, Andy, and David Chalmers. 1998. "The Extended Mind." *Analysis* 58: 7–19.

Clark, William Roberts, Michael J. Gilligan, and Matt Golder. 2006. "A Simple Multivariate Test for Asymmetric Hypotheses." *Political Analysis* 14: 311–31.

Clarke, Kevin A. 2002. "The Reverend and the Ravens: Comment on Seawright." *Political Analysis* 10: 194–97.

Cleland, Carol E. 2002. "Differences between Historical Science and Experimental Science." *Philosophy of Science* 69: 474–96.

———. 2013. "Is a General Theory of Life Possible? Seeking the Nature of Life in the Context of a Single Example." *Biological Theory* 7: 368–79.

Clemens, Elisabeth S., and James M. Cook. 1999. "Politics and Institutionalism: Explaining Durability and Change." *Annual Review of Sociology* 25: 441–66.

Cohen, G. A. 1995. *Self-Ownership, Freedom, and Equality*. New York: Cambridge University Press.

Coleman, James. 1982. *The Asymmetric Society*. Syracuse, NY: Syracuse University Press.

———. 1990. *Foundations of Social Theory*. Cambridge, MA: Belknap Press.

Coley, John D., Douglas L. Medin, and Scott Atran. 1997. "Does Rank Have Its Privilege? Inductive Inference within Folkbiological Taxonomies." *Cognition* 64: 73–112.

Coley, John D., and Kimberly D. Tanner. 2012. "Common Origins of Diverse Misconceptions: Cognitive Principles and the Development of Biology Thinking." *CBE: Life Sciences Education* 11: 209–15.

Collier, Andrew. 1994. *Critical Realism: An Introduction to Roy Bhaskar's Philosophy*. London: Verso.

Collier, David. 2011. "Understanding Process Tracing." *PS: Political Science and Politics* 44: 823–30.

Collier, David, Henry E. Brady, and Jason Seawright. 2010. "Sources of Leverage in Causal Inference: Toward an Alternative View of Methodology." Pp. 161–99 in Brady and Collier, *Rethinking Social Inquiry*.

Collier, David, and John Gerring, eds. 2009. *Concepts and Method in Social Science: The Tradition of Giovanni Sartori*. London: Routledge.

Collier, David, and Steven Levitsky. 1997. "Democracy with Adjectives: Conceptual Innovation in Comparative Research." *World Politics* 49: 430–51.

Collier, David, and James Mahon. 1993. "Conceptual 'Stretching' Revisited: Adapting Categories in Comparative Research." *American Political Science Review* 87: 845–55.

Collins, Harry. 1981. "Stages in the Empirical Programme of Relativism." *Social Studies of Science* 11: 3–10.

Collins, John, Ned Hall, and L. A. Paul, eds. 2004. *Causation and Counterfactuals*. Cambridge, MA: MIT Press.

Collins, Patricia Hill. 2019. *Intersectionality as Critical Social Theory*. Durham, NC: Duke University Press.

Collins, Randall. 1994. *Four Sociological Traditions*. New York: Oxford University Press.

Colyvan, Mark. 2001. *The Indispensability of Mathematics*. Oxford: Oxford University Press.

Connolly, William E. 1974. *The Terms of Political Discourse*. Princeton, NJ: Princeton University Press.

Copi, Irving M. 1954. "Essence and Accident." *Journal of Philosophy* 51: 706–19.

Copi, Irving M., and Carl Cohen. 1994. *Introduction to Logic*. 9th ed. London: Macmillan.

Copley, Bridget, and Heidi Harley. 2015. "A Force-Theoretic Framework for Event Structure." *Linguistics and Philosophy* 38: 103–58.

Cosmides, Leda. 1989. "The Logic of Social Exchange: Has Natural Selection Shaped How Humans Reason? Studies with the Watson Selection Task." *Cognition* 31: 187–276.

Costner, Herbert L., and Robert K. Leik. 1964. "Deductions from 'Axiomatic Theory.'" *American Sociological Review* 29: 819–35.

Cox, R. T. 1946. "Probability, Frequency and Reasonable Expectation." *American Journal of Physics* 14: 1–13.

Crane, Tim, and D. H. Mellor. 1990. "There Is No Question of Physicalism." *Mind* 99: 185–206.

Crick, Francis, and Christof Koch. 2003. "A Framework for Consciousness." *Nature and Neuroscience* 6: 119–26.

Crocker, David A. 2008. *Ethics of Global Development: Agency, Capability, and Deliberative Democracy*. Cambridge: Cambridge University Press.

Cyr, Jennifer. 2019. *Focus Groups for the Social Science Researcher*. Cambridge: Cambridge University Press.

Dahl, Robert A. 1957. "The Concept of Power." *Behavioral Science* 2: 201–15.

———. 1971. *Polyarchy: Participation and Opposition*. New Haven, CT: Yale University Press.

D'Andrade, Roy. 1995. "Moral Models in Anthropology." *Current Anthropology* 36: 399–408.

Danks, David. 2009. "The Psychology of Causal Perception and Reasoning." Pp. 448–70 in Beebee, Hitchcock, and Menzies, *Oxford Handbook of Causation.*

David, Marian. 2016. "The Correspondence Theory of Truth." *Stanford Encyclopedia of Philosophy,* Fall edition.

David, Paul A. 1985. "Clio and the Economics of QWERTY." *American Economic Review* 75: 332–37.

Davidson, Donald. 1967. "Causal Relations." *Journal of Philosophy* 64: 691–703.

Davis, Kingsley, and Wilbert E. Moore. 1945. "Some Principles of Stratification." *American Sociological Review* 10: 242–49.

Dawkins, Richard. 1986. *The Blind Watchmaker: Why the Evidence of Evolution Reveals a Universe without Design.* New York: Norton.

De Freitas, Julian, Kevin P. Tobia, George E. Newman, and Joshua Knobe. 2017. "Normative Judgments and Individual Essence." *Cognitive Science* 41 (S3): 382–402.

De León, Jason. 2015. *The Land of Open Graves: Living and Dying on the Migrant Trail.* Berkeley: University of California Press.

Demey, Lorenz, Barteld Kooi, and Joshua Sack. 2013. "Logic and Probability." *Stanford Encyclopedia of Philosophy,* Fall edition.

Dennett, Daniel C. 1987. *The Intentional Stance.* Cambridge, MA: MIT Press.

———. 1990. "The Interpretation of Texts, People and Other Artifacts." *Philosophy and Phenomenological Research* 1: 177–94.

Derrida, Jacques. 1982. *Margins of Philosophy.* Brighton, UK: Harvester Press.

Dessler, David. 1991. "Beyond Correlations: Toward a Causal Theory of War." *International Studies Quarterly* 35: 337–55.

Deutsch, Harry, and Pawel Garbacz. 2018. "Relative Identity." *Stanford Encyclopedia of Philosophy,* Fall edition.

DeWitt, Bryce S., and Neill Graham, eds. 1973. *The Many-Worlds Interpretation of Quantum Mechanics.* Princeton, NJ: Princeton University Press.

Diamond, Jared. 1997. *Guns, Germs, and Steel: The Fates of Human Societies.* New York: Norton.

Diesendruck, Gil, Rebecca Goldfein-Elbaz, Marjorie Rhodes, Susan Gelman, and Noam Neumark. 2013. "Cross-Cultural Differences in Children's Beliefs about the Objectivity of Social Categories." *Child Development* 84: 1906–17.

Dion, Douglas. 1998. "Evidence and Inference in the Comparative Case Study." *Comparative Politics* 30: 127–45.

Divers, John. 2002. *Possible Worlds.* London: Routledge.

Dodge, Ellen, and George Lakoff. 2005. "Image Schemas: From Linguistic Analysis to Neural Grounding." Pp. 57–92 in *From Perception to Meaning: Image Schemas in Cognitive Linguistics,* edited by Beate Hampe. Berlin: Walter de Gruyter.

Douglas, Mary. 1966. *Purity and Danger: An Analysis of the Concepts of Pollution and Taboo.* London: Routledge.

Dowding, Keith. 1991. *Rational Choice and Political Power.* Bristol, UK: Bristol University Press.

———. 2006. "Three-Dimensional Power: A Discussion of Steven Luke's *Power: A Radical View.*" *Political Studies Review* 4: 136–45.

———. 2019. *Rational Choice and Political Power.* Rev. ed. Bristol, UK: Bristol University Press.

Dowe, Phil. 2000. *Physical Causation.* New York: Cambridge University Press.

———. 2009. "Causal Process Theories." Pp. 213–33 in Beebee, Hitchcock, and Menzies, *Oxford Handbook of Causation.*

Dowling, John, and Jeffrey Pfeffer. 1975. "Organizational Legitimacy: Social Values and Organizational Behavior." *Pacific Sociological Review* 18: 122–36.

Downing, Brian M. 1992. *The Military Revolution and Political Change: Origins of Democracy and Autocracy in Early Modern Europe*. Princeton, NJ: Princeton University Press.

Drèze, Jean, and Amartya Sen. 1989. *Hunger and Public Action*. Oxford: Oxford University Press.

Driver, Julia. 2014. "The History of Utilitarianism." *Stanford Encyclopedia of Philosophy*, Winter edition.

Du Bois, W. E. B. 1995. *W. E. B. Du Bois: A Reader*. Edited by David Levering Lewis. New York: Henry Holt.

Dul, Jan. 2016. "Necessary Condition Analysis (NCA): Logic and Methodology of Necessary but Not Sufficient Causality." *Organizational Research Methods* 19: 10–52.

Dupré, John. 1981. "Natural Kinds and Biological Taxa." *Philosophical Review* 90: 66–90.

———. 1993. *The Disorder of Things*. Cambridge, MA: Harvard University Press.

———. 2002. "Is 'Natural Kind' a Natural Kind Term?" *Monist* 85: 29–49.

Durkheim, Émile. 1893/1964. *The Division of Labor in Society*. New York: Free Press.

———. 1895/1982. *Durkheim: The Rules of the Sociological Method and Selected Texts on Sociology and Its Method*. Edited by Steven Lukes. Translated by W. D. Halls. New York: Free Press.

———. 1912/1961. *The Elementary Forms of Religious Life*. New York: Collier.

Duster, Troy. 2001. "The 'Morphing' Properties of Whiteness." Pp. 113–37 in *The Making and Unmaking of Whiteness*, edited by Birgit Brander Rasmussen, Eric Klinenberg, Irene J. Nexica, and Matt Wray. Durham, NC: Duke University Press.

Dweck, Carol S. 1998. "The Development of Early Self-Conceptions: Their Relevance for Motivational Processes." Pp. 257–80 in *Motivation and Self-Regulation across the Life Span*, edited by Jutta Heckhausen and Carol S. Dweck. Cambridge: Cambridge University Press.

Dweck, Carol S., and Ellen L. Leggett. 1988. "A Social-Cognitive Approach to Motivation and Personality." *Psychological Review* 95: 256–73.

Dworkin, Ronald. 2000. *Sovereign Virtue*. Cambridge, MA: Harvard University Press.

Earman, John. 1992. *Bayes or Bust? A Critical Examination of Bayesian Confirmation Theory*. Cambridge, MA: MIT Press.

Edelman, Gerald M., and Giulio Tononi. 2000. *A Universe of Consciousness: How Matter Becomes Imagination*. New York: Basic Books.

Edwards, A. W. F. 2004. *Cogwheels of the Mind: The Story of Venn Diagrams*. Baltimore: Johns Hopkins University Press.

Eickmeier, Sandra, and Christina Ziegler. 2008. "How Successful Are Dynamic Factor Models at Forecasting Output and Inflation?" *Journal of Forecasting* 27: 237–65.

Eidlin, Barry. 2018. *Labor and the Class Idea in the United States and Canada*. Cambridge: Cambridge University Press.

Eisenstadt, S. N. 1964. "Institutionalization and Change." *American Sociological Review* 29: 235–47.

Elder-Vass, Dave. 2012. *The Reality of Social Construction*. Cambridge: Cambridge University Press.

Elga, Adam. 2007. "Isolation and Folk Physics." Pp. 106–19 in *Causation, Physics, and the Constitution of Reality: Russell's Republic Revisited*, edited by Huw Price and Richard Corry. Oxford: Oxford University Press.

Eliason, Scott R., and Robyn Stryker. 2009. "Goodness-of-Fit Tests and Descriptive Measures in Fuzzy-Set Analysis." *Sociological Methods and Research* 38: 102–46.

Ellis, Brian. 1996. "Natural Kinds and Natural Kind Reasoning." Pp. 11–28 in *Natural Kinds, Laws of Nature and Scientific Methodology*, edited by Peter J. Riggs. Dordrecht, the Netherlands: Kluwer.

———. 2001. *Scientific Essentialism*. Cambridge: Cambridge University Press.

———. 2009. *The Metaphysics of Scientific Realism*. Montreal: McGill-Queen's University Press.

Elman, Colin, John Gerring, and James Mahoney, eds. 2020. *The Production of Knowledge: Enhancing Progress in Social Science*. Cambridge: Cambridge University Press.

Elster, Jon. 1978. *Logic and Society: Contradictions and Possible Worlds*. Chichester, UK: Wiley.

———. 1983. *Sour Grapes*. Cambridge: Cambridge University Press.

———. 1985. *Making Sense of Marx*. Cambridge: Cambridge University Press.

———, ed. 1986a. *The Multiple Self*. Cambridge: Cambridge University Press.

———, ed. 1986b. *Rational Choice*. New York: New York University Press.

———. 1998. "A Plea for Mechanisms." Pp. 45–73 in *Social Mechanisms: An Analytical Approach to Social Theory*, edited by Peter Hedström and Richard Swedberg. Cambridge: Cambridge University Press.

———. 1999. *Alchemies of the Mind: Rationality and the Emotions*. Cambridge: Cambridge University Press.

Emigh, Rebecca. 1997. "The Power of Negative Thinking: The Use of Negative Case Methodology in the Development of Sociological Theory." *Theory and Society* 26: 649–84.

Emirbayer, Mustafa. 1997. "Manifesto for a Relational Sociology." *American Journal of Sociology* 103: 281–317.

Emirbayer, Mustafa, and Ann Mische. 1998. "What Is Agency?" *American Journal of Sociology* 103: 962–1023.

English, Robert. 2007. "Perestroika without Politics: How Realism Misunderstands the Cold War's End." Pp. 237–60 in Goertz and Levy, *Explaining War and Peace*.

Epstein, Steven. 1996. *Impure Science: AIDS, Activism, and the Politics of Knowledge*. Berkeley: University of California Press.

———. 2007. *Inclusion: The Politics of Difference in Medical Research*. Chicago: University of Chicago Press.

Escobar, Arturo. 1995. *Encountering Development: The Making and Unmaking of the Third World*. Princeton, NJ: Princeton University Press.

Esteva, Gustavo. 1992. "Development." Pp. 6–25 in *The Development Dictionary: A Guide to Knowledge as Power*, edited by Wolfgang Sachs. London: ZED Books.

Evans, Peter. 1995. *Embedded Autonomy: States and Industrial Transformation*. Princeton, NJ: Princeton University Press.

Evans, Vyvyan. 2006. "Lexical Concepts, Cognitive Models, and Meaning-Construction." *Cognitive Linguistics* 17: 491–534.

———. 2013. *Language and Time: A Cognitive Linguistics Approach*. Cambridge: Cambridge University Press.

Fagen, Richard R. 1969. *The Transformation of Political Culture in Cuba*. Stanford, CA: Stanford University Press.

Fair, David. 1979. "Causation and the Flow of Energy." *Erkenntnis* 14: 219–50.

Fairfield, Tasha. 2013. "Going Where the Money Is: Strategies for Taxing Economic Elites in Unequal Democracies." *World Development* 47: 42–57.

Fairfield, Tasha, and Andrew Charman. 2017. "Explicit Bayesian Analysis for Process Tracing: Guidelines, Opportunities, and Caveats." *Political Analysis* 25: 363–80.

———. Forthcoming. *Social Inquiry and Bayesian Inference: Rethinking Qualitative Research*. Cambridge: Cambridge University Press.

Falleti, Tulia G. 2006. "Theory-Guided Process-Tracing: Something Old, Something New." *APSA-CP: Newsletter of the Organized Section in Comparative Politics of the APSA* 17: 9–14.

Falleti, Tulia G., and Julia H. Lynch. 2009. "Context and Causal Mechanisms in Political Analysis." *Comparative Political Studies* 42: 1143–66.

Falleti, Tulia G., and James Mahoney. 2015. "The Comparative Sequential Method." Pp. 211–39 in Mahoney and Thelen, *Advances in Comparative-Historical Analysis*.

Fanon, Frantz. 1963/2004. *The Wretched of the Earth*. Translated by Richard Philcox. New York: Grove.

Fassin, Didier. 2008. "Beyond Good and Evil? Questioning the Anthropological Discomfort with Morals." *Anthropological Theory* 8: 333–44.

Fauconnier, Gilles. 1994. *Mental Spaces: Aspects of Meaning Construction in Natural Language.* Cambridge: Cambridge University Press.

Fauconnier, Gilles, and Mark Turner. 2002. *The Way We Think: Conceptual Blending and the Mind's Hidden Complexities.* New York: Basic Books.

Fay, Brian. 1975. *Social Theory and Political Practice.* New York: Routledge.

Feagin, Joe R. 2009. *The White Racial Frame: Centuries of Racial Framing and Counter-Framing.* London: Routledge.

Fearon, James. 1991. "Counterfactuals and Hypothesis Testing in Political Science." *World Politics* 43: 169–95.

———. 1996. "Causes and Counterfactuals in Social Science: Exploring an Analogy between Cellular Automata and Historical Processes." In *Counterfactual Analysis in World Politics*, edited by P. Tetlock and A. Belkin. Princeton, NJ: Princeton University Press.

Fearon, James, and David Laitin. 2008. "Integrating Qualitative and Quantitative Methods: Putting It Together Again." Pp. 1166–85 in *The Oxford Handbook of Political Science*, edited by Robert E. Goodin. Oxford: Oxford University Press.

Feyerabend, P. K. 1958. "An Attempt at a Realistic Interpretation of Experience." *Meeting of the Aristotelian Society* 58: 143–70.

Field, Hartry. 2016. *Science without Numbers: A Defense of Nominalism.* 2nd ed. Oxford: Oxford University Press.

Fillmore, Charles J. 1975. "An Alternative to Checklist Theories of Meaning." Pp. 123–31 in *Proceedings of the First Annual Meeting of the Berkeley Linguistics Society.* Berkeley, CA: Berkeley Linguistics Society.

Firth, Roderick. 1967. "The Anatomy of Certitude." *Philosophical Review* 76: 3–27.

Fligstein, Neil, and Douglas McAdam. 2012. *A Theory of Fields.* Oxford: Oxford University Press.

Flusberg, Stephen J., and James A. McClelland. 2017. "Connectionism and the Emergence of the Mind." Pp. 69–90 in *The Oxford Handbook of Cognitive Science*, edited by Susan E. F. Chipman. Oxford: Oxford University Press.

Fodor, Jerry A. 1975. *The Language of Thought.* Cambridge, MA: Harvard University Press.

———. 1983. *The Modularity of the Mind.* Cambridge, MA: MIT Press.

———. 1984. "Observation Reconsidered." *Philosophy of Science* 51: 23–43.

———. 1988. "A Reply to Churchland's 'Perceptual Plasticity and Theoretical Neutrality.'" *Philosophy of Science* 55: 188–98.

———. 1998. *Concepts: Where Cognitive Science Went Wrong.* New York: Oxford University Press.

Foucault, Michel. 1975/1995. *Discipline and Punish: The Birth of the Prison.* 2nd ed. Translated by Alan Sheridan. New York: Vintage.

———. 1982. "The Subject and Power." *Critical Inquiry* 8: 777–95.

Fraser, Nancy. 1989. *Unruly Practices: Power, Discourse, and Gender in Contemporary Social Theory.* Minneapolis: University of Minnesota Press.

Freedman, David. 1999. "From Association to Causation: Some Remarks on the History of Statistics." *Statistical Science* 14: 243–58.

———. 2008. "On Types of Scientific Enquiry: The Role of Qualitative Reasoning." Pp. 300–318 in Box-Steffensmeier, Brady, and Collier, *Oxford Handbook of Political Methodology.*

———. 2010. *Statistical Models and Causal Inference.* New York: Cambridge University Press.

Freeman, Samuel. 2019. "Original Position." *Stanford Encyclopedia of Philosophy*, Summer edition.

Frege, Gottlob. 1884/1960. *The Foundations of Arithmetic: A Logico-Mathematic Enquiry into the Concept of Number.* Translated by J. L. Austin. New York: Harper.

Fuchs, Stephen. 2001. *Against Essentialism: A Theory of Culture and Society*. Cambridge, MA: Harvard University Press.

Fulbrook, Mary, and Theda Skocpol. 1984. "Destined Pathways: The Historical Sociology of Perry Anderson." Pp. 170–210 in *Vision and Method in Historical Sociology*, edited by Theda Skocpol. Cambridge: Cambridge University Press.

Furniss, Norman, and Timothy Tilton. 1977. *The Case for the Welfare State: From Social Security to Social Equality*. Bloomington: Indiana University Press.

Gadenne, Volker. 2015. "Critical Rationalism." Pp. 271–76 in *International Encyclopedia of the Social and Behavioral Sciences*, 2nd ed., edited by James D. Wright. Amsterdam: Elsevier.

Gagnon, John H., and William Simon. 1973. *Sexual Conduct: The Social Sources of Human Sexuality*. Chicago: Aldine.

Galavotti, Maria Carla. 2005. *Philosophical Introduction to Probability*. Stanford, CA: CSLI Publications.

Galluzzo, Gabriele. 2015. "A Kind Farewell to Platonism: For an Aristotelian Understanding of Kinds and Properties." Pp. 85–113 in Galluzzo and Loux, *The Problem of Universals*.

Galluzzo, Gabriele, and Michael J. Loux, eds. 2015. *The Problem of Universals in Contemporary Philosophy*. Cambridge: Cambridge University Press.

Gandhi, Jennifer. 2008. *Political Institutions under Dictatorship*. New York: Cambridge University Press.

Gärdenfors, Peter. 2000. *Conceptual Spaces: The Geometry of Thought*. Cambridge, MA: MIT Press.

———. 2007. "Representing Actions and Functional Properties in Conceptual Spaces." Pp. 241–69 in *Body, Language, and Mind*, vol. 1, *Embodiment*, edited by Tom Ziemke, Jordan Zlatev, and Roslyn M. Frank. Berlin: Mouton de Gruyter.

———. 2014. *The Geometry of Meaning: Semantics Based on Conceptual Spaces*. Cambridge, MA: MIT Press.

Gardina Pestana, Carla. 2006. "Nineteenth-Century British Imperialism Undone with a Single Shell Fragment." Pp. 197–202 in Tetlock, Lebow, and Parker, *Unmaking the West*.

Garfinkel, Alan. 1981. *Forms of Explanation: Rethinking the Questions of Social Theory*. New Haven, CT: Yale University Press.

Garfinkel, Harold. 1967. *Studies in Ethnomethodology*. Englewood Cliffs, NJ: Prentice Hall.

Gaventa, John. 1980. *Power and Powerlessness: Quiescence and Rebellion in an Appalachian Valley*. Urbana: University of Illinois Press.

Geddes, Barbara. 2003. *Paradigms and Sandcastles: Theory Building and Research Design in Comparative Politics*. Ann Arbor: University of Michigan Press.

Geertz, Clifford. 1973. *The Interpretation of Cultures: Selected Essays*. New York: Basic Books.

———. 1974. "'From the Native's Point of View': On the Nature of Anthropological Understanding." *Bulletin of the American Academy of Arts and Sciences* 28: 26–45.

———. 1988. *Works and Lives: The Anthropologist as Author*. Stanford, CA: Stanford University Press.

Gelman, Susan A. 2003. *The Essential Child: Origins of Essentialism in Everyday Thought*. Oxford: Oxford University Press.

———. 2013. "Artifacts and Essentialism." *Review of Philosophy and Psychology* 4 (3): 449–63.

Gelman, Susan A., and Gil Diesendruck. 1999. "A Reconsideration of Concepts: On the Compatibility of Psychological Essentialism and Context Sensitivity." Pp. 79–102 in *Conceptual Development: Piaget's Legacy*, edited by Ellin Kofsky Scholnick, Katherine Nelson, Susan A. Gelman, and Patricia H. Miller. Mahwah, NJ: Lawrence Erlbaum.

Gelman, Susan A., and Lawrence A. Hirschfeld. 1999. "How Biological Is Essentialism?" Pp. 403–46 in *Folkbiology*, edited by Douglas L. Medin and Scott Atran. Cambridge, MA: MIT Press.

Gelman, Susan A., and Steven O. Roberts. 2017. "How Language Shapes the Cultural Inheritance of Categories." *PNAS* 114: 7900–7907.

Gentner, Dedre, Brian F. Bowdle, Phillip Wolfe, and Consuelo Boronat. 2001. "Metaphor Is Like Analogy." Pp. 199–253 in *The Analogical Mind: Perspectives from Cognitive Science*, edited by Dedre Gentner, Keith J. Holyoak, and Biocho N. Kokinov. Cambridge, MA: MIT Press.

Gentner, Dedre, and Francisco Maravilla. 2018. "Analogical Reasoning." Pp. 186–203 in *International Handbook of Thinking and Reasoning*, edited by Linden J. Ball and Valerie A. Thompson. New York: Psychology Press.

George, Alexander L., and Andrew Bennett. 2005. *Case Studies and Theory Development in the Social Sciences*. Cambridge, MA: MIT Press.

Gerring, John. 2012. *Social Science Methodology: A Unified Framework*. Cambridge: Cambridge University Press.

———. 2017. *Case Study Research: Principles and Practices*. 2nd ed. Cambridge: Cambridge University Press.

Geser, Hans. 1992. "Towards an Interaction Theory of Organizational Actors." *Organizational Studies* 13: 429–51.

Gibbs, Jack. 1965. "Norms: The Problem of Definition and Classification." *American Journal of Sociology* 70: 586–94.

Giddens, Anthony. 1979. *Central Problems in Social Theory: Action, Structure and Contradiction in Social Analysis*. Berkeley: University of California Press.

———. 1984. *The Constitution of Society*. Berkeley: University of California Press.

———. 1991. *Modernity and Self-Identity*. New York: Polity.

Giere, Ronald N. 2006. *Scientific Perspectivism*. Chicago: University of Chicago Press.

Gilbert, Margaret. 1987. "Modelling Collective Belief." *Synthese* 73: 185–204.

———. 1992. *On Social Facts*. Princeton, NJ: Princeton University Press.

Gil-White, Francisco J. 2001. "Are Ethnic Groups Biological 'Species' to the Human Brain?" *Current Anthropology* 42: 515–54.

Girle, Rod. 2003. *Possible Worlds*. Montreal: McGill-Queen's University Press.

Glanzberg, Michael G., ed. 2018a. *Oxford Handbook of Truth*. Oxford: Oxford University Press.

———. 2018b. "Truth." *Stanford Encyclopedia of Philosophy*, Fall edition.

Gleick, James. 1987. *Chaos: Making a New Science*. New York: Penguin.

Glennan, Stuart S. 1996. "Mechanisms and the Nature of Causation." *Erkenntnis* 44: 49–71.

———. 2009. "Mechanisms." Pp. 315–25 in Beebee, Hitchcock, and Menzies, *Oxford Handbook of Causation*.

Glymour, Clark. 2001. *The Mind's Arrows: Bayes Nets and Graphical Causal Models in Psychology*. Cambridge, MA: MIT Press.

Glymour, Clark, David Danks, Bruce Glymour, Frederick Eberhardt, Joseph Ramsey, Richard Scheines, Peter Spirtes, Choh Man Teng, and Jiji Zhang. 2010. "Actual Causation: A Stone Soup Essay." *Synthese* 175: 169–92.

Glymour, Clark, and Frank Wimberly. 2007. "Actual Causes and Thought Experiments." Pp. 43–68 in *Causation and Explanation*, edited by Joseph Keim Campbell, Michael O'Rourke, and Harry Silverstein. Cambridge, MA: MIT Press.

Go, Julian. 2011. *Patterns of Empire: The British and American Empires, 1688 to the Present*. Cambridge: Cambridge University Press.

Gödel, Kurt. 1947. "What Is Cantor's Continuum Problem?" *American Mathematical Monthly* 54: 515–25.

Godfrey-Smith, Peter. 2009. "Causal Pluralism." Pp. 326–37 in Beebee, Hitchcock, and Menzies, *Oxford Handbook of Causation*.

Goertz, Gary. 2003a. "Cause, Correlation, and Necessary Conditions." Pp. 47–64 in Goertz and Starr, *Necessary Conditions*.

———. 2003b. "The Substantive Importance of Necessary Condition Hypotheses." Pp. 65–94 in Goertz and Starr, *Necessary Conditions*.

———. 2006a. "Assessing the Trivialness, Relevance, and Relative Importance of Necessary or Sufficient Conditions in Social Science." *Studies in Comparative International Development* 41: 88–109.

———. 2006b. *Social Science Concepts: A User's Guide*. Princeton, NJ: Princeton University Press.

———. 2020. *Social Science Concepts and Measurement*. New and revised ed. Princeton, NJ: Princeton University Press.

Goertz, Gary, and Jack S. Levy. 2007a. "Causal Explanation, Necessary Conditions, and Case Studies." Pp. 9–45 in Goertz and Levy, *Explaining War and Peace*.

———, eds. 2007b. *Explaining War and Peace: Case Studies and Necessary Condition Counterfactuals*. London: Routledge.

Goertz, Gary, and James Mahoney. 2005. "Two-Level Theories and Fuzzy-Set Analysis." *Sociological Methods and Research* 33: 497–538.

———. 2012. *A Tale of Two Cultures: Qualitative and Quantitative Research in the Social Sciences*. Princeton, NJ: Princeton University Press.

Goertz, Gary, and Harvey Starr, eds. 2003. *Necessary Conditions: Theory, Methodology, and Applications*. Lanham, MD: Rowman and Littlefield.

Goffman, Erving. 1969. *The Presentation of Self in Everyday Life*. London: Allen Lane.

Goldhagen, Daniel Jonah. 1996. *Hitler's Willing Executioners: Ordinary Germans and the Holocaust*. New York: Knopf.

Goldstone, Jack A. 1991. *Revolution and Rebellion in the Early Modern World*. Berkeley: University of California Press.

———. 1998a. "Initial Conditions, General Laws, Path Dependence, and Explanation in Historical Sociology." *American Journal of Sociology* 104: 829–45.

———. 1998b. "The Problem of the 'Early Modern World.'" *Journal of Economic and Social History of the Orient* 41: 249–84.

———. 2006. "Europe's Peculiar Path: Would the World Be 'Modern' if William III's Invasion of England in 1688 Had Failed?" Pp. 168–96 in Tetlock, Lebow, and Parker, *Unmaking the West*.

Goldthorpe, John H. 1991. "The Uses of History in Sociology: Reflections on Some Recent Tendencies." *British Journal of Sociology* 42: 211–30.

———. 1997. "Current Issues in Comparative Macrosociology: A Debate on Methodological Issues." *Comparative Social Research* 16: 1–26.

Gómez-Torrente, Mario. 2019. *Roads to Reference: An Essay on Reference Fixing in Natural Language*. Oxford: Oxford University Press.

Gonzalez-Ocantos, Ezequiel, and Jody LaPorte. Forthcoming. "Process Tracing and the Problem of Missing Data." *Sociological Methods and Research*.

Goodman, Nelson. 1947. "The Problem of Counterfactual Conditionals." *Journal of Philosophy* 44: 113–28.

———. 1951. *The Structure of Appearance*. Cambridge, MA: Harvard University Press.

———. 1978. *Ways of Worldmaking*. Indianapolis, IN: Hackett.

Goodman, Nelson, and W. V. Quine. 1947. "Steps toward a Constructive Nominalism." *Journal of Symbolic Logic* 12: 105–22.

Gopnik, Alison, Clark Glymour, David M. Sobel, Laura E. Schulz, Tamar Kushnir, and David Danks. 2004. "A Theory of Causal Learning in Children: Causal Maps and Bayes Nets." *Psychological Review* 111: 3–32.

Gorski, Philip S. 2013. "What Is Critical Realism and Why Should You Care?" *Contemporary Sociology* 42: 658–70.

Gould, Stephen J., and Niles Eldredge. 1977. "Punctuated Equilibria—The Tempo and Mode of Evolution Reconsidered." *Paleobiology* 3: 115–51.

Gouldner, Alvin W. 1962. "Anti-Minotaur: The Myth of a Value-Free Sociology." *Social Problems* 9: 199–213.

Gourevitch, Peter. 1986. *Politics in Hard Times: Comparative Responses to International Economic Crises.* Ithaca, NY: Cornell University Press.

Gowans, Chris. 2018. "Moral Relativism." *Stanford Encyclopedia of Philosophy*, Winter edition.

Grady, Joseph E. 2005. "Image Schemas and Perception: Refining a Definition." Pp. 35–56 in *From Perception to Meaning: Image Schemas in Cognitive Linguistics*, edited by Beate Hampe. Berlin: Walter de Gruyter.

Grandy, Richard E. 2007. "Artifacts: Parts and Principles." Pp. 18–32 in Margolis and Laurence, *Creations of the Mind.*

Granovetter, Mark. 1978. "Threshold Models of Collective Behavior." *American Journal of Sociology* 83: 1420–43.

Graßhoff, Gerd, and Michael May. 2001. "Causal Regularities." Pp. 85–114 in *Current Issues in Causation*, edited by Wolfgang Spohn, Marion Ledwig, and Michael Esfeld. Münster: Mentis.

Graziano, Michael S. A. 2019. *Rethinking Consciousness: A Scientific Theory of Subjective Experience.* New York: Norton.

Green, Christopher G., and John Vervaeke. 1997. "The Experience of Objects and the Objects of Experience." *Metaphor and Symbol* 12: 3–17.

Green, Donald P., Shang E. Ha, and John G. Bullock. 2010. "Enough Already about 'Black Box' Experiments: Studying Mediators Is More Difficult than Most Suppose." *Annals of the American Academy of Political and Social Science* 628: 200–208.

Greene, Brian. 2004. *The Fabric of the Cosmos.* New York: Knopf.

———. 2011. *The Hidden Reality: Parallel Universes and the Deep Laws of the Cosmos.* New York: Knopf.

Greene, Joshua. 2013. *Moral Tribes: Emotion, Reason, and the Gap between Us and Them.* New York: Penguin.

Griffin, Larry J. 1992. "Temporality, Events, and Explanation in Historical Sociology: An Introduction." *Sociological Methods and Research* 20: 403–27.

———. 1993. "Narrative, Event-Structure, and Causal Interpretation in Historical Sociology." *American Journal of Sociology* 98: 1094–1133.

Griswold, Wendy. 2012. *Cultures and Societies in a Changing World.* 4th ed. Thousand Oaks, CA: Sage.

Grosholz, E. R. 1985. "Two Episodes in the Unification of Logic and Topology." *British Journal for the Philosophy of Science* 36: 147–57.

Gross, Neil, and Zachary Hyde. 2017. "Norms and Mental Imagery." Pp. 361–91 in *Social Theory Now*, edited by Claudio E. Benzecry, Monika Krause, and Isaac Ariail Reed. Chicago: University of Chicago Press.

Grusky, David, ed. 2001. *Stratification in Sociological Perspective.* Boulder, CO: Westview Press.

Grzymala-Busse, Anna. 2011. "Time Will Tell? Temporality and the Analysis of Causal Mechanisms and Processes." *Comparative Political Studies* 44: 1267–97.

Hackett, Edward J., Olga Amsterdamska, Michael Lynch, and Judy Wajcman, eds. 2008. *The Handbook of Science and Technology Studies.* Cambridge, MA: MIT Press.

Hacking, Ian. 1979. "What Is Logic?" *Journal of Philosophy* 6: 285–319.

———. 1981. "The Archaeology of Foucault." *New York Review of Books*, May 14, 27–40.

———. 1991. "A Tradition of Natural Kinds." *Philosophical Studies* 61: 109–26.

Hacking, Ian. 1995a. "The Looping Effects of Human Kinds." Pp. 351–83 in *Causal Cognition: A Multidisciplinary Approach*, edited by Dan Sperber, David Premack, and Ann J. Premack. Oxford: Clarendon Press.

———. 1995b. *Rewriting the Soul: Multiple Personality and the Sciences of Memory*. Princeton, NJ: Princeton University Press.

———. 1999. *The Social Construction of What?* Cambridge, MA: Harvard University Press.

———. 2001. *An Introduction to Probability and Inductive Logic*. Cambridge: Cambridge University Press.

———. 2007. "Natural Kinds: Rosy Dawn, Scholastic Twilight." *Royal Institute of Philosophy Supplements* 61: 203–39.

———. 2014. *Why Is There a Philosophy of Mathematics at All?* Cambridge: Cambridge University Press.

Hájek, Alan. 2012. " Interpretations of Probability." *Stanford Encyclopedia of Philosophy*, Winter edition.

Hale, Bob. 1987. *Abstract Objects*. Oxford: Blackwell.

———. 2013. *Necessary Beings: An Essay on Ontology, Modality, and the Relations between Them*. Oxford: Oxford University Press.

Hall, Ned. 2004. "Two Concepts of Causation." Pp. 181–203 in Collins, Hall, and Paul, *Causation and Counterfactuals*.

Hall, Peter A. 2006. "Systematic Process Analysis: When and How to Use It." *European Management Review* 3: 24–31.

Hall, Peter A., and Rosemary C. R. Taylor. 1996. "Political Science and the Three New Institutionalisms." *Political Studies* 44: 936–57.

Hallam, A., and P. B. Wignall. 1997. *Mass Extinctions and Their Aftermath*. New York: Oxford University Press.

Halpern, Joseph Y. 2016. *Actual Causality*. Cambridge, MA: MIT Press.

Halpern, Joseph Y., and Christopher Hitchcock. 2010. "Actual Causation and the Art of Modeling." Pp. 383–406 in *Heuristics, Probability, and Causality*, edited by R. Dechter, H. H. Geffner, and J. Y. Halpern. London: College Publishers.

Halpern, Joseph Y., and Judea Pearl. 2005. "Causes and Explanation: A Structural-Model Approach. Part I: Causes." *British Journal for the Philosophy of Science* 56: 843–87.

Hanna, Robert. 2006. *Rationality and Logic*. Cambridge, MA: MIT Press.

Hardin, Garrett. 1968. "The Tragedy of the Commons." *Science* 162: 1243–48.

Harman, Gilbert. 1996. "Moral Relativism." Pp. 3–64 in *Moral Relativism and Moral Objectivity*, edited by Gilbert Harman and Judith Jarvis Thompson. Cambridge, MA: Blackwell Publishers.

Harré, Rom. 1974. "Some Remarks on 'Rule' as a Scientific Concept." Pp. 143–84 in *Understanding Other Persons*, edited by Theodore Mischel. Oxford: Blackwell.

———. 2002. "Social Reality and the Myth of Social Structure." *European Journal of Social Theory* 5: 111–23.

Harré, Rom, and Michael Krausz. 1996. *Varieties of Relativism*. Oxford: Blackwell.

Harré, Rom, and E. H. Madden. 1975. *Causal Powers: A Theory of Natural Necessity*. Oxford: Blackwell.

Harré, Rom, and Secord, P. F. 1972. *The Explanation of Social Behavior*. Lanham, MD: Rowman and Littlefield.

Hart, H. L. A., and A. M. Honoré. 1959. *Causation in the Law*. Oxford: Oxford University Press.

Hart, H. L. A., and Tony Honoré. 1985. *Causation in the Law*. 2nd ed. Oxford: Oxford University Press.

Harvey, Frank P. 2012. *Explaining the Iraq War: Counterfactual Theory, Logic, and Evidence*. Cambridge: Cambridge University Press.

———. 2015. "'What If' History Matters: Comparative Counterfactual Analysis and Policy Relevance." *Security Studies* 24: 413–24.

Haslam, Nick. 1998. "Natural Kinds, Human Kinds, and Essentialism." *Social Research* 65: 291–314.

Haslam, Nick, and Donald Ernst. 2002. "Essentialist Beliefs about Mental Disorders." *Journal of Social and Clinical Psychology* 21: 628–44.

Haslam, Nick, Elise Holland, and Minoru Karasawa. 2013. "Essentialism and Entitativity across Cultures." Pp. 17–37 in *Culture and Group Processes*, edited by Masaki Yuki and Marilynn Brewer. Oxford: Oxford University Press.

Haslam, Nick, and Sheri R. Levy. 2006. "Essentialist Beliefs about Homosexuality: Structure and Implications for Prejudice." *Personality and Social Psychology Bulletin* 32: 471–85.

Haslam, Nick, Louis Rothschild, and Donald Ernst. 2000. "Essentialist Beliefs about Social Categories." *British Journal of Social Psychology* 39: 113–27.

———. 2004. "Essentialism and Entitativity: Structures of Beliefs about the Ontology of Social Categories." Pp. 61–78 in *The Psychology of Group Perception: Perceived Variability, Entitativity, and Essentialism*, edited by Vincent Yzerbyt, Charles M. Judd, and Olivier Corneille. Washington, D.C.: Psychology Press.

Haward, Paul, Laura Wagner, Susan Carey, and Sandeep Prasada. 2018. "The Development of Principled Connections and Kind Representations." *Cognition* 176: 255–68.

Haydu, Jeffrey. 1998. "Making Use of the Past: Time Periods as Cases to Compare and as Sequences of Problem Solving." *American Journal of Sociology* 104: 339–71.

Hechter, Michael, and Karl-Dieter Opp, eds. 2001. *Social Norms*. New York: Russell Sage Foundation.

Hedström, Peter, and Richard Swedberg, eds. 1998. *Social Mechanisms: An Analytical Approach to Social Theory*. Cambridge: Cambridge University Press.

Helmke, Gretchen, and Steven Levitsky. 2004. "Informal Institutions and Comparative Politics: A Research Agenda." *Perspectives on Politics* 2: 725–40.

Helpman, Elhanan, and Paul Krugman. 1985. *Market Structure and Foreign Trade*. Cambridge, MA: MIT Press.

Hempel, Carl G. 1942. *Aspects of Scientific Explanation and Other Essays in the Philosophy of Science*. New York: Free Press.

———. 1965. *Aspects of Scientific Explanation and Other Essays in the Philosophy of Science*. 2nd ed. New York: Free Press.

———. 1980. "Comments on Goodman's *Ways of Worldmaking*." *Synthese* 45: 193–99.

Hempel, Carl G., and Paul Oppenheim. 1948. "Studies in the Logic of Explanation." *Philosophy of Science* 15: 135–75.

Hendry, Robin Findlay. 2006. "Elements, Compounds, and Other Chemical Kinds." *Philosophy of Science* 73: 864–75.

Hernández-Conde, José V. 2017. "A Case against Convexity in Conceptual Spaces." *Synthese* 194: 4011–37.

Hexter, J. H. 1979. *On Historians*. Cambridge, MA: Harvard University Press.

Hicks, Alexander M. 1999. *Social Democracy and Welfare Capitalism: A Century of Income Security Politics*. Ithaca, NY: Cornell University Press.

Hirschfeld, Lawrence A. 1996. *Race in the Making: Cognition, Culture, and the Child's Construction of Human Kinds*. Cambridge, MA: MIT Press.

Hirschman, Albert O. 2013. "Morality and the Social Sciences: A Durable Tension." Pp. 331–44 in *The Essential Hirschman*, edited by Jeremy Adelman. Princeton, NJ: Princeton University Press.

Hitchcock, Christopher. 2018. "Probabilistic Causation." *Stanford Encyclopedia of Philosophy*, Fall edition.

Hobbes, Thomas. 1651/2012. *Leviathan*. Edited by Noel Malcolm. 3 vols. Oxford: Oxford University Press.

Hodges, Wilfrid. 2018. "Tarski's Truth Definitions." *Stanford Encyclopedia of Philosophy*, Fall edition.

Hoffman, Donald. 2019. *The Case against Reality: Why Evolution Hid the Truth from Our Eyes*. New York: Norton.

Hoffman, Donald, Manish Singh, and Chetan Prakash. 2015. "The Interface Theory of Perception." *Psychonomic Bulletin and Review* 22: 1480–1506.

Holland, Paul W. 1986. "Statistics and Causal Inference." *Journal of the American Statistical Association* 81: 945–60.

Holt, Jim. 2018. *When Einstein Walked with Gödel: Excursions to the Edge of Thought*. New York: Farrar, Straus and Giroux.

Homans, George C. 1967. *The Nature of Social Science*. New York: Harcourt, Brace and World.

Hood, Bruce. 2012. *The Self Illusion: How the Social Brain Creates Identity*. Oxford: Oxford University Press.

Hoover, Kenneth R. 1984. *Elements of Social Scientific Thinking*. 3rd ed. New York: St. Martin's.

Hudson, Robert G. 1994. "Background Independence and the Causation of Observations." *Studies in History and Philosophy of Science* 25: 595–612.

Hume, David. 1777/1975. *Enquiries concerning Human Understanding and concerning the Principles of Morals*. Oxford: Oxford University Press.

Humphreys, Macartan, and Alan Jacobs. 2015. "Mixing Methods: A Bayesian Approach." *American Political Science Review* 109: 653–73.

———. Forthcoming. *Integrated Inferences*. Cambridge: Cambridge University Press.

Hunt, Shelby D. 1994. "A Realist Theory of Empirical Testing: Resolving the Theory-Ladenness/Objectivity Debate." *Philosophy of the Social Sciences* 24: 133–58.

Huntington, Samuel P. 1968. *Political Order in Changing Societies*. New Haven, CT: Yale University Press.

Hurvich, Leo. 1981. *Color Vision*. Sunderland, MA: Sinauer Associates.

Immergut, Ellen M. 1998. "The Theoretical Core of the New Institutionalism." *Politics and Society* 26: 5–34.

Isaac, Jeffrey C. 1987a. "Beyond the Three Faces of Power: A Realist Critique." *Polity* 20: 4–31.

———. 1987b. *Power and Marxist Theory: A Realist View*. Ithaca, NY: Cornell University Press.

Isaac, Larry W., Debra A. Street, and Stan J. Knapp. 1994. "Analyzing Historical Contingency with Formal Methods: The Case of the 'Relief Explosion' and 1968." *Sociological Methods and Research* 23: 114–41.

Itzigsohn, José, and Karida L. Brown. 2020. *The Sociology of W. E. B. Du Bois: Racialized Modernity and the Global Color Line*. New York: NYU Press.

Izard, Carroll E. 2007. "Basic Emotions, Natural Kinds, Emotion Schemas, and a New Paradigm." *Perspectives on Psychological Science* 2: 260–80.

Jackendoff, Ray. 1983. *Semantics and Cognition*. Cambridge, MA: MIT Press.

———. 1987. *Consciousness and the Computational Mind*. Cambridge, MA: MIT Press.

———. 1990. *Semantic Structures*. Cambridge, MA: MIT Press.

———. 1992. *Languages of the Mind: Essays on Mental Representation*. Cambridge, MA: MIT Press.

———. 2002. *Foundations of Language: Brain, Meaning, Grammar, Evolution*. Oxford: Oxford University Press.

Jackson, Patrick Thaddeus. 2020. "The Dangers of Interpretation: C. A. W. Manning and the 'Going Concern' of International Society." *Journal of International Political Theory* 16: 133–52.

James, William. 1890. *The Principles of Psychology*. New York: Henry Holt.

Jasso, Guillermina. 1988. "Principles of Theoretical Analysis." *Sociological Theory* 6: 1–20.

Jaynes, E. T. 2003. *Probability Theory: The Logic of Science.* Cambridge: Cambridge University Press.

Jech, Thomas. 2011. "Set Theory." *Stanford Encyclopedia of Philosophy*, Winter edition.

Jepperson, Ronald L. 1991. "Institutions, Institutional Effects, and Institutionalism." Pp. 143–63 in Powell and DiMaggio, *New Institutionalism.*

Johnson, Chalmers. 1966. *Revolutionary Change.* Boston: Little, Brown.

Johnson, Mark. 1987. *The Body in the Mind: The Bodily Basis of Meaning, Imagination, and Reason.* Chicago: University of Chicago Press.

Jussim, Lee. 1986. "Self-Fulfilling Prophecies: A Theoretical and Integrative Review." *Psychological Review* 93: 429–45.

Kant, Immanuel. 1781/1998. *Critique of Pure Reason.* Edited by Paul Guyer and Allen W. Wood. Cambridge: Cambridge University Press.

Kapiszewski, Diana, Lauren M. MacLean, and Benjamin I. Read. 2015. *Field Research in Political Science: Practices and Principles.* Cambridge: Cambridge University Press.

Karasawa, Minoru, Nobuko Asai, and Koichi Hioki. 2019. "Psychological Essentialism at the Explicit and Implicit Levels: The Unique Status of Social Categories." *Japanese Psychological Research* 61: 107–22.

Karl, Terry Lynn. 1997. *The Paradox of Plenty: Oil Booms and Petro-States.* Berkeley: University of California Press.

Kashima, Yoshihisa, Emiko Kashima, Chi-Yue Chiu, Thomas Farsides, Michele Gelfand, Ying-Yi Hong, Uichol Kim, Fritz Strack, Lioba Werth, Masaki Yuki, and Vincent Yzerbyt. 2005. "Culture, Essentialism, and Agency: Are Individuals Universally Believed to Be More Real Entities than Groups?" *European Journal of Social Psychology* 35: 147–69.

Katznelson, Ira. 2003. "Periodization and Preferences: Reflections on Purposive Action in Comparative Historical Social Science." Pp. 270–301 in Mahoney and Rueschemeyer, *Comparative Historical Analysis.*

Kay, Paul, and Chad McDaniel. 1978. "The Linguistic Significance of the Meanings of Basic Color Terms." *Language* 54: 610–46.

Keet, C. Maria, and Alessandro Artale. 2008. "Representing and Reasoning over a Taxonomy of Part-Whole Relations." *Applied Ontology* 3: 91–110.

Keil, Frank C. 1989. *Concepts, Kinds, and Cognitive Development.* Cambridge, MA: MIT Press.

Keleman, Deborah, and Susan Carey. 2007. "The Essence of Artifacts: Developing a Design Stance." Pp. 212–30 in Margolis and Laurence, *Creations of the Mind.*

Kelley, Harold H. 1973. "The Processes of Causal Attribution." *American Psychologist* 28: 107–28.

Kendall, Patricia L., ed. 1982. *The Varied Sociology of Paul F. Lazarsfeld.* New York: Columbia University Press.

Kim, Jaegwon. 1974. "Noncausal Connections." *Noûs* 8: 41–52.

Kimeldorf, Howard. 1988. *Reds or Rackets? The Making of Radical and Conservative Unions on the Waterfront.* Berkeley: University of California.

King, Gary, Robert O. Keohane, and Sidney Verba. 1994. *Designing Social Inquiry: Scientific Inference in Qualitative Research.* Princeton, NJ: Princeton University Press.

Kirksey, S. Eben, and Stefan Helmreich. 2010. "The Emergence of Multispecies Ethnography." *Cultural Anthropology* 25: 545–76.

Kitcher, Philip. 1989. "Explanatory Unification and the Causal Structure of the World." Pp. 410–505 in *Scientific Explanation*, edited by Philip Kitcher and Wesley C. Salmon. Minneapolis: University of Minnesota Press.

Knight, Jack. 1992. *Institutions and Social Conflict.* Cambridge: Cambridge University Press.

Knobe, Joshua, Sandeep Prasada, and George E. Newman. 2013. "Dual Character Concepts and the Normative Dimension of Conceptual Representation." *Cognition* 127: 242–57.

Knorr Cetina, Karin. 1999. *Epistemic Cultures: How the Sciences Make Knowledge*. Cambridge, MA: Harvard University Press.

Kohli, Atul. 2012. *State-Directed Development: Political Power and Industrialization in the Global Periphery*. New York: Cambridge University Press.

Koivu, Kendra L. 2016. "The Sufficiency of Offensive Doctrine: Counterfactual Analysis and the New History of World War I." Manuscript, University of New Mexico.

Kornblith, Hilary. 1993. *Inductive Inference and Its Natural Ground: An Essay in Naturalistic Epistemology*. Cambridge, MA: MIT Press.

Koslicki, Kathrin. 2008. *The Structure of Objects*. Oxford: Oxford University Press.

Kripke, Saul A. 1980. *Naming and Necessity*. Cambridge, MA: Harvard University Press.

Krishna, Daya. 1971. "'The Self-Fulfilling Prophecy' and the Nature of Society." *American Sociological Review* 36: 1104–7.

Kuhn, Thomas. 1970. *The Structure of Scientific Revolutions*. Chicago: University of Chicago Press.

Kukla, Andre. 1994. "The Structure of Self-Fulfilling and Self-Negating Prophecies." *Theory & Psychology* 4: 5–33.

Kurtz, Marcus J. 2013. *Latin American State Building in Comparative Perspective: Social Foundations of Institutional Order*. Cambridge: Cambridge University Press.

Laakso, Aarre, and Garrison Cottrell. 2000. "Content and Cluster Analysis: Assessing Representational Similarity in Neural Systems." *Philosophical Psychology* 13: 47–76.

Lakoff, George. 1987. *Women, Fire, and Dangerous Things: What Categories Reveal about the Mind*. Chicago: University of Chicago Press.

Lakoff, George, and Mark Johnson. 1980. *Metaphors We Live By*. Chicago: University of Chicago Press.

———. 1999. *Philosophy in the Flesh: The Embodied Mind and Its Challenge to Western Thought*. New York: Basic Books.

Lakoff, George, and Rafael E. Núñez. 2000. *Where Mathematics Comes From: How the Embodied Mind Brings Mathematics into Being*. New York: Basic Books.

Lamont, Michèle, and Vírag Molnár. 2002. "The Study of Boundaries in the Social Sciences." *Annual Review of Sociology* 28: 167–95.

Lange, Marc. 2002. *Introduction to the Philosophy of Physics: Locality, Fields, Energy, and Mass*. Oxford: Blackwell.

Lange, Matthew. 2009. *Lineages of Despotism and Development: British Colonialism and State Power*. Chicago: University of Chicago Press.

Laplace, Pierre-Simon, Marquis de. 1814/1952. *Philosophical Essay on Probabilities*. Translated by E. T. Bell. New York: Dover.

LaPorte, Joseph. 2004. *Natural Kinds and Conceptual Change*. Cambridge: Cambridge University Press.

Lasswell, Harold D., and Abraham Kaplan. 1950. *Power and Society: A Framework for Political Inquiry*. New Haven, CT: Yale University Press.

Latour, Bruno, and Steve Woolgar. 1986. *Laboratory Life: The Construction of Scientific Facts*. Princeton, NJ: Princeton University Press.

Lauria-Santiago, Aldo A. 1999. *An Agrarian Republic: Commercial Agriculture and the Politics of Peasant Communities in El Salvador, 1823–1914*. Durham, NC: Duke University Press.

Lawler, Janet, and David Waldner. Forthcoming. "Interpretivism versus Positivism in an Age of Causal Inference." In *Oxford Handbook of the Philosophy of Political Science*, edited by Harold Kincaid and Jeroen Van Bouwel. Oxford: Oxford University Press.

Lebow, Richard Ned. 2007. "Contingency, Catalysts and Nonlinear Change: The Origins of World War I." Pp. 85–111 in Goertz and Levy, *Explaining War and Peace*.

———. 2010. *Forbidden Fruit: Counterfactuals and International Relations*. Princeton, NJ: Princeton University Press.

Leng, Mary. 2010. *Mathematics and Reality*. Oxford: Oxford University Press.

Leslie, Alan M., and Stephanie Keeble. 1987. "Do Six-Month-Old Infants Perceive Causality?" *Cognition* 25: 265–88.

Leslie, Alan, Fei Xu, Patrice D. Tremoulet, and Brian J. Scholl. 1998. "Indexing and the Object Concept: Developing 'What' and 'Where' Systems." *Trends in Cognitive Sciences* 2: 10–18.

Levi, Margaret. 1988. *Of Rule and Revenue*. Berkeley: University of California Press.

Lévi-Strauss, Claude. 1949/1969. *The Elementary Structures of Kinship*. Boston: Beacon Press.

Levy, Jack S. 2008. "Counterfactuals and Case Studies." Pp. 627–44 in Box-Steffensmeier, Brady, and Collier, *Oxford Handbook of Political Methodology*.

———. 2015. "Counterfactuals, Causal Inference, and Historical Analysis." *Security Studies* 24: 378–402.

Levy, Jack S., and William R. Thompson. 2010. *Causes of War*. Oxford: Wiley-Blackwell.

Lewis, David. 1973. *Counterfactuals*. Oxford: Blackwell.

———. 1979. "Counterfactual Dependence and Time's Arrow." *Noûs* 13: 455–76.

———. 1983. "New Work for a Theory of Universals." *Australasian Journal of Philosophy* 61: 343–77.

———. 1984. "Putnam's Paradox." *Australasian Journal of Philosophy* 62: 221–36.

———. 1986a. *On the Plurality of Worlds*. Oxford: Blackwell.

———. 1986b. *Philosophical Papers*. Oxford: Oxford University Press.

———. 1990. "Noneism or Allism?" *Mind* 99: 23–31.

———. 2000. "Causation as Influence." *Journal of Philosophy* 97: 182–97.

Li, Ming, and Paul Vitányi. 1997. *An Introduction to Kolmogorov Complexity and Its Applications*. New York: Springer.

Libet, Benjamin. 1985. "Unconscious Cerebral Initiative and the Role of Conscious Will in Voluntary Action." *Behavioral and Brain Sciences* 8: 529–66.

Lichbach, Mark Irving, and Alan S. Zuckerman, eds. 1997. *Comparative Politics: Rationality, Culture, and Structure*. New York: Cambridge University Press.

———, eds. 2009. *Comparative Politics: Rationality, Culture, and Structure*. 2nd ed. New York: Cambridge University Press.

Liebowitz, S. J., and Stephen E. Margolis. 1990. "The Fable of the Keys." *Journal of Law and Economics* 33: 1–25.

Lijphart, Arend. 1971. "Comparative Politics and the Comparative Method." *American Political Science Review* 65: 682–93.

Linsky, Bernard, and Edward N. Zalta. 1991. "Is Lewis a Meinongian?" *Australasian Journal of Philosophy* 69: 438–53.

Linz, Juan J. 1978. *The Breakdown of Democratic Regimes: Crisis, Breakdown, and Reequilibration*. Baltimore: Johns Hopkins University Press.

Lipset, Seymour Martin, Martin Trow, and James Coleman. 1956. *Union Democracy: The Inside Politics of the International Typographical Union*. New York: Free Press.

Little, Daniel. 2009. *Microfoundations, Method, and Causation*. New Brunswick, NJ: Transaction Publishing.

Livio, Mario. 2009. *Is God a Mathematician?* New York: Simon and Schuster.

Locke, John. 1690/1975. *An Essay concerning Human Understanding*. Edited by Peter H. Nidditch. Oxford: Clarendon.

———. 1690/1980. *Second Treatise of Government*. Edited by C. B. MacPherson. Indianapolis, IN: Hackett.

Lowe, E. J. 2006. *The Four-Category Ontology: A Metaphysical Foundation for Natural Science*. Oxford: Clarendon Press.

Luebbert, Gregory M. 1991. *Liberalism, Fascism, or Social Democracy: Social Classes and the Political Origins of Regimes in Interwar Europe*. New York: Oxford University Press.

Lukes, Steven. 1974. *Power: A Radical View*. London: Macmillan.

Lustick, Ian. 1996. "History, Historiography, and Political Science: Multiple Historical Records and the Problem of Selection Bias." *American Political Science Review* 90: 605–18.

Lyotard, Jean-François. 1979. *The Postmodern Condition*. Manchester, UK: Manchester University Press.

Mackie, John L. 1965. "Causes and Conditions." *American Philosophical Quarterly* 2: 245–64.

———. 1977. *Ethics: Inventing Right and Wrong*. London: Penguin.

———. 1980. *Cement of the Universe: A Study of Causation*. Oxford: Oxford University Press.

MacKinnon, Catherine A. 2001. *Sex Equality*. New York: Foundation Press.

Maddy, Penelope. 1990. *Realism in Mathematics*. Oxford: Clarendon Press.

Maeyer, Jenine, and Vicente Talanquer. 2010. "The Role of Intuitive Heuristics in Students' Thinking: Ranking Chemical Substances." In section "Learning," edited by Michael Ford and Maria Varelas. *Science Education* 94: 963–84.

Mahoney, James. 1999. "Nominal, Ordinal, and Narrative Appraisal in Macrocausal Analysis." *American Journal of Sociology* 104: 1154–96.

———. 2000. "Path Dependence in Historical Sociology." *Theory and Society* 29: 507–48.

———. 2001. *The Legacies of Liberalism: Path Dependence and Political Regimes in Central America*. Baltimore: Johns Hopkins University Press.

———. 2003. "Long-Run Development and the Legacy of Colonialism in Spanish America." *American Journal of Sociology* 109: 51–106.

———. 2004. "Revisiting General Theory in Historical Sociology." *Social Forces* 83: 459–90.

———. 2010. *Colonialism and Postcolonial Development: Spanish America in Comparative Perspective*. New York: Cambridge University Press.

———. 2012. "The Logic of Process Tracing Tests in the Social Sciences." *Sociological Methods and Research* 41: 566–90.

Mahoney, James, and Laura Acosta. Forthcoming. "A Regularity Theory of Causality for the Social Sciences." *Quality and Quantity*.

Mahoney, James, and Gary Goertz. 2004. "The Possibility Principle: Choosing Negative Cases in Comparative Research." *American Political Science Review* 4: 653–69.

Mahoney, James, Erin Kimball, and Kendra Koivu. 2009. "The Logic of Historical Explanation in the Social Sciences." *Comparative Political Studies* 42: 114–46.

Mahoney, James, and Dietrich Rueschemeyer, eds. 2003. *Comparative Historical Analysis in the Social Sciences*. Cambridge: Cambridge University Press.

Mahoney, James, and Richard Snyder. 1999. "Rethinking Agency and Structure in the Study of Regime Change." *Studies in Comparative International Development* 34: 3–32.

Mahoney, James, and Kathleen Thelen, eds. 2010. *Explaining Institutional Change: Ambiguity, Agency, and Power*. New York: Cambridge University Press.

———, eds. 2015. *Advances in Comparative-Historical Analysis*. Cambridge: Cambridge University Press.

Mamdani, Mahmood. 1996. *Citizen and Subject: Contemporary Africa and the Legacy of Late Colonialism*. Princeton, NJ: Princeton University Press.

Mandalaywala, Tara M., David M. Amodio, and Marjorie Rhodes. 2018. "Essentialism Promotes Racial Prejudice by Increasing Endorsement of Social Hierarchies." *Social Psychology and Personality Science* 9: 461–69.

Mandelbaum, Maurice. 1955. "Societal Facts." *British Journal of Sociology* 6: 305–17.

———. 1987. *Purpose and Necessity in Social Theory*. Baltimore: Johns Hopkins University Press.

Mandler, Jean Matter. 1984. *Stories, Scripts, and Scenes: Aspects of Schema Theory*. Hillsdale, NJ: Lawrence Erlbaum.

———. 1992. "How to Build a Baby II: Conceptual Primitives." *Psychological Review* 99: 587–604.

———. 2004. *The Foundations of Mind: Origins of Conceptual Thought*. Oxford: Oxford University Press.

———. 2012. "On the Spatial Foundations of the Conceptual System and Its Enrichment." *Cognitive Science* 36: 421–51.

Mandler, Jean M., and Cristóbal Pagán Cánovas. 2014. "On Defining Image Schemas." *Language and Cognition* 6: 510–32.

Manicas, Peter T. 1981. "Review of *States and Social Revolutions: A Comparative Analysis of France, Russia, and China*, by Theda Skocpol." *History and Theory* 20: 204–18.

Mann, Michael. 1986. *The Sources of Social Power*. Vol. 1, *A History of Power from the Beginning to A.D. 1760*. Cambridge: Cambridge University Press.

Marcus, Gary F. 2001. *The Algebraic Mind: Integrating Connectionism and Cognitive Science*. Cambridge, MA: MIT Press.

Margolis, Eric, and Stephen Laurence, eds. 1999. *Concepts: Core Readings*. Cambridge, MA: MIT Press.

———, eds. 2007a. *Creations of the Mind: Theories of Artifacts and Their Representation*. Oxford: Oxford University Press.

———. 2007b. "The Ontology of Concepts—Abstract Objects or Mental Representations?" *Noûs* 41: 561–93.

Markman, Ellen M., and Jeffrey Seibert. 1976. "Classes and Collections: Internal Organization and Resulting Holistic Properties." *Cognitive Psychology* 8: 561–77.

Martin, John Levi. 2003. "What Is Field Theory?" *American Journal of Sociology* 109: 1–49.

Marx, Karl. 1972. "Revolutionary Program and Strategy." Part 3 of *The Marx-Engels Reader*, edited by Robert C. Tucker. New York: Norton.

Marx, Karl, and Friedrich Engels. 1848/2012. *The Communist Manifesto*. New Haven, CT: Yale University Press.

Mayntz, Renate. 2004. "Mechanisms in the Analysis of Social Macro-Phenomena." *Philosophy of the Social Sciences* 34: 237–54.

Mayr, Ernst. 1982. *The Growth of Biological Thought: Diversity, Evolution, and Inheritance*. Cambridge, MA: Harvard University Press.

———. 1988. *Toward a New Philosophy of Biology: Observations of an Evolutionist*. Cambridge, MA: Harvard University Press.

McAdam, Doug. 1982. *Political Process and the Development of Black Insurgency, 1930–1970*. Chicago: University of Chicago Press.

McAdam, Douglas, Sidney Tarrow, and Charles Tilly. 2001. *Dynamics of Contention*. New York: Cambridge University Press.

McCall, Leslie. 2005. "The Complexity of Intersectionality." *Signs* 30: 1771–1800.

McCloskey, Michael. 1983. "Intuitive Physics." *Scientific American* 248 (4): 122–30.

McDermott, Michael. 2002. "Influence versus Sufficiency." *Journal of Philosophy* 99: 84–101.

McDonnell, Erin Metz. 2017. "Patchwork Leviathan: How Pockets of Bureaucratic Governance Flourish within Institutionally Diverse Developing States." *American Sociological Review* 82: 476–510.

———. 2020. *Patchwork Leviathan: Pockets of Bureaucratic Effectiveness in Developing States*. Princeton, NJ: Princeton University Press.

McGinn, Colin. 1983. *The Subjective View: Secondary Qualities and Indexical Thoughts*. Oxford: Clarendon Press.

McGinn, Colin. 1999. *The Mysterious Flame: Conscious Minds in a Material World.* New York: Basic Books.

McKeown, Timothy J. 1999. "Case Studies and the Statistical Worldview: Review of King, Keohane, and Verba's *Designing Social Inquiry.*" *International Organization* 53: 161–90.

McMullin, Ernan. 1984. "Two Ideals of Explanation in Natural Science." *Midwest Studies in Philosophy* 9: 205–20.

McShane, Blakeley B., David Gal, Andrew Gelman, Christian Robert, and Jennifer L. Tackett. 2019. "Abandon Statistical Significance." *American Statistician* 73 (supplement 1): 235–45.

Mead, George Herbert. 1934. *Mind, Self, and Society.* Chicago: University of Chicago Press.

Medin, Douglas. 1989. "Concepts and Conceptual Structure." *American Psychologist* 44: 1469–81.

Medin, Douglas, and Andrew Ortony. 1989. "Psychological Essentialism." Pp. 183–96 in *Similarity and Analogical Reasoning,* edited by Stella Vosniadou and Andrew Ortony. Cambridge: Cambridge University Press.

Melamed, Yitzhak Y., and Martin Lin. 2020. "Principle of Sufficient Reason." *Stanford Encyclopedia of Philosophy,* Spring edition.

Mellor, D. H. 1977. "Natural Kinds." *British Journal for the Philosophy of Science* 28: 299–312.

Menzel, Christopher. 2015. "Possible Worlds." *Stanford Encyclopedia of Philosophy,* Spring edition.

Menzies, Peter. 2004. "Difference Making in Context." Pp. 139–80 in Collins, Hall, and Paul, *Causation and Counterfactuals.*

———. 2009. "Platitudes and Counterexamples." Pp. 341–67 in Beebee, Hitchcock, and Menzies, *Oxford Handbook of Causation.*

———. 2011. "The Role of Counterfactual Dependence in Causal Judgments." Pp. 186–207 in *Understanding Counterfactuals, Understanding Causation: Issues in Philosophy and Psychology,* edited by Christoph Hoerl, Teresa McCormack, and Sarah R. Beck. Oxford: Oxford University Press.

Merrill, G. H. 1980. "The Model-Theoretic Argument against Realism." *Philosophy of Science* 47: 69–81.

Merton, Robert K. 1945. "What Is Sociological Theory?" *American Journal of Sociology* 50: 462–73.

———. 1948. "The Self-Fulfilling Prophecy." *Antioch Review* 8: 193–210.

Metzinger, Thomas. 2009. *The Ego Tunnel: The Science of the Mind and the Myth of Self.* New York: Basic Books.

Meyer, John W., and Brian Rowan. 1977. "Institutionalized Organizations: Formal Structure as Myth and Ceremony." *American Journal of Sociology* 83: 340–63.

Mill, John Stuart. 1843/1911. *A System of Logic: Ratiocinative and Inductive.* London: Longmans, Green.

———. 1861/1998. *Utilitarianism.* Edited by Roger Crisp. Oxford: Oxford University Press.

Miller, Richard W. 2000. "Half-Naturalized Social Kinds." *Philosophy of Science* 67 (supplement): S640–S652.

Millikan, Ruth Garrett. 1999. "Historical Kinds and the 'Special Sciences.'" *Philosophical Studies* 95: 45–65.

Minsky, Marvin. 1975. "A Framework for Representing Knowledge." Pp. 211–77 in *The Psychology of Computer Vision,* edited by Patrick Henry Winston. New York: McGraw-Hill.

Moore, Barrington, Jr. 1966. *Social Origins of Dictatorship and Democracy: Lord and Peasant in the Making of the Modern World.* Boston: Beacon Press.

Moore, G. E. 1922. *Philosophical Studies.* London: Routledge.

Moore, K. E. 2006. "Space-to-Time Mappings and Temporal Concepts." *Cognitive Linguistics* 17: 199–244.

Morgan, Stephen L., and Christopher Winship. 2007. *Counterfactuals and Causal Inference: Methods and Principles for Social Research.* Cambridge: Cambridge University Press.

———. 2015. *Counterfactuals and Causal Inference: Methods and Principles for Social Research.* 2nd ed. Cambridge: Cambridge University Press.

Morning, Ann. 2009. "Toward a Sociology of Racial Conceptualization for the 21st Century." *Social Forces* 87: 1167–92.

Morris, Aldon D. 1984. *The Origins of the Civil Rights Movement: Black Communities Organizing for Change.* New York: Free Press.

Morriss, Peter. 2002. *Power: A Philosophical Analysis.* 2nd ed. Manchester, UK: Manchester University Press.

Mukherjee, Siddhartha. 2016. *The Gene: An Intimate History.* New York: Scribner.

Mumford, Stephen. 1998. *Dispositions.* Oxford: Clarendon.

———. 2009. "Causal Powers and Capacities." Pp. 265–78 in Beebee, Hitchcock, and Menzies, *Oxford Handbook of Causation.*

Mumford, Stephen, and Rani Lill Anjum. 2011. *Getting Causes from Powers.* Oxford: Oxford University Press.

Nagel, Ernst. 1961. *The Structure of Science: Problems in the Logic of Scientific Explanation.* New York: Harcourt, Brace and World.

———. 1979. *The Structure of Science: Problems in the Logic of Scientific Explanation.* 2nd ed. Indianapolis, IN: Hackett.

Nagel, Thomas. 1974. "What Is It Like to Be a Bat?" *Philosophical Review* 83: 435–50.

———. 1986. *The View from Nowhere.* Oxford: Oxford University Press.

———. 1991. *Equality and Partiality.* Oxford: Oxford University Press.

———. 1997. *The Last Word.* New York: Oxford University Press.

Nash, John. 1997. *Essays on Game Theory.* Cheltenham, UK: Edward Elgar.

Nelson, Alan. 1994. "How Could Scientific Facts Be Socially Constructed?" *Studies in History and Philosophy of Science* 25: 535–47.

Nersessian, Nancy J. 2010. *Creating Scientific Concepts.* Cambridge, MA: MIT Press.

Newman, George E., and Joshua Knobe. 2019. "The Essence of Essentialism." *Mind and Language* 34: 585–605.

Nietzsche, Friedrich. 1886/1966. *Beyond Good and Evil: Prelude to a Philosophy of the Future.* Translated by Walter Kaufman. New York: Vintage.

Niiniluoto, Ilkka. 1998. "Verisimilitude: The Third Period." *British Journal for the Philosophy of Science* 49: 1–29.

Nobles, Melissa. 2000. *Shades of Citizenship: Race and Census in Modern Politics.* Stanford, CA: Stanford University Press.

North, Douglass C. 1981. *Structure and Change in Economic History.* New York: Norton.

———. 1990. *Institutions, Institutional Change, and Economic Performance.* Cambridge: Cambridge University Press.

Nozick, Robert. 1974. *Anarchy, State, and Utopia.* New York: Basic Books.

Nussbaum, Martha. 1992. "Human Functionary and Social Justice: In Defense of Aristotelian Essentialism." *Political Theory* 20: 202–46.

———. 1999. *Sex and Social Justice.* Oxford: Oxford University Press.

———. 2000. *Women and Human Development: The Capabilities Approach.* Cambridge: Cambridge University Press.

———. 2011. *Creating Capabilities.* Cambridge, MA: Harvard University Press.

Oana, Ioana-Elena, Carsten Q. Schneider, and Eva Thomann. Forthcoming. *Qualitative Comparative Analysis (QCA) with R.* Cambridge: Cambridge University Press.

O'Brien, Gerard, and Jon Opie. 2006. "How Do Connectionist Networks Compute?" *Cognitive Processes* 7: 30–41.

Oddie, Graham. 1981. "Verisimilitude Reviewed." *British Journal for the Philosophy of Science* 32: 237–65.

———. 1986. "The Poverty of the Popperian Program for Truthlikeness." *Philosophy of Science* 53: 163–78.

Odell, James J. 1998. *Advanced Object-Oriented Analysis and Design Using UML*. Cambridge: Cambridge University Press.

Oderberg, David S. 2007. *Real Essentialism*. New York: Routledge.

O'Donnell, Guillermo. 1973. *Modernization and Bureaucratic-Authoritarianism: Studies in South American Politics*. Berkeley: Institute of International Studies, University of California.

O'Donnell, Guillermo, and Philippe Schmitter. 1986. *Tentative Conclusions about Uncertain Democracies*. Baltimore: Johns Hopkins University Press.

Ogden, C. K., and I. A. Richards. 1923. *The Meaning of Meaning*. London: Kegan Paul.

Olson, Mancur. 1965. *The Logic of Collective Action: Public Goods and the Theory of Groups*. Cambridge, MA: Harvard University Press.

Orren, Karen. 1991. *Belated Feudalism: Labor, the Law, and Liberal Development in the United States*. Cambridge: Cambridge University Press.

Ortner, Sherry B., and Harriet Whitehead, eds. 1981. *Sexual Meanings: The Cultural Construction of Gender and Sexuality*. Cambridge: Cambridge University Press.

Ostrom, Elinor. 1986. "An Agenda for the Study of Institutions." *Public Choice* 48: 3–25.

———. 1990. *Governing the Commons: The Evolution of Institutions for Collective Action*. New York: Cambridge University Press.

———. 2009. *Understanding Institutional Diversity*. Princeton, NJ: Princeton University Press.

Paige, Jeffery M. 1997. *Coffee and Power: Revolution and the Rise of Democracy in Central America*. Cambridge, MA: Harvard University Press.

Palmer, Stephen E. 1999. *Vision Science: Photons to Phenomenology*. Cambridge, MA: MIT Press.

Palmer, Trevor. 1999. *Controversy: Catastrophism and Evolution—The Ongoing Debate*. New York: Kluwer Academic.

Panksepp, Jaak. 2000. "Emotions as Natural Kinds within the Mammalian Brain." Pp. 137–56 in *Handbook of Emotions*, 2nd ed., edited by M. Lewis and J. M. Haviland-Jones. New York: Guilford.

Parsons, Talcott. 1937. *The Structure of Social Action*. New York: McGraw-Hill.

———. 1951. *The Social System*. Glencoe, IL: Free Press.

Pater, Joe. 2019. "Generative Linguistics and Neural Networks at 60: Foundation, Friction, and Fusion." *Language* 95: 41–74.

Pattillo, Mary. 2013. *Black Picket Fences: Privilege and Peril among the Black Middle Class*. 2nd ed. Chicago: University of Chicago Press.

Paul, L. A., and Ned Hall. 2013. *Causation: A User's Guide*. Oxford: Oxford University Press.

Pearl, Judea. 2000. *Causality: Models, Reasoning, and Inference*. Cambridge: Cambridge University Press.

———. 2009. *Causality: Models, Reasoning, and Inference*. 2nd ed. Cambridge: Cambridge University Press.

———. 2018. *The Book of Why: The New Science of Cause and Effect*. New York: Basic Books.

Pickering, Andrew. 1984. *Constructing Quarks: A Sociological History of Particle Physics*. Chicago: University of Chicago Press.

Pierson, Paul. 1998. "Not Just What, but When: Issues of Timing and Sequence in Comparative Politics." Paper prepared for presentation at the Annual Meeting of the American Political Science Association, September, Boston.

———. 2004. *Politics in Time: History, Institutions, and Social Analysis*. Princeton, NJ: Princeton University Press.

Pierson, Paul, and Theda Skocpol. 2002. "Historical Institutionalism in Contemporary Political Science." Pp. 693–721 in *Political Science: State of the Discipline*, edited by Ira Katznelson and Helen V. Milner. New York: Norton.

Pinch, Trevor J., and Wiebe E. Bijker. 1989. "The Social Construction of Facts and Artifacts: Or How the Sociology of Science and the Sociology of Technology Might Benefit Each Other." Pp. 17–47 in *The Social Construction of Technological Systems: New Directions in the Sociology of Technology and History*, edited by Wiebe E. Bijker, Thomas P. Hughes, and Trevor J. Pinch. Cambridge, MA: MIT Press.

Pinker, Steven. 1994. *The Language Instinct*. New York: W. Morrow.

———. 1997. *How the Mind Works*. New York: Norton.

———. 2002. *The Blank Slate: The Denial of Human Nature in Modern Intellectual Life*. New York: Viking.

———. 2007. *The Stuff of Thought: Language as a Window into Human Nature*. New York: Viking.

———. 2011. *The Better Angels of Our Nature: Why Violence Has Declined*. New York: Viking.

———. 2018. *Enlightenment Now: The Case for Reason, Science, Humanism, and Progress*. New York: Viking.

Piore, Michael J., and Charles Sabel. 1984. *The Second Divide: Possibilities for Prosperity*. New York: Basic Books.

Plummer, David. 1999. *One of the Boys: Masculinity, Homophobia, and Modern Manhood*. New York: Hawthorn Press.

Pomeranz, Kenneth. 2001. *China, Europe, and the Making of the Modern World Economy*. Princeton, NJ: Princeton University Press.

Popper, Karl. 1934/1968. *The Logic of Scientific Discovery*. New York: Harper and Row.

———. 1945/2013. *The Open Society and Its Enemies*. Princeton, NJ: Princeton University Press.

———. 1963. *Conjectures and Refutations*. London: Routledge.

———. 1976. "A Note on Verisimilitude." *British Journal for the Philosophy of Science* 27: 147–59.

Potter, Jonathan. 1996. *Representing Reality: Discourse, Rhetoric, and Social Construction*. London: Sage.

Potter, Michael. 2004. *Set Theory and Its Philosophy*. Oxford: Oxford University Press.

Poulantzas, Nicos. 1975. *Political Power and Social Classes*. London: NLB.

Powell, Walter W. 1991. "Expanding the Scope of Institutional Analysis." Pp. 183–203 in Powell and DiMaggio, *New Institutionalism*.

Powell, Walter W., and Paul J. DiMaggio, eds. 1991. *The New Institutionalism in Organizational Analysis*. Chicago: University of Chicago Press.

Prentice, Deborah A., and Dale T. Miller. 2007. "Psychological Essentialism of Human Categories." *Current Directions in Psychological Science* 16: 202–6.

Presnell, Jenny L. 2013. *The Information-Literate Historian: A Guide to Research for History Students*. 2nd ed. New York: Oxford University Press.

Prinz, Jesse J. 2002. *Furnishing the Mind: Concepts and Their Perceptual Basis*. Cambridge, MA: MIT Press.

———. 2014. *Beyond Human Nature: How Culture and Experience Shape the Human Mind*. New York: Penguin.

———. 2015. "The Return of Concept Empiricism." Pp. 931–50 in *Categorization and Cognitive Science*, 2nd ed., edited by Henri Cohen and Claire Lefebvre. Amsterdam: Elsevier.

Przeworski, Adam. 1985. *Capitalism and Social Democracy*. Cambridge: Cambridge University Press.

Przeworski, Adam, and Henry Teune. 1970. *The Logic of Comparative Social Inquiry*. New York: John Wiley.

Psillos, Stathis. 2002. *Causation and Explanation*. Montreal: McGill-Queen's University Press.

Psillos, Stathis. 2009. "Regularity Theories." Pp. 131–58 in Beebee, Hitchcock, and Menzies, *Oxford Handbook of Causation*.

Putnam, Hilary. 1970. "Is Semantics Possible?" *Metaphilosophy* 1: 187–201.

———. 1975. *Mind, Language, and Reality*. New York: Cambridge University Press.

———. 1979. "What Is Mathematical Truth?" Pp. 60–78 in *Mathematics, Matter and Method*, vol. 1, 2nd ed. Cambridge: Cambridge University Press.

———. 1981. *Reason, Truth, and History*. Cambridge: Cambridge University Press.

Putnam, Robert. 2000. *Bowling Alone: The Collapse and Revival of American Community*. New York: Simon and Schuster.

Quadagno, Jill, and Stan J. Knapp. 1992. "Have Historical Sociologists Forsaken Theory? Thoughts on the History/Theory Relationship." *Sociological Methods and Research* 20: 481–507.

Quillien, Tadeg. 2018. "Psychological Essentialism from First Principles." *Evolution and Human Behavior* 39: 692–99.

Quine, W. V. 1943. "Notes on Existence and Necessity." *Journal of Philosophy* 40: 113–27.

Quinn, Naomi. 1991. "The Cultural Basis of Metaphor." Pp. 56–93 in *Beyond Metaphor: The Theory of Tropes in Anthropology*, edited by J. W. Fernandez. Stanford, CA: Stanford University Press.

Rabinow, Paul, and William M. Sullivan, eds. 1987. *Interpretive Social Science: A Second Look*. Berkeley: University of California Press.

Radcliffe-Brown, A. R. 1952. *Structure and Function in Primitive Societies*. London: Cohen and West.

Ragin, Charles C. 1987. *The Comparative Method: Moving beyond Qualitative and Quantitative Strategies*. Berkeley: University of California Press.

———. 1992. "Introduction: Cases of 'What Is a Case?'" Pp. 1–18 in *What Is a Case? Exploring the Foundations of Social Inquiry*, edited by Howard S. Becker and Charles C. Ragin. Chicago: University of Chicago Press.

———. 2000. *Fuzzy-Set Social Science*. Chicago: University of Chicago Press.

———. 2008. *Redesigning Social Inquiry: Fuzzy Sets and Beyond*. Chicago: University of Chicago Press.

Ragin, Charles C., and Peer C. Fiss. 2017. *Intersectional Inequality: Race, Class, Test Scores, and Poverty*. Chicago: University of Chicago Press.

Railton, Peter. 1978. "A Deductive-Nomological Model of Probabilistic Explanation." *Philosophy of Science* 45: 206–26.

Rawls, John. 1971/1999. *A Theory of Justice*. Rev. ed. Cambridge, MA: Harvard University Press.

Reed, Baron. 2011. "Certainty." *Stanford Encyclopedia of Philosophy*, Winter edition.

Reed, Isaac. 2008. "Justifying Sociological Knowledge: From Realism to Interpretation." *Sociological Theory* 26: 101–29.

———. 2011. *Interpretation and Social Knowledge: On the Use of Theory in the Human Sciences*. Chicago: University of Chicago Press.

Reisch, George. 1991. "Chaos, History, and Narrative." *History and Theory* 30: 1–20.

Resnik, Michael D. 1997. *Mathematics as a Science of Patterns*. Oxford: Oxford University Press.

Rhodes, Marjorie, and Susan A. Gelman. 2009. "A Developmental Examination of the Conceptual Structure of Animal, Artifact, and Human Social Categories across Two Cultural Contexts." *Cognitive Psychology* 59: 244–74.

Rhodes, Marjorie, Sarah-Jane Leslie, and Christina M. Tworek. 2012. "Cultural Transmission of Social Essentialism." *Proceedings of the National Academy of Sciences* 109: 13526–31.

Rhodes, Marjorie, and Tara Mandalaywala. 2017. "The Development and Developmental Consequences of Social Essentialism." *WIREs Cognitive Science* 8 (4): e1435.

Ridgeway, Cecilia L., and Shelley J. Correll. 2004. "Unpacking the Gender System: A Theoretical Perspective on Gender Beliefs and Social Relations." *Gender and Society* 18: 510–31.

Riedl, Rachel Beatty. 2014. *Authoritarian Origins of Democratic Party Systems in Africa.* New York: Cambridge University Press.

Rigney, Daniel. 2001. *The Metaphorical Society: An Invitation to Social Theory.* Lanham, MD: Rowman and Littlefield.

Rihoux, Benoît, and Charles C. Ragin, eds. 2009. *Configurational Comparative Methods: Qualitative Comparative Analysis (QCA) and Related Techniques.* Thousand Oaks, CA: Sage.

Rips, Lance J. 1989. "Similarity, Typicality and Categorization." Pp. 21–59 in *Similarity and Analogical Reasoning,* edited by Stella Vosniadou and Andrew Ortony. Cambridge: Cambridge University Press.

Rips, Lance J., Sergey Blok, and George Newman. 2006. "Tracing the Identity of Objects." *Psychological Review* 113: 1–30.

Roberts, Clayton. 1996. *The Logic of Historical Explanation.* University Park: Penn State University Press.

Roberts, Kenneth M. 2014. *Changing Course in Latin America: Party Systems in the Neoliberal Era.* New York: Cambridge University Press.

Robertson, Teresa. 2009. "Essential vs. Accidental Properties." *Stanford Encyclopedia of Philosophy,* Spring edition.

Robeyns, Ingrid. 2016. "The Capability Approach." *Stanford Encyclopedia of Philosophy,* Winter edition.

Rodney, Walter. 1972. *How Europe Underdeveloped Africa.* London: Bogle-L'Ouverture Publications.

Roemer, John E. 1996. *Theories of Distributive Justice.* Cambridge, MA: Harvard University Press.

Rohlfing, Ingo. 2012. *Case Studies and Causal Inference: An Integrative Approach.* Basingstoke, UK: Palgrave Macmillan.

———. 2013. "Bayesian Causal Inference in Process Tracing: The Importance of Probably Being Wrong." Paper presented at the Annual Meeting of the American Political Science Association, August 29–September 1, Chicago.

Romer, Paul M. 1986. "Increasing Returns and Long-Run Growth." *Journal of Political Economy* 94: 1002–37.

Rorty, Richard. 1979. *Philosophy and the Mirror of Nature.* Princeton, NJ: Princeton University Press.

———. 1991. *Objectivity, Relativism, and Truth.* Philosophical Papers, vol. 1. Cambridge: Cambridge University Press.

Rosch, Eleanor. 1973. "Natural Categories." *Cognitive Psychology* 4: 328–50.

———. 1978. "Principles of Categorization." Pp. 27–48 in *Cognition and Categorization,* edited by Eleanor Rosch and B. B. Lloyd. Hillsdale, NJ: Lawrence Erlbaum.

———. 1999. "Reclaiming Concepts." *Journal of Consciousness Studies* 6 (11–12): 61–77.

———. 2011. "'Slow Lettuce': Categories, Concepts, Fuzzy Sets, and Logical Deduction." Pp. 89–120 in *Concepts and Fuzzy Logic,* edited by Radim Belohlavek and George J. Klir. Cambridge, MA: MIT Press.

Rose, David. 2015. "Persistence through Function Preservation." *Synthese* 192: 97–146.

Rose, David, and Shaun Nichols. 2019. "Teleological Essentialism." *Cognitive Science* 43: 1–19.

Rose, David, and Jonathan Schaffer. 2017. "Folk Mereology Is Teleological." *Noûs* 51: 238–70.

Rosenfeld, Gavriel D. 2005. *The World Hitler Never Made: Alternative History and the Memory of Nazism.* Cambridge: Cambridge University Press.

Rothbart, Myron, and Marjorie Taylor. 1992. "Category Labels and Social Reality: Do We View Social Categories as Natural Kinds?" Pp. 11–36 in *Language, Interaction and Social Cognition,* edited by Gün R. Semin and Klaus Fiedler. London: Sage.

Roy, William G. 1997. *Socializing Capital: The Rise of the Large Industrial Corporation in America.* Princeton, NJ: Princeton University Press.

Rozenblit, Leonid, and Frank Keil. 2002. "The Misunderstood Limits of Folk Science: An Illusion of Explanatory Depth." *Cognitive Science* 26: 521–62.

Rubin, Donald B. 1974. "Estimating Causal Effects of Treatments in Randomized and Nonrandomized Studies." *Journal of Educational Psychology* 66: 688–701.

Rubinow, I. M. 1913/1969. *Social Insurance, with Special Reference to American Conditions.* New York: Arno Press.

Rueschemeyer, Dietrich. 1986. *Power and the Division of Labour.* Stanford, CA: Stanford University Press.

———. 2003. "Can One or a Few Cases Yield Theoretical Gains?" Pp. 305–36 in Mahoney and Rueschemeyer, *Comparative Historical Analysis.*

———. 2009. *Usable Theory: Analytic Tools for Social and Political Research.* Princeton, NJ: Princeton University Press.

Rueschemeyer, Dietrich, and Peter B. Evans. 1985. "The State and Economic Transformation: Toward an Analysis of the Conditions Underlying Effective Intervention." Pp. 44–77 in *Bringing the State Back In,* edited by Peter B. Evans, Dietrich Rueschemeyer, and Theda Skocpol. Cambridge: Cambridge University Press.

Rueschemeyer, Dietrich, Evelyne Huber Stephens, and John D. Stephens. 1992. *Capitalist Development and Democracy.* Chicago: University of Chicago.

Rupert, Robert D. 2009. *Cognitive Systems and the Extended Mind.* Oxford: Oxford University Press.

Russell, Bertrand. 1913. "On the Notion of Cause." *Proceedings of the Aristotelian Society* 13: 1–26.

———. 1948. *Human Knowledge.* New York: Simon and Schuster.

Said, Edward W. 1978. *Orientalism.* New York: Random House.

Salmon, Wesley. 1998. *Causality and Explanation.* New York: Oxford University Press.

Santibáñez, Francisco. 2002. "The Object Image-Schema and Other Dependent Schemas." *Atlantis* 24: 183–201.

Sartori, Giovanni. 1970. "Concept Misformation in Comparative Politics." *American Political Science Review* 64: 1033–53.

———. 1975. "The Tower of Babel." Pp. 7–38 in *Tower of Babel: On the Definition and Analysis of Concepts in the Social Sciences,* edited by Giovanni Sartori, Fred W. Riggs, and Henry Teune. International Studies Association, Occasional Paper no. 6, University of Pittsburgh.

———. 1984. "Guidelines for Concept Analysis." Pp. 15–85 in *Social Science Concepts: A Systematic Analysis,* edited by Giovanni Sartori. Beverly Hills, CA: Sage.

Saslaw, Janna. 1996. "Forces, Containers, and Paths: The Role of Body-Derived Image Schemas in the Conceptualization of Music." *Journal of Music Theory* 40: 217–43.

Sayer, Andrew. 1992. *Method in Social Science: A Realist Approach.* 2nd ed. London: Routledge.

———. 1997. "Essentialism, Social Constructionism, and Beyond." *Sociological Review* 45: 453–87.

———. 2000. *Realism and Social Science.* 2nd ed. London: Sage.

Schaffer, Jonathan. 2000. "Trumping Preemption." *Journal of Philosophy* 97: 165–81.

———. 2003. "Overdetermining Causes." *Philosophical Studies* 114: 23–45.

Schank, Roger C., and Robert P. Abelson. 1977. *Scripts, Plans, Goals and Understanding: An Inquiry into Human Knowledge Structures.* Hillsdale, NJ: Lawrence Erlbaum.

Scheffer, Marten, Jordi Bascompte, William A. Brock, Victor Brovkin, Stephen R. Carpenter, Vasilis Dakos, Hermann Held, Egbert H. van Nes, Max Rietkerk, and George Sugihara. 2009. "Early-Warning Signals for Critical Transitions." *Nature* 461: 53–59.

Schelling, Thomas. 1978. *Micromotives and Macrobehavior.* New York: Norton.

Scheper-Hughes, Nancy. 1995. "The Primacy of the Ethical: Propositions for a Militant Anthropology." *Current Anthropology* 36: 409–40.

Schmidt, Vivien A. 2008. "Discursive Intuitionalism: The Explanatory Power of Ideas and Discourse." *Annual Review of Political Science* 11: 303–26.

Schneider, Carsten Q. 2018. "Idealists and Realists in QCA." *Political Analysis* 26: 246–54.

Schneider, Carsten Q., and Ingo Rohlfing. 2013. "Combining QCA and Process Tracing in Set-Theoretic Multi-Method Research." *Sociological Methods and Research* 42: 559–97.

———. Forthcoming. "A Unifying Framework for Causal Research in Set-Theoretic Multi-Method Research." *Sociological Methods and Research.*

Schneider, Carsten Q., and Claudius Wagemann. 2012. *Set-Theoretic Methods for the Social Sciences: A Guide to Qualitative Comparative Analysis.* Cambridge: Cambridge University Press.

Schubert, Thomas W. 2005. "Your Highness: Vertical Position as Perceptual Symbols of Power." *Journal of Personality and Social Psychology* 89: 1–21.

Schutz, Alfred. 1970. *On Phenomenology and Social Relations.* Chicago: University of Chicago Press.

Scott, James C. 1998. *Seeing like a State: How Certain Schemas to Improve the Human Condition Have Failed.* New Haven, CT: Yale University Press.

Scott, Joan W. 1986. "Gender: A Useful Category of Historical Analysis." *American Historical Review* 91: 1053–75.

———. 1999. *Gender and the Politics of History.* New York: Columbia University Press.

Scott, W. Richard. 1991. "Unpacking Institutional Arguments." Pp. 164–82 in Powell and DiMaggio, *New Institutionalism.*

Scriven, Michael. 1959. "Truisms as the Grounds for Historical Explanations." Pp. 443–75 in *Theories of History,* edited by Patrick Gardiner. Glencoe, IL: Free Press.

Searle, John R. 1964. "How to Derive 'Ought' from 'Is.'" *Philosophical Review* 73: 43–58.

———. 1995. *The Construction of Social Reality.* New York: Free Press.

———. 2008. "Language and Social Ontology." *Theory and Society* 37: 443–59.

———. 2015. *Making the Social World: The Structure of Human Civilization.* Oxford: Oxford University Press.

Seawright, Jason. 2010. "Regression-Based Inference: A Case Study in Failed Causal Assessment." Pp. 247–71 in Brady and Collier, *Rethinking Social Inquiry.*

———. 2015. *Multi-Method Social Science.* New York: Cambridge University Press.

Seawright, Jason, and David Collier. 2010. "Glossary." Pp. 313–59 in Brady and Collier, *Rethinking Social Inquiry.*

Sen, Amartya. 1992. *Inequality Reexamined.* Cambridge, MA: Harvard University Press.

———. 1999. *Development as Freedom.* New York: Knopf.

———. 2002. *Rationality and Freedom.* Cambridge, MA: Harvard University Press.

———. 2009. *The Idea of Justice.* Cambridge, MA: Harvard University Press.

Sen, Amartya, and Bernard Williams, eds. 1982. *Utilitarianism and Beyond.* Cambridge: Cambridge University Press.

Sewell, William H., Jr. 1992. "A Theory of Structure: Duality, Agency, and Transformation." *American Journal of Sociology* 98: 1–29.

———. 1996. "Historical Events as Transformations of Structures: Inventing Revolution at the Bastille." *Theory and Society* 25: 841–81.

———. 2005. *Logics of History: Social Theory and Social Transformation.* Chicago: University of Chicago Press.

Shadish, William R., Thomas D. Cook, and Donald T. Campbell. 2002. *Experimental and Quasi-Experimental Designs for General Causal Inference.* Boston: Houghton Mifflin.

Shapiro, Stewart. 1991. *Foundations without Foundationalism: A Case for Second-Order Logic.* Oxford: Clarendon Press.

Shapiro, Stewart. 1997. *Philosophy of Mathematics: Structure and Ontology*. New York: Oxford University Press.

———. 2007. "Philosophy of Mathematics and Its Logic: Introduction." Pp. 1–28 in *The Oxford Handbook of Philosophy of Mathematics and Logic*, edited by Stewart Shapiro. Oxford: Oxford University Press.

Sheehy, Paul. 2006. *The Reality of Social Groups*. Hampshire, UK: Ashgate.

Sher, Gila. 2013. "The Foundational Problem of Logic." *Bulletin of Symbolic Logic* 19: 145–98.

Shin, Sun-Joo, Oliver Lemon, and John Mumma. 2018. "Diagrams." *Stanford Encyclopedia of Philosophy*, Winter edition.

Shotter, John. 1993. *Conversational Realities*. London: Sage.

Shtulman, Andrew. 2006. "Qualitative Differences between Naïve and Scientific Theories of Evolution." *Cognitive Psychology* 52: 170–94.

Silver, Nate. 2012. *The Signal and the Noise: Why So Many Predictions Fail—But Some Don't*. New York: Penguin Press.

———. 2016. "Why FiveThirtyEight Gave Trump a Better Chance than Almost Anyone Else." https://fivethirtyeight.com, November 13.

Simmel, Georg. 1907/1978. *The Philosophy of Money*. Edited by Tom Bottomore and David Frisby. London: Routledge.

Singer, Peter. 1981. *The Expanding Circle: Ethics, Evolution, and Moral Progress*. Princeton, NJ: Princeton University Press.

Sinnott-Armstrong, Walter. 2015. "Consequentialism." *Stanford Encyclopedia of Philosophy*, Winter edition.

Skinner, B. F. 1953. *Science and Human Behavior*. New York: Free Press.

Skocpol, Theda. 1979. *States and Social Revolutions: A Comparative Analysis of France, Russia and China*. Cambridge: Cambridge University Press.

———. 1992. *Protecting Soldiers and Mothers: The Political Origins of Social Policy in the United States*. Cambridge, MA: Belknap Press.

———. 1994. "Cultural Idioms and Political Ideologies in the Revolutionary Reconstruction of State Power: A Rejoinder to Sewell." Pp. 199–211 in *Social Revolutions in the Modern World*. Cambridge: Cambridge University Press.

Skyrms, Brian. 1984. "EPR: Lessons for Metaphysics." *Midwest Studies in Philosophy* 9: 245–55.

———. 2014. *The Evolution of the Social Contract*. 2nd ed. Cambridge: Cambridge University Press.

Slater, Dan. 2010. *Ordering Power: Contentious Politics and Authoritarian Leviathans in Southeast Asia*. New York: Cambridge University Press.

Slater, Dan, and Erica Simmons. 2010. "Informative Regress: Critical Antecedents in Comparative Politics." *Comparative Political Studies* 43: 886–917.

Slater, Matthew H., and Andrea Borghini. 2011. "Introduction: Lessons from the Scientific Butchery." Pp. 1–32 in *Carving Nature at Its Joints: Natural Kinds in Metaphysics and Science*, edited by Joseph Keim Campbell, Michael O'Rourke, and Matthew H. Slater. Cambridge, MA: MIT Press.

Sloman, Steven. 2005. *Causal Models: How People Think about the World and Its Alternatives*. Oxford: Oxford University Press.

Smith, Adam. 1759/2002. *The Theory of Moral Sentiments*. Edited by Knud Haakonssen. Cambridge: Cambridge University Press.

Smith, Christian. 2010. *What Is a Person? Rethinking Humanity, Social Life, and the Moral Good from the Person Up*. Chicago: University of Chicago Press.

Smith, Edward E., and Douglas L. Medin. 1981. *Categories and Concepts*. Cambridge, MA: Harvard University Press.

Smith, Edward E., and Daniel N. Osherson. 1984. "Conceptual Combination with Prototype Concepts." *Cognitive Science* 8: 337–61.

Smolensky, Paul. 1988. "On the Proper Treatment of Connectionism." *Behavioral and Brain Sciences* 11: 1–74.

Smolin, Lee. 2001. *Three Roads to Quantum Gravity*. New York: Basic Books.

———. 2006. *The Trouble with Physics: The Rise of String Theory, the Fall of Science, and What Comes Next*. Boston: Houghton Mifflin Harcourt.

Soifer, Hillel David. 2012. "The Causal Logic of Critical Junctures." *Comparative Political Studies* 45: 1572–97.

———. 2015. *State Building in Latin America*. New York: Cambridge University Press.

———. 2018. "Choosing Units of Analysis: The Modifiable Areal Unit Problem in Political Science." Manuscript, Temple University.

Somers, Margaret S. 1998. "'We're No Angels': Realism, Rational Choice, and Rationality in Social Science." *American Journal of Sociology* 104: 722–84.

Sperber, Dan. 1994. "The Modularity of Thought and the Epidemiology of Representations." Pp. 39–67 in *Mapping the Mind: Domain Specificity in Cognition and Culture*, edited by Lawrence A. Hirschfeld and Susan A. Gelman. Cambridge: Cambridge University Press.

Sprites, Peter, Clark Glymour, and Richard Scheines. 1993. *Causation, Prediction, and Search*. New York: Springer.

Stalnaker, Robert C. 2003. *Ways a World Might Be: Metaphysical and Anti-Metaphysical Essays*. Oxford: Clarendon Press.

———. 2012. *Mere Possibilities: Metaphysical Foundations of Modal Semantics*. Princeton, NJ: Princeton University Press.

Steinhardt, Paul J. 2019. *The Second Kind of Impossible: The Extraordinary Quest for a New Form of Matter*. New York: Simon and Schuster.

Steinmetz, George. 1998. "Critical Realism and Historical Sociology: A Review Article." *Comparative Studies in Society and History* 40: 170–86.

———. 1999. *State/Culture: State Formation after the Cultural Turn*. Ithaca, NY: Cornell University Press.

———. 2007. *The Devil's Handwriting: Precoloniality and the German Colonial State in Qingdao, Samoa, and Southwest Africa*. Chicago: University of Chicago Press.

Stevens, S. S. 1946. "On the Theory of Scales of Measurement." *Science* 103: 677–80.

Stich, Stephen P. 1983. *From Folk Psychology to Cognitive Science: The Case against Belief*. Cambridge, MA: MIT Press.

Stinchcombe, Arthur L. 1968. *Constructing Social Theories*. Chicago: University of Chicago Press.

Stoll, Robert S. 1961. *Set Theory and Logic*. New York: Dover.

Strawson, Galen. 1989. *The Secret Connexion: Causation, Realism, and David Hume*. Oxford: Clarendon Press.

Streeck, Wolfgang, and Kathleen Thelen. 2005. "Introduction: Institutional Change in Advanced Political Economies." Pp. 1–39 in *Beyond Continuity: Institutional Change in Advanced Political Economies*, edited by Wolfgang Streeck and Kathleen Thelen. Oxford: Oxford University Press.

Strevens, Michael. 2000. "The Essentialist Aspect of Naïve Theories." *Cognition* 74: 149–75.

Stryker, Robin. 1994. "Rules, Resources, and Legitimacy Processes: Some Implications for Social Conflict, Order, and Change." *American Journal of Sociology* 99: 847–910.

Sundholm, Göran. 2000. "Inference versus Consequence." Pp. 26–35 in *The Logica Yearbook 1997*, edited by Timothy Childers. Prague: Filosofia.

Suppes, Patrick. 1970. *A Probabilistic Theory of Causality*. Amsterdam: North-Holland.

Swedberg, Richard. 2014. *The Art of Social Theory*. Princeton, NJ: Princeton University Press.

Swedberg, Richard. 2017. "Theorizing in Sociological Research: A New Perspective, a New Departure?" *Annual Review of Sociology* 43: 189–206.

Sweetser, Eve E. 1987. "The Definition of a Lie: An Examination of the Folk Models Underlying a Semantic Prototype." Pp. 43–66 in *Cultural Models in Language and Thought*, edited by Dorothy Holland and Naomi Quinn. Cambridge: Cambridge University Press.

Swidler, Ann. 1986. "Culture in Action: Symbols and Strategies." *American Sociological Review* 51: 273–86.

Szwedek, Aleksander. 2017. "The OBJECT Image Schema." Downloaded at researchgate.net, https://www.researchgate.net/publication/325793581_The_OBJECT_image_schema, July 19, 2018.

Talmy, Leonard. 1988. "Force Dynamics in Language and Cognition." *Cognitive Science* 12: 49–100.

Tannenwald, Nina. 2007. *The Nuclear Taboo: The United States and the Non-Use of Nuclear Weapons since 1945*. Cambridge: Cambridge University Press.

Tansey, Oisín. 2007. "Process Tracing and Elite Interviewing: A Case for Non-Probability Sampling." *PS: Political Science and Politics* 40: 765–72.

Tarski, Alfred. 1944. "The Sematic Conception of Truth." *Philosophy and Phenomenological Research* 4: 341–76.

Tawney, R. H. 1912. *The Agrarian Problem in the Sixteenth Century*. New York: Sentry Press.

———. 1941. "The Rise of the Gentry, 1558–1640." *Economic History Review* 11: 1–38.

Taylor, Charles. 1985. "Interpretation of the Sciences of Man." Pp. 15–57 in *Philosophy and the Human Sciences*, vol. 2. Cambridge: Cambridge University Press.

Taylor, Marianne G. 1996. "The Development of Children's Beliefs about Social and Biological Aspects of Gender Differences." *Child Development* 67: 1555–71.

Taylor, Marianne G., Marjorie Rhodes, and Susan A. Gelman. 2009. "Boys Will Be Boys; Cows Will Be Cows: Children's Essentialist Reasoning about Gender Categories and Animal Species." *Child Development* 80: 461–81.

Taylor, Michael, ed. 1988. *Rationality and Revolution*. Cambridge: Cambridge University Press.

Tegmark, Max. 2014. *Our Mathematical Universe: My Quest for the Ultimate Reality*. New York: Vintage.

Temin, Peter. 1991. "Free Land and Federalism: American Economic Exceptionalism." Pp. 71–93 in *Is America Different? A New Look at American Exceptionalism*, edited by Byron E. Shafer. Oxford: Clarendon Press.

Tetlock, Philip E. 2005. *Expert Political Judgment: How Good Is It? How Can We Know?* Princeton, NJ: Princeton University Press.

Tetlock, Philip E., and Aaron Belkin. 1996a. "Counterfactual Thought Experiments in World Politics: Logical, Methodological, and Psychological Perspectives." Pp. 3–38 in Tetlock and Belkin, *Counterfactual Thought Experiments in World Politics*.

———, eds. 1996b. *Counterfactual Thought Experiments in World Politics: Logical, Methodological, and Psychological Perspectives*. Princeton, NJ: Princeton University Press.

Tetlock, Philip E., Richard Ned Lebow, and Geoffrey Parker, eds. 2006. *Unmaking the West: "What If?" Scenarios That Rewrite World History*. Ann Arbor: University of Michigan Press.

Tetlock, Philip E., and Geoffrey Parker. 2006. "Counterfactual Thought Experiments: Why We Can't Live without Them and How We Must Learn to Live with Them." Pp. 14–44 in Tetlock, Lebow, and Parker, *Unmaking the West*.

Thelen, Kathleen. 1999. "Historical Institutionalism in Comparative Politics." *Annual Review of Political Science* 2: 369–404.

———. 2003. "How Institutions Evolve: Insights from Comparative Historical Analysis." Pp. 305–36 in Mahoney and Rueschemeyer, *Comparative Historical Analysis*.

———. 2004. *How Institutions Evolve: The Political Economy of Skills in Germany, Britain, the United States, and Japan*. Cambridge: Cambridge University Press.

Thelen, Kathleen, and Sven Steinmo. 1992. "Historical Institutionalism in Comparative Politics." Pp. 1–32 in *Structuring Politics: Historical Institutionalism in Comparative Analysis*, edited by Sven Steinmo, Kathleen Thelen, and Frank Longstreth. New York: Cambridge University Press.

Thiem, Alrik. 2017. "Standards of Good Practice and the Methodology of Necessary Conditions in Qualitative Comparative Analysis." *Political Analysis* 24: 478–84.

Thiem, Alrik, Michael Baumgartner, and Damien Bol. 2016. "Still Lost in the Translation! Misunderstandings between Configurational Comparativists and Regressional Analysts." *Comparative Political Studies* 49: 742–74.

Thomann, Eva, and Martino Maggetti. 2020. "Designing Research with Qualitative Comparative Analysis (QCA): Approaches, Challenges, and Tools." *Sociological Methods and Research* 49: 356–86.

Thomasson, Amie L. 2003. "Realism and Human Kinds." *Philosophy and Phenomenological Research* 67: 580–609.

Tichý, Pavel. 1978. "Verisimilitude Revisited." *Synthese* 38: 175–96.

Tilly, Charles. 1984. *Big Structures, Large Processes, Huge Comparisons*. New York: Russell Sage Foundation.

———. 1998. *Durable Inequality*. Berkeley: University of California Press.

Tomasello, Michael, Malinda Carpenter, Josep Call, Tanya Behne, and Henrike Moll. 2005. "Understanding and Sharing Intentions: The Origins of Cultural Cognition." *Behavioral and Brain Sciences* 28: 721–27.

Tooley, Michael. 1987. *Causation: A Realist Approach*. Oxford: Oxford University Press.

———. 2003. "Causation and Supervenience." Pp. 386–434 in *Oxford Handbook of Metaphysics*, edited by Michael J. Loux and Dean W. Zimmerman. Oxford: Oxford University Press.

Toulmin, Stephen. 1972. *Human Understanding*. Princeton, NJ: Princeton University Press.

Tsukamoto, Saori, Yoshihisa Kashima, Nick Haslam, Elise Holland, and Minoru Karasawa. 2017. "Entitativity Assumptions of Individuals and Groups across Cultures." Pp. 335–51 in *The Psychological and Cultural Foundations of East Asian Cognition: Contradiction, Change, and Holism*, edited by Julie Spencer-Rodgers and Kaiping Peng. Oxford: Oxford University Press.

Tudor, Maya. 2013. *The Promise of Power: The Origins of Democracy in India and Autocracy in Pakistan*. New York: Cambridge University Press.

Turner, Stephen P. 1994. *The Social Theory of Practices: Tradition, Tacit Knowledge and Presuppositions*. Chicago: University of Chicago Press.

———. 2002. *Brains/Practices/Relativism*. Chicago: University of Chicago Press.

Tversky, Amos. 1977. "Features of Similarity." *Psychological Review* 84: 327–52.

Vance, Carole S. 1989. "Social Construction Theory: Problems in the History of Sexuality." Pp. 13–34 in *Homosexuality: Which Homosexuality?* edited by A. van Kooten Nierkerk and T. Van Der Meer. Amsterdam: An Dekker.

Van Evera, Stephen. 1997. *Guide to Methods for Students of Political Science*. Ithaca, NY: Cornell University Press.

Van Horn, Kevin S. 2003. "Constructing a Logic of Plausible Inference: A Guide to Cox's Theorem." *International Journal of Approximate Reasoning* 34: 3–24.

Varela, Francisco J., Evan Thompson, and Eleanor Rosch. 2016. *The Embodied Mind: Cognitive Science and Human Experience*. Rev. ed. Cambridge, MA: MIT Press.

Varzi, Achille. 2016. "Mereology." *Stanford Encyclopedia of Philosophy*, Winter edition.

Vervaeke, John, and Christopher D. Green. 1997. "Women, Fire, and Dangerous Theories: A Critique of Lakoff's Theory of Categorization." *Metaphor and Symbol* 12: 59–80.

von Neumann, John, and Oskar Morgenstern. 1944. *Theory of Games and Economic Behavior*. Princeton, NJ: Princeton University Press.

von Wright, Georg Henrik. 1971. *Explanation and Understanding*. Ithaca, NY: Cornell University Press.

Voss, Kim. 1993. *The Making of American Exceptionalism: The Knights of Labor and Class Formation in the Nineteenth Century*. Ithaca, NY: Cornell University Press.

Waldner, David. 1999. *State Building and Late Development*. Ithaca, NY: Cornell University Press.

———. 2007. "Transforming Inferences into Explanations: Lessons from the Study of Mass Extinctions." Pp. 145–76 in *Theory and Evidence in Comparative Politics and International Relations*, edited by Richard Ned Lebow and Mark Irving Lichbach. New York: Palgrave Macmillan.

———. 2012. "Process Tracing and Causal Mechanisms." Pp. 65–84 in *The Oxford Handbook of Philosophy of Social Science*, edited by Harold Kincaid. Oxford: Oxford University Press.

———. 2017. "Schrödinger's Cat and the Dog That Didn't Bark: Why Quantum Mechanics Is (Probably) Irrelevant to the Social Sciences." *Critical Review* 29: 199–233.

Walker, Henry A., and Bernard P. Cohen. 1985. "Scope Statements: Imperatives for Evaluating Theories." *American Sociological Review* 50: 288–301.

Wallerstein, Immanuel. 1974. *The Modern World System*. Vol. 1, *Capitalist Agriculture and the Origins of the European World-Economy in the Sixteenth Century*. Berkeley: University of California Press.

Waltz, Kenneth. 1979. *Theory of International Politics*. Reading, MA: Addison-Wesley.

Walzer, Michael. 1983. *Spheres of Justice: A Degree of Pluralism and Equality*. New York: Basic Books.

Warglien, Massimo, and Peter Gärdenfors. 2013. "Semantics, Conceptual Spaces, and the Meeting of Minds." *Synthese* 190: 2165–93.

Warner, Richard. 1989. "Why Is Logic *A Priori*?" *Monist* 72: 40–51.

Wartenberg, Thomas E. 1990. *The Forms of Power: From Domination to Transformation*. Philadelphia: Temple University Press.

Wax, Murray L. 1967. "On Misunderstanding Verstehen: A Reply to Abel." *Sociology and Social Research* 51: 323–33.

Waxman, Sandra R. 2010. "Names Will Never Hurt Me? Naming and the Development of Racial and Gender Categories in Preschool-Aged Children." *European Journal of Social Psychology* 40: 593–610.

———. 2012. "Social Categories Are Shaped by Social Experience." *Trends in Cognitive Sciences* 16: 531–32.

Weber, Max. 1949. "Objective Possibility and Adequate Causation in Historical Explanation." Pp. 164–88 in *The Methodology of the Social Sciences*. Glencoe, IL: Free Press.

———. 1978. *Economy and Society*. Edited by Guenther Roth and Claus Wittich. 2 vols. Berkeley: University of California Press.

Wegner, Daniel M. 2018. *The Illusion of Conscious Will*. New ed. Cambridge, MA: MIT Press.

Wendt, Alexander. 1998. "On Constitution and Causation in International Relations." *Review of International Studies* 24: 101–17.

———. 1999. *Social Theory of International Politics*. Cambridge: Cambridge University Press.

———. 2004. "The State as a Person in International Theory." *Review of International Studies* 30: 289–316.

———. 2015. *Quantum Mind and Social Science: Unifying Physical and Social Ontology*. Cambridge: Cambridge University Press.

Weston, Thomas. 1987. "Approximate Truth." *Journal of Philosophical Logic* 16: 203–27.

———. 1992. "Approximate Truth and Scientific Realism." *Philosophy of Science* 59: 53–74.

Whitehead, Alfred North, and Bertrand Russell. 1910–13/1956. *Principia Mathematica*. 3 vols. Cambridge: Cambridge University Press.

Wiarda, Howard. 1973. "Toward a Framework for the Study of Political Change in the Iberic-Latin Tradition: The Corporative Model." *World Politics* 25: 206–35.

Wilkerson, T. E. 1988. "Natural Kinds." *Philosophy* 63 (243): 29–42.

Williamson, Timothy. 2000. *Knowledge and Its Limits.* Oxford: Oxford University Press.

Wilson, Robert A. 1999. "Realism, Essence, and Kind: Resuscitating Species Essentialism?" Pp. 187–202 in *Species: New Interdisciplinary Essays,* edited by Robert A. Wilson. Cambridge, MA: MIT Press.

———. 2004. *Boundaries of the Mind: The Individual in the Fragile Sciences.* Cambridge: Cambridge University Press.

Wilson, Robert A., Matthew J. Barker, and Ingo Brigandt. 2007. "When Traditional Essentialism Fails: Biological Natural Kinds." *Philosophical Topics* 35: 189–215.

Wittgenstein, Ludwig. 1922/1972. *Tractatus Logico-Philosophicus.* Translated by Paul Kegan. London: Routledge.

———. 1953/2001. *Philosophical Investigations.* 3rd ed. Oxford: Blackwell.

———. 1956/1978. *Remarks on the Foundations of Mathematics.* Rev. ed. Oxford: Blackwell.

Wolf, Eric R. 1982. *Europe and the People without History.* Berkeley: University of California Press.

Wolff, Phillip. 2007. "Representing Causation." *Journal of Experimental Psychology: General* 136: 82–111.

Wolff, Phillip, and Robert Thorstad. 2017. "Force Dynamics." Pp. 147–68 in *Oxford Handbook of Causal Reasoning,* edited by Michael Waldmann. Oxford: Oxford University Press.

Wolff, Phillip, and Matthew Zettergren. 2002. "A Vector Model of Causal Meaning." *Proceedings of the Annual Meeting of the Cognitive Science Society* 24: 1–6.

Woodward, James. 2003. *Making Things Happen: A Theory of Causal Explanation.* Oxford: Oxford University Press.

Wright, Erik Olin. 1997. *Class Counts: Comparative Studies in Class Analysis.* Cambridge: Cambridge University Press.

Wright, Richard W. 1985. "Causation in Tort Law." *California Law Review* 73: 1735–1828.

———. 2011. "The NESS Account of Natural Causation: A Response to Criticisms." Chap. 14 in *Perspectives on Causation,* edited by Richard Goldberg. Oxford: Hart Publishing.

Wright, Robert. 2000. *Nonzero: The Logic of Human Destiny.* New York: Random House.

———. 2013. "Why Can't We All Just Get Along? The Uncertain Biological Basis of Morality." *The Atlantic,* November.

Xu, Fei, and Susan Carey. 1996. "Infants' Metaphysics: The Case of Numerical Identity." *Cognitive Psychology* 30: 111–53.

Yablo, Stephen. 2004. "Advertisement for a Sketch of an Outline of a Prototheory of Causation." Pp. 119–37 in Collins, Hall, and Paul, *Causation and Counterfactuals.*

Yanow, Dvora, and Peregrine Schwartz-Shea, eds. 2015. *Interpretation and Method: Empirical Research Methods and the Interpretive Turn.* 2nd ed. London: Routledge.

Yashar, Deborah J. 1997. *Demanding Democracy: Reform and Reaction in Costa Rica and Guatemala, 1870s–1950s.* Stanford, CA: Stanford University Press

Zadeh, Lofti A. 1965. "Fuzzy Sets." *Information and Control* 12: 338–53.

———. 1972. "A Fuzzy-Set-Theoretic Interpretation of Linguistic Hedges." *Journal of Cybernetics* 2 (3): 4–34.

Zaks, Sherry. 2017. "Relationships among Rivals (RAR): A Framework for Analyzing Contending Hypotheses in Process Tracing." *Political Analysis* 25: 344–62.

Zucker, Lynn G. 1983. "Organizations as Institutions." *Perspectives in Organizational Sociology* 2: 1–47.

Zuckerman, Alan S. 1997. "Reformulating Explanatory Standards and Advancing Theory in Comparative Politics." Pp. 277–310 in Lichbach and Zuckerman, *Comparative Politics.*

INDEX

The following index arranges categories in a form that is intended to be useful to the main readers of this book—that is, social scientists and other scholars interested in the practice of social science. The index does not list many substantive terms (e.g., names of countries) that may be important outside of this context.

A NOTE ON THE TYPE

This book has been composed in Adobe Text and Gotham.
Adobe Text, designed by Robert Slimbach for Adobe,
bridges the gap between fifteenth- and sixteenth-century
calligraphic and eighteenth-century Modern styles.
Gotham, inspired by New York street signs, was designed
by Tobias Frere-Jones for Hoefler & Co.

Printed and bound by CPI Group (UK) Ltd, Croydon, CR0 4YY